Partisans of the Southern Press

Partisans of the Southern Press

Editorial Spokesmen
of the
Nineteenth Century

Carl R. Osthaus

THE UNIVERSITY PRESS OF KENTUCKY

Library of Congress Cataloging-in-Publication Data

Osthaus, Carl R.
    Partisans of the Southern press : editorial spokesmen of the
nineteenth century / Carl R. Osthaus.
       p.   cm.
    Includes bibliographical references and index.
    ISBN 0-8131-1875-1
    1. Press—Southern States—History—19th century. 2. Newspaper
editors—Southern States. 3. Press and politics—Southern States.
I. Title.
PN4893.O88 1994
071'.5'09034—dc20   94-16880

in memory of

Gerald C. Heberle

Contents

Acknowledgments

One of the delights in completing this book is the opportunity to recognize people and institutions that have supported my research and given me encouragement, advice, and constructive criticism. Oakland University has been generous with fellowships, travel grants, and sabbatical leaves in support of my work, and the interlibrary loan staff of Kresge Library, Oakland University, has been unfailingly helpful and diligent in my behalf. At a crucial time the American Philosophical Society granted me travel funds for the completion of my work on the *Charleston Mercury* and *Charleston Daily Courier*. Along the way the staffs at many libraries and archives offered the benefit of their expertise, but none more so than the staff of the manuscripts division at the Perkins Library, Duke University, Durham, North Carolina. James McPherson and William McFeely aided in helping me secure research funds, and at an early stage Theodore H. Baker reviewed my New South chapters. Paul Escott and Michael O'Brien read an earlier version of this manuscript, offering encouragement and the kind of criticism that one would pay for dearly if a price tag could be put on it. I am especially appreciative of their comments. I owe special thanks to my former student, my friend, and now my colleague Cara Shelly. Although her own work was pressing, she devoted countless hours to a careful reading of my book and improved it with her knowledge of Southern history and her sensitivity to English prose. My wife, Wendy, carefully read the manuscript, offering her usual discerning comments and giving me a clear message to get it done. She also packed and moved our household while I was applying the finishing touches. I owe her big-time.

I doubt that I would have completed this manuscript without the aid and friendship of the late Gerald C. Heberle. Over the years I bene-fited immensely from his keen intelligence, wise counsel, delightful sense of humor, and unsurpassed understanding of the English lan-guage. It was fun to laugh with him at the exploits of "my editors" or the problems of my research and writing. I miss him.

Most of all, I am grateful to my lovely daughters, Laura and Amy, who "took care of business" and gave me support when it was most needed.

Introduction

This book examines the careers of important and powerful Southern editors. The subjects were chosen because they were significant as individuals and because their work, considered collectively, illuminates key aspects of Southern daily newspaper history in the nineteenth century. Some readers will be disappointed that I have not included their favorite editor or a number of other very able editors outside the mainstream. Typical country editors spoke for communities existing in the backwash of a Richmond or Charleston yet followed in the footsteps of their city cousins. Reform editors, however, represented an alienated community; they embraced protest and a cultural tradition hostile to the established interests and the promotional orientation of the elite journals.[1] Black leaders during and after Reconstruction edited scores of weeklies which demanded equal rights, defended the interests of nearly four million newly freed slaves, and celebrated the achievements of those ignored by the dominant white press. Such editors are unquestionably worthy of study, but I sought a project that was both workable and illustrative of the major thrust of the powerful urban dailies. The mainstream editors who are the focus of this study sought state and regional power, recognition as Southern spokesmen, endorsement by the political, commercial, and industrial elite, journalistic fame, and increased circulation and financial success.

My essays begin with Thomas Ritchie, the best example of influential, antebellum Southern political editing and the constructive potential of partisan journalism in the Age of Jackson.[2] In many ways he set standards of influence for those who followed. His difficulties as editor of the *Washington Daily Union* from 1845 to 1851 heralded sectionalism's disruptive impact on Southern journalism.

The South's most successful "modern," antebellum venture, the *New Orleans Daily Picayune* (founded and edited by George Wilkins Kendall and Francis Asbury Lumsden), was a natural for inclusion. The *Picayune* was a notable example of that sprightly penny press journalism that invigorated American press development in the 1830s and 1840s.

The South's sectional journalism of the 1850s produced a host of strong editorial voices but none that stood apart from the throng and were considered representative of the best in the South. I chose to examine sectional journalism in the crisis of the Union through the contrasting styles of Robert Barnwell Rhett's *Charleston Mercury* and Aaron Willington and Richard Yeadon's *Charleston Daily Courier*, South Carolina's most ultra radical and conservative papers, respectively. Rhett's style, justifiably or not, helped mold the Northern view of Southern journalism, and yet the rival *Courier* was always the more successful newspaper, having greater circulation, larger profits, and better news coverage.

During the Civil War the press in both the North and the South rallied the people in support of the war while simultaneously criticizing weaknesses and bungling among the civilian directors of the war effort. Next to the fire-eating Robert Barnwell Rhett, the most famous (and more influential and knowledgeable) rebel editor was the misanthropic John M. Daniel, whose *Richmond Examiner* both helped and hindered the Southern cause in daily blasts from the Confederate capital.

Of the myriad voices calling for resistance to Yankee Reconstruction, none was more sure or significant than that of John Forsyth of the *Mobile Daily Register*, who damned Republican political power and the freedmen's pretensions while celebrating the reemergence of white Democratic power and unity. The South has lived by many myths, that of Southern unity being the most prominent. If, in the mythical view, the South spoke as one in rejecting Yankee rule, editors like Forsyth were in large part responsible. Historians today recognize the diversity of voices from the Reconstruction era; the black press and the Republican press arose to challenge Forsyth's white Democracy. Their defeat smoothed the way for elite rule and helped enshrine the myth of unity.

Finally, if Ritchie is the alpha of nineteenth-century Southern journalism, surely the omega would be the triumvirate of New South editors who heralded the arrival of modernization and reconciliation, Henry Watterson (*Louisville Courier-Journal*), Francis Warrington Dawson (*Charleston News and Courier*), and Henry Grady (*Atlanta Constitution*).

I have chosen to concentrate on editors not only because they were powerful and colorful but because the editor completely dominated journalism and monopolized the dissemination of news (or what passed for "news"). According to Pulitzer Prize-winning journalist Harry Ashmore, writing editorials in recent years is "like pissing in a blue serge suit. It gives a momentary feeling of warmth, but nobody notices."[3] Such was not the case in the nineteenth century, for when political editors spoke, partisans listened. Often the editorial was the most original matter in the paper. Although the South's papers had only a fraction of the circulation of those of the major Northern urban centers, a few exceptional Southerners such as Thomas Ritchie and Henry Watterson rivaled the greatest of the Northern editors in national impact. The South had its editorial giants, but the majority of their Southern colleagues had to be content with local and regional significance. The journalists discussed herein were the South's editorial giants.

In the mid-nineteenth century several Northern cities proved capable of supporting mass circulation newspapers reflecting a diversity of reader interests, but not so the South. There the major urban dailies spoke for planters, slaveholding professionals, and commercial interests. The editor was the voice of the politically active and economically significant segment of the community; the editorial giants of the South responded to this readership, preserving and extending values long entrenched in Southern society. Like the section's political leaders, Southern editors, in the final analysis, had to reaffirm and reiterate, not reform or crusade. Southern editors simultaneously served three major functions, as narrators (reporting events), as advocates (advancing arguments), and as weathercocks (indicating the prevailing views of the elite and a relatively small, middle-class readership), but the greatest of these was the last.[4]

By mid-century, a formative age in American journalism, the Southern press had become obsessed with sectional politics and threats to the racial status quo and the rights of the states. In this atmosphere every Southern editor became a paladin of Southern virtue and a critic of Northern culture. This trend arose with sectionalism and continued as long as sectionalism survived. If Northerners dominated the schools, pulpits, literature, and commerce, Southerners lamented, then the press must speak for the South, combatting Northern arrogance and redressing the grievances of a wronged people.

1
The World of
the Southern Editor

Newspapers vie with each other in
gas and grandiloquence.

George Templeton Strong

The history of Southern newspapers before 1900 falls, very roughly, into three chronological periods. Southern journalism was much the same as Northern journalism from the 1790s up to the 1850s. In the second period, when sectional conflict dominated politics and journalism, a number of characteristics came to be especially, if not uniquely, associated with Southern newspapers; it was not that Southern newspapers had changed but rather that Northern papers were revolutionizing the profession while the South carried on in the old tradition. In the last phase of the century, however, the leading Southern papers, those publicizing the so-called New South, adapted themselves more and more to the most modern standards of journalism and narrowed the gap between themselves and the most advanced Northern papers.

The nineteenth century was an age of personal journalism, when strong, colorful personalties dominated "viewpapers" devoted to politics and quarrels, not necessarily in that order. Until the twentieth century all Southern papers, in contrast to Northern dailies, were still small enough that a single strong editor could dominate every column, and thus personal journalism lasted longer in the South than elsewhere. Bold editor-owners stamped their principles, interests, values, and prejudices on all aspects of the newspaper world.[1] Many of the most successful editors did a variety of work that in later years would require a staff of specialists—one South Carolinian concluded that successful editors needed the constitution of a horse, the obduracy of a mule, and the endurance of a starving anaconda.[2]

For the first half-century of journalism in the American republic, most generalizations are equally valid for newspapers in any part of the country. American journalism began with the "printer-essayist-editor" who filled the four-page sheets of the 1790s with months-old European news, lengthy political essays, shipping notices, and miscellaneous articles and notices. There was very little local news. Editorial opinion at first appeared in letters signed by pen names and in brief exchanges in news columns; but by 1796 Noah Webster's *American Minerva* had an editorial column, and by 1800 the *Philadelphia Aurora* was using its second page as an editorial page and regularly using the editorial "we."[3]

Party patronage often defrayed the modest cost of establishing a paper. Though it was easy to found a partisan journal, it was more difficult to keep it going. In 1803 a diarist noted that "the increase of Gazettes is excessive. I have several times attempted to count the whole number, but they appear and disappear and change places so often that the exact number I cannot ascertain."[4] Circulation, advertising, and profits were never very large. Subscribers commonly ignored pleas to pay what they owed; shortly before the Civil War a *Charleston Mercury* editor bitterly observed that gentlemen who paid their grog bills as a matter of honor blithely ignored the printer's bills.[5] Owner-editors were common in the nineteenth century, and hosts of them went bankrupt along with their papers. Poverty was endemic, especially among country editors. A saying in North Carolina suggested that "one cut-away coat lasts a country editor through three generations of trousers"; the long coat fortunately concealed a multitude of trouser patches.[6] Had not the political parties established newspapers, it is difficult to see how extensive journalism could have developed in this period.

American politics had still to develop a tradition of restraint and toleration; the early Federalists and Republicans unleashed their journalistic partisans to wage rancorous warfare. As one contemporary put it, the press was "abominably gross and defamatory." A fairly typical offender might accuse his enemies of "bribery, blackmail, venality, concupiscence, intrigue, mendacity, and whatever other crimes his fertile vocabulary could put a name to."[7] Many a founding father was shocked by what resulted from the freedom of the press. Benjamin Franklin, tongue-in-cheek, defended the liberty of the press as long as liberty of the cudgel—the sole remedy for press abuse—was maintained as well.[8] Editors themselves routinely editorialized against press abuses and promised temperate, dignified political discussion, only to resume the mudslinging in the next moment of political strife.[9]

Historian of journalism Frank Luther Mott described the youthful world of newspaperdom as a kind of Donnybrook Fair of broken heads and skinned knuckles and labeled the years from 1801 to 1833 the "Dark Ages of Partisan Journalism."[10] In spite of its excesses, however, the press did establish a public forum for discussions vital to the working out of the new Constitution and political practices of the young republic.

From the 1820s into the 1850s the most influential journalists were political editors, surrogates of the candidates who rallied the shock troops of party conflict, and their policy was often pure, blinkered partisanship.[11] This was merely an intensification of the earlier pattern. Although more commercial papers existed than had earlier, political papers remained more numerous, and even the commercial journals were heavily involved in politics. Everything, it seemed, was politically relevant. John W. Forney of the *Philadelphia Press*, advising a friend on how to orate about the virtues of a local fire company, said he would dwell upon "the fine, self-denying heroism of these firemen's devoted lives; of their protection of our homes, and I would adjure them to remember Douglas and follow Walker, and never cease to war upon the infamies of Lecompton."[12]

The typical political journal of the 1830s, expensive at five to ten dollars a year, paid in advance, addressed its sophisticated political essays and endless didactic editorials to small audiences of 1,500 to 3,000. Only people of substance or deep political involvement read the papers; it was a rare editor whose circulation and advertising revenues sufficed for a healthy financial independence. Frequently, editors of this era were even more dependent on party patronage than in the 1790s. If the party failed to come through with the necessary federal or state printing contract or the timely subvention from party funds, the paper might well collapse. A few editors were party insiders who, in an age of spoilsmen, helped shape policy and made presidents, congressmen, cabinet officers, and all the party officials. Most editors, however, were small-time hacks, dutifully repeating the party line as it came from Washington or the state capital.[13] If an editor's sentiments failed the test of purity (i.e., if he got out of step with the power brokers or party majority) then he faced annihilation; rarely did an editor's career survive a change of party. His function, concludes historian J. Mills Thornton III, "was constantly to apply party principles to developing circumstances in such a way as to accord with the prejudices of the community."[14]

One result of partisanship in journalism was the multiplication of newspapers. There had to be at least as many papers in the community as there were parties. Thus throughout the South up to the Civil War, papers competed in virtually every sizable market. Such would not be the case during and after the Civil War.

In composition, the political paper of the Jacksonian period resembled its predecessors more closely than its successors. They were still four-page sheets, though the stronger ones had expanded to six or seven columns. The proceedings, laws, and debates of various legislative bodies, political and miscellaneous essays, letters to the editor, commercial notices, and advertising constituted the bulk of the paper. Newspaper exchanges were absolutely essential.[15] Many a noteworthy editor assembled his paper with scissors, paste, and copies of other newspapers, reserving his real energies for the fire and brimstone of his own editorial columns. If he managed to squeeze out even half a column of his own material each day, he was considered an editor of great talent.[16] In a moment of candor, one editor confessed that scissors and paste journalism properly conducted could create a superior journal. The key was careful selection: "it was better to reprint good material from the exchanges than to write bad material."[17] That a historian in the 1970s could refer to this practice as "mutual journalistic plagiarism" connotes twentieth-century values;[18] nineteenth-century editors were enthusiastically dedicated to publishing the best exchanges and lamented the poverty of their columns when the mails failed to bring timely "news."

For the editors of this era there was seldom more than one side to any question. The idea of opening the columns of a paper to opposing views or objective criticism seems never to have occurred to many journalists. Adversarial relations must not be compromised by open-mindedness; the public must be protected from influences that might give rise to independent thought. It was common, intoned the *Philadelphia Public Ledger*, for papers to mystify the truth and inflame the feelings of the readers.[19] News reporting in such a system had little room to develop. Editors generally lacked interest in anything outside politics, and they could rely on letter-writers or unpaid essayists to fill whatever nonpolitical space was wanted. Politics itself was propaganda and partisanship, not probing questions and objective investigations. Party newspapers were expected to be loyal soldiers, not critics or defenders of some nonpartisan public interest. Editors were to manufacture facts or give coloring to those already established. An impartial press would do its readers a great injustice; partisan readers paid for partisan papers. One contemptuous reader who failed to find conviction and fire in the *National Intelligencer* sneered at "Mr. Silky Milky Smith's National Smoothing Plane."[20]

The politico-journalistic style of the Age of Jackson was intolerant, bigoted, and fanatical; editorial quarrels and abusive personal exchanges—one of the earliest forms of the much deplored, nineteenth-century press sensationalism—were the characteristic features of Jacksonian journalism. Sometimes they were acted out like a stylized ritual. Many an editor discovered that editorial violence pleased his readers; press vilification was often bad for his health but good for circulation. In small towns and cities, rival editors might interest the public in their squabbles and thus contrive to live where one alone might die.[21] Thomas Baker noted in the *Memphis Commercial Appeal* that much rivalry was perhaps designed to boost circulation by dressing up a dull sheet with witty barbs. "Editors who denounced each other's politics were often the best of personal friends, and the entire press corps formed a close, mutually cooperative group, with a conscious sense of unity." [22] Baker overstates this relationship. Editorial clashes engendered an endless list of brawls, canings, and bloody duels, especially in the South. The public supposedly deplored the abuses of press freedom, but according to one mid-nineteenth-century journalist, the people relished the articles that were the most defamatory and personal and the least instructive and valuable. [23]

Partisan rhetoric ranged from the merely bombastic to the vindictive and vulgar. A political victory would be heralded as a "Glorious Victory—the Country Saved," so that a stranger to this land might reasonably conclude that the party in power consisted of tyrants in no way responsible to the people. [24] Many editors typically assailed their opponents as villains of the worst depravity. "I do not say," remarked an old-time Federalist in Connecticut, "that all democrats are horse thieves, but I do aver that all horse thieves are democrats." [25] Some editors were celebrated for their rich vocabularies of invective. Samuel Bowles of the *Springfield Republican* remembered that "'[p]imp,' 'liar,' 'blockhead,' 'leper,' 'thief,' and 'blackleg' were terms which fell with practiced use from editors' pens, and, by the fifties, 'villain' and 'scoundrel' had spent their offensive power." [26]

The style was national, not peculiar to the South. Charles Dickens captured the essence of a certain class of American papers when in *Martin Chuzzlewit* he christened New York papers with such names as the *New York Sewer*, the *New York Stabber*, and the *New York Plunderer*. [27] Southern editors, resentful and envious of New York's financial and journalistic domination, frequently depicted the nation's largest city as the center of newspaper licentiousness, [28] but perhaps the worst nineteenth-century example of abusive journalism was Wilbur Storey's writing in the *Detroit Free Press* and *Chicago Times*. Storey seems to have become a journalist so that he could destroy the reputations of his many opponents. According to his biographer, soul-consuming hatred filled his columns and brought out the worst in his rivals, who replied in kind, calling Storey a pimp, labeling his paper a sluiceway of calumny, and charging that he had installed a Chicago prostitute in his home. [29]

The blackguard editor was something of a stock figure in the novelist's gallery. [30] In John Pendleton Kennedy's *Quodlibet*, a desperate group of Quodlibetarian Democrats, being smote hip and thigh by the Whig *Thorough Blue Whole Team*, must hire their own journalist for retaliatory purposes. The job applicant begins his interview lugubriously, "I am in want of employment"; he is "a thin, faded little fellow, whose clothes seemed to be somewhat too large for him. His eye was gray and rather dull, his physiognomy melancholy, his cheek sunken, his complexion freckled, his coat blue, the buttons dingy, his hair sandy and like un-twisted rope. The first glance at the person of this new comer gave every man of the club the assurance that here was an editor indeed."[31] The editor assures the committee that failure, rejection, poverty, and deri-sion have long since curdled the milk of human kindness in his bosom. He promises to make the *Quodlibet Whole Hog* a monument of partisan rancor. One Quodlibetarian remarks admiringly that the fellow sounds like "a gouger when his bile's fresh."[32]

Mark Twain, as well, delighted in satirizing the life of editors; in "Journalism in Tennessee" an old editor, fresh from a shooting, advises his young assistant who will be in charge of the office: "Jones will be here at three—cowhide him. Gillespie will call earlier, perhaps—throw him out of the window. Ferguson will be along about four—kill him. . . . The cowhides are under the table, weapons in the drawer, ammunition there in the corner, lint and bandages up there in the pigeonholes. In case of accident, go to Lancet, the surgeon, downstairs. He advertises; we take it out in trade."[33]

The failings of the American press and its editorial corps—generally referred to as the licentiousness of the press—received considerable at-tention in the antebellum era. Critics lashed out against the tyranny of the press—the irresponsible attacks on individuals and gross partisan-ship—but they also denounced journalists' errors and blunders and the shoddiness of many papers slapped together in excessive haste.[34] Haste as well as poor handwriting (the mark of a veteran editor?) created many an embarrassing moment, as when a *Charleston Daily Courier* compositor substituted "destructive and defective" for "distinctive and definitive," or when Henry Watterson's "from Alpha to Omega" was transformed into "from Alton to Omaha."[35]

Journalism as a recognized profession was only beginning to emerge by the Civil War. Charles Congdon, a veteran editor on Horace Greeley's *New York Tribune*, described the situation prior to the 1850s: "Men drifted into the management of newspapers out of other callings. Having done this they trifled. Never for a moment did they think of leading. They joked and bantered and sneered; they used the scissors and paste-brush much more than the pen; there was no method, no system, no manage-ment, no earnest purpose, nothing but personal scolding and partisan wrath."[36] Ignorance supposedly characterized the press rank and file. A Southern paper regaled its readers with the story of a Toledo reporter who failed to recognize a July 4 oration as the Declaration of Indepen-dence and enthusiastically took notes on "the greatest speech, by jingo, that he had ever heard." The resulting write-up was so highly embellished that his editors failed to recognize the Declaration until they encountered the names of the signers as "the committee of arrangement."[37]

Journalists, as a group, were socially suspect. The printer's transient life and the journalist's strange hours and hard drinking gave newspapermen an almost-Bohemian air of disreputability. The unscrupulous tactics and vulgar language of the political press discredited many an editor in the eyes of polite society.[38] Editors were low-class people, pronounced South Carolinian James Henry Hammond, a successful politician and planter, and himself a former editor: "In this country I scarcely know one who has . . . been able to lift himself above it [the editor's post]."[39] Yet many Southern editors, like Hammond himself, became community leaders, and thus in at least one respect antebellum Southern journalism was probably somewhat superior to the national norm—in the social standing and prestige attached to editing important newspapers. All Southern editors of the topmost rank were state or regional spokesmen. Self-made men like George Wilkins Kendall, Aaron Willington, and Francis Warrington Dawson, joined editors born to the purple, such as Thomas Ritchie, Robert Barnwell Rhett, Jr., John M. Daniel, John Forsyth, and Henry Watterson, in the upper levels of the Southern hierarchy.[40] Hammond used his position as editor of the radical *Southern Times* to make a name for himself in politics, and at the height of his journalistic power he gave up the rigors of newspaper work to marry a Charleston socialite.[41]

Perhaps the sharp verbal exchanges and occasional brawls or duels of Southern newspapermen should be seen in part as efforts to prove their manhood and demonstrate worthiness as community leaders.[42] Honor and public opinion were synonymous, so it is not surprising that, as Edward L. Ayers concludes, most duels in the Old South were fought not between established planters but by young professionals seeking social advancement and dependent upon the manipulation of language and image—men in law, politics, and journalism.[43] Hammond again offers a case in point. To win journalistic success and the chance for upward mobility, he tangled with other distinguished public figures and got himself involved in a duel, precipitated in part by an exchange of epithets—blackguard versus a person of "reeking foulness." But here, too, he recognized opportunity—opportunity to portray himself as fearless, honorable, and dedicated to principled action.[44]

Doubtless many antebellum political journals were not unfairly satirized in *Quodlibet*, but among the best papers there did exist a tradition of serious and constructive journalism. Editors sought to stamp their image on the community. Samuel Bowles of the *Springfield Republican*, for example, advanced a commonplace (and self-serving) view when he claimed the power of journalism to be superior to that of pulpit, platform, and schoolhouse.[45] Papers such as Gales and Seaton's *National Intelligencer*, Niles's *Weekly Register*, William Cullen Bryant's *New York Evening Post*, and Thomas Ritchie's *Richmond Enquirer* aspired to raise a free, competitive press to the level of public statesmanship.[46]

In Washington the *National Intelligencer*, the *Globe*, and the *Union* set an agenda for the press of the state capitals by publishing in-depth reports and accounts of Congressional proceedings. Battling Washington journals created sharp debate and established a national dialogue on vital issues such as western land policies, internal improvements, the Second Bank of the United States, the Specie Circular, the Mexican War, and the conflict between nationalism and states' rights.[47]

Beginning in the 1830s, but gaining tremendous momentum in the 1850s and 1860s, eastern metropolitan newspapers addressed to a mass audience revolutionized American journalism. Steam-driven technology made possible extraordinary economies in the mass production of papers, while the tastes of the new middle- and working-class readers dictated a drastic change in style and content in the penny press. Huge production for huge markets, in turn, necessitated huge financial investments. Given the right conditions, a giant urban daily could reap unprecedented profits with the price lowered to one penny a copy.

By the 1850s, New York City, with its three eight-page dailies, the *Herald*, the *Tribune*, and the *Times*, became America's newspaper capital, with James Gordon Bennett's *Herald* blazing the way. Bennett assembled a large staff, hired reporters to cover regular assignments, and set everyone to toiling throughout the night to capture a "picture of the day," which, as it happened, was an exposition—sometimes an exposé—of the bewildering world of modern city life. Seeking out colorful human interest accounts of the latest happenings, he made his paper into a great department store of news, but the bargain basement exploitation of sex, crime, and scandal was its biggest draw.[48] Bennett did not toady to any clearly defined readership; his *Herald* pursued an independent path, exhibited an anti-aristocratic bias, and rose in part by opposing the local power structure. Employing choice labels such as "tricksters," "loafers," "frauds," "parasites," and "thieves," Bennett ridiculed politicians, exposed their schemes, and made them look foolish and criminal. "Over the years," concludes Douglas Fermer, "he sought to make his paper almost a fourth element in the constitutional system by invoking the power of the people to preserve the democratic system against the 'party wire pullers' who sought to 'beguile the masses.'"[49] And the masses responded. Booming circulation—77,000 by 1860—attracted lucrative advertising, and by 1860 the *Herald* had the size and financial power to be truly independent.

Other papers, following in the *Herald*'s footsteps, modernized their facilities and newspaper columns, and because their commercial announcements and economic analyses were as important to the elite as their sensationalism was to the man on the street, they soon rivaled and then displaced the old, purely commercial sheets. Huge circulations resulted in freedom from mercantile or political domination; some owner-editors prized and maintained their freedom while others became the slaves of sensationalism.

The Civil War completed the newspaper revolution in the North. Thereafter the single most important function of the great dailies was timely news gathering.[50] In 1895 one pundit summarized the changes wrought in a single generation:

The old theory that it was the chief province of the newspaper to publish political essays, and help politicians to get offices, has been exploded, and in the place of it we have the demonstrated fact that it is the essential business of a newspaper to tell daily and as accurately as possible the many-featured story of current events, with such comments as shall serve to instruct and entertain. It must pursue a ceaseless and vigilant quest for late things, novel things, interesting things; it must ransack the universe for the unexpected that is always happening somewhere. The spirit of public curiosity and anticipation is imperative and insatiable and will have what it craves.[51]

As will be seen, Southern newspapermen held their own in American journalism when politics, passion, partisanship, and constitutionalism dominated the editor's world and when news arrived inexpensively through the newspaper exchanges. When these conditions changed, the Southern press became a distinctive, much derided entity in American journalism because it was left behind. Though the South had once supported some of the liveliest and best political journals, rapid technological change and Northern urban growth gave Northern newspapermen distinct advantages just at a time when sectionalism forced Southern editors to hew to a narrowly ideological line emphasizing resistance. Southern journals might represent the most cosmopolitan elements in their society, but these elements were weak relative to those in the North. The professions in the South presented few opportunities for upward mobility; for the vast majority, agriculture was the only realistic calling. According to the 1850 census, "Georgia had only 190 newsmen, whereas Maine, a comparably rural, underpopulated state, boasted 258. In the southwest printers were exceedingly few: thirty in Alabama, thirty-four in Mississippi."[52] Sizable Southern cities were few, and much of the Southern population was illiterate. Newspapers were to be kept out of the hands of slaves, and free blacks were never targeted by white editors as subjects for sympathetic news coverage or as a potential sales market. Antebellum Southern cities reflected the agricultural outlook of the South as a whole. A Southern urban lifestyle moved to an agricultural rhythm, and the urban press frequently pushed agrarian interests as it sought to secure the business of the countryside. Even in the growing Southern cities late in the nineteenth century the rural-urban symbiosis remained.[53]

Finally, slavery and sectional politics, like a great incubus, had stifled independent thought on the great public issues. Instead of showing imagination and enterprise, the Southern press after midcentury conformed to a narrow sectional orthodoxy. No Southern editor dared appeal to a mass of readers by assuming the stance of the common man in serious opposition to the propertied and powerful elite. Southern editors survived by joining, or at least ingratiating themselves with, the establishment.

Freedom to dissent in print dwindled in the fifties and vanished in the sixties and early seventies. What one newspaper authority called "the spirit of public curiosity" was a dangerous thing for an editor to toy with in an embattled South. Thus even the few Southern newspapers (like the *New Orleans Picayune* in its earliest years) that copied some elements of the penny press style were miniscule in size and tamely inoffensive in content as compared with the eastern press.[54] The South lacked both the money and the freedom for aggressive news gathering. Nationally New York City in the two decades before the Civil War came to dominate the dissemination of news, but of all regions except the far frontier, the South seemed most dependent upon the great metropolis since news flow remained a function of modernism: steamships, high trade volume, the telegraph, and railroads.[55] Provincial status and dependency rankled; in 1860 the *Charleston Mercury*, exponent of the most radical and intolerant creed of Southernness, complained, "We have to go to New York papers for news of our own affairs."[56]

On the eve of the Civil War, Southern journalism was old-fashioned; when it emerged from Reconstruction it was positively archaic. Thomas Ritchie, Southern voice of Jacksonian Democracy, had no successors. Increasingly, antebellum Southern papers abandoned political for sectional journalism, scrambling to the defense of their region against Northern majoritarians or equalitarian abolitionists and "black Republicans." At the dawn of a modern era of journalism, when Northern editors responded to growing cities, increasingly diverse readerships, new journalistic standards pioneered by news-seeking, mass-circulation penny papers, and new technology, the Southern press embraced orthodoxy in substance and style. The closed society of the South from the 1850s through the 1870s reflected a closed press reinforcing and reiterating community views. The collapse of parties, the destruction of war, and the rise of a one-party South destroyed even the limited financial base of support for many newspapers and helped fasten press orthodoxy on the South. Postbellum Northern editors of the giant metropolitan presses understandably sneered at the general run of Southern papers as provincial, brawling, fire-eating absurdities.

In the last two decades of the century, it was the task of New South editors—Dawson, Grady, and Watterson especially—to alter this opinion, and this they did surprisingly well. Their newspapers became significant forces for economic development, social improvement, and political moderation. Still they were hampered by the restrictions of their region and their audience. In the final analysis, they, too, were Southern editors; like their predecessors they had to explain, justify, and protect the South's interests. Perhaps they looked more innovative, by contrast with their colleagues, than they really were. It is surprisingly difficult, in fact, to find anything substantially new in, say, Henry Grady's New South ideas. Even a modest shift in emphasis and rhetoric was impressive in the context of Southern Reconstruction journalism.

The most eminent nineteenth-century Southern editors were prophets who knew how to gain honor in their own country; they made prophecies that pleased those who awarded or denied the honors even when their prophecies proved fallacious or disastrous or both. This is not to defame the editors as mere chameleons; on the contrary, most of them were men of remarkable individuality. In every case they shared the basic values of the Southern ethos they championed, but also in every case they had to struggle to reconcile some of their personal convictions with the pressures of Southern conformity. Precisely because journalism in that era was so personal, editors were held accountable for everything their papers said and even for what they left unsaid. No Southern editor rose to the top of the profession by being noncommittal. Each had to find his own technique of accommodation to his society, and therein lay the greatest challenge of journalism. No thinking man could always be at one with Southern society through the endless series of changes, reversals, and crises. How was an editor to express his own strength, talent, intelligence, and ambition while never losing contact with a conservative, suspicious, intolerant Southern elite? That contact was essential to the life of a newspaper and (sometimes literally) of its editor. There was no other constituency in the South whose support could sustain a major journalistic enterprise. Slaves, freedmen, poor whites, and other underclass Southerners did not buy newspapers, and advertisers hardly would pay to solicit their patronage.[57] Such diversity and dissent as editors pronounced was always comprehended within the governing classes.

2

Between Nationalism and Nullification

The Editorial Career of Thomas Ritchie

There is no book published in the United States
of equal importance in its effects upon public opinion as a
well conducted newspaper of extensive circulation.

Southern Review, 6 August 1830

"He held the politics of the Old Commonwealth in the hollow of his hand," declared the *New York Times*.[1] To his political friends and opponents he was Old Father Ritchie, Old "Nous Verrons" (after a favorite editorial saying), the Napoleon of the press, or, less charitably, the dictator of Virginia politics.[2] The subject of such superlatives was Thomas Ritchie, the Democratic editor of the *Richmond Enquirer* from 1804 to 1845, and of the *Washington Daily Union* from 1845 until 1851. With pardonable exaggeration, one admirer remarked that Ritchie taught Virginians "to think his own thoughts, to speak his own words, to weep when he wept, to wreath their faces with his smiles, and, over and above all, to vote as he voted."[3]

Every respectable reading room in the United States carried Ritchie's *Enquirer*; nearly every Democratic paper in the country copied from it, and Whig papers had to respond to it. It spread Ritchie's influence, and eventually he became a major force in the Democratic party and in national politics. One contemporary recalled that when an important question was before the country, hundreds of people in the South and West asked "what course the Richmond Enquirer would pursue."[4] Aspirants for the highest offices courted Ritchie; some observers thought him instrumental in keeping Henry Clay and John C. Calhoun out of the White House and putting James K. Polk into it.[5] Martin Van Buren ascribed to the *Enquirer* "an influence greater than any other press in the Union," and upon Ritchie's death in 1854 the *Daily Albany Argus*, a powerful state organ, editorialized: "So large a share of public confidence as he enjoyed, had never been extended to any other individual of his profession, in this or in any other country."[6]

But Ritchie had his detractors. Waspish John Randolph called him a "double-faced villain . . . a Bug hardly worth the effort of crushing." Andrew Jackson, a former Ritchie ally, warned Polk in 1844 not to trust him.[7] At Ritchie's death, Horace Greeley's *New York Tribune* belittled his career; Greeley, having little appreciation of conflict within Virginia, thought it took no great ability to control the policies of a slaveholding society.[8]

Greeley notwithstanding, friend and foe alike admitted that Ritchie was a figure of no small importance in American politics and journalism; most historians have agreed. It remains to be explained just how the editor of a Richmond semiweekly with a circulation of 5,000 or less could achieve such national acclaim and set the standard for future Southern editors. The answer surely has to do with his mastery of Virginia politics and with the nature of political journalism in the Age of Jackson. The political editor—if he was the spokesman of a party, if he was located in a state capital, and if he represented a state or section— could affect national policy.[9] Until Ritchie removed to Washington and sectional antagonism laid him low, he spoke the views of the Virginia Democracy and the states' rights principles of much of the South. His *Enquirer* was partisan but not parochial; it helped set the political agenda of the nation and imposed order and purpose on an unpredictable electorate. If bias, vulgarity, and scurrility were the standard fare of Jacksonian journalism, Ritchie's *Enquirer* stood forth as a reliable, informative journal of public affairs which had the potential to make democracy work. In Ritchie centered the best elements of political journalism in the Age of Jackson.

No one could foresee the establishment of one of the nation's foremost journals when on May 9, 1804, twenty-five-year-old Thomas Ritchie and his partner and printer, William W. Worseley, published the first issue of the semiweekly *Richmond Enquirer*. It was a Republican paper built upon the ruins of the *Richmond Examiner*, formerly the principal Jeffersonian organ in Virginia. From the beginning the *Enquirer* enjoyed modest success; within fourteen months circulation jumped from 500 to 1,150, and on July 30, 1805, Ritchie bought out Worseley, establishing himself as sole proprietor.[10]

The new editor doubted his preparation for a position in public affairs, but in fact his background and training were more than adequate for early nineteenth-century journalism.[11] Although his father, a wealthy Scottish merchant, died when he was six, Ritchie grew up within a circle of family, friends, and relatives that included some of the most able scholars and thinkers in Virginia. Young Ritchie received a gentleman's education, studying the classics and learning enough science to review scientific and technical books later in the *Enquirer*. Like many nineteenth-century journalists, Ritchie became an editor only after dabbling in a number of other careers. All the while he read widely in politics and political economy; he later found plenty of use for his study of Smith, Ricardo, Malthus, Voltaire, Rousseau, and Paine. Ritchie's youth in the late 1790s and early 1800s was a fascinating time in the growth of American political life. He was especially affected by the crisis created by the Alien and Sedition Acts and by the Virginia and Kentucky Resolutions of 1798 and 1799. In countless editorials over nearly half a century he would celebrate the principles of '98-'99 and carry republicanism on to future generations. In time, he would receive recognition as Virginia's constant defender of states' rights.

Money from his parents' estate enabled Ritchie to finance his share of the *Richmond Enquirer*. The common belief that President Jefferson influenced the establishment of the *Enquirer* has never been documented. At this time Jefferson and Ritchie were not close. Ritchie obtained some federal printing contracts for publishing the laws of the United States, but the far more lucrative state printing patronage went to a rival Republican editor until 1814. After his rival died, Ritchie received the state printing contract, which he retained for the next twenty years.[12]

In appearance, Ritchie's four-page *Enquirer* differed little from other political papers of the early 1800s. The political and mercantile news it delivered came from other newspapers and private letters, virtually the only sources of outside information at that time. The *National Intelligencer*, the semi-official organ of the Jefferson, Madison, and Monroe administrations, figured prominently in the *Enquirer*'s reports, as it did in those of journals throughout the country. The *Enquirer* published verbatim the speeches, laws, and proceedings of the Virginia legislature and Congress. A political journal was expected to provide facts as well as opinion. Except for coverage of state and city government, local news (which everyone was supposed to know) appeared only by accident in the advertisements and the announcements of organizations.[13]

The first issue was typical of the early *Enquirer*. Extracts from speeches celebrating the anniversary of Jefferson's inauguration covered all of page one and part of page two. "Foreign Intelligence"—mainly letters on the war in Europe—appeared on page two. On pages two and three the editor published laws of the United States. Ritchie's first editorial appeared on page three, and a modest amount of advertising filled the remainder of the paper. Ritchie promised to labor for the enlightenment of society and "to encourage as much of the spirit of party as may be necessary for the elucidation of unfettered truths, without mixing up with it any of the grossness of vulgar or personal abuse." Rather modestly, he claimed no special knowledge of worldly affairs, but in return for his readers' forbearance he promised honesty and zeal.

Bland as it was, Ritchie's first editorial was something of a departure in American journalism. In 1804 the editorial page had not yet appeared in American newspapers; editorial material invariably was anonymous and usually less than a column in length. Often, papers had none at all. But Ritchie included editorial comment in several forms, and by 1810 a "direct editorial appeared in nearly every issue."[14] Soon the authority of Ritchie's editorials and the superior quality of the essays contributed by distinguished Virginians set the paper apart and captured a healthy circulation. According to a study by Bert Marsh Mutersbaugh, from the beginning the *Enquirer* depended on its own excellence, not on political patronage, whose role in the party journalism of the Jeffersonian period has been exaggerated. "It was the quality and range of its essays and the sheer hard work and care with which Ritchie conducted the paper which accounted for its success," concludes Mutersbaugh.[15] Ritchie's first editorial was at least accurate; zeal and honest motives would make their mark.

Ritchie worked with extraordinary energy, his contemporaries agreed. Proprietor and senior editor or sole editor of the *Enquirer*, and later the *Washington Daily Union*, Ritchie, like other early nineteenth-century editors, was also his own chief reporter (normally covering the Virginia House of Delegates), book review editor, proofreader, layout supervisor, and jack-of-all-trades. He read literally hundreds of newspapers (the exchanges) from which he clipped items for inclusion in the *Enquirer*; in 1850 he told his son that he had skimmed 225 papers in one day. Between 1816 and 1833 he also edited the *Richmond Compiler*, a politically neutral, weekly booster paper which advocated city and state economic development.[16]

Ritchie could do anything with a newspaper except run it as a business. Perhaps because of overwork, perhaps because of an obsessive concern for politics, or perhaps because he was bored by routine, he was an inefficient, indifferent businessman. He was called to journalism by a desire to participate in public affairs, not to run a business. In 1846 the business manager of the *Washington Daily Union* inquired wistfully, "Is it impossible for us to have some system about our paper?"[17] Many of Ritchie's subscription accounts, the main source of revenue for the *Enquirer* in the early years, went uncollected and eventually amounted to many thousands of dollars. Occasionally he gave voice to that unpopular litany of the political press of the early republic: a plea for delinquent subscribers to pay up, which they rarely did. A New Orleans editor once remarked that Ritchie's cornucopia was overflowing with subscriptions, but not with money.[18] Few figures on his finances exist, but it appears that his papers were more prestigious than profitable. He perpetually borrowed money from friends, and at least twice had to sell a part interest in his paper and then later float loans to buy out his partners. Ritchie seems to have suffered an absolute lack of commercial instincts; when a business partner died in the 1830s, Ritchie discovered that the man was $16,000 in debt to the office. In 1842 Ritchie owed banks between $12,000 and $15,000, and he was still in debt when he left for Washington in 1845.[19]

Throughout his lengthy career, as presidents and governors came and went and the Virginia dynasty gave way to the Age of Jackson, Ritchie's newspaper reached out to an elite reading public in town and country. Ritchie proceeded with the elite's approval. He assayed to speak for all Virginians of the better sort, whether in Tidewater, Piedmont, the Valley, the trans-Allegheny West, or his hometown of Richmond. Planters and the better-off, politically-attuned farmers, urban professionals, and merchants composed his constituency. Virginia at the close of the 1820s was "a complex, heterogeneous society, a region of extremes both in lands and in peoples."[20] Virginians divided on many issues, among them suffrage extension, internal improvements, the apportionment of representation in the legislature, the burden of taxation, and the future of slavery. Sectionalism was almost as much a fact of life in Virginia as in the nation at large.

Ritchie spoke as a moderate and conciliator, addressing an educated audience with the hope of finding a consensus which would accommodate change without turmoil as population shifted westward and the Tidewater elite slowly lost influence. His was not the voice of Richmond (most of which was Whig anyway) or the cities or the Tidewater or Piedmont planters or any other group or special interest, but of all of them. His family heritage, his ties to Essex County and his daughter's estate, Brandon, on the James River, and his path to prominence as a Richmond editor and social leader placed him in an ideal position to understand and speak for the leadership elements in sectionally divided Virginia.

Ritchie was a leading member of Richmond's interlocking urban elite, which controlled most aspects of urban life, from government and business to church and charity. Merchants, professionals, bankers, and a landed oligarchy with homes in Richmond were beginning to share power with newly arisen entrepreneurs. A major part of the Richmond elite had its roots in the country, as did Ritchie, and the interests of Richmond were not distinct from those of the country. Agriculture was commerce, and vice versa as David Goldfield has shown, and there was considerable urban-rural cooperation throughout the era.[21]

Ritchie's journalism, directed toward Virginia's powerful elite, was serious, demanding, overwhelmingly political, and almost devoid of humor (except for some of the personal exchanges), sensationalism, or anything smacking of the human interest angle. His *Enquirer* served as a forum for the debate of public issues and for airing political and sometimes personal controversies. Because Ritchie was on intimate terms with the leaders of Virginia, he could draw upon such unpaid subscriber-correspondents as Judge Spencer Roane (a cousin), Senator William C. Rives, Speaker of the House Andrew Stevenson, Senator and essayist John Taylor of Caroline, Judge Richard E. Parker, Senator L. W. Tazewell, Governor William Branch Giles, Dr. John Brockenbrough (a cousin and president of the Bank of Virginia), and even Madison and Monroe. Their writings, studded with classical allusions and appearing under Greek or Roman pseudonyms, crowded the columns of the *Enquirer*.[22] Ritchie himself seems frequently to have contributed anonymous pieces. The *New York Times* claimed that "he appeared in the lists, alternately, with lance in rest as the editor of the *Richmond Enquirer*, and with visor down under the *nomme de plume* [*sic*] of some Roman patriot or Grecian philosopher, and if he found no opposing champion worthy of his steel, he would even controvert the postulates of his own pen."[23] Many essays dwelt on esoteric points of constitutional history and economic theory. One particularly arcane piece, for example, pondered the possible use of a colon or semicolon in the constitution and what this punctuation portended for the expanded power of the central government.[24]

Ritchie devoted far more space to essays and letters from Virginia's leading figures than to his own editorials.[25] Many "letters to the editor" arrived unsolicited and were anonymous, though the identities of a few famous writers were easily determined. Often Ritchie specifically solicited contributions, occasionally even giving advice on how a particular subject should be approached, while at other times he might issue a public invitation.[26] Once, for example, he invited gentlemen versed in constitutional law to respond to the question: "How the 'judicial power of the United States' ought to be so organized, that its laws may be duly carried into effect, without an unnecessary addition to its expence, and its influence?"[27]

The *Enquirer* also supplied the latest political gossip, most of which Ritchie culled from his voluminous correspondence and reshaped for publication.[28] His periodic apologies for violating the confidences in letters marked "private" suggest that sometimes the editor in him overcame the gentleman.[29] A disconcerted President Polk later complained of Ritchie's "constitutional infirmity," his inability to keep a secret. Polk grumbled, "All he knows, though given him in confidence, he is almost certain to put into his newspaper."[30]

And Ritchie had much to put in. He was at the center of social as well as public affairs, an advantage of no small import in an age when newspapers employed few staff members to gather news. No Richmond public figure enjoyed greater popularity than the editor of the *Enquirer*. Ritchie turned up everywhere. He served, for instance, on a committee to raise funds to liquidate Jefferson's debts and on the board of trustees of Richmond's Lancasterian school.[31] If there was a public meeting to protest the *Chesapeake-Leopard* outrage, a meeting to encourage manufactures, a committee to draw up resolutions for Greek independence from the Turks, or a gathering for virtually anything, Ritchie invariably was the secretary.[32] He and his growing family (ten of his twelve children lived to adulthood) joined in the city's "busy round of parties, balls, evenings of whist, and musical entertainments;" Jonathan Daniels, the celebrated, twentieth-century North Carolina editor, rather facetiously identified Ritchie as a noted dance leader and perennial toastmaster. Ritchie could preside at a Richmond testimonial dinner attended by merchants and tobacconists, yet still lead the Jacksonian planters and yeoman of rural Virginia, where his *Enquirer* had its greatest circulation. The mansion of Ritchie's associate and cousin Dr. John Brockenbrough was as much a gathering place for the politically prominent as was the nearby state capitol.[33]

The *Enquirer* was a political paper through and through, but Ritchie also felt it his duty to raise the general intellectual standards of society. In the early years especially, he published articles about literature and science in almost every issue. After the War of 1812 there was a strong interest in reform and modernization in education, transportation, the banking system and other institutions; for weeks Ritchie filled his columns with the essays of the advocates of progressive change.[34] Always he championed increased educational opportunities for the common folk and on occasion raised the issue of women's education. Whenever Congress and the Virginia legislature were not in session, the *Enquirer* included more nonpolitical material. Occasionally—particularly after hard-fought political campaigns—Ritchie would trumpet his intention to balance politics by expanding his coverage of literature, education, and agricultural and industrial development. Ritchie was a lifelong sponsor of state-supported internal improvements, especially those designed to open the West to development. As a city father and booster of Richmond and Virginia, he and the *Enquirer* were advocates of all good causes and a force for modernization. Within Virginia his reputation for liberalism survived into the twentieth century.[35]

Still, one must agree with historian Richard B. Davis that, in season and out, seven-eighths of the paper was news and essays about politics.[36] Ritchie could focus almost single-mindedly on politics in the *En-*

quirer because urban development and boosterism, which were so much a part of nineteenth-century journalism of the big cities, could be shunted off to his aptly named *Compiler*, a commercial booster paper. The *Enquirer* specialized in what mattered—politics, especially domestic politics. Its coverage of foreign affairs was highly selective. Threats of war between the United States and either Great Britain or France, and European or Latin American revolutions were worth comment during the Jefferson and Madison administrations, but from the mid-1820s through the 1840s, European affairs shrank to insignificance in the *Enquirer*'s columns.[37] Politics was becoming a national pastime; for Ritchie it was a consuming passion. In 1849, when the penny press boasted a growing circulation and healthy profits, future president James Buchanan argued that too much editorial and other political matter in Ritchie's *Daily Union* left it void of appeal as a family paper and offered little to attract the ladies.[38] Ritchie scorned such criticism.

With the rise of a serious political opposition in the 1820s and the Whigs in the 1830s, Ritchie had realized that he and the *Enquirer* had "many humbugs to dissipate, many insidious appeals to overthrow."[39] To that end, he rallied the Democrats against the common enemy. The endless political battles of the Jacksonian era crowded the four pages of the paper.[40] In 1833 Ritchie informed his importunate correspondents: "Our Communications crowd so fast upon us, that we cannot do justice to our guests, without yielding our own place at the Board. We have many views to express, many blows to parry; and several hits to return, but there is a time for all things. . . . We must have patience ourselves; and our Correspondents must practice the same virtue. The Telegraph— and the Pennsylvanian are baying at our heels—but we shall have time enough to kick back the unmannerly curs."[41]

Ritchie relished his triumphs in party battles and delighted in thumping his political opponents, so it is surprising to discover that he condemned the reigning standards of editorial abuse and fanatical partisanship. Early in his career he wrote that "the station of a public editor is itself a high, a dignified, a commanding one. . . . In this country, where librarians are so few and books so little read; where the people look to their public prints for the most solid information; that station is exalted."[42] As an earnest young editor he viewed journalism as a public calling, and he never abandoned this concept, whatever the squalid realities of daily partisan warfare. The *Enquirer* was to be a "brief abstract and chronicle of the times." It was to inform the people of the acts of their government, and through the columns of the *Enquirer*, the opinions of the people "would be transmitted with sufficient force to check their representatives." A free society, Ritchie concluded, would be impossible without a free press.[43]

According to Ritchie's editorial code, a political newspaper should be a public journal, an open paper. It could be partisan, but it must publish all important government news and major speeches and communications even if contrary to the editor's views. Its policies must reflect the editor's conscience and party principles rather than competition for the spoils of office.[44]

Ritchie paid more than lip service to this standard of editorial integrity; he denounced press licentiousness, petty editorial bickering, and the eternal partisan insult and recrimination which lowered editorial dignity and increased public disrespect for the profession of journalism.[45] Though he often compromised these ideals, contemporaries and historians have given Ritchie relatively high marks for minimizing personal rancor and scurrility. Ritchie succeeded in raising the *Enquirer* well above the typical hack newspaper.

Ritchie proved that "pungency did not need to be scurrilous to be effective."[46] Still, his attacks could sting. He once observed that two of his editorial opponents, who usually were at odds with one another, had decided to "pig together in the same truckle bed"; he dismissed the speech of an angry Whig as "an expression of splendid bile"; and he referred to Duff Green, the editor of the *United States Telegraph*, as a "miserable driveller and servile sycophant of Mr. Calhoun."[47] A "venomous attack" upon John Taylor of Caroline in 1809 has been called "the most scurrilous, certainly the least excusable, personal vendetta in which Ritchie ever engaged."[48] Taylor was no helpless target; he had charged that Ritchie's "pitiful malignity was only surpassed by his unblushing effrontery, his inordinate vanity and consumate arrogance." Yet the exchange of insults did not prevent a later reconciliation.[49] In 1824 Ritchie waged a furious battle against Ninian Edwards, who, Ritchie believed, had tried by underhanded means to ruin William Crawford's presidential chances. "This miserable Mar-plot; this anonymous assassin of honest men's reputation, this pusillanimous 'Parthian who shoots his arrows as he flies'; is likely to meet with the recompence which his conduct deserves."[50]

Examples such as these cannot make of Ritchie the typical mudslinging editor. In the context of nineteenth-century American journalism, when editors were expected to blacken their opponents' names, Ritchie's lapses from his higher standard were relatively rare. Embarrassed by editorial brawls in which the public press became a public nuisance, he found such conduct grossly insulting to the nation and damaging to the image of the press.[51] In 1838 Ritchie played a major role in assembling a convention of editors which resolved to remove personal controversy as much as possible from editorial exchanges. On that occasion he scolded, "We misrepresent each other's motives—we heap opprobrious epithets upon each other's heads—we do not recollect that violence is not energy, and that virulence is anything but dignity. How can we expect to be treated as gentlemen, if we do not conduct ourselves as gentlemen?" Ritchie urged the editors to understand that it was their duty to make the press "*pure* as well as *free, dignified* as well as *independent, respectable* as well as *interesting*."[52] Like earlier and later editorial conventions, this one achieved no lasting reforms. "The fraternal sentiments then expressed," remarked one Virginian, "evaporated with the fumes of the wine in which they were drunk."[53] That Ritchie, like other outstanding editors, could not always live up to his deeply held beliefs was simply one of the hazards of the profession and the times.

In the light of Ritchie's high-minded intentions and his opposition to duelling, it is ironic that the Ritchie name should be associated with one of the most sanguinary and squalid editorial brawls of the century. For twenty-one years Ritchie had argued and riposted with a powerful editorial rival on the *Richmond Whig*, John Hampden Pleasants, and their cacophonous duet had fostered a healthy spirit of controversy that helped preserve a competitive political system. Lester Cappon described the Ritchie-Pleasants focus of Virginia journalism as "a veritable training-school in politics and argumentation for the growing ranks of readers."[54] These editorial combatants joshed each other and challenged each other's pretensions to political influence in the best tradition of nineteenth-century personal journalism. Pleasants called Ritchie "the old mesmerized driveller of the Enquirer," lampooned his gullibility when he fell for a hoax, wrote his political obituary after he had backed a losing presidential candidate in 1824, and flung accusations of political lunacy year after year; for his part, Ritchie labeled Pleasants the oracle of the Clay clique, denounced his aristocratic pretensions, and ridiculed Pleasants's editorial slips and blunders.[55] Unfortunately, the fencing degenerated into bitterness and the pungency into malignancy. In the early forties Ritchie denounced Pleasants's "dirty work"; the *Whig* editor, Ritchie wrote, was motivated by sheer malice, and his words were the deadly "insinuations of an indecent and factious slang-whanger."[56] The exchanges escalated dangerously and in 1843 resulted in a challenge to Pleasants by Ritchie's oldest son, William—a challenge fortunately withdrawn after the intervention of a third party.[57] Three years later Ritchie's sons took over the *Enquirer* and soon drew Pleasants into a quarrel resulting in a tragic duel. Thomas Ritchie, Jr., killed Pleasants in a barbaric dawn shootout which bore faint resemblance to any affair of honor.[58]

On a more constructive level, openness was a novel characteristic of Ritchie's journalism.[59] As promised, he published the speeches and views of his opponents, such as Henry Clay's lengthy defense of the

American System, which the states' rights Richmond editor considered anathema. He also occasionally included letters personally critical of himself and rebuttals ridiculing his own editorial stand. During the presidential campaign of 1808 the young editor printed a letter accusing himself of inconsistency and incompetence and describing his writing as inane, priggish, and dull.[60] Also during that campaign Ritchie published the letters of Monroe's supporters while he himself backed Madison. Harry Ammon concludes that "in an age of intense partisan journalism such conduct was nearly unprecedented. Had it not been for this gesture . . . the minority element would have lacked a public forum."[61] In the nullification crisis, Ritchie gave space to the South Carolina nullifiers' views and to Andrew Stevenson's speech denying the right of secession, though he disagreed with both positions.[62]

Ritchie's tolerance was not only high-minded but also expedient. Was there a better way to forestall the establishment of a rival press than by printing the opposition's speeches and letters? His approach yielded other benefits as well. When no well-formulated opinion had coalesced, Ritchie reported all views while waiting for majority sentiment to emerge.[63]

Virginia was anything but monolithic and harmonious. In some of the key political battles in Virginia in the late 1820s and 1830s—battles over suffrage extension, the democratization of representation in the general assembly, and gradual emancipation—conservative, slaveholding bastions in eastern and southern Virginia faced off against more populous, small-farming regions across the state. In these confrontations neither conservatives nor reformers had a comfortable majority. Ritchie played the role of moderator, adopting a centrist position, albeit one which accepted and even endorsed change.[64] His advocacy of a moderately reformist position was usually conciliatory rather than antagonistic.

Behind the scenes Ritchie worked to bring feuding Democrats together; publicly he invited the discussion of all viewpoints in his paper. Regarding the banking controversy of 1837, the *Enquirer* announced: "The Democrats are taking the field under various names, and with different banners—and so long as they contend with the *weapons* of argument, not the fiery arrows of denunciation, the discussion may profit our country, without injuring our party." As one Virginia politician put it, Ritchie was a good model of an editor who suppressed animosities.[65] Ritchie survived for decades amid shifting coalitions by adopting the appearance and, as much as possible, the practice of being fair to all.

His critics, of course, said he simply lacked courage. They thought he marked time until a majority appeared and then embraced it.[66] This criticism was unfair. At times he was courageously independent. In 1818, for example, he jeopardized his own popularity by denouncing Andrew Jackson's invasion of Florida, even demanding the return of the Florida spoils won by the hero of New Orleans.[67] Although he later provided reliable support for the Jackson and Van Buren administrations, Ritchie criticized Jackson's use of patronage, the interpretation of the Constitution enunciated in the Nullification Proclamation, and the removal of the deposits from the Bank of the United States.[68] In an upheaval over state banking in 1837, Ritchie pushed his own middle-ground program of protecting the banks but severely restricting their operations. In so doing he bucked the Democratic hard-money majority; some Democrats were so angered as to talk loosely of establishing a rival, hard-money paper. Conservative wrath was not abated by Ritchie's radical critics; in fact, conservatives still thought Ritchie nuts for hard money. On the national scene, Ritchie opposed Van Buren's Sub-Treasury scheme in 1837-38, advocating instead the establishment of special state deposit banks. Over this issue Ritchie broke with friends and longtime political associates who turned on him with considerable bitterness. He pushed his program as a compromise, but when it was rejected he continued to oppose Van Buren. Friends warned him that he was committing political suicide, but he persisted. After months of tension—when he finally realized that no compromise was possible—he surrendered and got right with the national Democracy.[69] James Buchanan praised Ritchie's about-face: his "recent conduct has merit enough in it to cover all his past sins."[70] Yet Ritchie knew he had made enemies. Jackson later called Ritchie a good but unsafe editor who went off half-cocked and did the party great injury before he could be set aright, and a former associate editor complained that "the Enquirer has thrown cold water on every prominent and efficient measure of the Administration; Its doubts, difficulties and conscientious objections! have proven more injurious than all the abuse and slangwhanging of all the opposition presses put together."[71]

Ritchie's readers seem to have believed in the sincerity of his beliefs and the honesty of his motives.[72] As long as he remained a loyal Democrat—supporting Democrats at election time and the few fundamental issues which party regularity required—readers tolerated a certain amount of dissent. After the battles ended, Ritchie even enjoyed the esteem and friendship of his political adversaries.[73]

On one issue, however, there was little toleration and generosity of spirit. That issue was slavery. As a young editor inspired by belief in press freedom, Ritchie once had announced his intention to publish a full account of the Haitian revolt led by Jean Jacques Dessalines, but he quickly was intimidated by an angry public.[74] Thereafter he adhered to the Southern orthodoxy on the peculiar institution except for a brief episode in 1831-32. In the aftermath of the Nat Turner rebellion, the

Virginia House of Delegates debated the gradual emancipation of slaves in Virginia, and Ritchie, his Whig rival John Hampden Pleasants, and other editors not only printed the debates but also endorsed gradual emancipation. Ritchie gingerly coupled his critique of slavery as socially and economically debilitating with an orthodox defense of the moral integrity of Virginians and their financial stake in black servitude. His editorials and selected letters to the editor, protective as they were of Southern rights, interests, and sensibilities were conservative and cautious.[75] Appealing to Virginians' sense of fair play, he emphasized how on this subject he had kept faith with the public for twenty-seven years, but now it was time for the press to speak its mind. He pleaded that "something must be done"; "it is the part of no honest man to deny it— of no free press to effect to conceal it." Ritchie asked his readers to seek "gradual, systematic and discreet means to reduce the mass of this evil."[76]

For a brief time antislavery sentiment welled up in the South in a way surprising to contemporaries and historians. Alison Freehling has shown that, in the 1831-32 debates, Virginia's antislavery delegates represented the views of a majority of white Virginians. Nevertheless, the antislavery debates were exceptional and brief.[77]

Both antislavery sentiment and the openness of debate in the press shocked conservatives. Ritchie, as well as Pleasants and others, defended press freedom, and Ritchie insisted that "we can trust our cause to a cool jury of our countrymen, and fearlessly abide the issue."[78] His countrymen, however, were about to demand an end to the debate, and Ritchie was forced to seek a middle position. Conservatives were adamant; it was clear that the price of gradual emancipation in any form was dissolution of the state. A retreat from antislavery, with elements of a vengeful backlash, was soon underway. Within Virginia, Ritchie faced a movement to cancel *Enquirer* subscriptions. Referring to Virginia papers as abolition presses loaded with effusions of inflammatory matter, "Appomattox" spurned Ritchie's plea for independence of the press as dangerous, harmful, and tantamount to the establishment of an absolute dominion over slaveholders. The people should exercise their independence, "Appomattox" urged, by withdrawing their subscriptions from something so threatening to the safety of Virginians.[79] In South Carolina the fire-eaters denounced Ritchie as the "apostate traitor, the recreant and faithless sentinel, the cringing parasite, the hollow-hearted, hypocritical advocate of Southern interests . . . who has scattered the firebrands of destruction everywhere in the South."[80]

Ritchie's apostasy was brief. The *Enquirer* recanted its mild antislavery position after the defeat of gradual emancipation in the Virginia House of Delegates and lapsed into silence on the slavery problem. In the April 1832 elections to the general assembly, candidates and the press sidestepped the issue of emancipation, and soon attention focused on the presidential campaign. Silence reigned. If the South Carolina ethos exhibited fanatical devotion to the positive good theory of slavery, Virginia's was rather tepid, reflecting silence, anxiety, and a certain fatalism about the continuation of the peculiar institution.[81] Years later, the silence was broken in the dispute between Pleasants and Ritchie's sons as the charge of antislavery sentiment was bandied about. Pleasants, seeing the charge as little less than an accusation of treason to the South, demanded retraction or satisfaction.[82] Albeit essentially bogus, the charge had lethal consequences. No Southerner could continue in public life with a reputation for being soft on slavery.

Whether the elder Ritchie's long-lasting silence on slavery proves an exception to his rule of moderate independence, or whether his unusual flouting of majority opinion in 1831-32 supports a tradition of dissent, is moot. It is almost certain that Ritchie would not have questioned the conventional wisdom had Pleasants, his chief rival, not temporarily joined him. Ritchie, like others, briefly took a stand on a novel and ultimately threatening measure, abandoning it when self-destruction loomed.

Journalistic integrity and openness were fine in their way, but Thomas Ritchie's reputation in Southern journalism was based above all on his advocacy of political and constitutional principles. Ritchie became one of the great antebellum popularizers of Southern constitutional orthodoxy. Through victory and defeat, from 1804 to 1851, Ritchie heralded the principles of 1798 and 1799—the compact theory of the government, the sovereign rights of the states, and the danger to American liberty from a consolidated government. These principles became the *Enquirer*'s sacred liturgy in battles against Federalists and Whigs, against the aggrandizement of a central government, against a costly system of federal internal improvements, against the Bank of the United States, against anything that derogated from the ascendancy of Virginia. And the South responded to his pen.[83] The wife of an Alabama senator recalled from her childhood that she had been religiously taught three lessons: "To be proud alike of my name and blood and section; to read my Bible; and last, to know my *Richmond Enquirer*."[84]

In the early 1810s, the triumphs of Jefferson and Madison and the strong spirit of nationalism arising from the War of 1812 temporarily diverted Ritchie from strict constructionism. Ever the flag-waving patriot and as militant as any of the celebrated War Hawks of 1811-12, Ritchie belligerently defended American interests against British arrogance and aggression. Once the war began, he advocated a draft, demanded that Congress adopt new tools of war, such as mines and submarines, denounced editors who were lukewarm toward the cause, and damned New England governors who refused to part with their state militias. In the age of Virginia's dynasty, which perhaps hid the reality of Virginia's relative economic and population decline, the *Enquirer* for a short time exhibited a mild economic nationalism, even accepting a small measure of protection for American industry.[85]

In the late 1810s the *Enquirer* led Virginia's return to Jeffersonian strict construction. Many Virginians, like Ritchie, had become alarmed at Virginia's declining influence in federal affairs and were moving toward conservatism. They were outraged by the power of the Second Bank of the United States, an unequal and oppressive tariff, and the centralizing decisions of John Marshall's Supreme Court, which the *Enquirer* blasted by publishing Judge Spencer Roane's protests against *Martin* v. *Hunter's Lesee* and *McCulloch* v. *Maryland*.[86]

A sense of a loss of mastery became acute when Virginians confronted a crisis which they could view only as Northern aggression—the attempt to exclude slavery from the territories.[87] In the Missouri Crisis in 1820, Ritchie and most Virginians adopted militant states' rights views and stirred up the fires of sectional discord whereas, paradoxical as it seems in retrospect, Calhoun and South Carolina sought to quench them.[88] In May 1819, Ritchie was one of the first to take a stand. As he saw it, the controversy was not about slavery itself, which he declared "an evil . . . we know not how to get rid of." [89] Instead the issue was states' rights. Ritchie denounced the Missouri Compromise as unconstitutional, revolutionary, and destructive of the equality of the states. By excluding slaveholding Southerners from the territories obtained by common sacrifice, taxing them for costly manufactures, and abolishing the slave representation guaranteed by the federal constitution, Northern sectionalists violated every fundamental principle of political justice.[90]

The passage of the compromise was a grievous blow, and Ritchie and his fellow Virginians for a time remained unreconciled. As always, Ritchie published the opinions of a few opponents, but he drew closer to such extreme Southern rights spokesmen as John Randolph of Roanoke and John Taylor of Caroline. In 1820 his press issued John Taylor's *Construction Construed*, an elaborate defense of states' rights which Ritchie, in a laudatory introduction, described as a breath of political life from the founding fathers. In 1821 he "broke one of the best kept secrets of American politics, Jefferson's authorship of the Kentucky resolutions," and five years later published a new, combined edition of the Virginia and Kentucky Resolutions.[91]

Yet it would be wrong to view Ritchie's *Enquirer* as merely a purveyor of states' rights obstructionism. Ritchie was a strict constructionist, and in the Missouri Crisis he appears vulnerable to the charge of extremism. Nevertheless, he eventually did accept the compromise. As his anger cooled, he announced in the *Enquirer* that the Union was too dear to be torn asunder and that it had never really been in danger during the Missouri controversy.[92]

Sharing habits of mind common to most Americans of his time, Ritchie thought of the United States as the special trustee of the cause of liberty. His political theory identified the Union, the federal system, and states' rights as equally essential, neutralizing a natural tendency of government to evolve toward the extremes of centralization and tyranny or decentralization and anarchy. In 1828 he wrote that the *Enquirer* "will continue to uphold the constitution of the country according to the good old school of '98 and '99. The principles of human liberty, the Union of the States, the due powers of the general government, the rights of the States and the rights of the people, will ever be as they ever have been the shibboleth of its faith. Men are of subordinate consideration, but principles are eternal." One of his favorite mottoes was "as much scope as possible to the liberties of the people, and as much limitation to the powers of the government," but another was equally popular: "The Rights of the States and the Union of the States."[93]

Although Ritchie's preeminence as an editor grew in part from his constant advocacy of constitutional principles and in part from his reputation for responsible and sober journalism, his involvement in practical politics secured an audience for his ideas. Southerners were not likely to take seriously the constitutional or political commentary of ivory-tower theoreticians. Editors needed inside political information and access to political chieftains. Editors of national significance had to speak for presidents, presidential aspirants, or powerful party factions, laying down the party line for followers in the provinces. Ritchie of course publicized the orthodox views of the Democratic party, but he was not merely a mouthpiece for those of influence and power—he was a man of influence and power himself.

In the Jacksonian era, parties were built around state leadership. Ritchie was central to Virginia's Democracy, and his power within the Jacksonian coalition helped assuage those Virginians who acknowledged and lamented Virginia's fall from the glory days of Jefferson, Madison, and Monroe.[94] Virginia went Democratic in every presidential election before 1860, and the Democrats controlled the state legislature throughout this long period.[95] Historian Joseph Harrison, Jr., argues that in a large state divided by east-west sectional tensions and operating under a decentralized constitution, this record of Democratic dominance is remarkable.[96]

The Democrats owed much of their success to an effective party press dominated by the *Enquirer*. "The Enquirer and the Enquirer only is taken everywhere and almost in every cabin in the State," complained a member of President John Quincy Adams's cabinet, with some exaggeration.[97] The *Enquirer* spoke for a small group of influential Virginians known collectively as the Richmond Junto. Preserving from the colonial period an aristocratic legacy of disinterested leadership and public service, this loosely organized steering committee of wealthy and socially prominent Virginians exercised remarkable influence in Virginia politics—particularly in presidential politics—for nearly forty years.[98] Ties of blood, marriage, and friendship bound the Junto together. Though it represented planters from east of the Blue Ridge Mountains, almost all of its prominent members were business and professional people who lived in Richmond for at least part of the year.[99] The Junto arose out of the central corresponding committee of the legislative caucus, which communicated with county leadership and drew up the slate of Virginia's presidential electors. In addition to family and personal influence, key elements in its domination of the political process included control over political appointments, minimal rotation in office, a centralized and irresponsible judiciary, and the weight of corporations, especially banks.[100]

From the beginning Ritchie's family connections and ties to the capital's intellectual community drew him to the Junto, whose members gave him inside political information and wrote political and literary essays for his paper.[101] Ritchie's elder cousin, Judge Spencer Roane, whose states' rights essays became the political gospel of many a Virginia Republican, was the Junto's strongest leader in the 1810s.[102] Two other cousins, John and William Brockenbrough, were prominent members. John Brockenbrough served as president of the Bank of Virginia from 1811 to 1843, and the Junto used its control over state financial operations to the considerable advantage of the Bank. Though the *Enquirer* was strongly pro-Bank, it is to Ritchie's credit that he opened his columns to the Bank's critics.[103]

Relatively little is known of the Junto's operations. Not until 1823 did the first public criticism of it appear in the press, much of it aimed directly at Ritchie.[104] Ritchie always denied the existence of the Junto, labeling it a phantom and suggesting that Virginians were hardly the sort to be led around by a wicked editor.[105]

The membership of the Junto, always informal, changed over the years, but Ritchie remained an insider and the Junto's spokesman. His stabilizing presence supplied an essential element of continuity as Virginia politics evolved from the "simple, stable oligarchy" of the eighteenth century into the "complex, turbulent, contentious, emerging democracy" of the Jacksonian era. As Virginia politics changed, conservatives believed, their leadership became essential in channeling public affairs along a safe course. Here was Ritchie's opportunity.[106] Invariably he was the secretary of the legislative caucuses in Richmond where presidents, governors, senators, and other officeholders were made and unmade. Frequently Ritchie appeared in the House of Delegates as official reporter, and often delegates congregated at his desk to confer with him and iron out legislative proposals.

Within the Junto, Ritchie worked for unity and conciliation, apparently achieving considerable unity on national questions as the Junto judged national issues and candidates by the single standard of states' rights. The Junto strongly supported Madison in 1808, backed Monroe somewhat reluctantly in 1816, fought hard for Crawford in 1823 and 1824, rejected Adams and then buttressed the Jackson, Van Buren, and Polk administrations.[107] Ritchie and the Junto were largely responsible for turning back Calhounian influence in Virginia.[108]

In matters other than presidential politics and patronage—matters such as internal improvements, intrastate sectional representation, education—the Junto was anything but united.[109] Ritchie's democratic leanings made him probably the most progressive member of the Junto. He was consistent in his advocacy of internal improvements for the west, and since the 1810s he had spoken for the west's demand for suffrage reform. His support of suffrage reform in the state constitutional convention in 1829-30 especially rankled conservatives but won the *Enquirer* enduring support from western Virginia. For a time conservatives expressed considerable interest in establishing a rival press, so strongly did their feelings run against Ritchie.[110] Junto disagreements were probably major reasons for the openness of the *Enquirer* and Ritchie's consistent drive for conciliation and toleration for dissenters. Fundamental to Ritchie's power in the party (in addition to the basic unity of conservatives and reformers in presidential politics) was his ability to draw support both from reform-minded Virginians and powerful eastern Junto conservatives.

Because Ritchie was a power in Virginia politics he could aspire to national leadership. The Jacksonian coalition had two centers of strength: at Albany, New York, where Edwin Croswell's *Albany Argus* spoke for the Van Buren wing of the party; and at Richmond, where Ritchie's *Enquirer* voiced the views of the Junto and the southern wing of the party.[111] Ironically, earlier Ritchie had considered General Jackson little less than a tyrant. Many Southerners thought Jackson's constitutional and economic views unsound. His apparent disregard of international law in Florida had frightened Ritchie and many Junto allies; they thought him too rash, too quick to anger, disrespectful of civilian authorities, and too ignorant of politics and government to occupy the office once held by Jefferson and Madison.[112] Ritchie never entirely overcame such fears. At the time of the Bank veto, recalled Martin Van Buren, Ritchie "scarcely ever went to bed . . . without apprehension that he would wake up to hear of some *coup d'etat* by the General which he would be called on to explain or defend."[113]

Nevertheless, by the mid-1820s the danger of Jackson had seemed negligible in comparison with the damage resulting from the Adams administration and Clay's American System. When the Adams-Clay candidate for Virginia's U.S. Senate seat triumphed over Ritchie's favorite, the Richmond editor turned to an alliance with the Van Burenites and Jackson in early 1827.[114] Ritchie's historic reversal on the hero of New Orleans soon had him praising the firm and incorruptible patriot and denying that Jackson had ever been essentially a "Military Chieftain."[115] If Ritchie was embarrassed by the flip-flop, he did not show it. The Richmond editor always would admit that at times he had been wrong about men, but never about principles.[116]

Ritchie saw obvious benefits in the revival of the Virginia-New York axis in politics. Though never forgiven or trusted by Jackson, Ritchie became one of the most influential press spokesmen of the Democratic party (the others being Francis P. Blair and John C. Rives of the *Globe* and Edwin Croswell of the *Albany Argus*). Ritchie hoped that the Democrats would restore to Washington the timeless principles of '98-'99. In fact, the major thrust of the Jackson and Van Buren administrations, especially in slaying the monster bank and in discouraging abolitionism, did reflect concern for states' rights sentiments. Whenever they broke with the ideology of '98-'99 and the defense of slavery and the South, the *Enquirer* did not hesitate to publicize Virginia's protest.[117] But on most major issues the party was right, and it was the party, adhering to the sacred principles, which could preserve liberty, the rights of the states, and the union of the states.

Ritchie's power was widely recognized. In 1824 Ritchie's fellow editors on the *National Intelligencer*, Joseph Gales, Jr., and William W. Seaton, urged Ritchie to publicize a certain candidate "because, there being no national central committee, you come the nearest to the character of such a committee."[118] Four years later Virginia's leading Jacksonian congressman, William C. Rives, wrote of the *Enquirer*:

There is not a political aspirant in the nation who does not anxiously court the countenance of such a paper, and at this moment, Van Buren, I know, and most probably Calhoun, and all the rest of the candidates for the presidential purple, are in close correspondence with Ritchie, and suing for his support. Great as has been the influence of the *Enquirer* heretofore, circumstances are likely to increase rather than diminish it, (abroad at least), for the next four years. Virginia is the *stake* that will be more eagerly played for by the political gamblers, who wish to succeed Jackson, than, probably any other electoral voter in The Union.

The power therefore that has the *reputation* of influencing Virginia, will be courted with increased ardour and assiduity.[119]

Rives's prediction was right. Ritchie's influence grew throughout the 1830s despite serious disagreements with the Jackson and Van Buren administrations. Jackson's Force Bill and hasty removal of the deposits and Van Buren's independent treasury scheme occasioned serious revolts in the Virginia Democracy. Ritchie voiced the complaints of many Virginia Democrats, suffered minor defeats within the state, and earned a reputation for being erratic, but he always remained true to the party as he saw it and a dominant power. Ritchie was instrumental in destroying the Bank of the United States, achieving compromise and outmaneuvering the nullifiers in 1833, destroying Calhoun in Virginia, and electing Van Buren in 1836. His associates prospered politically as well. Ritchie's friend David Campbell became governor in 1837, and his brother-in-law Richard E. Parker advanced to the Senate. When Parker resigned shortly thereafter, Ritchie's cousin William Henry Roane succeeded him.[120]

Ritchie kept Virginia in the Democratic column even when the party went down to defeat nationally in 1840. In opposition, Ritchie attributed Democratic losses to Democratic apathy and Whig humbugging, which featured "their glorious insignia of coonskins and hard cider."[121] Urging compromise among Democrats, Ritchie rallied his party for the next contest upon a new issue, the annexation of Texas, which Ritchie considered essential for national as well as Southern security.[122] In 1844 Ritchie reached the culmination of his power when he became the unofficial field marshal of the Polk forces in the general election. Ritchie "probably contributed more than any other man in the union towards elevating Mr. Polk toward the presidency," concluded *Niles' Weekly Register*.[123]

As an advocate of party loyalty and independence of judgment, the spokesman for states' rights and union, an architect of the Virginia-New York Democratic alliance, and a veteran of the vicissitudes of Virginia coalition politics, Ritchie learned that the key to power was unity through compromise and conciliation. Within Virginia, Ritchie's willingness to compromise eased the east-west sectional conflict and conservative-reform clashes while uniting the various Democratic factions. As Ritchie rose to national prominence, he realized even more the necessity of moderation to hold together the Democratic coalition of nonslaveholding Northern farmers and mechanics and Southern slaveholding planters and farmers. His slogan for preserving the Democratic party was "Union, harmony and concession."[124] He would support all Democrats except anti-expansionists and extremists who would divide the party. As long as moderates controlled the Democratic party and maintained the Virginia-New York axis and its philosophy of states' rights, Virginia, the South, and slavery would be secure within the Union.[125]

Ritchie believed that the peace and order of the nation depended on the willingness of factions and sections to negotiate, and he took considerable risks in playing the role of honest broker. A study of one case in some detail may show how the editor operated in crisis situations. In the sectional blowup over the tariff and South Carolina's nullification in 1832 and 1833, the separate strands of his editorial genius—his emphasis on constitutional principles, his journalistic integrity and openness, his political clout, as well as his desire for conciliation and moderation—served his country well while preserving and advancing his own interests.

South Carolina's nullification and Jackson's swift response put Ritchie's journalistic leadership and moderate course to a severe test. From the beginning Ritchie denounced nullification as unconstitutional, an absurd and mischievous heresy which could result only in anarchy; thus he tended to side with the Jacksonians,[126] although he agreed with most Virginians that the tariff hurt the South and was an indefensible exercise of power. His stance demanded courage, for Southern anger at the tariff was growing even if a majority of Virginians had no stomach for the extremism of nullification. Furthermore, a significant number of Calhounites populated the Virginia Democracy, and Calhoun's theories acquired a large following.[127] At any moment Jackson's celebrated temper might destroy the moderates and unite all Southerners in a constitutional crisis one step short of the battlefield.

The *Enquirer* proclaimed Jackson correct on nullification, and until December seemed master of the volatile situation. But then Jackson issued the Nullification Proclamation, which to most Southerners embraced a Federalist form of centralism, denied the compact theory of the government, and negated the rights of the states. The proclamation placed Jackson's Southern supporters on the defensive, but when the president followed with a request for additional military powers in the Force Bill, they faced utter ruin. Ritchie immediately criticized Jackson's proclamation and opposed the Force Bill, all the while trying to emphasize the real villains of the piece, the Northern tariffites, whose ruthlessness violated the goodwill upon which the American union depended.[128]

Opposition to Jackson and Ritchie sprang up within the Virginia Democracy and throughout the South. For a time it seemed as if everyone, nullifiers as well as tariffites, reviled the fence-sitter in Richmond. Jackson himself was displeased by Ritchie's course. Nullifiers called Ritchie a Federalist, and nationalists called him a Nullifier. The wife of the governor of Virginia "was certain that he took his cue from the Albany regency"; and the governor himself "spoke of him and others of the Junto as 'wretches' who had 'deserted their principles and liberties of the people' for the smiles of a tyrant."[129] The *Augusta* (Ga.) *Chronicle* abused the *Enquirer* as a pimp and a parasite, charging it with attempting to enforce the tariff at the point of a bayonet.[130] The way of the peacemaker was hard.

Ritchie exerted all of his party influence to move Jackson toward conciliation. He fired off numerous letters to Martin Van Buren, Francis P. Blair, Senator William Rives, and others, imploring them to influence the administration to adopt a policy of forbearance along with an adamant rejection of nullification. Prudence must preside, he warned Blair, while to Senator Rives he prophesied the destruction of the Jacksonian party in the South should there be any more rash action in the White House. His pleadings hinted at panic.[131] Publicly, however, Ritchie stressed the chances for peaceful settlement and minimized extremist rhetoric. The tariff was unjust, he wrote, but hardly harmful enough to justify so revolutionary a step as nullification. Surely President Jackson would propitiate the aggrieved states.[132] The *Enquirer* criticized Virginia Governor John Floyd and others who stirred up anti-administration feeling, and it ridiculed the irresponsible press element which shouted nonsense about Jacksonian tyranny and suggested disunion.[133]

As political alignments shifted in the midst of the crisis, Ritchie was tolerant, sometimes even respectful, of his leading Calhounite opponents. Occasionally, as was his custom, he admitted his opponents' letters to his columns,[134] apparently thinking that placating the Calhounites might encourage a retreat from nullification, while insult, ridicule, and threats would harden their resolve. Ritchie backed wholeheartedly the efforts of the state legislature to send a Virginia mediator to South Carolina to break the impasse; he liked the idea that the interposition of a mediating state might serve as a "new via medicatrix in our complicated political system" to preserve the union, as well as the rights of the states.[135] Along with conciliatory words, the *Enquirer* kept the pressure on South Carolina by emphasizing—not unjustly—the unpopularity of nullification. Every paper in Virginia save one, Ritchie reported, opposed this extremism.[136] The *Enquirer* published the resolutions of Virginia county meetings, which were decidedly hostile to nullification, thus further separating South Carolina opinion from majority sentiment in the South.[137]

On the other side Ritchie repudiated Jackson's Nullification Proclamation as unconstitutional insofar as it denied the compact theory of government and the right of secession under any circumstances. Airing his own belief in the compact theory of the government and the rights of the states, Ritchie reestablished his Southern credentials: this public disagreement with an administration that he had backed for four years drew support throughout the South. Secession, wrote Ritchie, was the *ultima ratio* of the Federal system, but it was a right to be exercised only as a last resort—after exhausting all amicable expedients.[138]

Knowing full well that crises are resolved not on an ideological level but, rather, by practical expedients, Ritchie worked for the enactment of a compromise tariff, launching a press campaign to force the North to face the South's genuine anger over unjust tariffs and using his connections to move the administration toward concessions. He convinced Van Buren of the depth of Southern anger, and, in Congress, support for the president's hard-line stand crumbled under the impact of opposition from state leaders. Soon Jackson had little choice but to moderate his views and endorse the compromise tariff orchestrated by his arch-enemy, Kentuckian Henry Clay.[139]

When the compromise tariff and South Carolina's repeal of its nullification ordinance resolved the immediate crisis, Ritchie sought to heal the wounds within the party and nation by searching for constitutional consensus and by disparaging the nullifiers. The latter was easy enough; Calhoun was an old enemy. Every editor was versed in rallying his own against a common foe whose motives were partisan rather than principled; now *Enquirer* readers learned that the Carolina nullifier had provoked the crisis to create a party which he could ride into power and that the emerging anti-abolition agitation was a similar gambit.[140]

Calhoun could be dispatched with a few pointed editorials, but the more refractory constitutional issues continued to divide the Democracy. In regard to Jackson, his proclamation, and his penchant for force, Ritchie was clear: the president, a patriot, not a tyrant, had been misled. The Southern Democracy would support his correct measures, but not his wrong ones. Here was a damning admission in an age in which editors simply did not criticize their party's leader and provide the opposition with potentially lethal ammunition. Party unity was the *sine qua non* of electoral success. The party leader could not remain "wrong" in the eyes of other powerful members. There had to be a resolution.

In September Blair and Rives's *Globe* introduced a gloss on the proclamation's disputed doctrinal points on sovereignty in an effort to satisfy Ritchie and the guardians of the principles of '98-'99. An "authorized exposition"—which Jackson never authorized—altered the language of the disagreement and superficially reconciled the irreconcilable. "[T]he language of 'compact,' which the proclamation treated with indifference, was returned to favor," concludes historian Merrill Peterson, "and although both nullification and secession were rejected, the right of state interposition on the principles of the Resolutions of '98 (which the proclamation had neglected to mention) was clearly affirmed." Ritchie heralded the exposition as Jackson's recantation. "No one can hereafter pretend to affirm, that the President adopts the idea of a consolidated, instead of a federal government," thundered the *Enquirer*.[141]

Interest in the federal-state confrontation in 1832-33 had been so intense that the tariff crisis almost crowded the Bank War and the presidential campaign of 1832 from the *Enquirer*'s columns. As editors before and after Ritchie learned, public excitement on current affairs translated into increased circulation.[142] So it was with the *Enquirer*, despite that paper's plethora of highly erudite offerings on constitutionalism and tariff history. However unattractive to modern readers, such material was interesting to nineteenth-century readers and, more than that, vital to a resolution of the crisis.

The victory of political moderation owed as much to Thomas Ritchie as to any other single person. Throughout the months of crisis the editor had addressed the perils of party division and disunion, combatted the extremists on both sides, and kept the lines of communication open. Ritchie's *Enquirer* had a national reputation for credibility. His readers North and South believed the *Enquirer*'s reportage stressing the importance of states' rights feelings, the anger of the South, and the unpopularity of nullification. Ritchie had proven the constructive possibilities of a responsible press.

Ritchie seemingly reached the pinnacle of his editorial career in 1845 when, in the aftermath of Polk's victory, the president himself tapped the Richmond editor to ascend to the administration organ in the capital, to be called the *Washington Daily Union*. The capital's administration and opposition papers—especially the *National Intelligencer* and the *Globe* but others as well—had dominated political journalism in the United States since the early days of the republic. Supported by government contracts—the only means to allay their heavy expenses—these newspapers had little need for crowd-pleasing fare and could concentrate on an elite, political audience, reporting congressional proceedings and debates, printing new legislation, and publishing special reports of the national government. These journals gave direction to policy and set forth party principles and programs in lengthy, informed editorials highlighted by access to party and government officials of the highest order. The capital's patronage presses were actors as well as narrators in the business of government, and selection to join this elite group was a signal honor.[143]

Naturally, most assumed that forty-one years of experience had prepared the Richmond editor for this great opportunity, but suddenly Ritchie's entire editorial career was placed in jeopardy. What should have been the culmination of a distinguished career turned out to be a fiasco.[144] With the exception of his contribution to the Compromise of 1850—an important exception—his six-year watch at the helm of the *Washington Daily Union* marked a decline in his political and editorial stature. Despite all his experience, Ritchie floundered in the nation's capital, the victim of sectionalism, political factionalism, and the unaccustomed environs of Washington journalism. An astute correspondent of the *Baltimore Patriot* remarked at his arrival, "An editor who exercises an influence in abstracted Virginia, will find himself in a strange atmosphere, when he launches unfledged on a new career at Washington. Mr. Ritchie, as the head of the Enquirer, has been accustomed to dictate to his party in his state, and is looked up to there, as one of her big men; but he will soon find that even a great man's shadow is very small here."[145]

Finances played a major role in Ritchie's decision to exchange a secure and politically successful position for the rather hazardous opportunities beckoning in a very different journalistic environment, and finances played a role in his downfall. Ritchie, at least initially, did not want the *Daily Union* job; indeed, he rejected the first two offers from Polk because of his reluctance to leave Richmond. But Polk was desperate to replace the *Washington Globe*, which editors Francis P. Blair and John C. Rives had made the standard-bearer of the Van Buren Democrats. Polk especially distrusted Blair because of the editor's antislavery leanings and opposition to the annexation of Texas. Moreover, Polk suspected Blair would devote the next four years to efforts to control the Democratic presidential succession in 1848. Blair, Polk concluded, would divide the party. Whether any editor could unite the party while being spokesman for the administration was not certain. Ritchie was one of several who refused the job.

Finally, in a complex and secret deal, Polk's friend from Tennessee, Major John P. Heiss, obtained from Simon Cameron and other influential politicians the sum, reputedly thirty-five thousand dollars, necessary to buy out Blair and Rives.[146] While Heiss approached Ritchie, Polk and others forced Blair out by threatening to withhold the lucrative government printing contracts. When President Polk and Ritchie conferred, Polk assured the Virginian that he had read the *Enquirer* for years and that on all important matters they were in essential agreement. Ritchie, apprehensive about dependence on a political clique, slowly succumbed. His president and party said they needed his services; the purchase money came from third parties whom he did not know; government printing contracts beckoned; and apparently there were no strings attached to the transaction. Probably the deciding factor was financial, since Ritchie, now in the twilight of his career, was much concerned about the security of his family. When Blair, whom Ritchie respected, gave assurances that there would be no hard feelings, Ritchie at last accepted.[147]

For a little over a year the *Daily Union* made all the money Ritchie could have hoped. The *Union* nearly doubled the *Globe*'s subscription list of four thousand in the first two months. In October 1846 John Heiss, the business manager, reported total profits of $108,758.87, but factionalism, sectionalism, and political grudges—some aimed directly at Ritchie—soon led Congress to alter the contract system for publishing government documents, which traditionally by vote of Congress had gone to one printing establishment. The *Union* had such a contract for two years, from 1845 until 1847. In 1846 Whig Congressmen and a small group of dissident Democrats pushed successfully for the adoption of a lowest bid system, and Ritchie and Heiss were shut out for the remaining two years of Polk's term.

Between 1849 and 1851, Ritchie, now leading an opposition press, received a major portion of the government business (which was still a mainstay of the capital press), but his bids were ruinously low.[148] His incompetence as a business manager was notorious. The limitations of the Washington newspaper field abetted Ritchie's financial collapse. Elsewhere in the largest cities, huge, low-priced, popular journals based on mass circulation and lucrative advertising arrangements forged ahead with record sales, profits, and security, but in the nation's capital an elite press could not rely on mass circulation or business support. The duties and responsibilities of the capital's political press were many; its sources of support limited to government largesse. As John Forney recalled: "In former times what was called the national organ was liberally sustained by the advertising and the printing of the Government. . . . No class of men do harder work for less pay than the political writers at Washington, and none, if properly sustained, can exert a wider or better influence. Proprietors of newspapers at the national capital must now spend vast sums of money for editorial assistance, news correspondence, etc. yet their incomes are comparatively small. They have no large population around them, and as yet no active, progressive states South of them." Ritchie undoubtedly would have seconded Forney's wistful recommendation for resumption of the old system of contracting or establishment of another "by which, under proper regulations, the profits of the public printing could be secured to the organ of the party in the majority";[149] but no such system fell into place.

Ritchie continued his struggle until 1851, at first trying to expand circulation to defray his huge annual expenses (twelve to fifteen thousand dollars for reporters alone) and finally appealing to Congress for a special appropriation to pay off his debts incurred in government contract work. In March 1851, when relief did not materialize, Ritchie was forced to sell the *Union* for twenty thousand dollars. Then Congress, recognizing the losses sustained by the *Union* in printing government documents and proceedings, put politics aside to provide the elderly editor the relief he so desperately needed.[150]

Ritchie's future, however, had looked bright on May 1, 1845, when he rushed to the capital and in less than twenty-four hours produced his first *Union* editorial, trumpeting the benefits of liberty and union, constitutional federalism based on the "good old Jeffersonian standard," and the importance of party unity in support of the Polk administration.[151] Ritchie's daughter, enchanted by her father's promotion and apparent success, wrote that he was idolized by the Democracy.[152] Not everyone agreed, especially the Van Buren wing, who viewed Ritchie's appointment as a southward shift, perhaps toward Calhoun.[153] The new editorial arrangement, Forney later concluded, began the disruption of the Democratic party.[154] Forney spoke from hindsight, but a few of Ritchie's contemporaries foresaw the party's disintegration. Blair, for instance, predicted privately that Ritchie's arrival would divide the party along sectional lines within a year.[155]

In form and coverage Ritchie's Washington paper was similar to the old *Enquirer*. Political essays and letters were featured prominently, as were lengthy partisan editorials. The *Union*'s political focus was if anything even narrower and more obsessive than the *Enquirer*'s; Secretary of State James Buchanan complained of too much editorial matter and a paucity of interesting material from other papers.[156] The *Union* contained more foreign news than did the *Enquirer*, and it naturally covered Congressional proceedings and national politics more thoroughly.

It was in policy and style that the *Daily Union* diverged most sharply from the *Enquirer*; regrettably, Ritchie abandoned most of the high-minded journalistic practices that had made him a giant among editors in his time. As always, Ritchie's paper was the life of the party (to borrow a phrase from Bernard Weisberger),[157] but now his idea of party rose no higher than a slavish adulation of the Polk administration. He became a mouthpiece for the president, or in the words of the *New Orleans Daily Picayune*, a party hack.[158] The independent critic of yesteryear who had stood up to Jackson and Van Buren flattered and toadied to Polk in the pages of his paper. The champion of the open press in Richmond excluded critics of the administration from the *Daily Union*.[159] In his first week in Washington Ritchie wrote a defense of Polk's appointment of Democratic editors to high office, conveniently forgetting that the *Enquirer* had condemned Jackson for the same thing on the grounds that it jeopardized the integrity of the press.[160] Like an obedient underling, Ritchie followed every turn and twist of Polk's policy. He wrote, for example, on March 16, 1846, that the president's conduct of foreign policy "has been alike calm and fearless. . . . At the very moment of his inauguration a conflict was menaced on the part of Mexico, a weaker power. Profoundly sensible that the policy of honorable peace is the policy of civilization, and the only one worthy of a friend to the best interests of humanity, all his efforts were bent to accomplish the annexation of Texas without an armed collision." [161] Less than two months later Ritchie swallowed whole Polk's one-sided justification of war and assured readers that "Mexico has commenced offensive war by the invasion of our territory and the slaughter of a detachment of our regular army within our own borders." [162]

In Washington Ritchie's anti-Whig partisanship was pure, invariable, almost a mindless reflex. His Washington rival, the *National Intelligencer*, could always draw Ritchie's fire. [163] John W. Forney remembered that practical jokers in the Whig press took great delight in worrying old Father Ritchie with hoaxes and humbugs, "and it was amusing to note how the most trifling allusion to the President and his cabinet would quicken his facile pen, and how he would pour his almost unintelligible manuscript into the hands of the printer." [164]

While his attacks upon the Whig journals were not particularly personal, they were harsh and tiresome. When Ritchie persisted in referring to his Whig rival as the subservient tool of the British interests on the Oregon question or, later, as the organ of Mexican interests, repetition dulled the effectiveness of the editorials. [165] During and after the presidential campaign of 1848 the *Daily Union* preserved an unblemished record of small-minded partisanship. [166] In Richmond Ritchie had announced that the organ of a government "ought to be ever stately and ceremonious," [167] but the standards of the organ he edited in Washington were vastly inferior to those which his *Enquirer* had preached.

If the *Daily Union* fell well short of the highest journalistic standards, it was still worth reading for Ritchie's unrivaled supply of inside political information, his coverage of Congress, his announcement of the administration's foreign policy views, his news of the Mexican War (since he was the first journalist to see the official dispatches), and, most important, information gleaned through his ties to Polk. Polk relied upon the *Union* to present his views to the public and keep recalcitrant Democrats in line. [168] Of necessity, then, Democratic leaders had to subscribe to the *Union* to remain abreast of the administration line and the latest capital gossip.

Despite Ritchie's crippling sacrifices for his relationship with Polk, Polk presently came to distrust his editor. Ritchie wanted so much to appear to be the executive organ, Polk concluded, that he blabbed everything in his paper. The president finally decided that it was not always prudent to trust Ritchie with sensitive information, but the occasions when Polk withheld information were the exceptions rather than the rule.[169]

As the prestige of Ritchie's Virginia triumphs evaporated, Washington politicians, editors, and major segments of the public came to see him as just another partisan editor. He had no editorial eminence and no political base of his own now to offset the enmities he incurred as Polk's man. This was a dangerous position for the supporter of a one-term president—particularly when elements of his own party turned on him. Several Democrats aspiring to succeed Polk hoped to win over the *Union* editor and became Ritchie's opponents when that effort failed.[170] Some Democrats were angered when Ritchie sought to whip them into line.[171] Once again, as in the Richmond days, Ritchie antagonized the Calhoun faction in the Senate, this time by his Mexican War stand; in fact, angry Calhounites joined with the Whigs and a few other senators who were fed up with Ritchie's lecturing ("as if they were school-boys subject to his ferule") to expel Ritchie from the Senate floor in 1847.[172] To some congressmen, Ritchie made the national Democratic organ too Southern, and they compelled him to accept the services of a Northern assistant. There was even a demand to bring Blair back.[173] To Southern extremists, on the other hand, Ritchie was a turncoat who had attempted to expel Robert Barnwell Rhett from the party because he abandoned Polk on the Oregon issue.[174]

Polk defended Ritchie, but as critics charged that Ritchie's paper was simply the president's tool, the defense did the editor little good. The charges may have been more substantial than the defense in any case. Ritchie was under tight control by the White House. His first business in Washington had been to submit the prospectus for the *Daily Union* for Polk's approval. Though Ritchie and Polk agreed philosophically on most matters, they sometimes differed over tactics, but Ritchie invariably bent to the administration's course. When he ran afoul of White House policy, Polk or some other Democrat would rebuke him, whereupon he would offer apologies and perhaps even publish a retraction absolving the president and cabinet of responsibility for his error. In April 1846, for example, Ritchie had to apologize to Polk for a hastily prepared editorial which aroused considerable dissatisfaction among congressional Democrats. The blunder (actually that of an assistant whose essay Ritchie failed to review) had to be rectified, so the *Union* printed an emollient essay by the president. "It is," Polk wrote in his diary, "the second or third time since I have been President that I have sketched an article for the paper. I did so in this instance to allay if possible the excitement which I learned the article in yesterday's Union has produced." A few months later Ritchie blundered again. "I told him," wrote Polk, "I regretted exceedingly the appearance of an article in the Union of last evening on the Oregon question, because it did not present the administration truly."[175]

Trying to account for his precipitous decline from the great Richmond days, some critics suggested that the sixty-nine-year-old Ritchie had outlived his abilities. Certainly the switch from the semiweekly or triweekly *Enquirer* to a daily added immeasurably to his editorial burden. Forney, for one, believed Ritchie "had lived too long in a narrow sphere to figure on the national stage"; he was "the kindest and most genteel old fogy who ever wore nankeen pantaloons, high shirt-collars, and broad-brimmed straw hats." But other observers noted his youthful appearance and apparently abundant energies. His Washington work schedule—hectic days spent receiving fifteen to twenty callers and late nights working until two or three in the morning—would have burdened anyone, but Ritchie seems to have taken the strain well.[176]

Perhaps it is easier to account for Ritchie's loss of independence by noting the radical change in his own political position. In Richmond his editorial strength rested on his power in the Junto and in the Virginia Democratic party; in Washington he was just another editor, economically and politically dependent on Polk and the Democrats in Congress.[177] Always devoted to moderation, compromise, and party unity, Ritchie may have felt that the editor of the administration's paper must, as a matter of loyalty, subordinate his own will to that of the president. With his prestige dissipated and an alien administration in the White House, Ritchie, by the time of the 1850 sectional crisis, was a sitting duck.

Whenever Ritchie had encountered sectional divisiveness, his response had always been to stress the principles of 1798-99, the rights of the states, and the permanency of the Union. This course was predicated on the existence of a moderate Democratic consensus, a centrist majority which could, with shrewd tactics, isolate and dominate the political extremes. Perhaps the events of 1832-33 vindicated this analysis; by 1850 the center was much smaller, and the extremes were much more extreme. In Robert Barnwell Rhett, for example, Ritchie claimed to have discovered a monster indeed—a disunionist, a fanatic as mischievous as the abolitionists of the North.[178]

Ritchie wrecked what remained of his career by fighting for what became the Compromise of 1850; he accepted the admission of California as a free state (since this was essentially a *fait accompli* by Californians themselves), advocated the principle of government nonintervention in the territories (specifically in Utah and New Mexico), defended slavery in the District of Columbia, and fought for tough new laws guaranteeing the return of fugitives. All of this aligned Ritchie with the compromise-seeking Whigs. He and Henry Clay, enemies for thirty years, worked together for the compromise—secretly at first and then publicly. Ritchie found himself defending both Clay and Webster against the attacks of many Southerners.[179]

Inevitably politicians and editors from both sides of the Mason-Dixon line attacked the *Union*. In vain did Ritchie proclaim a policy which would be fair to both North and South. How could he be charged with disloyalty to the Union, he demanded, given his forty-year record and his attacks on nullifiers and disunionists? And how could the South misjudge him so, given his defense of Southern rights?[180] Bearing down hard on the necessity of securing justice for the South, Ritchie asserted,

the North has done great injustice to the South by its assault upon an institution existing in the South before the Union was established, and which was recognized by the constitution on which the Union is founded. The tendency of the conduct of fanatics of the North has been to excite insurrection in the South. Its legislatures have sent to those of the South insulting and impertinent resolutions and messages. In many States of the North obstacles have been thrown in the way of the recapture of fugitive slaves, which is a violation of an express stipulation in the constitution.[181]

Such editorials inflamed Northerners but did not appease the South. The middle position was almost untenable by 1850. The *Union*'s associate editor, Edmund Burke, a New Hampshire politician, astounded Ritchie by accusing him of following the Calhoun line toward secession. Out of this dispute came an agreement that each was to peruse the editorials of the other prior to publication. Not surprisingly, Burke resigned four months later.[182]

Southern opposition, however, disturbed Ritchie the most. The *Mississippian*, which he had considered a friendly paper, lumped together the *Union* and the *Intelligencer* as papers bought by Northern patronage. The *Columbus* (Georgia) *Times* denounced Ritchie's abandonment of Southern principles since he had become editor of a national party paper.[183] Ritchie protested, "We do not see how our being 'the organ of a national democratic party' has prevented the senior editor from carrying out the strict States-rights principles of the Jefferson school."[184]

Many if not most Southern Democrats found Ritchie's protestations unconvincing. Sixty-four Southern Congressmen—both Whigs and Democrats—struck directly at Ritchie by calling for the establishment of a Southern newspaper. These Congressmen sneered that Washington papers like the *Union* and the *Intelligencer* made "the maintenance of political parties their supreme and controlling object, *but* [there are] *none which consider the preservation of sixteen hundred millions of property, the equality and liberty of fourteen or fifteen States, the protection of the white man against African equality, as paramount over or even equal to the maintenance of some political organization which is to secure a President, and* [sic] *who is an object of interest, not because he will certainly rule or perhaps ruin the South, but chiefly for the reason that he will possess and bestow office and spoils."* [185] This call, entitled "The Southern Address," further charged the Washington press with selling out to Northern influence and favors and lulling the South into a false sense of security. Ritchie fought back with all his customary arguments for party unity, but they had little impact on those who demanded a Southern newspaper. Representative James Green of Missouri argued that "a political paper is so absorbed with the questions of party politics that it cannot bestow that time, space, and attention to the discussion of this subject [slavery and Southern rights] which its merits and importance demand." R.H. Stanton of Kentucky concluded that "the moral and political condition of the slave States, are not understood by those who assail our rights" and maintained that "good can be done in enlightening the people of the North upon these subjects, by means of their calm and temperate investigation in a newspaper devoted exclusively to that object." Ritchie replied that Northerners would never read a Southern rights paper. [186]

The *Southern Press*, edited by Elwood Fisher and Edwin DeLeon, two somewhat obscure Southern journalists who backed the movement for Southern unity and the Nashville Convention, first appeared on June 17, 1850. Ostensibly created to give tone and animation to the cause of Southern unity, it launched violent attacks on Virginia, Maryland, Kentucky, and those, especially Ritchie, who backed the compromise. [187] The *Southern Press* was not well received. While Southerners could agree with the general purpose of protecting Southern rights, the means to this end were always controversial. From the beginning many Southern newspapers recognized the *Southern Press* as the tool of the fire-eaters, and they were quick to denounce its presumption to speak for all Southerners. The tone of the *Southern Press* was especially galling, for as one historian has emphasized, it "was not calculated to promote good will. Never persuasive, never conciliatory, but always dogmatic, self-righteous, belligerent, it invited damning by being quick to damn." [188]

Predictably, the new radical sheet expired in August 1852. Disdaining partisanship as harmful to Southern unity, the *Southern Press* lacked the financial backing of a party. Dedicated to opposing the Compromise of 1850, and edited by a Whig and a Democrat, it maintained harmony in its own office by refusing to endorse a candidate and by essentially having no policy during the 1852 campaign, when both Whigs and Democrats endorsed the Compromise. Accenting its adamant anti-Compromise arguments with hints of disunionism, it failed to secure Congressional printing contracts. And speaking on national issues to a largely nonpaying audience across the South, it failed to attract local subscribers and Washington's commercial and professional interests.[189]

The short-lived *Southern Press* may have provoked some journals to a more vigorous defense of Southern rights, but its own extremism may have encouraged a reaffirmation of unionism. Almost certainly Fisher and DeLeon viewed with satisfaction two occurrences during their months on the journalistic firing line—the death of Ritchie's *Union* and the disappearance of any truly national political organ in Washington.[190]

As political parties strained and fractured under the pressures of 1846-50, so also did official party organs, which could no longer fill the role of party unifiers and spokesmen.[191] A number of developments account for the decline of the patronage system and the powerful administration organ in the capital. Finance of course played a major role; the economic liabilities of the political press were harder to tolerate in an age of surging mass circulation papers that enjoyed both profits and influence. In the late 1840s, furthermore, papers throughout the nation began to rely increasingly on their own Washington-based correspondents as the spread of the telegraph made possible the rapid flow of information.[192] The simultaneous heightening of sectional divisiveness meant that there was less possibility of a unified, controlled discussion of events in Washington, and Thomas C. Leonard has argued that "reporting that achieved national circulation outside the control of canny party operatives . . . made the political system less stable."[193] Coinciding with these developments, the selection of Ritchie over Blair as editor of the Democratic organ was both a symbol and partial cause of increasing sectional tension.

The crises of these years shook Ritchie badly. The political quarrels of 1850 damaged his chances for additional government printing contracts and the possibility of congressional reimbursement for his losses on previous contracts. What remained of his editorial reputation had been shredded.[194] Especially resenting the idea that he had been derelict in defending Southern rights, he later wrote: "I came to Washington with some little influence in the South. In attempting to save the Union I have been shorn of some of that moral force which I had gained on another theatre."[195]

In April 1851, Ritchie announced his retirement from public life in a valedictory summarizing the major themes of his long editorial career. He warned both North and South of the dangers of sectionalism—a force which had largely ruined the concluding chapter of his journalistic career—and emphasized the importance of upholding the Union by preserving the recent compromise. He declared, "We must preserve all the great pillars of our prosperity—the *Liberty of the People, the Rights of the States, and the Union of the States.*" His closing paragraph reaffirmed the other great cause of his career—the integrity of the press—which he identified as editorial independence, liberality, courtesy, and decency.[196]

Perhaps it is best to consider Ritchie's *Enquirer* as his real contribution to journalism and to regard him as miscast in Washington. Charles Ambler, Ritchie's early-twentieth-century biographer, concluded that "to Ritchie more than to anyone of his contemporaries the press of to-day owes a debt of gratitude for high ethical conceptions which he brought to and made a part of his profession."[197] The *Enquirer* ranked among a select group of political papers which transcended the hack journalism of the age to inform and instruct an elite readership. In addressing daily the questions agitating all minds and raising questions about the nature and framework of American government, Ritchie, like a handful of other able editors, helped make newspapers a necessity and journalism an integral part of the political system. His *Enquirer* brought a degree of order to the confusing world of politics. It organized the party faithful and provided a means for electioneering, it won adherents to a cause and rallied them against a common political enemy, and it promoted political ideals and principles and discussed issues openly and critically.[198] Virginians accepted the *Enquirer*'s directing role. Many, wrote an *Enquirer* reader, "have taken your paper for more than a quarter of a century and have continued their patronage because you have always stood up for the rights of the people—because you have discussed the great political questions of your day in the good temper and distinguished ability and because you have uniformily treated your political opponents with the courtesy and delicacy of a gentleman."[199] Upon Ritchie's death in 1854, the *Daily Picayune* remembered that his *Enquirer* "came to be received as an authority on constitutional and political questions; and enjoyed throughout the country and especially in Virginia, and the South generally, a weight of influence which few can appreciate now. . . . With these advantages of position and his discreet management, indefatigable industry and ready tact, and a certain agreeable fluency of style, the Richmond Enquirer was the acknowledged representative of Virginia, when Virginia was the leading state in the Union."[200]

Yet few today recall that a Richmond editor was one of the giants of American journalism. A very different image of the Southern editor had come to dominate Northern thought by the 1850s if not, as Clement Eaton suggests, earlier. "After Jefferson's death," Eaton claims, "Southern journalism became so partisan and violent that the cartoon of a Southern editor with a quill in one hand and a dueling pistol in the other was not entirely out of line with reality."[201] In the era of the Civil War and Reconstruction, there was much to support such an interpretation. Southern press extremism kept pace with the perceived threat to a

Southern way of life, and the partisan press became the sectional press—
a phenomenon absent in Northern journalism because of the greater diversity in Northern life and the assurance that Northern ways would
dominate the nation. The South's sectional press continued the functions
of a partisan press, except that by the 1850s the press's goal was sectional
victory, which had a Union-sundering impact, rather than party victory
with its implied preservation of the Union.

3

The Rise of a
Metropolitan Giant

The *New Orleans Daily Picayune*,
1837-1850

The *New Orleans Picayune* debuted on a rainy day in late January 1837. With seventy-five dollars and a borrowed press, the paper's two editor-proprietors ran off one thousand copies of the four-page paper, eleven by fourteen inches—about big enough to wrap a loaf of bread.[1] If the tiny paper appeared to be cheaply made, it was also cheaply sold—for one Spanish "picayon" (hence the paper's name), a silver coin common in New Orleans and worth six and a quarter cents. While the *Picayune*'s cost far exceeded that of New York City's new penny press, it was a sensational reduction for a city in which no other daily sold for less than ten cents.[2]

Because it was a new departure in Southern journalism, the *Picayune*'s creators deliberately made it unique in size and cost. The new-comer was a journal of entertainment, an "audacious little sheet . . . full of witticism as one of Thackeray's dreams after a light supper."[3] Of partisan politics there was nothing, although the prospectus perfunctorily announced devotion to the Union and abhorrence of abolitionism. The *Picayune* delighted readers, accustomed as they were to the ponderous horse-blanket sheets filled with constitutional pedantry, partisan vitriol, and commercial statistics. When the second issue sold out, the editors knew they were onto a good thing and advised commercial advertisers to take notice. In a short time the *Picayune* ran fifteen hundred copies and the editors had to buy a new, double-cylinder Napier press.[4]

The *Picayune* represented a new phenomenon in American journalism. The first of its kind in the South, it was consciously modeled on the penny press of the Northeast.[5] Upstart tabloids like the *New York Sun*, James Gordon Bennett's *New York Herald*, and the *Philadelphia Public Led-*

ger only a few years before had burst on the scene with a fresh, flippant style and an emphasis on local, human-interest, and sometimes sensational stories. Unlike the expensive, elitist journals, often (quite rightly) assumed to be bought and paid for by special interests, penny papers spoke as the *vox populi*, exposing abuses by the privileged few and defending the public interest. They stressed local issues over national concerns, brief, sprightly paragraphs over lengthy, verbatim reports and speeches, news columns over editorials, facts over opinion, and reporting over editorializing. They loved murders and disasters, frauds, scandals, and peccadilloes of the rich and respectable, and picturesque misfortunes of thieves, drunks, and streetwalkers appearing before the police court. The *Picayune* would fulfill its promise to report "earthquakes, anecdotes, suicides, marriages, murders, sea serpents, conflagrations, cholera, sad accidents, mermaids, shipwrecks, melancholy catastrophes, terrible afflictions, laughable occurrences, nick nacks, pic nics, and even politics, Millerism, Mesmerism, and Mormonism."[6] Politically neutral if not indifferent to politics, penny papers aimed to amuse the middle and working classes.[7] They spoke to the moment, not for the ages. The *Picayune* once cheerfully remarked, "We leave profundity to those who prefer profound sleep."[8]

The rise of the penny press coincided with several key developments in Jacksonian America. The gradual advance of literacy made possible a mass reading public, the spread of an egalitarian outlook encouraged newspapers which championed the public good, and the growth of new means of communication and transportation—the steamship, the railroad, and the telegraph—quickened the flow of news. New printing and papermaking technology made mass production of cheap newspapers possible. The *Philadelphia Public Ledger* announced its intent to place a "newspaper in the hands of every man . . . and even of every boy old enough to read." Around 1830 the average circulation of the daily press numbered between twelve and seventeen hundred subscribers, but a decade later penny papers in the large eastern cities realistically aimed at a circulation five to ten times greater.[9]

The penny press developed only in big cities such as New Orleans, which had a population of 102,000 in 1840, making it the third largest city in the country and incontestably the leading city of the South. In commerce it ranked second only to New York City, and in per capita wealth some placed it first.[10] During the golden age of river transport, New Orleans carried the commerce of nearly thirty thousand miles of inland waterways; railroads did not yet pose a serious challenge to the vast water system that drew the trade of half a continent to New Orleans.[11]

There would have been no penny press in New Orleans, however, had the people of the city been what outsiders imagined them to be. The

Creole myth of a city of upper-class, native-born, French-descended aristocrats besieged by aliens endured long after such a society had faded to a faint glimmer in the city's romantic past. By the 1840s Creole-Anglo friction was not severe; the ruling class, a composite of all groups, was clearly open to self-made men. New Orleans had a large immigrant population, chiefly German and Irish, and a large middle class, composed of professional men, business managers, skilled workers, clerks, grocers, and similar groups.[12]

On the other hand, the city had a well-earned reputation for filth, disease, and death. Dead animals, garbage, and even night soil were dumped on mostly unpaved streets. With only rudimentary drainage, no sewage system, and little thought of sanitation, yellow fever epidemics and cholera outbreaks were frequent.[13] A certain rawness would continue to be associated with New Orleans, and as late as midcentury a visitor described it as located halfway between civilization and California.[14]

Besides the dirt and pestilence, New Orleans was known for a special grace and color and a certain sophistication. Among the city's distinctive features was enthusiastic support for the theater and the opera. New Orleans attracted some of the finest European operatic talent, and it was the first American city to have a regular opera season.[15]

Unlike most other American cities (Washington and some other Southern ports excepted), New Orleans lived only six months a year. In the healthy, busy season between October and April, ships often stood two and three deep at the wharfs, newcomers bustled about the city, and the race courses, theaters, and the opera drew throngs of citizens. From May to October business dwindled to almost nothing, outsiders shunned the city, and residents who could afford it took extended vacations or abandoned the city at the first hint of fever. Still, nothing stopped the surging population of the fastest growing marketplace west of the Appalachians. Between 1835 and 1838 several new hotels, churches, and public buildings were completed, and in the boom year prior to the founding of the *Picayune*, eight new banks were established, issuing paper money, as it later turned out, far in excess of their specie reserves.[16]

Among the thousands attracted to the great Southwestern metropolis were two printers, Francis Asbury Lumsden of North Carolina and George Wilkins Kendall of Vermont, who would found the *New Orleans Picayune*. Lumsden had served his apprenticeship with Joseph Gales, Jr., on the *Raleigh Register*. When Gales moved to Washington to edit what many considered the nation's most influential journal, the *National Intelligencer*, he took Lumsden along. For part of his nine years as a printer on the *National Intelligencer*, Lumsden worked with Kendall, and they renewed their friendship when they became foremen of composing rooms in New Orleans in 1835. Soon the young but experienced printers were planning to bring out their own paper.[17] Lumsden became the *Picayune*'s senior editor, and although he wrote for the paper, he served primarily as its general manager. Kendall emerged as the paper's star writer and reporter; it was he who created the special *Picayune* flavor. A man of tremendous energy, imagination, and resourcefulness, Kendall was born to be a reporter—he was impatient with routine, always restlessly searching for something new, something different.[18] Kendall would have a brilliant, creative career in journalism and would later become a Texas pioneer, developer, and sheep rancher who contributed enormously to his adopted state.[19] Lumsden, although less colorful than Kendall, would become a New Orleans institution, beloved by his adopted city as were few others. After retiring from the *Picayune* in 1851, Lumsden devoted his last years to public service. He served on the board of administrators of the public schools and was elected several times to the state legislature and the municipal council of New Orleans.[20]

The immediate success of these two printers—lacking as they were in capital and political connections—was not a matter of mere luck. They had observed firsthand the phenomenal success of the penny press and had worked on old-fashioned papers for years. Lumsden and Kendall had their own notions of what made good journalism: "To make the paper interesting is our sole desire."[21] They would captivate the reader with "dashes of good sound sense, set down brief and sprightly, intermingled with facts, current events, solid intelligence. . . . It should not be always light, nor should it ever be too dry."[22] Readers' time was short in a fast-paced utilitarian age, too short to waste on digesting the "politico-philosophico-absurdities" of the mammoth elitist journals, swollen into a "shapeless, overgrown conglomerated mass of inanimate matter."[23] Kendall and Lumsden's impatient readers had "nothing to do but take a look at the Picayune, for instance, and they can swallow it . . . in a mouthful, without the trouble of mastication."[24]

The *Picayune* was everything that Thomas Ritchie's *Enquirer* was not. Traditional papers like Ritchie's were long-winded, didactic, self-important, and if they occasionally varied their political or mercantile fare with stories and poems, they still advanced an exclusive literature for polite society. The *Picayune*, however, winked and promised, "It shall be our delight to crack jokes, to tell stories in our own way, to ridicule folly, and to correct the manners of the age by exciting laughter against them."[25] Here was a language and literature for the masses, incorporating dialect, slang, colloquialisms, and folk tales. *Picayune* readers, whose number more than doubled in the first three months, were treated to tales about droll Irishmen, a Kentucky backwoodsman who saw the elephant in wicked New Orleans, a wild levee brawl (entitled "Chickens and Bowie Knives"), and imaginary New Orleans "worthies" such as Nathaniel O.

Drinkwater, Salathiel Swipes, and Thomas Jefferson Benjamin Franklin Stubbs.[26] Ludicrous anecdotes and tall tales about ducks born with chicken feet during a drought or steamboats that jumped over sandbars delighted the *Picayune* staff.[27] A *Picayune* writer explored the feelings of a man facing the gallows—"pretty pokerish" was the conclusion.[28] The irreverent editors adored puns, the worse the better. An eye-catching title, "Snodgrassiana," undoubtedly attracted many a reader who learned that "Snodgrass is a whig.—A political opponent asked him the other day, what he had to say in favor of Mr. Wise's late speech in Congress. He replied, 'go thou, and do *like-wise.'*" A two-stanza poem about a lady reclining on a sofa and reciting a favorite song, "The Legacy," ended with her beau's confession that he much admired the "leg-I-see"![29] One- or two-line gags filled a whole column; if the reader didn't like one, there were always plenty of others. The *Picayune* indulged in undertaker jokes even in the midst of a yellow fever epidemic: "We doubt, after all, if he gives universal satisfaction, for he has never been employed to work for the same person a second time. He puts *down* more than the most skillful debater, and, though no politician, is an active *clay* man. . . . To say that he is a *grave* man would be repeating a threadbare pun, but whether he be grave or gay he is the last man that people call on for his services."[30] Women were made fun of too, and all the antediluvian male jests about females' clacking tongues, etc., were in the paper. The *Picayune* gravely debated the question of which woman was prettier, the one in a white check apron, making warm biscuits for supper, or the other with a brick-bat in one hand and a cabbage stalk in the other, chasing a hog out of the dooryard.[31]

The *Picayune* exuded a gargantuan self-confidence. One historian has noted how its columns throbbed with the enthusiasm of youth.[32] Some might call it brashness. In the early days Kendall and Lumsden put themselves in the paper, recounting their travels and troubles and laughing at the incidents which befell them as they searched for news. The *Picayune* reported, for example, that Lumsden caught an eighty-three pound catfish that was so mean and ugly it reminded him of several gentlemen about town. The editors boasted of their scoops and twitted their rivals. One week after the paper's founding the editors claimed the largest circulation in the city and predicted that within a month the *Picayune* would outstrip all other New Orleans papers combined. It was too bad about the others, "but how can we help it? The people will have the Picayune, and it is not in our nature to refuse them." The *Picayune*'s new printing equipment had to be, of course, the best in New Orleans: "Here goes for a brag—a bare-faced puff direct." "Do you hear us crow? Cock a dookle doo-oo!"[33]

Lumsden and Kendall even had the nerve to put out a *Picayune* on

Sunday. As expected, the clergy emitted wrathful protests which the *Picayune* calmly dismissed; the paper published no Monday edition, and the Sunday edition was prepared on Saturday, so what was the fuss about? The religious folk of New Orleans, however, also claimed to be affronted by the *Picayune's* "racy" stories about the underside of society. A self-styled Association of Gentlemen compared the *Picayune* somewhat incongruously to Judas Iscariot and uttered vague threats against the editors for violating public decency. The editors responded by apologizing in the next issue for their lack of original reading matter that day, explaining that the "Christian threats" had diverted their time to making out their last will and testament.[34]

The editors loved to deflate the self-important and pompous. Many a country editor seeking an exchange was firmly refused, the *Picayune* said, because such papers were boring and of absolutely no use.[35] Once the exasperated *Picayune* lambasted the *Mobile Chronicle* as the poorest and most spiritless exchange received during the past two weeks, and asked eagerly, "Can't the Mobilians stir up the Chronicle and make it spit a little fire—breathe a little enthusiasm?"[36] Those who wrote letters to the *Picayune* did so at their own risk. Anonymous correspondents frequently found their best efforts not only rejected but publicly ridiculed. Fifty or sixty letters to the editor were ceremonially burned one afternoon because, as the editors claimed, they were all exceedingly dull.[37] *Picayune* criticism was not necessarily constructive: "Sedgwick's poetry is too sentimental, and More Anon's story is too long. Clitus is an ass." "Carolus had better give up writing poetry and take to digging clams."[38]

Not surprisingly, the *Picayune* found other New Orleans newspapers absurd and more than a little contemptible. Readers enjoyed watching editors abusing each other if they showed wit and style. The *Picayune* slammed the *True American*, thought the *Commercial Bulletin* made good wrapping paper, and excoriated the *Bee* for its attacks on the city's merchants and banks. When the editor of the *Bee* retaliated by physically attacking Lumsden on the street, the *Picayune* crowed that the *Bee's* editor had at last revealed himself as a blackguard and coward. The *Picayune's* most serious quarrel in its first year was with the *Commercial Herald*, whose editor was called a great puff and a liar: "Like the little dog of smooth skin, with sonorous voice and little sagacity, he runs barking about town and finds that even the kennel will not notice him." The *Herald*, concluded Kendall and Lumsden, was not worth a "Picayune."[39]

The *Picayune's* attitude toward combat among editors, however, changed completely within a year or so. Instead of sneers and lampoons for their rivals, the *Picayune's* editors began to denounce "coarsely vulgar and indecent personal abuse," editorial boasting, and disparagement of other newspapers. From 1838 on, almost all injurious personal remarks, personal abuse, and editorial quarrels disappeared from the *Picayune*'s columns.[40] It is not easy to account for the reversal. Perhaps the flippant, combative style was only a temporary tactic designed to build circulation quickly and to be discarded when that goal was achieved. Even while picking quarrels of their own, they had banned the kind of letters full of private pique and personal invective that most papers encouraged. It is, of course, possible that the editors were more fearful for their personal safety than they had admitted. Kendall and Lumsden were certainly aware that editorial taunting and ridicule often degenerated into uncontrollable hatred and vicious feuding; this was not the kind of entertainment they wanted to give readers. After 1838 they ridiculed editorial thrashings, happily reporting that a St. Louis editor had been fined twenty dollars and court costs for assaulting a rival—now journalists knew "at what cost they may indulge in the luxury of flogging each other."[41]

Most objectionable was the vulgarity and bad taste of the eastern penny press, especially Bennett's *New York Herald*.[42] By contrast, the *Picayune* claimed, "In point of decency, dignity and courtesy the press of New Orleans stands at the head of all others in the Union." The *Picayune*, if not its New Orleans contemporaries, deserved this self-bestowed compliment.[43]

Lumsden and Kendall knew very well that a successful newspaper had to be more than fun and froth; they would take up major issues, but never with the doctrinaire style much in vogue at the time. In 1837 no issue was more important than the banking crisis and what should be done about the suspension of specie payments. The *Picayune* derided the get-rich-quick schemes that had precipitated the panic, but it also scoffed at the locofocos who indiscriminately attacked all banks and merchants as aristocratic oppressors.[44] In short, the *Picayune* opted for a middle course: "We have not been the advocates of banking without proper bounds, nor the ultra defenders of an exclusive metallic currency. We never did think that either the Pope or Nicholas Biddle was infallible, nor were we blind believers in the doctrine that Tom Benton possessed the alchemic power to make gold float up the Mississippi, or that the United States Bank was a great "monster," with one eye in the centre of its forehead like a large ball of fire, and a pair of huge horns surpassed only in size and ugliness by those of his Satanic Majesty."[45]

The *Picayune* thought that if the government helped the sound banks to resume specie payments, then the economy would right itself, and in the long run moderate reforms and natural attrition would pare banking down to a realistic level.[46] Hostile editors, doubtless resentful of the *Picayune*'s competition, accused it of defending an aristocratic elite and attacking the working class. The *Picayune* editors proclaimed that they were mechanics themselves and believers in the principles of Thomas Jefferson; nevertheless, they could see little sense in attacking the city's commercial interests.[47] The newspaper fight over banking policy came to naught, but it showed that the *Picayune*, for all its wry humor, had to be taken seriously as a controversialist.

The flamboyant *Picayune* impressed newsmen around the country and, in New Orleans, touched off a price war and a struggle over circulation. As in other penny press towns, New Orleans editors advanced boastful claims about their respective paper's superior accuracy, completeness, liveliness, and timeliness. Readers were enchanted with the *Picayune*'s innovations, especially with its informal style, and several papers—the *New Orleans Delta*, *New Orleans Crescent*, and the *St. Louis Reveille*, for example—were created or refashioned in the *Picayune*'s image.[48] Nationally many editors eagerly exchanged with the *Picayune* and copied from it habitually, with or without due credit.[49] In Georgia a literary publication regularly featured *Picayune* clippings, labeling them "Picayuneana."[50]

Of course not everyone applauded the *Picayune*'s style. A Pensacola paper thought it relied excessively on witticisms,[51] and the sober-sided Philadelphia *Saturday Evening Post* called the *Picayune* "a chronicle of iniquitous accomplishments, pot-house witticisms, horse racing, elaborate indecencies, and the annals of a gambling community."[52] More typical, though, was the reaction of Anne Royal, who wrote in her magazine, the *Huntress*, that the *Picayune* was the most amusing and time-killing paper in New Orleans. "The editor is inimitable; it is impossible to do justice to an editor of his rich imagination and genius. His mind is a *magazine* of wit and humor, of which he is no Niggard, and few [sic], if any paper, is more quoted, more read, or more admired. It is just the thing."[53]

The public's reception of penny journals suggests that many people were fed up with partisan political papers. Made skeptical by endless hyperbole and outright lying, turned cynical by detours and shifts in party positions, irked by small-mindedness and the divisiveness of exclusive partisanship, and bored by the endless repetition of fulsome praise for friends and nasty insult for enemies, readers were delighted by the creation of an alternative journalism. Party spirit, the *Picayune* argued, choked everything and made a mockery of the people's rights. A steady diet of hyperbole and whoppers, it maintained, eventually resulted in public disbelief of the press even on those rare occasions when partisan writers chanced to hit upon the truth. George Wilkins Kendall clearly disliked politics and distrusted politicians.[54] The *Picayune* complained frequently that its exchanges, especially the eastern papers, contained nothing but politics; "Ritchie is at his nous verrons—Pleasants writing for the liberty of unborn millions, etc."[55] Often the *Picayune* lampooned party excesses, congressional speechifying, and campaign bombast, especially of the 1840 hard-cider, log-cabin variety. Once the *Picayune* observed that Congress looked "like a drunken drayman whose horse has floundered in the mud."[56]

For all the *Picayune*'s playfulness, Kendall and Lumsden were committed to a high ideal of journalism. Theirs was a nonpartisan organ. They owed nothing to anyone but the public. They were proud of their independence and their ability to resist the pressures of politicians and subscribers who, during a political contest, would order, "Stop my paper." They need never cut, slant, distort, or invent the news to promote party orthodoxy, party unity, or party victory.[57] "The independent press," the editors argued, "aims to discuss public questions with an eye to the general welfare of the whole country; whilst the party press owes a fealty which may at times interfere with its usefulness."[58] The *Picayune* found and criticized plenty of examples of such interference.

The early *Picayune* was very careful in covering politics. It published announcements of Democratic and Whig political meetings and election returns, often relying for its facts upon the *Baltimore American*, which it described as a temperate and dignified journal. It briefly noted political news and gossip but rejected lengthy political essays and partisan diatribes.[59] The editors insisted that they kept their readers *au courant* with the political news of the day, and they resented the condescension of partisan contemporaries who believed that neutrals knew nothing of politics. There must be some reason, the *Picayune* hinted, why the political journals of New Orleans got half their political communications from the columns of the *Picayune*.[60]

What party politics was to other journals, the improvement of New Orleans was to the *Picayune* in its early years. Largely ignoring national politics, Kendall and Lumsden saw themselves not as defenders of the South but, rather, as advocates of the public good and spokesmen for civic improvement in New Orleans. Kendall and Lumsden would needle the city into action in their best Picayunish style. The third issue, for example, gravely reported, "A friend has informed us that the city authorities are about to employ an able and efficient corps of engineers to take soundings of the holes in the public streets, and to submit estimates and plans for the construction of bridges over them, as soon as they can find bottom for the construction of middle piers."[61] Here was the opening round of a major campaign against the vile condition of the streets; it was quickly followed by other editorial blasts attacking the problem of "mud, mud, mud" and by an advertisement for citizens to join a Rat Catching Club.[62] "What's the matter with New Orleans?" sounded obliquely through many a column. "Is it Nobody's Business,"

or rather, "whose business is it?" inquired the *Picayune*, that two un-
sightly, smelly, mountains of oyster shells had accumulated on the levee
directly opposite several business establishments.[63] Two beatings of respectable citizens by the city's night watchmen provoked a furious
blast. The editors described the attacks as "wanton and murderous"
and referred to the night watchmen as the '"brutal and bloody' minions
of a badly administered system of police."[64] Speeding draymen, the
mismanaged post office, and a host of other nuisances caught the *Picayune*'s eye. The city council, said the paper, should be ashamed of failing to provide a new ferry for the second municipality. And what about
building a levee plank road? Why didn't the council take some action to
protect New Orleans against flooding? And so on. To be sure, when
public officials did do something worthwhile the *Picayune* was quick to
praise them (and to claim some credit for itself as civic gadfly).[65]

The *Picayune* often showed concern for the improvement of public
morals and civility. It decried rowdyism and gambling houses which became public nuisances, and complained of loafers who idled about, af-
fronting respectable society with their vile language. It denounced gentlemen who leaned out their windows and engaged in crude badinage
with female domestics on opposite balconies.[66] Bathers who flaunted
their nudity before respectable folk out for a drive enraged the *Picayune*:
"An offense so gross deserves a higher punishment than the law metes
out to it, but whatever penalty the law does adjudge should be rigidly
exacted."[67]

The *Picayune* adopted most reformist causes of the time. After some
good-natured spoofing of the alleged evils of drink, the *Picayune* in the
early 1840s gradually embraced temperance.[68] It wholeheartedly supported the abolition of imprisonment for debt, attacked the use of cor-
poral punishment in the military, and endorsed a manual labor school
for boys.[69] The *Picayune* asked for subscriptions to build chapels for sea-
men and boatmen, a class in dire need of improvement.[70] The cause
dearest to its heart, however, was public education. The editors publicized their visits to the schools, reported student accomplishments at
exam time, and consistently advocated greater expenditures for public
education, especially higher teachers' salaries.[71]

The most controversial of the *Picayune*'s commitments was its campaign against duelling. Though Lumsden and Kendall at first said nothing against duelling in general, they firmly renounced the practice for
themselves. If challenged, they wrote in their third issue, they would
apologize if wrong; but if, as they fully expected, they were in the right,
they preferred some trial of skill, perhaps a foot race, to satisfy honor. If
they lost, they would "frankly acknowledge ourselves shot through
with a pistol ball, or thrust through with a small sword, or, what is still

worse, cut in halves by a broadsword. How extremely unpleasant to think of such things."[72]

As they recorded one fatal affray after another, the editors came to see duelling as "a custom which disgraces the worst annals of barbarism."[73] But reader response to their dramatic 1837 campaign against the practice was disappointing. Thereafter the editors returned intermittently to the issue, but in a slightly more diplomatic way. The *Picayune* sought to soften public opinion by relentlessly noting "fatal affrays," and "bloody rencontres," of which New Orleans had plenty.[74] It described the tragic deaths of young, respectable citizens and the pathos of grieving widows, children, and friends.[75] Although the editors conceded that a gentleman excited by passion could be motivated to participate in a duel,[76] they continued to argue that duelling was a relic of barbarism, rejecting the idea that the practice softened manners and refined polite society.[77]

Picayune columns were open to other critics of duelling, such as "Lycurgus," who insisted that hatred, not honor, drove men to commit premeditated murder on the duelling field. "Lycurgus" even sneered at the concept of honor, relating a mechanic's comment about a duellist: "I wish his high sense of honor had induced him to call at my shop and pay me his bill before he consented to stand the fire of a rifle and peril his existence."[78] One doubts that any New Orleans gentleman, with a gentleman's attitude toward paying tradesmen's bills, would have cared for Lycurgus's values.

As "Lycurgus" implied, death by duelling was legally homicide. But judges and juries proved reluctant to convict defendants. The *Picayune* therefore advocated legislation to prohibit the carrying of concealed weapons and to disfranchise participants in a duel.[79] As was usually the case, however, the paper was most effective when it used its wits. Was duelling a gentlemanly ritual? The *Picayune* laughed at a story of the "pokeberry duel," which featured a drunken quarrel about dogs, a dawn meeting between sobered-up young men witless with fright, a shrewd second, pistols loaded with powder but no ball, and plenty of pokeberry juice to fake a gory wound.[80] The paper reported a formal encounter between gentlemen using effective but nontraditional double-barrelled shotguns. And was there really a duel, as the *Picayune* claimed, between blacks ("Nigger, whe'ye gwyne? To de field ob honor.")?[81]

The honor of duelling was vindicated, if one believed the *Picayune*, in a series of essays by "Lucius O'Trigger" and "Ramrod Snaplock, Jr." Lucius O'Trigger described how the merest puppies could become boorish louts and find fame on the field of honor.[82] But was there glory in duelling? Of course, cried Lucius: "Nothing raises you higher in the estimation of the ladies. When you have lost your arms, or your legs, or other important organs, the ladies can always tell, as by intuition, whether you lost them on the field of honor or by the railroad cars running over you when *corned*."[83] The nit-picking pedant of duelling lore, Ramrod Snaplock, Jr., was conjured up by the *Picayune* to settle certain subtle problems with the O'Trigger text: "Errata.—By reference to the writings of Lucius O'Trigger, I find the words 'challenger' and 'cowhider', occurring in Prop IX, are typographical errors. They should be challengee and cowhidee, words much used in his 'Treatise on the art of Bullying.' In 'Honor's Epistolary Formulary,' I find the following grammatical principle: 'Nouns representing persons of the masculine gender, said persons being gentlemen of honor, are divided into Active; as: cowhider, challenger, nosepuller; Passive; as: cowhidee, challengee, nosepullee.'"[84]

By ridiculing the foolishness and hypocrisy of a practice associated with the South's ruling elite, the *Picayune* appealed to the man in the street who would not be found, dead or alive, on the field of honor. In other ways, too, the early *Picayune*'s outlook and composition rejected aristocratic pretensions in favor of urban, bourgeois values, and little of the fabled plantation South appeared in its columns. The *Picayune*, like other penny press papers, sought to attract a broad reading public[85] and was proud to be called "the People's friend."[86] Kendall and Lumsden were not loathe to explain their intent; their paper courted popular favor by endeavoring to please all sorts of people. "The merchant, confined to his counting room takes it [the *Picayune*] to see what's going on 'out of doors;' the tradesman takes it to see what's doing in the country—to learn the state of the crops, etc.; ladies take it to read the 'pretty stories;' nice young men take it to see what is 'funny;'—and loafers take it to see if they be 'shewn up.' In fact, the Picayune is like the 'dews of heaven,'—its information, humor and usefulness descends on all."[87]

Until the mid-forties Kendall and Lumsden spoke for the class from which they arose—the hardworking, urban middle class. They largely ignored the country. Moreover, by occasionally attacking dull country editors, suggesting that country folk had no interest in city elections, and criticizing rural voters who spurned New Orleans's need for levee appropriations, they expressed a hostility to rural sensibilities most unusual in the Southern press.[88]

Although Kendall and Lumsden proved their moral courage and independent spirit by denouncing duelling, and although they contributed to the growth of a journalistic tradition of exposing and criticizing public problems, in at least two vitally important areas, they dropped well below their own standard of journalistic excellence. Like most major urban dailies, especially the commercial and penny papers, the *Picayune* was an optimistic city booster. The editors forced the city to notice its relatively small and correctable lapses but failed to confront New Orleans with several of its most grievous and threatening problems— among them, the railroads' menace to New Orleans's commercial volume and the serious public health hazards of the city.

In the 1840s the rise of the railroads, some thought, might divert traffic from the great river and leave New Orleans on the commercial fringe. For a long time the *Picayune* scoffed at the doomsayers:

The natural depot for the commerce of the West is at our wharfs. Efface New Orleans from the face of the earth tomorrow—let Charleston, Savannah and Mobile be connected by railroads with Louisville, Memphis and Natchez, and before ten years shall have elapsed a city, as large and as prosperous as that which is now menaced by an "occasional correspondent" with ruin and dilapidation, will line the banks of the Mississippi, not a hundred miles from the Balize; and that, too, without making use of railroads extending to that interior of whose trade certain of our seaboard cities are so amorous.[89]

Not until very late, in 1850 and afterward, did the *Picayune* realize the threat posed to New Orleans's commerce. The *Picayune* belatedly fought for railroads for New Orleans, New Orleans-owned steamship lines to Vera Cruz and New York, and a railroad across the isthmus of Tehuantepec to protect and further the city's California trade.[90] The *Picayune*'s railroad campaign of the 1850s has been described as "impressive and unrelenting."[91] Its conversion may, however, have come too late. When at last the paper and farsighted citizens pushed for railroad development, they faced deadening inertia for which the *Picayune* was partly responsible.

The *Picayune* and other papers faced an even worse situation with regard to public health. Notoriously unhealthy even in normal times, New Orleans was also subject to devastating epidemics every few years. Between 1803 and 1900 there were no fewer than thirty-seven epidemics of yellow fever alone.[92] The subject aroused endless controversy and recrimination, for few accurate figures were available on sickness and death (certainly none were readily accessible). The stakes were high: should the city destroy its own business for a considerable period by warning people of the pestilence, or should it go on with business as usual while people who might have fled stayed and died? A common pattern emerged in press treatment of the great epidemics of 1837, 1842, and 1847. Most New Orleans papers belittled the early reports of fever, sometimes rejecting them entirely, often claiming that they really concerned only unacclimated newcomers. When the tide of death finally overwhelmed the city, the New Orleans press had no choice but to publicize the ravages of yellow fever and rather belatedly warn travelers and residents to stay away. Newspapers that had been slow to announce the existence of an epidemic frequently accused their rivals of concealing news about the fever's outbreak. Controversy continued even when the disease diminished. When could papers declare the danger ended and tell residents and newcomers that it was safe to enter the city? When at last the first hard frost definitely ended the epidemic, the press immediately forgot about it and tried to rebuild the city's image by boosting business prospects.[93]

The *Picayune*'s treatment of epidemic disease was no better than that of any other journal in New Orleans or in other antebellum cities.[94] In fact, in 1839 the *Picayune* admitted that it had suppressed news of the first outbreaks, excusing its action on the specious ground that such news would alarm the public, and that fear would predispose people to catch the fever! Rather self-righteously it reminded readers that the press should supply accurate information and not exaggerate reports of the disease.[95] The public, for obvious reasons, was highly skeptical about anything it read in the papers relating to disease.[96] All sorts of rumors circulated, and the *Picayune* had as little success as any other paper in quelling them. On this critical test of integrity and courage, the *Picayune* dismally failed its self-appointed public service function. By the 1850s the *Picayune* had lost the ability to convince New Orleans of the city's actual state of health.

Despite this unhappy record, the *Picayune* was one of a tiny number of pre-Civil War papers that appreciated the value of good reporting. Except for the occasional bit of commercial news, traditional journals had little need for reporters. The *Picayune*, however, eschewed customary column-stuffers and set out to report in its own special style the doings of New Orleans. The fact that New Orleans was virtually moribund six months of every year made energetic reporting all the more challenging.

Lumsden and Kendall pledged "to find something new for our paper every day during the summer, and keep up an excitement for the benefit of the languishing and dying."[97] It took some ingenuity to put out an interesting *Picayune* when theaters were closed, elections over, races run, the levee dead, commerce stagnant, and many of the wealthier people out of town. If the mail failed to get through, as frequently happened, there were no gleanings from the exchanges. Lumsden and Kendall creatively looked for news in the ordinary events of their city, finding a story, for example, in "an unfathomable abyss of mud" in what should have been New Orleans's streets. They, and presently their staff, haunted the recorder's court, hoping to sniff out an entertaining felony or human interest story.[98]

During the lively New Orleans season, the *Picayune* had almost too much to report—racing, life along the levee, crops and markets, duels, crimes, plays, concerts, opera performances (reviewed frankly and sometimes brutally), and a thousand other things in the South's most colorful city. Such coverage required first-rate reporters and writers. The editors worked closely with their reporters, urging them to "give us facts, incidents, occurrences, at the earliest moment."[99] In an age when reporters were commonly derogated as riff-raff, keyhole snoopers, bohemians, or drunkards, the *Picayune* demanded respect for the reporter as "a gentleman and a man of the world; by education, talent, industry and character, inferior to none whom he meets in his daily and nightly rounds."[100] Lumsden himself was a good reporter, when he found the time, but Kendall was among the nation's truly great ones. The initials G.W.K. on letters from Mexico, New York City, Paris, or Brussels would later set the standard for good correspondence.[101]

Although the *Picayune* relied on exchanges for news from around the country, the editors were fastidious in choosing material and usually condensed and rewrote it. Unlike other editors they never filled the columns with gobbets from other papers—once they claimed to have searched 150 papers for the right material for a single paragraph.[102]

Lumsden and Kendall recruited a large and able press staff. Exclusive of the proprietors, in 1850 the *Picayune* employed eight editorial writers.[103] Over the years several staff members left to join or found other journals; Denis Corcoran, a reporter who specialized in humorous sketches of police court scenes (and whose writings sometimes were attributed to Kendall), was the most important to leave. In 1845 Corcoran and three other former *Picayune* employees established the *New Orleans Delta*, which for many years was Kendall and Lumsden's chief rival.[104] The most important addition to the *Picayune* staff, on the other hand, was a Vermonter like Kendall, Alva Morris Holbrook, who arrived in New Orleans in 1835. Trained in business, Holbrook was a member of a New Orleans mercantile firm when he bought an interest in the *Picayune* two years after its founding. He soon became the paper's business manager, and when Lumsden retired from active management in 1851, Holbrook took over. In 1862 the *New York Times* reported that nothing surfaced in the paper's columns unless it first passed through Holbrook's hands.[105]

Lumsden and Kendall aspired to be first with the news, and they generally were. When they got their first scoop by using a fast horse and rider in 1837, they boasted of their innovation with a woodcut of a horse, rider, and streaming banner proclaiming "You're too Late." Thereafter "Our Horse" announced the arrival of the *Picayune*'s express mail.[106] In the forties, especially in reporting the Mexican War, the *Picayune* extended its express system: it hired fast steamers and set type on board ship, made arrangements with the railroads, and organized pony express riders to fill gaps in the network. Consistently, the *Picayune*'s private express arrived twenty-four to forty-eight hours ahead of the U.S. mail, fulfilling the paper's earlier prediction that its horse would keep Cousin Amos's (Amos Kendall, U.S. Postmaster General) nag from browsing by the roadside. The *Picayune*'s system was even superior for some time to the telegraph.[107] Early telegraph reporting, it turned out, was sloppy and full of errors. The telegraph mistakes, said the editors, were "not only costly to the press, but they disturb and harass the public mind, and make the telegraph nearly useless as a reliable source of public intelligence, and at times a positive injury."[108]

In the mid-1840s, the *Picayune*, in part because of a key addition to the editorial staff but, more important, because of heightened interest in western expansionism, began to transform itself into a different kind of journal—one with a careful but purposeful focus on national affairs. In 1844 the *Picayune* hired the former political editor of the *New Orleans Bee*, Alexander C. Bullitt. A Kentucky Whig, resident in New Orleans since 1833, Bullitt expanded the *Picayune*'s political coverage and political editorials. The paper still adhered to an independent if not always neutral course, but it gradually adopted a Whiggish tone.[109]

The predominance of western expansionist issues in politics was the primary cause of the *Picayune*'s transformation; both geography and editorial decision dictated that New Orleans's greatest paper should become deeply involved with events in Texas, Mexico, California, and Oregon. Lumsden and Kendall had always had an interest in Texas and Mexico, especially after the failure of the Texas-sponsored Santa Fe expedition, which Kendall had joined in order to report the exploration of new territory and the opening of New Mexico to Texan and American trade. Captured by Mexican soldiers, members of the expedition, including Kendall, spent several months in Mexican prisons.[110] Kendall and his friends on the *Picayune* who worked for his release became specialists on Mexican affairs. More than any other American paper, the *Picayune* of the 1840s carefully reported on Mexico's politics and revolutions and the international minuet involving the fate of the Lone Star State, but the paper's coverage revealed little sympathy for Mexicans, whom it considered both arrogant and feeble. Despite this attitude, or perhaps because of it, the *Picayune* always pushed hard for annexation.[111]

Foreign news coverage had not always been a strong point of the *Picayune*. Thomas Ewing Dabney, historian of the *Times-Picayune*, poked fun at the editors' first irrelevant gleanings from the foreign exchanges, citing the following *Picayune* offering: "The sultan was planning to establish a naval base near Constantinople; the empress of Austria had the grippe; the queen of Portugal was *enceinte*."[112] Dabney conceded that brief, gossipy material possessed a human interest appeal for ordinary readers who ignored the turgid essays and political polemics of traditional editors. In the 1840s, however, because of its desire for Texas and fear of British meddling in the Southwest, the *Picayune* increased the scope and depth of its foreign reporting, spending large sums to secure correspondence from Vera Cruz, Tampico, Mexico City, Galveston, Houston, and various American cities—particularly Washington—attuned to foreign developments.[113]

Upon the outbreak of hostilities with Mexico in 1846, New Orleans became the assembly point for volunteers and war material. The *Picayune* immediately sent correspondents into the field and from the beginning dominated American press coverage of the war. In both Mexico and New Orleans the *Picayune* avidly sought news from its reporters and correspondents, soldiers and officers, travelers, steamboat captains, and local and foreign exchanges. The *Picayune* also examined the Mexican press, reviewing significant trends in *El Republicano*, *El Diario del Gobierno*, and *El Soldado de la Patria*, among others.[114]

The Mexican War was the first to be effectively covered by reporters. Of the eleven regular correspondents who were largely responsible for this development, six were *Picayune* writers, the most important being George Wilkins Kendall.[115] Kendall followed frontline troops into battle and filed dramatic accounts of the fighting, often complete with maps.[116] When all was quiet at the front, Kendall focused on human interest stories portraying the everyday life of soldiers in Mexico.[117] He produced a body of work whose quantity, quality, completeness, and accuracy impressed his generation of journalists.[118]

Writing stories at the front was only half the task; the other half was getting the news to the public. Here again Kendall and the *Picayune* excelled. Kendall arranged for pony express couriers to carry his letters to the coast. Although his riders were in constant danger from Mexican guerrillas, some being shot at, captured, or even killed, he maintained a successful service. Even army officers on occasion relied on Kendall's express to get their letters and dispatches out of Mexico.[119] The *Picayune*, in conjunction with the *Baltimore Sun* and sometimes the *New York Herald* and the *Charleston Courier*, created a private express using horses, trains, steamships, and the telegraph to speed the news to the Northeast.[120] Thanks to Kendall and the *Picayune*, newspaper readers frequently knew as much about the latest battle as did the Secretary of War.[121] It was Kendall's account of Buena Vista that informed an anxious President Polk of General Taylor's victory against heavy odds. Together the *Picayune* and *Baltimore Sun* later put news of the peace treaty on Washington streets before official Washington dispatches were made public.[122]

People often crowded into the *Picayune* office and jammed the street in front of the building waiting for the latest from Mexico. A *Charleston Courier* correspondent remarked that people asked, "Any news of the army?" in place of "how d'ye do?" The *Picayune*'s circulation boomed and six-page issues and extras became commonplace when war news was heavy.[123] In place of the kaleidoscopic variety of short, breezy news items, once a *Picayune* trademark, there was now a surfeit of war news, especially in the form of lengthy letters from special correspondents in Mexico and from army officers. All the letters were carefully identified as to source and time so as to document their accuracy.[124]

Even before the outbreak of war, the *Picayune* had become, at least in its own eyes, a pundit on Mexican and Southwestern affairs, and it had begun to print lengthy, serious editorials on foreign policy and other national issues. Now that its reporting of foreign affairs and war news had earned it the nation's attention, its editorials became dogmatic and assertive. Like others, the *Picayune*'s editors found writing editorials enjoyable and addictive. Of all the editorial voices of Young America and Manifest Destiny, the *Picayune*'s became one of the most insistent: Mexico was solely responsible for the war, having reneged on debts, launched murderous forays into Texas, refused to negotiate honorably with the United States, and concluded a long series of aggressions by invading American territory.[125] "National character demands that the scath [sic] of battle be felt near the vitals of Mexico. . . . If the United States do not have recourse to blood-letting upon a large scale, the effect will be deplorable in every respect."[126] The world must see a well-armed, vigorous American force in the western hemisphere and especially in the vacuum of Southwestern politics. Sensing nefarious British intrigues everywhere, the *Picayune* called for a display of American combat strength that would force the world to recognize the power and dignity of the United States.[127]

Some Americans of tender conscience had said that trouncing a weak, defenseless neighbor would make the United States a bully. Nonsense, thundered the *Picayune* in 1842: "It is sometimes salutary to punish the weak and pretending; . . . the feebleness of Mexico should no longer be a shield for her insolence and her dishonorable course."[128] When Mexico refused to call it quits after being soundly beaten, the *Picayune* pushed for the conquest of northern Mexico and hinted that more might be demanded.[129] A war of conquest, the editors argued, at least meant that methods of American expansion were more honest than those of European monarchies: rapacity was less loathsome than intrigue.[130]

As was to be expected, the *Picayune*'s influence drew it into political conflicts. When partisanship eventually intruded upon impartial coverage of the war, the *Picayune* was violently attacked on the grounds that its reporters slighted certain Democratic generals, particularly Gideon

Pillow, and exaggerated the achievements of their favorite Whig generals.[131] The controversy was brief but bitter. Contemporary newspapers, army officers, and modern day historians largely confirmed the accuracy of the *Picayune*'s battlefield reporting.[132] Even Ritchie's *Washington Daily Union*, the *Picayune*'s most influential critic, admitted the value of the *Picayune*'s work and relied on *Picayune* material.[133]

After the war, the nationalistic truculence of the *Picayune* rapidly subsided. Manifest Destiny fulfilled, the *Picayune* became the voice of reasonable moderation once again. No paper of its size presented a better variety of well-written material or covered foreign news more cogently. In 1848 Kendall won additional laurels for himself and his paper for his eyewitness reports of the revolutions in Europe, and the editors actually devoted more attention to the upheavals in Europe than to the presidential election at home.[134] The *Picayune* continued to speak to the nation in lengthy editorials and set an example of dignified journalism by avoiding quarrels and personalities. The flippant, wise-cracking *Picayune* was no more; it looked more and more like a Southern and nonpartisan precursor of the *New York Times* of the 1850s.

One feature common to the *Picayune* of 1837 and 1850 was the paper's profitability. As in the case of the best penny papers, financial success was a constant in the *Picayune*'s history. So great was the circulation increase in the first year that Lumsden and Kendall, because their presses couldn't meet the demand, turned away prospective subscribers and the many country editors seeking an exchange. The situation was soon corrected with new presses. *Picayune* editors then turned their attention to the Texas market, sending Lumsden to enroll Texas subscribers in 1838 and 1839. Though established in the panic year of 1837, the *Picayune* survived depression and grew steadily, becoming the largest daily in New Orleans in the early 1840s and the largest in the South by 1860, with a circulation of 12,600. This was a huge circulation for a Southern daily although it paled in comparison with the giants of the North. In 1838 Lumsden and Kendall added a weekly edition, which soon became as famous in the Southwest as the *New York Tribune*'s weekly in the northwest. In the following decade they steadily enlarged the size of the daily to accommodate more advertising, which all along had tended to crowd out reading matter. In 1848 an afternoon edition was introduced, and the *Picayune* began to appear seven days a week.[135] Between 1839 and 1844, Kendall, Lumsden, and Holbrook earned roughly fifty-nine thousand dollars from the daily, the weekly (which carried no advertising), and the job printing office.[136] Symbolic of both the *Picayune*'s prosperity and its permanence as a New Orleans institution, in 1850 the publishers erected an elegant, four-story, granite-faced office building to replace the old *Picayune* establishment which had been destroyed by fire.[137]

After the Mexican War the moderate, nonpartisan stance of the *Pica-yune* was difficult to maintain. Before the Wilmot Proviso and the crisis of 1850, the *Picayune*, in the main, studiously ignored the sectional conflict. From time to time the editors proclaimed their Southern loyalties but deprecated extremism.[138] In 1838, for example, Lumsden wrote, "We flatter ourselves that we are ourselves among 'the warmest advocates for Southern rights'—and, though we may not be very powerful champions, yet none are more cordially zealous. Born, and reared, and educated in the South, our sympathies and all our prejudices are with the South."[139] An assurance like this was mandatory, for Kendall was a Vermonter, as was later the third partner, Holbrook. The only topic that provoked the *Picayune* to characteristically Southern tirades was abolitionism. To the *Picayune* nothing was more ridiculous and dangerous than the prospect of blacks unleashed from the controls of servitude. The abolitionists were fanatics more destructive than fire, sword, and pestilence, and if any came south they should be hanged. So convinced were the editors that slavery was the *sine qua non* of Southern life and abolition a heretical abnormality that they denounced as pernicious and contrived the perpetual insinuations of Southern editors that any political opponent was secretly antislavery.[140]

In the crisis of 1850 the *Picayune* adopted a middle course, seeking to encourage Northern and Southern moderates and isolate and defeat extremists in both sections. Its interpretation of the news stressed the reasonableness and inevitability of compromise, and played up the weaknesses of extremism.[141] Although Northerners were encouraged to emulate Daniel Webster and to repudiate free soil enemies of peace such as Thaddeus Stevens and William H. Seward,[142] the *Picayune* was rather more critical of Southern than of Northern opponents of compromise. It denounced the Nashville Convention as potentially the vehicle of a small, unrepresentative group of Southern disunionists whose machinations would merely harden Northern sentiment against compromise. The *Picayune* sided unequivocally against disunionists; there was little pretense of journalistic impartiality.[143]

After passage of the Compromise measures, the *Picayune* evened the balance by denouncing Northern extremists (also few and unrepresentative) who attempted to obstruct the return of fugitive slaves. For the *Picayune*, the only issue now was adherence to the law. In late 1850 the *Picayune* actively campaigned for Southern Unionists. Deliberate treason against the Union, warned the *Picayune*, "ranks, in the popular abhorrence next to the crime of parricide, and will be reckoned with the same stern exaction of accountability."[144]

In the crisis of 1850 the *Picayune* emerged as the Southwest's most vigorous champion of the Union, a role it played until Lincoln's election forced it into a pragmatic acceptance of secession. The editors were committed to a policy, though not explicitly to a particular party. To their credit they preserved through the most difficult times the *Picayune* tradition of avoiding scurrility, hatred, and personal insult. Yet sectional tensions inexorably became the focus of editorial writers.

By the mid-1840s the once lighthearted, entertaining penny paper of the Crescent City had evolved into a serious journal of news, a celebrated, civic-minded institution. In the late 1830s and early 1840s Kendall and Lumsden's wit and irreverent tales struck the fancy of readers and exchange editors throughout the nation; a few years later its coverage of Texas and Mexico and advocacy of expansion won national recognition for authoritative news coverage and editorializing. For a time—and in a limited range of topics—the *Picayune* even reversed the South's traditional dependence on Northern publishing houses; for the *Picayune*, followed by other New Orleans papers, in the 1840s supplied the nation's clamor for news from the Southwest, and New York and Washington eagerly awaited the New Orleans exchanges.[145]

The *Picayune*'s evolution was hardly unique. Other penny papers which became major urban institutions—the *New York Herald*, for instance—also increased their reporting and news services as well as their prices after initial success as entertainers and gadflies. A few years after its founding the *Herald* developed a style more serious and responsible than that of other penny papers yet more lively and enterprising than that of the Wall Street horse-blankets.[146]

For Kendall and Lumsden, and a few other penny press editors, entertainment was an insufficient journalistic rationale, and they soon sought influence in public affairs. In so doing they addressed the needs and interests of a different audience; by the mid-forties the *Picayune* spoke more often for city fathers and commercial interests than for hard-working artisans.[147] Despite its origins, it was now an establishment press. The smorgasbord of light material disappeared; while humor and variety remained in limited form, timely news gathering, accurate reporting and original writing, editorials on expansionism, and articles advancing New Orleans's civic and commercial interests became *Picayune* trademarks. In these developments many of the best features of the penny press can be observed: the *Picayune* remained peculiarly an urban journal covering and advancing local interests, one of which happened to be Southwestern expansion. Though drawn into politics, often on the Whig side, it gloried in its independence.

Few Southern papers could be like the early *Picayune*. The New Orleans journalistic field was unique; no other Southern city offered a readership so large, a working class and middle class so substantial and diverse, a mercantile community so prosperous and optimistic, or natural endowments so compelling. Few Southern papers could entertain the public with the eccentricities of local leaders or curiosities of its waterfront denizens, unravel the mysteries or explain the customs of a great city, or campaign for civic progress in addition to reporting to the nation stirring events in Texas and Mexico. A typical Southern daily addressed a limited field in which a single clientele was all important—planters and slaveholding professionals. Finally, the editorial team (and how many Southern papers had an editorial team?) of Kendall, Lumsden, Bullitt, and Holbrook might have been the best in the South.

Although many would expect the *Picayune* to march with the giant urban journals of the North into a modern newspaper era in the decades after 1850, a different fate awaited the New Orleans daily. New Orleans suffered a relative decline in growth and prosperity; the port stagnated with the onset of the railroad age; and sectionalism, the dominant issue of the 1850s, became the great incubus of the editorial mind. War and Reconstruction followed, and the *Picayune* could not hold its position in the forefront of American journalism.

Still, the *Picayune* had established its reputation. Holbrook, who dominated the *Picayune* management after Lumsden's retirement in 1851, provided continuity from the 1850s into the 1870s.[148] Although Kendall was abroad or in Texas from the 1850s until the end of the Civil War, the traditions of excellent reporting and writing and political moderation were maintained. With the Republican triumph in 1860, the *Picayune* had little choice but to go with the people and support secession and the Confederacy. War brought extreme hardship, including two brief shutdowns by military authorities during the occupation. Never given to fanaticism or fire-eating, the *Picayune* accommodated itself to the Union occupation and accepted a return to unionism while defending the best interests of the South. Not surprisingly, the *Picayune*, though a critic of Radical Rule and social change in the postwar South, avoided the bitter-end resistance so destructive of effective journalism, and thus became the only antebellum, English-language paper in News Orleans to survive the war and Reconstruction.[149] Holbrook died in 1876, but the *Picayune*—although facing a number of new, Democratic journals and weakened by debts and recent turmoil—struggled along into the late nineteenth century.[150] In 1914 it merged with the *Times-Democrat* to become the *Times-Picayune*, "the dominant New Orleans paper of the twentieth century."[151]

4

The Triumph of Sectional Journalism

The *Charleston Daily Courier* and *Charleston Mercury* on the Eve of Secession

Freedom of the press is guaranteed
only to those who who own one.

A. J. Liebling

"We doubt not that many persons South as well as North, have formed an idea that the editor of the *Mercury* is a sort of Capt. Kidd, or Blue Beard, or gigantic Ogre, whose supreme delight consists in treason, stratagem and spoils."[1] Though the *Mercury* snickered, this characterization was not very wide of the mark. Both contemporaries and recent historians agree that in 1860 the *Mercury*, edited by Robert Barnwell Rhett, Jr., was the leading secessionist organ and that the family's head, Rhett, Sr., was the dean of Southern fire-eaters. Widely quoted throughout the North as the voice of Southern extremism, the *Mercury* secured for the Rhetts a lasting national reputation for political influence and power.[2] The secession of South Carolina seemed to prove their leadership in breaking up the Union.

In reality, 1860 was an aberration; never before or after did the Rhetts or the *Mercury* enjoy such success and popularity. From the early 1830s to the 1850s the *Mercury* was the political organ of a frequently distrusted, extremist faction that preached states' rights, nullification, and eventually secession. In these years the *Mercury* more often suffered defeat than enjoyed victory, and in the mid-fifties, after Calhoun's death, its popularity and influence declined dramatically.

Successful South Carolina journalism was better represented by the *Mercury*'s traditional rival, the *Charleston Daily Courier*. The antebellum *Courier* was a prosperous commercial paper that featured an attractive mixture of news, business, and cultural information. Politically it preferred a neutral course while leaning toward unionism. In most public matters it adopted a moderate tone. But in 1850 and again in 1860 the *Courier* was helpless to resist the maelstrom of political crisis and was swept into the vortex of secessionist extremism. Charleston was no place for journalistic moderation during sectional crises.

Though a leading city of the South, Charleston existed on the periphery of national and international trade. With forty-two thousand inhabitants in 1850, Charleston was less than half the size of New Orleans, and by 1860 its population had declined by almost three thousand.[3] Lacking markets of a populated hinterland or trade in diverse products, the city did not share in the national economic boom of the late forties and fifties but instead suffered from increased competition from Wilmington and Savannah.[4] Demographic and economic limitations did not bode well for newspaper success in Charleston, or, for that matter, for intellectual or cultural achievement of any kind. In 1839 Cincinnati, just a few years removed from the frontier, published more magazines and newspapers than all of South Carolina.[5] Visitors thought time stood still in quaint, old-fashioned Charleston. "We recollect," wrote a newspaper correspondent, "the feeling of disappointment with which we first beheld Charleston. We had been accustomed to consider her the first Southern city—though not the largest; but . . . we could only compare her to a decayed old woman. Though we were obliged to admit that even in her decay she was unmistakably a lady."[6]

Located in the heart of the tidewater black belt and closely integrated with the rural hinterland of the state, Charleston—despite its limitations—had no rival as the political, commercial, social, and cultural center of South Carolina.[7] Historian Michael Johnson has noted that "though the most prominent planters considered their plantations nice places to visit, . . . they lived where they wanted, in Charleston." Ruled by a merchant-businessman-planter partnership, Charleston was primarily a planters' city, and country gentlemen lorded over the rest of the state's population.[8] "Charlestonians who were not planters—the mechanics, merchants, lawyers, and doctors—served the agricultural community," William Freehling observes. "Urban Charleston re-emphasized the agrarian nature of South Carolina."[9]

No other state was so dominated by an elite or so dedicated to the protection of slavery, republicanism, and the Southern way of life as South Carolina. While recent scholars recognize that a republican ethos bound planters and farmers and that democratic forces were at work throughout the state, planters dominated both elective and appointive offices.[10] High voter turnout and active electioneering among yeomen and slaveholding farmers suggest a democratic process at work, but the campaigns of a slaveholding elite offered voters little choice. Here the function of campaigning and public opinion "was simply to ratify en masse the elite's decisions, giving them the force of community consensus."[11]

Yet the political ideology of Charleston and South Carolina differed only in intensity and timing from the Southern mainstream; where Charlestonians led, the South followed.[12] As Roy Nichols noted, Charleston was a kind of spiritual capital. "Here were the most fervid traditions of southern loyalty, the most elegant pattern of civilization. It was a Mecca which many southerners, whether they realized it or not, approached in a frame of mind resembling reverence."[13] The press of such a city would have great influence.

Widely recognized as South Carolina's outstanding dailies on the eve of the Civil War, the *Charleston Daily Courier* and the *Charleston Mercury* were products of distinctly different traditions. In 1862 a country paper aptly summarized the differences:

The *Courier* is practical and the *Mercury* speculative. The *Courier* deals with the present and the past, and the *Mercury* more with the future. The *Courier* is content to meet events as they occur, and the *Mercury* anticipates them. There is more diffusion in the *Courier*, and more compactness in the *Mercury*. The *Courier* is pleased to hold on the even tenor of its way; and the *Mercury* is bold, dashing, presumptive, and prophetic. The *Courier* is highly social in its character, sympathizing with all the little offices of humanity, cheering and blessing man's pilgrimage. The *Mercury* is highly political, and seldom if ever stoops to narrate domestic events. . . . [B]oth are popular. . . . The *Courier* . . . however is, and must be, ever more popular . . . [being] highly domestic, and more a favorite with families.[14]

The *Courier* was first in seniority, first in circulation, and first in profits. An important element in the *Courier*'s consistency of policy and style was the fact that one man, Aaron S. Willington, served with the paper from its founding as a Federalist sheet in 1803 until the upheaval of Civil War. Willington came to Charleston from Massachusetts, a circumstance his adopted city forgave but never forgot.[15] Northern roots were not uncommon, however, among the proprietors and editors of Southern journals. Even the most radical sheets like the *Mercury, Palmetto Banner*, and *Columbia Carolinian* had Northern-born editors at one time or another,[16] and in 1858 a *Mercury* employee lamented that "it was flung at the *Mercury* . . . that 3/4s of its editors were from the North."[17]

At first directing the *Courier*'s mechanical department, Willington soon superceded these duties, doing everything from typesetting and printing to editorial writing and collecting for subscriptions. During the War of 1812 he helped establish the *Courier*'s enduring reputation for innovative news gathering by personally boarding incoming ships beyond the bar of Charleston harbor in order to scoop his rivals with foreign news.[18] In 1813 Willington became sole proprietor of the *Courier* and set the formula that would make it a success. As the Federalist Party sank into oblivion, it was easy, perhaps even necessary, to move the paper toward neutrality; soon, the *Courier* emerged as a "commercial and business journal, and rather a medium of general intelligence and literature, than a political organ."[19]

Willington gradually built an able press staff to take over the day-by-day work of the paper, and in 1833 he added Richard Yeadon of Charleston and William S. King of New York as co-partners. The *Courier* established a solid and dignified personality. Readers liked its emphasis on brief, well-reported news items and, during the 1810s and 1820s, were not impatient with its blandly uncontroversial editorial voice.[20]

The nullification crisis, however, forced the *Courier* to break with its editorial tradition. Neutrality was impossible on so vital a question. The *Courier*, strongly opposed to nullification, went to war against the Calhounites and became the leading Unionist paper in the state, a reputation it would carry all the way to 1860. With delight it published Calhoun's 1816 speech in favor of a protective tariff and denounced the nullification ordinance as the "mad edict of a despotic majority."[21]

The *Courier*'s polar opposite was, of course, the *Mercury*, and although one authority has claimed that the *Courier-Mercury* contest was "not a particularly two-fisted battle" by editorial standards of the age, the *New York Courier and Enquirer* thought differently: "Nothing in the nature of a newspaper controversy . . . could be more pointed, or more pungent, than the weapons of warfare wielded by *The Charleston Courier*, in doing battle with the Calhoun cohorts in South Carolina. It is almost painful to stand by, and see the *execution* done by the grape and cannister which the *Courier* throws into the nullification ranks. Its shots tell, with fearful effect, upon the *Mercury* in particular."[22]

Courier-Mercury confrontations over the Test Oath, the Bank of the United States, the subtreasury, and other issues continued long after the nullification controversy ended with compromise in 1833.[23] The *Courier* emerged from these contests a somewhat different paper. It retained its commercial character and commitment to good reporting, but its editorial tone was more political and much more controversial. For this change, no man was more responsible than Richard Yeadon.

A native-born Charlestonian and a graduate of South Carolina College (that breeding ground of aristocratic South Carolina leadership), Richard Yeadon won his spurs in local journalism in 1830 as an aggressive, antinullification writer for William Gilmore Simms's Unionist Charleston *City Gazette*.[24] In 1832 he became *de facto* editor of the *Courier*, and on January 1, 1833, joined Willington and William King as co-owner. He soon overshadowed both.

Yeadon possessed in abundance all the weapons of editorial combat:

a sharp and piercing wit, a penchant for verbal abuse, a facile, productive pen, and a capacity for hard work. Editorial skills like these made *Courier* columns sparkle, but they led to controversy and quarrels.[25] But Yeadon was also a conscientious advocate of public causes. Admitted to the bar in 1824, by 1833 he was on his way to political and financial prominence among South Carolina's elite. He later had a distinguished career in the statehouse, engineering several practical measures for legal reform and public education. Meanwhile, although beginning life poor, he steadily amassed a fortune from newspaper work, handsome legal fees, the profits of a farm near Aiken, South Carolina, and astute investments in city, state, and railroad stocks and bonds. By the time of the Civil War, he was thought to be worth between three and four hundred thousand dollars.[26]

Yeadon faced rough going as an editor because his views had less and less support in South Carolina. He was typical of a small class of South Carolina business and professional men who espoused the Hamiltonian ideas rooted in the Union and Whig parties. As strict constructionism and belief in states' rights burgeoned under Calhoun's leadership, Yeadon supported the Federalist doctrine of divided sovereignty, proclaimed the Supreme Court the final arbiter in disputes between the central government and the states, defended the protective tariff and Bank of the United States, and argued that secession was revolutionary and treasonable if attempted by arms. In 1844 Yeadon battled for Henry Clay, only to see the Whigs collapse with less than eleven percent of the South Carolina vote.[27]

Newspapers cannot flout majority sentiment indefinitely, and Yeadon's unpopular causes were harming the *Courier*. In a three-column editorial on November 4, 1844, Yeadon confessed that the *Courier's* divided councils mandated political neutrality, a policy both unpleasant and inconsistent with his position before the community. He therefore announced his retirement from active direction of the *Courier*, though he would retain his share in the ownership.[28]

William King, who hated controversy almost as much as Yeadon enjoyed it, became editor.[29] Temperamentally suited to nonpartisanship and moderation and experienced as business and commercial editor, King provided ideal leadership for the new departure—or, rather, the return to the old course. The *Courier* was to be, as Yeadon announced in his valedictory, "a business or mercantile, as distinguished from a party or even a political paper, editorially prescribing neutrality in politics, but opening its columns to all parties for the admission, under editorial supervision, of well written and temperate considerations."[30] Under King's tutelage the *Courier* campaigned successfully to secure the first New York-to-Charleston steamship line and, in April 1847, an extension of the

"Electro Magnetic Telegraph" to Charleston.[31] During the Mexican War, King put together a pony express news service from Mobile to Charleston to deliver the latest war news ahead of the U.S. mail. As a result the *Courier* sold thousands of extras and handsomely increased its profits.

In 1850, however, political passions again engulfed the *Courier*. Although not a political paper, the *Courier* was expected to take a stand on the Compromise and the growing secessionist movement. Whereas in 1832-33 the *Courier* had boldly opposed the nullifiers, in 1850-51 it shrank from conflict, asking only to be let alone. But Charleston well knew the Unionist sympathies of Willington and King and would tolerate no dissent from the extremist states'-rights position. Robert Barnwell Rhett and the *Mercury* dominated the political and journalistic scene and, in effect, silenced their rivals. Every Charleston Unionist candidate for the state legislature went down to defeat in the election of 1850.[32] "No journal could be sustained in Charleston which should advocate acquiescence in the compromise," Yeadon wrote to his Unionist friend Benjamin Perry,[33] but the former *Courier* editor added that he would have advocated acquiescence if he had had charge of the paper. He was "ready for disunionism as a dire & hateful alternative & refuge from intolerable insult & worry—but I unhesitatingly prefer Clay's compromise to disunion, & will resolutely stand up to that mark."[34]

Fortunately for the *Courier*, Willington and King, though still Unionists at heart, had no stomach for martyrdom. Determined to save the paper at all costs, they gave way to secessionist pressure. The editors announced that secession appeared inevitable and placed the *Courier* in the ranks of cooperationists, those who supported secession in conjunction with other Southern states.[35] Cooperationism, to Willington and King, represented the lesser of two evils, or, to put it another way, the most moderate political stance Charleston would permit at the moment.

The *Courier*'s prudent choice in 1850 saved the paper. When South Carolina opted for cooperationism, the unilateral secessionists were discredited. Gradually, South Carolina returned to something like normalcy, and the *Courier* almost immediately recouped its popularity. Even the *Mercury* conceded that the *Courier* had recovered its primacy by the time of its fiftieth anniversary in 1853.[36]

Willington and King quickly restored old *Courier* editorial policies. Yeadon, who was still part owner, was understandably miffed when his own paper turned down his critique of the national administration on the grounds that the *Courier* should avoid political controversy. Despite a steady turnover among writers, editors, and managers in the 1850s, the paper's success continued. King died in 1852, and Willington was nearly blinded in 1855, but an unexpected, partial recovery eventually enabled him to visit the office every day and supervise the paper's business affairs. Deaths depleted the paper's editorial corps between 1856 and 1858.[37] Into the vacuum at the top stepped Richard Yeadon.

In abandoning a rather active retirement, Yeadon responded to the threat of a Republican presidential victory in 1856 as much as to his paper's needs. During King's reign Yeadon had kept an eye on newspaper developments in Charleston and published occasional essays (if King approved) in the *Courier*.[38] Upon his return to active duty, Yeadon launched a bold and, according to the *New York Herald*, scurrilous attack on Republican presidential candidate John C. Fremont.[39] Such outlets for Yeadon's political interest and contentious nature were acceptable to Charlestonians, as were his lively but inconsequential skirmishes with country editors on errors of grammar or spelling. But on occasion his quarrels were less welcome; he once touched off an explosion by introducing some qualifications on the right of secession.[40]

Although Yeadon's influence was perceptible in the *Courier*'s pages, the paper remained much as before. The *Courier* emphasized the news more than its editorial columns, and its editorials and leaders were often written by staff members other than Yeadon. Paid correspondents in Washington and New York sent lively, thrice-weekly reports. One reader praised "Pink," the New York correspondent, for his ability to "condense more matters of interest in a shorter space than any party in the same profession that we know of anywhere."[41] Reporting in the antebellum period was a little chancy: the *Courier*, to its embarrassment, once scooped other papers with an announcement of a nonexistent European war.[42] Fortunately, the mistake was an aberration.

The one news item the *Courier* exempted from its policy of accurate, timely reporting was the 1858 yellow fever epidemic in Charleston. Neither the *Courier* nor the *Mercury* reported the calamitous outbreak; in fact, both angrily denied Georgia newspaper reports of it. Not until the mayor proclaimed a day of public prayer did the papers notice the epidemic, and then they complained that reports of sickness had been much exaggerated. Truth crept into the *Courier*'s remarks only after the fever had completed its devastating course.[43]

For the most part, however, the *Courier* exemplified Willington's idea that a newspaper should "promote the welfare of the community by cooperating effectively with its commercial interests and presenting the news fully, accurately, and impartially, leaving its readers to form their own judgments and opinions."[44] The *Courier*, like Ritchie's *Enquirer*, printed the views of its critics and opponents. Even the position on popular sovereignty of South Carolina's *bete noire*, Stephen Douglas, was reported fairly in the *Courier*.[45]

In several ways the *Courier* resembled the mature *Daily Picayune*, the South's most prominent paper. The *Courier* and the mature *Picayune* stood with mainstream journals since political and commercial papers still dominated American journalism.[46] The *Courier*, like the *Picayune*, was financially strong, leading the state in circulation and commercial and business patronage and widely reputed to be a gold mine for its proprietors. Some stories placed its annual net profits at forty thousand dollars.[47] Of course the *Courier* could not match the *Picayune*'s overall strengths since Charleston's journalistic field was too limited, its readership too small, and its outlook too provincial.

One of the reasons for the paper's financial success was that, to a greater degree than the *Picayune*, it served rural interests—virtually every issue reported on the weather, crop conditions, agricultural production prospects throughout the South, and correspondence from farmers and planters. The *Courier* served and drew revenue from the whole state, and by the mid-1850s its fortunes had never been brighter.[48]

Personally these were years of triumph for Yeadon. Now recognized as senior among the state's editors, he presided over a host of charitable and civic organizations. He was widely acclaimed for his generosity and for his wit and speaking ability. Even crusty old secessionist Edmund Ruffin of Virginia was impressed by Yeadon, whom he styled a rare character and a most intelligent and agreeable gentleman. In 1856 the politically moderate editor was elected to the state legislature, leading the field of Charleston's thirty-two candidates with 2,532 votes—the highest number ever won by a Charleston candidate up to that time. Yeadon's victory launched a legislative career spanning, in all, nine years.[49]

As Yeadon's victory implies, Unionist elements, National Democrats, and those opposing immediate secession were riding high in 1856 and 1857. Despite widespread grumbling about Northern aggression, moderates were more popular than radicals.[50] After Buchanan's victory over Fremont, Yeadon decided it was time to take a firm stand against disunionists. When the *Mercury* published a speech by Robert Barnwell Rhett, Sr., defining true Southern statesmanship as action designed to break up the Union, the *Courier* published a Yeadon letter blasting the secessionists and the *Mercury* and followed up with a strong editorial a few days later. Rhett was too impetuous and rash, declared Yeadon, and out of touch with the times. "The City and the State, may have been inclined to Disunionism, in the event of Fremont's sectional and insulting elevation to the Presidency; but now that Buchanan and Breckinridge, and the Constitution, are triumphant, we doubt not that both City and State will go harmoniously for the Union too." The day had long since passed when the *Mercury* was the organ of the state, Yeadon announced.[51]

The *Mercury* may not have been the voice of South Carolina in 1856, but it had lived through a long and curious career very different from that of the *Courier*. In the mid-1850s, as Yeadon said, the *Mercury* was down and the *Courier* was up. Yet the *Mercury* had risen from the depths before; whatever its condition, politicians had always wanted to know what it had to say.

The *Mercury* lived for politics. Founded in 1822 as a politically neutral journal of miscellany and news, the *Mercury* soon turned to factional and sectional politics, the one form of journalism guaranteed success in South Carolina. Its subscription list would depend heavily on party support. The *Mercury* covered the routine material of antebellum journalism routinely. Its news gathering was inconsequential; its strength lay in its editorial voice.[52] Political papers were legion, but the Calhoun-Rhett connection placed the *Mercury* in a unique position. Only in the *Mercury* could South Carolinians and party leaders throughout the country be sure of finding views approved by the state's leaders. The *Mercury* was proud to speak for John C. Calhoun, and "the Senator's ideas found their most complete expression in this paper." The *Mercury* endorsed nullification as early as 1828, and by 1832, when it battled Charleston's three Unionist papers, it had won a lasting reputation for ultraism.[53]

Political journalism unfortunately featured all of the vices of politics. South Carolina's political climate accepted as standard the use of innuendo, the telling of half-truths, and the resort to clever manipulation. So too did the *Mercury*. Factionalism, personal ambition, duplicity, and violence were rife in South Carolina politics—so too in the columns of the *Mercury*.[54] Yet the *Mercury* was not merely the sum of the political villainies of the age, for setting it apart from the hack sheets burdened by personal spite and ambition was the paper's dual role as both a political and sectional journal. The editors sought to unify the state for extreme action in response to aggression from Washington. It was therefore imperative to win adherents within South Carolina and circumscribe political animosity by at least recognizing the worthy motives of fellow South Carolinians and blurring fundamental differences. In so doing *Mercury* editors could maintain hope for eventual agreement on a common course of action while still keeping ultraism alive. The sectional paper was a paper with a mission; its function was not merely to win and hold office.

Slavery and sectional conflict obsessed every *Mercury* editor. Commitment to Calhoun required a certain amount of editorial agility in order to follow the strategic turns of a perpetual presidential contender, but to the *Mercury* everything, even Calhoun, was a means to an end: the protection of slavery and the security of South Carolina and the South. The *Mercury* was the pioneer preacher of Southern separatism and the paladin of the plantation economy.[55]

Although generally the organ of Calhoun, the early *Mercury* often spoke with the spirit of younger, more radical politicians, chiefly Robert

Barnwell Rhett, Sr. For many years Calhoun's chief lieutenant and heir apparent, Rhett had long had a financial interest in the *Mercury*; for twelve years, from 1832 to 1844, his brother-in-law had held the top editorial post. Periodically Rhett and the *Mercury* became disgruntled with Calhoun's Fabian tactics and set off on their own, deducing from Calhoun's premises the logical conclusion of separate state secession. Such was the case in the Bluffton Movement of 1844, but Calhoun quickly rebuked Rhett and disciplined the *Mercury*. Rhett returned to orthodoxy, and within a year of Calhoun's death succeeded him in the Senate and in intellectual sway over the *Mercury*.[56] Rhett's credentials as a Southern diehard were impeccable. He owned two rice plantations and 190 slaves. Born and bred in the South Carolina Sea Islands, the most aristocratic slave culture in the South, Rhett took his rightful place as a lawyer-politician, serving in numerous state offices and six terms in Congress. His Colleton district was described as "the Faneuil Hall where the cradle of Southern sovereignty is constantly rocked."[57]

Though considered by family, friends, and even by some political opponents as a kind, courteous, and cordial gentleman, in public affairs Rhett was notorious for his domineering, abrasive personality. He claimed to abhor contention but inflamed it at every opportunity. To his son he lamented his lack of a moderate temperament; in debate he invariably became harsh and passionate, though to his credit he never resorted to personal insult. Even South Carolina grandees found him rash, presumptuous, offensively self-confident, unconquerably certain of his own rectitude, and utterly contemptuous of anyone who disagreed with him.[58] His much-publicized religious principles and puritanical opposition to immorality, alcohol, and duelling enhanced his reputation for extremism among a planter elite that seldom shunned the pleasures their money could buy or the perquisites their aristocratic status assured.[59] His friends praised his fearlessness, his selfless devotion to the South, and his sensitivity to honor. Even enemies conceded that he sought no personal preferment.[60] His devotion to principle was absolute, his mind hermetically sealed. The unconditional support of his devoted followers in the Colleton district made his power base virtually impregnable. When political crises predisposed people to accept his position, Rhett was a powerful leader; otherwise he probably deserved a contemporary's sneer, "[Rhett] is vain, self-conceited, impracticable . . . and by his ridiculous ambition to lead and dictate everything, has rendered himself odious in Congress and in the State."[61]

The "passion for purity and principle" of Rhett and the ultras was the animating spirit of the *Mercury*. One of the appeals of Rhett and the *Mercury* in presecession days was the sense that they were keeping faith with the past. Talk of "resistance," "submission," "consolidated empire," and "tyranny of the numerical majority," recalled the language of the nullifiers of twenty years earlier.[62] In the 1850s Rhett was the heir of Calhoun and other states' rights sachems, passing that inheritance to a younger generation of politicians who had never known harmonious relations with the federal government.[63]

In 1850 it seemed Rhett's time had come at last. In her biography of Rhett, Laura White remarks that he adopted "the air of a prophet justified—a pose as convincing to his followers as it was irritating to others."[64] Disgusted by the Nashville Convention's reluctance to take action, Rhett returned to South Carolina to launch an independent drive for secession. The *Mercury* urged unilateral state secession, and all South Carolina seemed ready for radical action under Rhett's leadership.[65]

William Gilmore Simms announced, "Rhett is our ruler" but added that he thought Rhett "rash, arrogant and a surface man, with one idea only—a good idea doubtless had it companionship."[66] Others shared Simms's reservations; the South was not ready for radicalism, and South Carolina found itself isolated. Soon the disunionists split over timing and tactics. In July 1851, opponents of separate state secession established their own daily, the *Southern Standard*, to combat Rhett and his *Mercury*. The *Standard* played upon the fears and prejudices of Charleston's conservative business community and ridiculed Rhett's cult as reanimated Bluffton boys, residents of Rhett's boggy Congressional district, Whippy Swamp, and "sundry other swamps, branches, and ponds."[67] Rhett and the cooperationists entertained no notions of compromise with each other. One cooperationist politician voiced the sentiments of many when he said he would never "consent to act with any party having Mr. Rhett as its leader and the Mercury as its exponent." Another wary cooperationist insisted, "If Rhett takes any part in a movement it is half dead the moment he touches it & whole dead when he embraces it. If the *Mercury* supports a measure it is suspected from one end of the South to the other."[68]

By October 1851, secession was defeated, Rhett repudiated, and the *Mercury*, "sulky and irreconcilable, was completely discredited as the organ of the state."[69] Many politicians who had stood with Rhett in the crisis later denied involvement.[70] Rhett was unbending; in April 1852, he resigned his Senate seat, which had been bestowed on him seventeen months earlier. His resignation made a profound impression. Though his principles had been repudiated—and some might add, his leadership rejected—South Carolina had to admire his personal honor, incorruptible integrity, and selfless devotion.[71]

The political fortunes of Rhett and the *Mercury* remained at low ebb through most of the fifties. The *Mercury* more than ever bore the mark of Rhett as it attacked National Democrats and sniped at cooperationists.

Though in retirement, Rhett maintained his influence on the paper through his nephew, William R. Taber, Jr. Taber was part owner and co-editor, with John Heart, until Taber's death in a duel in September 1856.[72] The duel resulted from an anonymous article in the *Mercury* written by Rhett's younger son, Edmund, attacking Judge A.G. Magrath.[73] Rhett's older son, Robert Barnwell Rhett, Jr., chortled over Edmund's "first fly in the Charleston cockpit," declaring Magrath a "gone chicken—beyond hope—dead politically." The Rhetts fully expected violence, and Robert, Jr., hoped his brother was "in good practice with the pistol."[74] As it happened, neither of the parties directly involved fought; instead Edward Magrath, the brother of the injured man, challenged Taber to a duel and killed him on the third shot. "The haste with which the duel was staged," concludes historian C.S. Boucher, "allowing no explanations as to the authorship of the articles, shows the bitterness of feeling."[75]

Rhett, Jr., aided by his brother, purchased Taber's interest in the *Mercury* in early 1857. A Phi Beta Kappa graduate of Harvard University and a successful Colleton rice planter, young Rhett presided over the editorial page while John Heart continued to manage the mechanical department.[76] The *Mercury* may have kept the faith politically in the ensuing years, but it slumped as a newspaper. William Gilmore Simms, who contributed to the *Mercury*'s literary department, spoke of poor editorship during this period and suggested that anybody could have done Rhett, Jr.'s, daily work in twenty minutes.[77]

The editorial policies and journalistic practices of the *Mercury* were, with one exception, precisely what anyone familiar with the Rhetts would expect. The exception was that the paper was surprisingly free of attacks on individuals. The *Mercury* generally lived up to its promise not to assail unnecessarily and without provocation; it did not respond in kind to the incessant personal attacks on its patrons and staff by other papers.[78] Such *ad hominem* exchanges were undignified, ungentlemanly, and, for Rhett, Sr., personally unpleasant. The *Mercury*'s personal attack on Judge Magrath was a departure from the norm. Perhaps chastened by having its editor shot dead, the *Mercury* seldom thereafter indulged in personalities except in cases like Lincoln, Sumner, Hamlin, and Douglas, where the "provocation" was overwhelming. These individuals were legitimate targets—that is, outsiders whose hostility, policies, and power posed a direct threat to South Carolina. Also threatening to the South were border-state congressmen who at heart were insufficiently proslavery. By contrast, all South Carolinians were potential allies who shared common principles on slavery and the need to protect the Palmetto State. Thus the language used to pillory Stephen Douglas—he was vulgar and lacking in decent self-respect—was never directed against South Carolinians. Richard Yeadon, in Rhett's eyes an unmitigated Unionist, was frequently wrongheaded in his political philosophies but nevertheless a talented patriot, honest, industrious, and ingenious.[79] Given such views, Rhett's hysterical denunciation of Texas Unionist Sam Houston in 1860 (a "drivelling schemer" and an "emasculated politician")[80]—or later his persistent warfare against the nationalistic president of the Confederacy—was as understandable as it was predictable.

In other respects, the *Mercury* remained completely in character as the voice of the ultras, editorializing in a fanatically opinionated style for its own cause and against any form of dissent. The *Mercury*'s policy was never to give a fair or objective statement of an opposing viewpoint.[81] For example, when it misled readers about what the results of an 1857 city election portended, it refused to print anything critical of its position.[82] The *Courier* riposted, "If the Press can utter what it pleases, and stifle all reply, then its boastful 'freedom' is tyranny."[83] The Rhetts disdained openness in journalism as a sign of a lack of principles and a species of moral cowardice.

Rhett, Jr., welcomed guest editorials of sound philosophy, i.e., conforming to the creed Rhett. From time to time, father and brother contributed editorials, as did Edmund Ruffin and many others. Ruffin was surprised to find that his letters to the *Mercury* appeared as unsigned editorials, but he was pleased since he considered editorials more influential than newspaper correspondence.[84] Edmund Rhett complained that his brother rewrote his articles, "striking out this, as irreligious, that blasphemous, a third harsh, a fourth improper, etc., etc." Edmund protested, "No paper can in these times pay that is not sharp, aggressive, and pungent. It is not possible to publish the views of the Charleston Mercury without giving offense to somebody. . . . I desire to edit the Paper to make it pay."[85]

Making the paper pay was a major problem. The Rhetts rejected Edmund's views on pungency, finding it advisable to moderate the *Mercury*'s editorial stance in order to increase its circulation—and also to regain the ear of South Carolinians. The *Mercury*'s finances had followed the paper's political fortunes downward from the peak of 1850-51. According to J.C.G. Kennedy's 1852 law register, the *Mercury*'s daily circulation for 1850 (when there was no weekly or triweekly edition) climbed to 5,000, equalling that of the *Courier*; a financial statement of January 1858, however, showed that circulation had fallen to 656 daily and 2,311 triweekly.[86] Rhett, Jr., with pardonable anger accused planters of failing to support the Southern press while the *New York Tribune*, "the chief organ of our Northern aggressors," had almost 200,000 paying subscribers. The four previous *Mercury* editors had faced financial hardships and ruin; such would be the fate of the present editor, warned Rhett, Jr., if the tens of thousands due the paper were not collected.[87] The *Mercury's* situation must have rankled all the more because not all Southern papers were unprofitable. Nonpolitical dailies such as the *Courier* and the *New Orleans Daily Picayune*, or penny papers like the *Richmond Dispatch*, made handsome profits. For political papers, however, the financial outlook was often chancy.

The *Mercury* had accumulated a huge debt, and in 1857-58 there were negotiations to sell the paper. A group of cooperationist friends of Heart, led by ex-Governor James Henry Hammond, I.W. Hayne, Simms, and others, carefully examined the *Mercury* and discussed its problems. Rhett, Jr., placed the *Mercury's* floating bank debt and bonded debt at $44,543; on paper, the *Mercury's* income from advertising and subscriptions stood at $48,113, but probably only half of that was collectible. Hayne, however, estimated that $76,000 was necessary to free the paper from all debt. Hayne suggested that the *Mercury* could be reorganized and made to earn a modest profit within two years; but in the end, the staggering debt prevented agreement on any plan of reorganization.[88]

The debt was a huge burden; another liability was the reputation of Robert Barnwell Rhett, Sr., and his progeny. Heart bluntly declared that the paper had lost ground because "it was supposed to be, & was called the Rhett organ."[89] Hammond remarked, "If the Mercury was free of the Rhetts & well conducted it would be the most influential paper in the South. . . . [T]here is no necessity for Croaking, for denouncing, for keeping our voices strained to the highest key & using no language but vituperation as the Rhetts do & can't help doing."[90] I.W. Hayne held a similar view. "The Mercury, from its selfishness, by indiscretions, does the cause it professes to advocate infinite mischief, and is fast driving this city if not the State into an extreme of opposition."[91]

Many South Carolinians were increasingly hostile to the single-minded radicalism of the Rhetts, and they were alarmed that so many took the Rhetts as representative of the state.[92] The *New York Times*, for instance, was writing of a particularly intemperate outburst by Rhett, Sr., "[T]he spirit of secession has taken such a hold of the mind of the South Carolinians that nothing will satisfy them."[93] Outside observers' identification of South Carolina with the Rhetts was all the more galling when the state was steadily rejecting Rhett's leadership. In an 1857 senatorial contest in which he was the only prominent extremist to run, Rhett, Sr., received less than five percent of the vote.[94] And when, in the aftermath of John Brown's raid, the legislature took no action except to pass cooperationist resolutions, Hammond intoned the Rhetts' political obituary: they were "dead and ought to be dead as a political clique in South Carolina."[95]

Although it proved impossible to put to rest fears about the Rhetts' radicalism, the Rhett family in 1858 addressed the problems of debts and ownership by purchasing Heart's interest. Rhett, Jr., became sole editor.[96] At the same time, the Rhetts purchased the cooperationist *Southern Standard*, which had twelve hundred subscribers and a net income of seventeen thousand dollars.[97] In announcing its purchase of the *Standard*, the *Mercury* astounded its most loyal readers by declaring that there was now no political difference between the journals. The *Mercury*, like the *Standard*, now stood with the Democratic party; it had "long abandoned the separate action of the State, and seeks bona fide the union of the South for action on any proper occasion."[98] At last the Rhetts were trying to accommodate their journal to the political realities of South Carolina in the late 1850s.

The new departure eased but did not eliminate the debt problem plaguing the *Mercury*. Purchase of the *Standard*'s subscription list provided an immediate boost in sales figures.[99] The new, conciliatory tactics may have helped for a while until worsening relations between North and South decisively increased the *Mercury*'s appeal. Charleston's most militant paper quickly restored its traditional tone. The *Mercury* quadrupled its circulation between the time of the Rhetts' takeover and 1861, and rising demand in late 1860 and 1861 forced the *Mercury* to purchase a new Hoe double cylinder press. Friend and foe alike had to read the *Mercury* to keep abreast of secessionist views.[100]

The *Mercury* saw the 1850s as a decade of retreat and defeat for the South. In some ways 1858 marked a turning point along the road to the resistance campaign of 1860, for in that year the Democratic split over Kansas made real the prospect of a final smash-up of the Union. At first Republicans were the villains of the Kansas outrage, but when Stephen Douglas and his Northern Democratic colleagues helped defeat the Lecompton Constitution,[101] the *Mercury* turned on its so-called political allies. "The repeal of the Missouri Compromise has been a thousand times referred to in the South, as a proof of the strength of the South in the Union, and of the ability and fidelity of the Democratic party to secure the rights and interests of the South. The rejection of the Lecompton Constitution in Kansas gives us a fitting occasion to consider its [the Democratic party's] operation and estimate properly its value."[102]

According to the *Mercury*, the value of the Democratic party was minimal; Northern Democrats would betray the South on every important issue—the tariff, internal improvements, Southern slave property, and the right of secession. The greatest enemy was Douglas, who, like other Northern Democrats, was as dangerous as any Republican. From 1858 on, the *Mercury* attacked Douglas, as the *New Orleans Delta* said, with "inordinate ferocity." [103]

The *Mercury* told the cotton states they would have to protect themselves; the border states could no longer be trusted, and the Democratic party was bankrupt. [104] In "Measures for Southern Resistance to Northern Rule," the Rhetts outlined a six-point program for united Southern resistance in the event of a Republican victory in 1860. The editorial pointed toward disunion. [105] In a letter to William Porcher Miles on January 29, 1860, Rhett, Jr., predicted with remarkable prescience the actual steps toward secession. Since Southern states'-rights men were not strong enough to control the Democratic Convention, they must fragment the party. They could use the issues of squatter sovereignty and the Douglas interpretation of the Dred Scott decision to provoke a walkout by the Alabama and Mississippi delegations. Rhett continued, "After the Charleston Convention we must have a Southern States' rights Democratic party organized on principles and with state-rights candidates upon whom to rally. This will ensure the defeat of the double faced 'National' Democracy so called—and make up the issue between the sections, with a resistance party already formed to meet the event of a Black Republican President elected by the North." [106]

The *Mercury*'s goal was Southern independence. It was among the first journals to emphasize the faithlessness of national parties, and in 1860 boasted publicly of its role in dividing the Democrats. In the final analysis, radical strategy looked to a Republican victory, for it was built on the premise that no slave state could abide a Republican president. [107]

The *Mercury* was essentially a one-idea paper. The Rhetts supplied answers to every aspect of the sectional problem, always assuring readers of the propriety, necessity, and justice of resistance and harping on the terrors of delay and submission. If not exactly claiming the gift of prophesy, they were not above figuratively saying "I told you so" by reprinting their old speeches and editorials that accurately predicted recent events. [108]

The *Mercury* had no enthusiasm for causes other than the sectional threat and resistance. Even much of the editor's economic and financial material reflected this obsession: there were columns on the power of Southern cotton to control the destiny of the North, on Northern commercial stagnation as the sure result of sectional warfare, and on the blossoming of Southern commerce as a consequence of independence. [109] *Mercury* editors discovered a sectional angle even in seemingly innocuous subjects. For example, when American naval ships captured two Mexican vessels off Vera Cruz, the *Mercury* saw a hidden effort to bolster American nationalism and brake the momentum of Southern resistance.[110] In an unconscious parody, one of the *Mercury*'s advertisers caught the style:

> Southern Rights!
> Southern Enterprise!
> and
> Southern Independence
> the
> South Carolina Steam Bakery
> Biscuits
> Crackers
> Candies
> Confectionery
> and
> Fireworks.[111]

For all its legendary reputation for hotheadedness and principled defense of Southern resistance, the *Mercury* was not above dissimulation and circuity in working toward its objective. A secession campaign was impossible in the mid-1850s; the lessons of 1851, the prominence of moderate politicians, and the shaky financial condition of the *Mercury* dictated caution and moderation.[112] The *Mercury* seldom openly avowed secession even as it launched its disunion campaign in 1858. Privately, the Rhetts were secessionists; publicly, they advocated Southern unity and defense of Southern rights without discussing where this might lead. The *Mercury*'s 1858 prospectus officially announced the paper's dedication to a rigid states'-rights position only slightly stronger than that which Thomas Ritchie's moderate *Enquirer* might have endorsed.[113] The *Mercury* rejected the pleas of some of its most loyal supporters for advocacy of separate state secession "because the State repudiated that policy on a very aggravating occasion." The *Mercury* "does not press disunion upon its readers, as there is no issue before the country to make that result in the least degree feasible. There is no occasion for such a course, and neither circumstances nor public opinion would justify it."[114]

Rhett, Jr., engaged in a friendly exchange of views with Senator Hammond and the moderates and sought rapprochement by stressing the issues on which all states'-rights men could agree. In Congress, he noted, all South Carolinians would oppose the protective tariff, appropriations for internal improvements, antislavery in any form, and all the insidious and oppressive measures of Black Republicans.[115] Looking ahead to the elections, the *Mercury* called vaguely for unity and resistance: "Should they [the Republicans] be successful, we have a right to suppose that those who are united in principle will be united in measures of redemption and security."[116]

As late as August 10, 1860, Rhett, Jr., still avoided an explicit endorsement of separate state secession in the *Mercury*:

We should go for the co-action of all the Southern States. If this cannot be obtained, then we should support the co-action of the Cotton States. If this fails, then we should strive to get the co-action of four, three, or two of the Cotton States. Should all these expedients fail—then, and not until then, fairly comes up the question—shall South Carolina submit to the rule of the Black Republican party in possession of the General Government, or shall she secede alone from the Union? When this alternative arises, we will be prepared to meet it. The past course of the Charleston Mercury, we presume, affords some assurance of its fidelity to the South and the state, in all emergencies.[117]

And on November 3, while urging the legislature to call a state convention to respond to certain Republican victory, the *Mercury* editor sidestepped the conflict on secession policy by arguing that the issue need not be discussed before the assembling of the convention. The essential thing, he concluded, was that secession of one or more states would with reasonable probability lead to creation of a Southern confederacy.[118]

Laura White concisely characterized the Rhetts' 1858-60 policy: "To rouse the people again to the resistance spirit of 1850, but to suppress or evade any definite proposals, any discussion of method, on which opinions would divide, until it was too late to draw back—this was the *Mercury*'s unmistakable purpose and real though unavowed policy."[119] The *Mercury* became indignant when Northerners attached the disunionist label to Southern resistance organizations.[120] When the *Mercury* argued that the real intent of Southern resistance efforts was to save, not destroy, the Union, the dissimulation apparently succeeded. Even Senator Hammond was misled—in September 1860 he told a friend that Rhett had come out for the Union.[121]

Nevertheless, the Rhetts found it hard to abandon habits of a lifetime, and there were moments of frankness. In 1858 a *Mercury* editorial damned abject Southerners who would cling to the Union while abolitionists rode to victory. In a July 4, 1859, speech, Rhett, Sr., proclaimed himself a secessionist and denounced delay as naked submission to unconstitutional misrule and "wicked imbecility." Brown's raid, blared the *Mercury*, showed Southerners that they must have exclusive power over the post office, the police, and the military—in short, over their own government. "The South must control her own destinies or perish."[122]

Although the *Mercury*'s circulation grew dramatically in 1860 and the Rhetts' public standing grew in direct proportion to fear of the Republicans, many South Carolinians still deeply distrusted the Rhetts, especially Rhett, Sr. I.W. Hayne, a longtime enemy, remarked, "The older I get the more I feel the force of John Randolph's aphorism that the nonsense of 'principles not men' is like 'love without women'—Rhett! Middleton! Burt! They would ruin any cause."[123] But events seemed to be moving Rhett's way, and, with the splintering of the Democratic party in Charleston, South Carolinians elected Rhett delegate-at-large to the ensuing bolters' convention meeting in Richmond. However, the Richmond convention rejected Rhett's extremist views and Southern delegates crept back to the Democratic Convention in Baltimore. Some thought Rhett himself caused the setback.[124] Senator Hammond wrote from Washington:

I knew Rhett had no popularity out of South Carolina, but I had no idea he was so utterly odious. Aaron Burr never was more so. When it was learned that he was chosen to the Richmond Convention there burst forth at Washington such a wail (for there was some grief in it) of indignant execration as I never knew any man to excite before. . . . What a pity that such fine talent should be thrown away on such a perverse temper. There is nothing the friends of Breckinridge & Lane dread more than that Rhett's name should become mixed up with their canvass. They prefer that South Carolina should hold in & would *pay* largely I believe if the Mercury would *attack them* so rampant have Rhett, Yancey & Co made *Unionism*.[125]

By late 1860 the *Mercury* was tired of restraining itself, and it began badgering legislators to call an early secession convention, hinting darkly at great public indignation welling up at the prospect of delay.[126] The first rule of revolution, Rhett, Sr., wrote to his son, was to avoid leaving excessive time for reaction by the people.[127] As Charleston prepared to elect delegates to a secession convention, the *Mercury* urged nomination of a single ticket of twenty-two men, all pledged to immediate secession.[128] The cry of *Mercury* dictatorship and arrogance immediately sounded. The *Mercury* fell back to demand that all convention candidates respond to public interrogatories and commit themselves to an immediate and permanent dissolution of the Union. It then published the list of candidates, arbitrarily dividing them into categories headed "explicit" or "non-explicit." The *Courier*, angry citizens, and several offended candidates protested the *Mercury*'s presumption and (somewhat fatuously) demanded fair play. The *Mercury* dismissed the whole matter as a little misunderstanding. At least one observer thought the Rhetts had blundered, noting, "The outrageous conduct of the *Mercury* in classifying the candidates came near losing R. B. Rhett his [own] election."[129]

The effort to rig the secession convention was entirely in keeping with the Rhetts' concept of leadership. South Carolinians, they believed, were timid because the state's public men had no stomach for the fight; politicians were paralyzed by the thought of failure and party proscription and were waiting for the people to give them a lead. True statesmen, the Rhetts insisted, made public opinion, not vice versa. A few bold men, willing to take risks, possessing "nerve and self-sacrificing patriotism," must shape the movement's course, "controlling and compelling their inferior contemporaries."[130] The *Mercury* was to be the voice of those few bold men. The Rhetts thought their Southern rivals effeminate, their rivals' plans productive of "postponement, delay, enervation, feebleness, halting, fainting, paralysis, submission—and the downfall of slavery, with the destruction of the South."[131]

As for Northerners, the Rhetts thought them beneath contempt. The *Mercury* was amused by the suggestion that war might follow secession: "That a people, like the people of the North, prone to civil pursuits and money-making, should get up and carry out the military enterprise of conquering eight millions of the only people on the continent, who, from education and habits, are a military people,—is one of those absurdities which none but a professed panic-maker could be capable of announcing."[132] Rhett, Sr., assured the people that "secession was a quiet and easy remedy for an intolerable tyranny." Yankees were a poor, pusillanimous, cowardly race "only fitted by nature and education to manufacture wooden nutmegs."[133] If the improbable occurred and the North declared war, argued the *Mercury*, the South would be unconquerable. Though an agricultural people, Southerners would not lack for the instruments of war because the volunteer spirit would supply everything needed.[134] Indeed, secession would usher in a new era of prosperity for the South; its ports would handle a roaring trade in the South's great staples, enriching merchant, mechanic, and planter alike while the North's economy collapsed.[135]

The *Mercury* of 1860 reflected the Southern press's longstanding resentment of Northern economic, financial, and cultural hegemony. Southern newspapers failed to thrive, propagandists had it, because of Northern competitors backed by huge populations and businesses. In truth there had always been a significant Northern press circulation in the South, and the demand for Northern publications added to a crisis of intellectual self-confidence and nagging doubts that Southerners were lagging culturally.[136]

Commercially, too, the South seemed deficient, lamented the *Mercury* and scores of other Southern sheets; Charleston, Savannah, Mobile, and New Orleans were satellites of New York, Philadelphia, and Boston—mere intermediaries for the transit of cotton to New York City and of foreign imports to Southern planters. Buy Southern and establish direct trade with Europe was the naive cry of many a journal. Patriotic Southerners urged city building as both good economics and loyalty to the South, and the rhetoric of sectionalism colored almost equally campaigns for political resistance, railroads, urban growth, and support of Southern newspapers and literature. Fearing Republican nationalistic economic policies and Yankee cultural domination, the *Mercury* easily made a case for a bright economic future and glorious republic outside the Union. This crusade sought a consensus of interests and prejudices among farmers, planters, and Charlestonians—in short, all South Carolinians who mattered.[137]

One-sided editorials endorsing extremist action were self-serving at best; at worst they were terribly wrong, with disastrous consequences for the South. There was an air of unreality about many *Mercury* editorials. Of course the Rhetts could not simultaneously urge secession and predict a long, bloody war of unknown result. Whether they consciously pushed a recognizable lie or, as true believers, saw only a powerful South with a secure, prosperous future, is impossible to document. Given their provincialism and their total dedication to the planters' way of life, however, one must conclude that their vision was probably honestly flawed. The Rhetts' myopia in fact reflected conventional wisdom. By the end of the decade, it was easier for Southern editors to voice sectional stereotypes than to resort to a painful self-analysis that could only thwart a goal so fondly desired.

Mercury editorials were couched in terms of Southern honor, pride, and self-respect. To submit meant degradation, virtual deracination: "A man and a people who surrender rights without resistance are unworthy of them. They are fit to be slaves—the poor tools of a party—and the base instruments of unscrupulous despotism."[138] The Rhetts' choice of language—suggestive always of conflict, hatred, violence, and extreme passion—surely excited the *Mercury*'s partisans and just as certainly frightened moderates across the South. In normal political times, few would be attracted to a popular "Rhettism" of 1860: "Success is no criterion of duty."[139]

The many Southerners who wanted compromise and the many Northern conservatives who were willing to guarantee protection of slavery were scarcely mentioned in the *Mercury*, except to have their foolishness rebuked. The *Mercury*'s Northern coverage was largely confined to Lovejoy, Garrison, Phillips, Greeley, abolitionists, and Black Republicans. To criticisms of its unvarying one-sidedness, the *Mercury* blandly responded, "We have endeavored to place matters and opinions before the public fairly, without bias or exaggeration."[140]

In the fall of 1860 the Rhetts launched their final push for secession. Day after day they published inflammatory speeches, reported fervent Southern rights meetings, and told and retold tales of Northern outrages.[141] In a single issue the editors featured "Abolition Outrages in the Slave States—Mr. Seward's Politics," "The Wide Awakes," and "What Would be the Effect of Lincoln's Election?"[142] The Rhetts arranged for special telegraphic dispatches to report the collapse of Union sentiment and the growth of secessionist fever elsewhere in the Cotton South.[143]

For over three decades the advocate of a forlorn hope, the elder Rhett was at last vindicated. By October secession was the only policy acceptable to South Carolina, and the Rhetts had done more than anyone to make it so. In that month, Rhett, Jr., was elected to the statehouse, easily beating his editorial rival, former Unionist leader Richard Yeadon.[144]

"The tea has been thrown overboard—the revolution of 1860 has been initiated," exulted the *Mercury* upon Lincoln's election. And when South Carolina left the Union, the *Mercury* had an extra on the streets only five minutes after the declaration of independence. Secessionists rallied at the *Mercury* office and serenaded the editors, who basked in the warm glow of their state's nearly unanimous enthusiasm for independence.[145]

The *Mercury*'s great Charleston rival, the *Courier*, followed a different path in crucial years of 1858-60, but perhaps that path was as characteristically Southern as the *Mercury*'s. Under Yeadon's editorship, the *Courier* went its moderate way, minimizing politics, reporting news, maintaining absolute orthodoxy on slavery, and making excellent profits.[146] Yeadon thought the *Mercury* served a useful purpose: "While we would ourselves steady the helm of our State and keep her in the track of union, we are not unwilling that Deltas [the *New Orleans Delta*], South's [the *Richmond South*] and Mercuries, should stand as sentinels at the masthead, and cry the alarm of enemies . . . although the clamor may be sometimes premature."[147] The *Courier* was not at all eager to heed the cry of the sentinel. In 1858, for example, when Kansas was lost, the *Courier* did not urge mobilization for resistance but instead heaved a sigh of relief that compromise had been achieved.[148]

The compromise had been bought at a heavy price; after 1858 the *Courier* turned its back on Stephen Douglas.[149] Never again would it be quite so confident about unionism, but the erosion of its faith was gradual. Until mid-1860 the *Courier* did not share the *Mercury*'s belief that the South faced imminent peril, nor did it encourage agitation or support the resistance campaign.[150] Yeadon shrugged off "the evanescent twaddle of the mere aspiring partisans, who prate incessantly of ruin and destruction—loss of character—loss of honor—loss of everything conducive to the well-being and happiness of the country."[151] The *Courier* placed its hope in the Union's willingness to respect states' rights. In early 1858 the *Courier*, quoting James M. Mason, declared the "Union under the Constitution" to be "one to live and die for—but a Union that would make serfs of Southerners is not the Union our patriot fathers bequeathed us, and we should [have] none of it."[152]

Deeply shocked by John Brown's raid and the Republican party's strength, the *Courier*, by mid-1860, was on the verge of losing faith in the Union and the Democratic party's ability to preserve states' rights. The *Courier* accepted the Southern walkout from the 1860 Democratic Convention, for the party had rejected Southern rights in the territories; yet the paper desperately urged a reassembly of the national convention in the hope of securing genuine compromise.[153] When Democrats nominated Stephen Douglas and refused to adopt a platform acceptable to the South, the *Courier* at last saw sectionalism and resistance as the only issues that really mattered.[154] In June 1860, it endorsed the Southern Rights candidates, Breckinridge and Lane, and in August asserted, "In the event, then of the election of Lincoln, we would favor a convention of the Southern States, or as many of them as can be got to act together, to present to the North the alternatives of a new and satisfactory understanding of our political compact, or a dissolution of the Union. We prefer the alternative of disunion, however sad, to any further submission to northern aggression."[155] It was a crucial turnabout, and the *Mercury* celebrated with a front-page editorial—"The Position of the Charleston Courier on Disunion."[156] At last the most conservative paper in the state was in step with the most ultra. The *Courier* had come to terms with its environment, and the South Carolina press, united as never before, was ready to usher the Palmetto State out of the Union.

Although the *Courier* printed an occasional conservative letter, by October the former bastion of Unionism was committed to secession and was busily attacking what remained of the opposition to it.[157] Lincoln's election, it pronounced, was a signal for action, not words.[158] The *Courier* predicted that the state would vote unanimously for secession, denounced all thought of compromise, and boasted of South Carolina's honor in the familiar *Mercury* style.[159] When secession at last swept over the state, the editors of the *Courier*—once the unsparing critics of Rhett's extremism—joined the press of South Carolina in celebrating the event of the century with patriotic gusto.[160]

Just as secession seemed to be a logical extension of the states'-rights philosophy, so the *Mercury*'s extremism (reflecting the marriage of partisan journalism and fanatical dedication to secession) was a logical extension of the battling Jacksonian partisan press style. Political and sectional papers were similar in style; both could be hysterical regarding threats to their interests and policies, but the sectional press (1) focused almost exclusively on sectionalism in public life, (2) discovered its mission in defending the South rather than in winning and holding office, (3) spoke for a state or region instead of a political party and even worked to destroy the national party system altogether, and (4) sought unity in its journalistic field by winning over or suppressing rival voices in order to confront danger from without.

Sectional papers regarded critics, dissenters, and rival politicians not as political opponents who could be trusted with power but as enemies whose triumph would revolutionize the constitutional system of the country and destroy the liberties of its citizens. Hence the ultraism of both means and ends. Historically the *Mercury's* reputation for ultraism rests of course on its ends, but its closed columns, blinkered vision, and air of doctrinaire omniscience were the necessary means. The *Mercury* inflamed passions, glossed over whatever did not fit its mission, suppressed press freedom and national loyalties, and propagandized in defense of slavery and in support of secession. In the crisis produced by Republican victory the *Mercury's* voice seemed prophetic. Suddenly the Rhetts were popular. Although for years their machinations and fulminations had limited their popularity and hindered as much as helped the cause of Southern resistance, proving especially counterproductive in staid Virginia, the *Mercury's* circulation, like that of many fire-eating sheets, leaped forward in the secession crisis. The voice of extremism, increasingly the rage, heralded the Union's doom. That voice, as Fred Hobson reminds us, was designed to persuade, to move to action, not to memorialize or lament; it was not afflicted with guilt. The extremist spoke with confidence because his cause was not lost but at hand. In Charleston in 1860 the editorial spokesman and the hour had met.[161]

In South Carolina, the press moved rapidly toward the final stage of sectionalism, a stage not reached by most newspapers until the emergence of the Confederacy in 1861. Indeed, the 1860 battles among Breckinridge, Bell, and Douglas papers were some of the most vitriolic in the antebellum South, but as radicalism grew during the presidential campaign and the Breckinridge press increased in numbers and influence, other Southern states moved toward the South Carolina model.[162] The triumph of the sectional press in South Carolina and then in the Confederacy was an important step in the rise of a solid South.

The journalism for which the South was *not* celebrated was found in the somewhat conciliatory, constructive, and hugely profitable columns of the *Courier*. Here was a journalism which recognized the South's limited means of resistance as well as legitimate sectional interests as it voiced a planter-businessman point of view. The *Courier* embodied a Whig-progressive style that later resurfaced in New South and early-twentieth-century progressive journalism, a journalism featuring industrial and urban development and cognizant of the basis of nation-state compromise and cooperation even as it defended Southern race relations, elitism, and planter interests.[163] The *Courier* tradition was both

Southern and American, and it was generally positive and constructive while the *Mercury*'s was largely negative and destructive. The rival journals remained true to character during the War.

After the Rhetts' apotheosis of 1860, the war was, for them, an anticlimax. They soon went into opposition, reviling the Davis administration for its incompetence, arrogance, and autocracy. Perhaps the Rhetts were born to oppose, not to support.[164] Not surprisingly, although South Carolinians were critical of the Davis administration, they found the *Mercury*'s carping criticisms and fanatical antigovernment diatribes reprehensible; such attacks divided the Confederacy, weakened the war effort, and encouraged the Northern enemy.[165] Robert Barnwell Rhett, Jr., failed to win one of twenty Charleston seats in the statehouse in 1862, and his father was defeated in a bid for the Confederate Congress in 1863.[166]

The *Courier*, on the other hand, came to the president's defense, thereby returning to its old, moderate style. Yeadon vigorously supported the Confederacy personally through his vast wealth and publicly through his editorial efforts in the *Courier*.[167] When Charlestonians rejected Rhett, Jr., in 1862, they honored Yeadon by electing him to the state legislature. As in the mid-1850s, the *Courier* in 1862 and 1863 understood South Carolina better than did the *Mercury*.[168]

Both papers suffered physical and financial hardship during the War and Reconstruction. The *Courier* survived to merge with the *Charleston News* in 1873, and the *News and Courier*, under the progressive leadership of Francis Warrington Dawson, carried on the *Courier*'s tradition. The *Mercury*, however, expired in 1868 from its accumulated financial burdens—much to the joy of Northerners who still feared the fire-eaters' potential for disruption. Several Northern journals saw in the *Mercury*'s demise the dawn of a new era.[169] Had these hostile newspapermen realized that the Rhetts' style would surface whenever Southern editors perceived a threat of Northern aggression, they would have been less sanguine. Later even the most progressive New South editors understood that they had to speak for the South. Perhaps there was latent Rhettism in every Southern editor. After all, even the *Courier* had come out for secession.

In his farewell, Robert Barnwell Rhett, Jr., showed that neither the War nor Reconstruction had modified the Rhett creed by a single iota:

The Charleston Mercury will no more be heard. Its voice, which for fifty years has mingled in the counsels of the imperiled South, is hushed. But will it be dead? Has it advocated no high principles of liberty which, in some warm-living heart, shall not be forgotten? Has it counselled no policy of stern resistance to wrong—of a brave defiance of tyranny—of a deathless effort for independence, with a spirit undaunted and an honor untarnished for the South—a policy which shall yet survive and triumph? . . . Amidst the afflictions and desolations in this our land, I have faith to believe in the future independence and prosperity of the South. I take my place among her ruined children—better so than to be the proudest and most honored of her successful enemies—and I wait, hoping, praying, expecting the bright coming of her final deliverance.[170]

5

A Study of
Wartime Journalism
John M. Daniel and the Confederacy

We must have something to eat, and the papers to read.
Everything else we can give up.

Oliver Wendell Holmes, 1861

Historians trying to rehabilitate the reputation of Confederate President
Jefferson Davis argue that while he was struggling to offset the overwhelming power brought to bear on the agrarian South by the industrial
North, the South's newspaper editors cruelly tormented him, negating
much of his work, and eroding Southern morale with irresponsible criticism. Historians argue that a longstanding tradition of strident, sadistic
editorializing carried over into the war and produced an opposition
press that helped destroy Confederate will. Along with the Rhetts of the
Charleston Mercury, foremost among the editors who can be accused of
such negativism is John Moncure Daniel, editor and proprietor of the
Richmond Examiner.[1] All but forgotten today, Daniel was a giant of Confederate journalism, and his career illuminates the role of the editor in
the Southern cause and the limitations and paradoxes of Confederate
press freedom.

The negative interpretation of Daniel's wartime role seems, in part,
valid;[2] but the traditional interpretation—exaggerated and one-sided—
ignores Daniel's efforts to sustain the cause of independence.[3] Daniel
was an eccentric, molded by the partisan and sectional warfare of the
antebellum period. Extremism in journalism, absolute intolerance of
politicians' mistakes, and satirical style came naturally to him. His *Examiner* publicized every flaw, real or imaginary, in the Davis administration's management of the war effort. And the wartime *Examiner* was
certainly influential. John Esten Cooke, chronicler of the "Lost Cause,"
wrote that the *Examiner* had become "the controlling power, almost, of
the epoch."[4] Influential, but not only for evil. Dearly as Southerners

cherished individualism and civil liberties, including press freedom, they would hardly have tolerated a lethal enemy within their ranks.

From Davis's viewpoint, Daniel may be seen as a danger to Confederate morale, but from a different perspective, Daniel might just as accurately be viewed as the soul of Confederate resistance. Day after day his journal joined such pro-administration papers as the *Charleston Courier*, the "Standard-Bearer of the Confederacy," in glorifying Southern independence and Southern arms, in advocating drastic war measures, and in idealizing the virtues of Southern civilization.[5] Daniel perceived a crucial distinction between the Southern cause and the Confederate administration, and so did many, if not most, Southerners.

Few would quarrel with historian J. Cutler Andrews's pronouncement that the *Examiner* was Daniel's formidable personality writ large.[6] Daniel was born in Stafford County, Virginia, in 1825, the son of a country doctor of modest means. Educated at home by his father and then in Richmond by his uncle, Judge Peter V. Daniel, young John was destined for a gentleman's career at the bar, despite his dislike of legal studies. But in 1845, his father's death forced him to become self-supporting.[7] He took a job as a librarian in Richmond, earning one hundred dollars a year and his lodging. The poverty and obscurity of his early manhood both toughened and scarred him, but he seized the opportunity to finish his education by devouring a library and mastering mid-nineteenth-century literature and ancient and European history. He excelled as a conversationalist; but like many famous, self-made, and self-educated men, he was notorious for dogmatic pronouncements, and he had an arrogant passion for playing the autocrat of letters. Journalist, author, and physician George Bagby recalled that during the war years Daniel entertained and dominated a diverse circle of admirers from a sort of elevated barber's seat, "as from a throne, he looked down upon and conversed with his visitors; and to me at least . . . his words descended from their elevation with a certain authority, as from a true *cathedra*."[8]

For a while Daniel embraced transcendentalism with a young man's passion; his cousin recalled the future editor urging him to read the works of Ralph Waldo Emerson and even making a brief effort to found a liberal church in Richmond. But philosophical inquiry crashed headlong into the slavery question. Fortunately for his career, Daniel's transcendentalist misgivings about slavery were completely and conveniently squashed by Thomas Carlyle's pamphlet, "The Nigger Question," which later was virtually emblazoned on the *Examiner*.[9] Emerson was not to be the mentor of Daniel, the Southern gentleman.

Privation and hardship warped this sensitive and high-strung young man, embittering him against the world. According to his cousin Moncure Conway, his cynicism resulted in a spiritual loneliness coupled with a brilliant, individualistic mind.[10] Although friends praised his brilliance, they readily acknowledged his cold, self-contained, gloomy, even repellent, nature.[11] "Half misanthrope, half genius,"[12] Daniel was an incurable bachelor who, supposedly spurned by his one true love, had little use for womankind. He had few family ties and fewer intimate friends.[13] Toward his dogs (whom he loved to torment into fighting for his visitors) and his slaves, he exhibited a cruel streak that paralleled the genuine magnanimity he showed toward his gentlemen peers and newspaper employees.[14] Afflicted with a weak constitution, Daniel worshipped strength of mind and body and despised fools and weaklings. He especially admired John C. Calhoun for strength of character and steady nerve.[15]

From an early age Daniel felt destined to be a gentleman of consequence.[16] "He would be rich, he would be powerful, he would be great, he would ride to victory, not amid the cheers and congratulations of friends, but over the envy and chagrin of those who . . . scorned and crushed him."[17] When he began amassing a fortune in wartime Richmond, Daniel revealed his life's dream to Dr. Bagby: "When I am rich, I shall buy the old family estate in Stafford County and shall add to it all the land for miles around. I shall build a house to my fancy, and, with my possessions walled in, I shall teach these people what they never knew—how to live like a gentleman."[18] And in a fashion he did just that, purchasing a fine home, collecting a large and costly library, and indulging his appetite for fine clothes and food—all the while urging self-sacrifice on his fellow rebels and denouncing the contemptible rats and sneaks who cared more for their own carcasses than for the triumph of the Confederacy.[19]

No Southerner who antagonized as many people as Daniel did could afford to be a coward, and no one ever doubted the editor's courage.[20] He fought several duels during the war[21] and twice abandoned the safety of his editorial sanctum to join the Confederate Army, where he served briefly as an aide to General John Floyd in 1861 and to General A.P. Hill in 1862.[22] Resplendent in the most fashionable dress uniform, Daniel was a study in military foppery, especially in comparison with slouchily dressed General Hill and other veteran officers; nevertheless, he earned an honorable wound (a slight wrist wound) at Gaines Mill and could retire to his editorial haven, a scarred war hero.[23]

If for every virtue Daniel possessed a corresponding vice, the latter marred his journalism not at all, but on the contrary seems to have given it resilience and drive. The antebellum editor's chair combined the podium of the statesman-politician, the lecture hall of the man of letters, the pulpit of the fiery preacher, and the squalid office of an impoverished, quarrelsome lawyer.[24] The job fit Daniel like a glove.

Daniel had become an editor in 1847. After leaving the library and gaining a bit of experience on an agricultural weekly, the *Southern Planter*, he had been hired as an editorial assistant for a struggling newcomer, the *Richmond Semi-Weekly Examiner*. Within months Daniel became editor-in-chief, and soon he borrowed enough money to buy the paper and issue it three times a week.[25] Launched as an independent Democratic journal in protest against the state machine, Daniel's *Examiner* addressed itself to the planter class rather than to the Democratic rank and file or the citizens of Richmond, who were largely Whig. Later Daniel would boast of the thinking gentlemen who formed his readership.[26] *Examiner* editorials so frequently alluded to antiquity, the scriptures, and European history that "readers of limited education and background would have found it difficult to follow his writings."[27] Although obviously a journal of politics, the *Semi-Weekly Examiner* contained solid reading matter on a wide variety of topics and at least a modicum of the best current literature, including some of Edgar Allen Poe's poems which first appeared there.[28]

Daniel's antebellum editorial career was as spectacular as it was brief. As Oscar Fitzgerald put it, Daniel's entrance "into the editorial ranks was like turning an electric eel into a fish-pond."[29] For two decades, Thomas Ritchie, Sr., and John Hampden Pleasants had stood at the pinnacle of Richmond's press. With Ritchie's removal to Washington and Pleasants's death, Daniel took their place; his *Examiner* became the talk of the state. "Its press could hardly supply the demand. At every table, at every street corner, the subject was Daniel's last article."[30] Through ridicule, sarcasm, outrageous epithets, and merciless allegories Daniel flayed and roasted his political opponents.[31] "Whether you approved or disapproved," recalled John Esten Cooke, "you read those tremendous satires. Not to see the Examiner in those days was to miss a history of the times."[32]

Rival editors who crossed Daniel's path could expect a shower of verbal brickbats. He launched personal attacks on nearly every notable man in Virginia and occasionally even lashed out at the Richmond townsfolk. When they went into a frenzy over the arrival of Jenny Lind, the Swedish Nightingale, Daniel denounced the "asininity of the Richmond public, their gullibility, their pitiful weakness for what is foreign, their adaptation for toadyism, [and] their rage for what is high." "Enter Quince, Snug, Bottom, Flute, Snout, and Starveling," he wrote.[33] Dr. Bagby described how, in turn, "he accepted cheerfully the odium of the community, and, indeed, of the whole State in which he lived. For the sake of power and a competency, he became an outcast from society. At one time he was literally hated or feared by everybody. In the whole world there was scarcely a human being who really liked him for himself. All this he brought upon himself, deliberately and for a purpose. He marked out an arduous course, and he followed that course resolutely to the last day of his life, accepting all the consequences."[34] A Richmond belle remembered Daniel as "a very unpopular man, a sort of social sphinx." Daniel's enemies, she noted, could only hope that *Examiner* assistants might occasionally "subdue the roar of that autocratic lion."[35]

The sectional struggle made the *Examiner* something more than a mere local journal. As the crisis worsened, newspaper circulation generally increased all over the South.[36] Hardly an issue passed in which Daniel did not address the struggle. In addition to Whigs, erring editors, and toadying townspeople, the *Examiner* now lambasted weak-kneed Southerners, Yankees, abolitionists, and free-soilers. Its special enemy with which it fought continuously was Horace Greeley's *New York Tribune*. Like his idol Calhoun, Daniel defended the right of secession but hoped to avoid a final confrontation. "If we organize and act," he implored his readers in April 1850, "we may save our rights, and with them the Union."[37]

Beginning without a cent in 1847, Daniel made the *Examiner* a power in Virginia, but for a few years influence was his sole reward. Retaining the editorship, Daniel had to sell the paper to cover his debts, probably in 1849, but he managed to repurchase it, again by borrowing, in the fall of 1851. "Since that time," he wrote a year later, "the paper has been quite profitable; and I have at this time a subscription list larger by seven hundred than any other newspaper in the State of Virginia."[38] But Daniel remained in debt and now faced the horrifying prospect that, at age twenty-seven, he had achieved fame without wealth or the accoutrements of the genteel life he coveted. It was not enough.

Daniel saw in the Democratic victory of 1852 his chance to accumulate some money by obtaining a diplomatic post in Europe. He bluntly demanded the support of Virginia Senator R.M.T. Hunter: "The year's salary [of a *chargé d'affaires's* post]," he told Hunter, "with $4,500 outfit and $2,000 infit, would pay all expenses and leave several thousand dollars in hand." Diplomatic service and foreign travel would also enhance his social prestige. He would leave the paper safely in Democratic hands and resume the editorship on his return.[39] The Pierce administration honored his request, bestowing upon the worthy partisan a sinecure as *chargé d'affaires* at the Court of Turin.[40]

In some ways Daniel's European tour of duty was successful and personally satisfying. He performed the drudgery of his office satisfactorily, wrote excellent accounts of European affairs for the State Department, traveled extensively, found leisure to broaden his reading, and purchased books and paintings.[41] But from the beginning his mission was not without its misadventures. Arriving in New York City preparatory to departure, Daniel was arrested and sued for libel by a Yankee peddler whom he had attacked in the *Examiner*. Although released on bail and permitted to sail for Europe while the trial proceeded in his absence, Daniel found the adverse publicity unpleasant and the trial an enormous worry. When the New York court levied on him a fine and court costs totaling nearly three thousand dollars, Daniel denounced the verdict as a product of Northern prejudice: a New York jury and a Yankee peddler had seen an easy opportunity to persecute a defenseless Southerner.[42]

Another incident almost concluded his diplomatic career before it had really begun. Distracted by the trial, sick from travel and strange food, and frustrated by language barriers and unaccustomed surroundings, Daniel inaugurated his Italian career by writing a scorching satire of Turinese society for the amusement of his Richmond associates.[43] Although the letter was marked confidential, a friend published it in the *Examiner*, and soon European journals delightedly reprinted this specimen of American bumptiousness. "I have dined with dukes," wrote Daniel, "jabbered bad grammar to countesses, and am sponged on for seats in my opera-box by counts who stink of garlick, as does the whole country. I receive visits from diplomats with titles as long as a flagstaff, and heads as empty as their hearts, and find the whole concern more trashy than I ever imagined."[44] The incident eventually blew over after Daniel apologized, but the humiliated diplomat grumbled, "Is my life to be a continued fight with malice, folly, and mortification? I begin to be sick of it all together."[45] Daniel found the post so lucrative that in 1856 he eagerly accepted another four-year term.[46] His second tour of duty was enlivened by his appearance at a diplomatic reception escorting a beautiful countess of most unsavory political and personal reputation.[47]

South Carolina's secession interrupted this interlude in Daniel's life, and Daniel hurried back to take over the *Examiner*'s secession campaign.[48] Rumors of his return had started early. In August 1858 the *Richmond South* warned that if Italy had not soothed him the public could expect "some d....d cutting and slashing."[49] Whatever doubts about secession he may have had earlier,[50] he returned to the United States a full-fledged Southern nationalist. He had observed at close range the emergence of Italian nationalism and was soon making the separateness of Southern culture and the glories of Southern civilization his stock in trade.[51] From February through April, the *Examiner*, now appearing daily, exhorted the South to action and denounced "submissionists" and all peace proposals and conferences.[52] Daniel ridiculed his opponents mercilessly; one, whom he styled "a curly-headed poodle . . . nearly overcome with dignity and fat," became so irate that city officials required him to post bond to keep the peace.[53] In March the *Examiner* carried a devastating satire of Virginia's Unionists, the "Parliament of Beasts," which compared them to magpies, jackals, opossums, and other even less illustrious members of the animal kingdom. Although unsigned, the article was universally regarded as pure Daniel; "to this day," wrote Bagby in 1867, the article "is remembered by almost every man, woman and child in Virginia."[54] Few have doubted Daniel's crucial contribution to Virginia's shift of opinion before tensions exploded at Fort Sumter.[55]

With secession an accomplished fact, Daniel found no more Southern enemies to berate but instead mirrored the South's call for unity against the odious Yankee aggressors. During the war's early months the *Examiner* so strongly supported President Davis as to be considered an administration organ; it called for strong presidential leadership, rejoiced at Davis's decision to come to Richmond, and denounced the very suggestion of an opposition party in wartime.[56] The honeymoon lasted less than a year, however, and the *Examiner* soon became notorious for its criticism of the government.

Though Daniel brutalized Davis on occasion in 1862 and from August 1863 to the war's end, most of the early administration battles were caused by policy disagreements, not personal animosity. The president was often treated with dignity and respect.[57] For example, in January 1863, long after its break with the administration, the *Examiner* offered a calm, judicious appraisal: "President Davis should confine his communication with the public to his State Papers. Speeches like those which he delivered at Vicksburg and other places are ill calculated to benefit his own reputation or that of the country; while his messages and proclamations are uniformly models of propriety, both in style and material, and have all produced a good impression at home and abroad. His present effort is the best among the good."[58]

The *Examiner*'s wartime tone differed noticeably from that of the bitter, antebellum partisan journal struggling for fame and readership.[59] Of course attacks on abolitionism, Lincoln, Ben Butler, and Yankees in general were poisonous diatribes typical of Daniel at his most venomous, and soon he would turn his wrath upon those Southerners whom he deemed responsible for military reverses. The closing of ranks against a common enemy, however, softened his attitude toward most fellow Southerners. To be sure, state and Confederate elections elicited a few snarls at the former Whigs, and late in 1861 Daniel still branded Governor Letcher and former Unionists as "disloyal submissionists."[60] Nevertheless, a new nonpartisan spirit emerged. Elections, said Daniel, should concern the problem-solving abilities of candidates, not former party allegiances.[61] Early in 1863 Daniel wrote: "The day on which the people of Virginia are required by the Constitution to elect a Governor is rapidly approaching. What was once the high holiday of the county politician has come to be viewed as the disagreeable duty of the country. No more elegant communications to the newspapers; no more trills and quavers of praise from the local 'organs'; . . . With half the state under the hoof of the Yankee, . . . [h]ow would the old rhetoric of past 'campaigns' sound now?"[62]

If there was more political bickering and less unity than Daniel and other editors proudly proclaimed, still the decline of personal combat and the lessening of old political and journalistic animosities stand in distinct contrast to wartime trends in the North. Established dailies in major Northern cities quarreled as in antebellum days and fought "principled battles" reflecting major wartime divisions within and between the parties and factions. The *Chicago Tribune* railed against the Copperhead *Chicago Times*. In New York City, the *Herald*, the *World*, the *Tribune*, the *Times*, and the *Evening Post*, to mention only the strongest dailies, jockeyed for influence and circulation, seldom agreeing on basic issues. Whether it was policy regarding Northern military strategy, emancipation, or a host of other issues, Northern papers reflected a great diversity of opinion. More important, there was an established antiwar press in the North, a press which had no Southern counterpart, and elections, with two-party combat and editorial hyperbole, ran on schedule.[63]

Wartime considerations in the South altered the news columns as well as stereotypical editorial quarreling. Political news—campaigns and partisan maneuvering—almost disappeared; but government proceedings, another mainstay of antebellum news, took on even larger significance as the *Examiner* reported actions of the Confederate congress and various administrative departments, presidential speeches, and news of the Virginia legislature. When active campaigning was underway, military news and speculation pushed government reports from the news columns. "To write or to think now of anything whatever, save the marching or the fighting of the day that passes is plainly impossible," declared the *Examiner* in June 1864.[64]

With so much important news, space was tight, and it became even tighter when the newsprint shortage forced the *Examiner* to cut back from four to two pages, from May 7, 1862, until the end of the conflict.[65] To save space for war items and editorial opinion, Daniel reduced the amount of advertising and eliminated light essays and literature.

Everyone demanded the latest war news, but lacking financial and physical resources, the *Examiner*, like other Southern papers, was long on discussion, speculation, and rumor, and short on news. By contrast, the Northern metropolitan press possessed the means to achieve its highest priority—the acquisition of current information; it spent vast amounts for correspondents, telegraphic news, and larger presses capable of satisfying mass audiences several times a day. Many dailies began to publish morning and evening editions, resorted frequently to extras, increased their size either by adding pages or columns or both, and often initiated a Sunday edition despite the clergy's strictures. By the war's end there was probably as much news in one issue of the average daily as there had been in a whole week's papers before 1860. In 1861 Oliver Wendell Holmes described the Northern public as living from edition to edition, and near the war's end, Philadelphia newspaperman John W. Forney emphasized for the benefit of the managing editor that "now is the time for news in great papers, it cannot be the time for essays."[66] Gone were the leisurely days of editorial columns filled with philosophical disputation and abstract constitutional theorizing.

Several daily newspapers in the Midwest originated during the war because the summaries of events provided by the New York weeklies were too sketchy and too slow in arriving. The *Chicago Tribune*, *Toledo Blade*, and *Cincinnati Commercial* challenged the leadership of the New York press—New York City's "advantage of geographical position had at last been neutralized."[67] The *Chicago Tribune* published thirty-six thousand copies of its Bull Run edition, the largest issue in that paper's history up to that time, but by 1864 the daily output averaged around forty thousand. Both costs and profits soared. Some papers, like the *New York Evening Post*, kept expenses down and declared dividends of 80 percent of capital invested, which made their proprietors wealthy men; others, like the *New York Tribune*, earned only nominal profits because of huge expenditures for correspondents and paper.[68]

Everywhere in the North the war brought change to journalism. The Civil War, argues Michael Schudson in *Discovering the News*, accelerated and intensified the trends in American journalism emerging since the 1830s; but J. Cutler Andrews, in *The North Reports the Civil War*, concludes that for Northern journalism the "war had brought about sweeping changes in journalistic practice, changes which may accurately be described as revolutionary."[69]

Southern newspapers, on the other hand, experienced no expanded opportunities or widened horizons as a result of the war. On the contrary, Confederate journalism reflected in microcosm the crisis of the South's agricultural society in something akin to total war. Newspapers were crippled by war conditions and everywhere reduced to half-sheets by the scarcity of newsprint, ink, and labor. Railroads broke down and mail (and also newspapers for country subscribers) arrived belatedly if at all; the telegraph, though invaluable, was unreliable, and wordage was limited. Irreplaceable machinery wore out. And as circulation in-

creased, so did the number of subscribers unable to pay the greatly
inflated costs of the newspapers.[70] Many newspapers went under; only
17 of 26 were still publishing in Florida in early 1862, and only 14 out of
73 in Mississippi, where two-thirds of the newspapermen had en-
listed.[71] Of about 120 Virginia newspapers, only 17 survived the first
two years of the war.[72] The *Examiner* was one of the few to hang on for
the duration, but it, too, suffered the pervasive inability to report fresh
war news.

Usually containing less than a column of telegraphic news, the *Examiner* showed little advancement over antebellum levels.[73] (Some Northern
papers had two or three pages of telegraphic news.) Probably employing
no more than one correspondent at any given time, the *Examiner* made
less effort to cover the war than other leading Southern dailies, perhaps
because it needed to cover congressional sessions and government action
in Richmond. Transmission of news gathered beyond the capital was slow
and uncertain. "So unreliable were the railroads," concludes an authority
on Virginia newspapers, "that, not infrequently news of a skirmish in a
remote part of Virginia or in the lower South reached Richmond first via
the northern press."[74] The *Examiner's* best exclusive sources were soldiers
and travelers, but they usually provided a belated version of the news.

Invariably the *Examiner* relied heavily on other newspaper reports,
Northern more than Southern. The *Examiner* avidly copied Northern
press items, especially from the *New York Herald* and *New York World*; in
fact, many issues contained more news from Northern newspapers (obtained on the flag of truce boat or from travelers crossing the lines) than
from any other source.[75] *Examiner* readers frequently were better informed of the doings of Lincoln, his cabinet, Vallandigham, and Cop-
perheads than of the Confederate armies' operations.[76] The scant foreign news in the *Examiner* was gleaned from foreign papers carried in by
blockade-runners or, in the majority of cases, was copied from the
Northern press. The *London Times*, which Daniel greatly admired and
wished to imitate, was the most frequently quoted.[77]

Often lacking hard news, Southern editors resorted to the opinion
page; but this was no hardship. They had always loved brandishing the
editorial weapon. Daniel's editorial page was the heart of his journalism, and he sacrificed everything to it: "He was," declared an aston-
ished George Bagby, "the only newspaper proprietor I ever heard of
who would throw out, without hesitation, paying advertisements, in
order to make room for editorials, or for contributions which particularly pleased him. Oftentimes his news columns were reduced to the
last point of compression to make room for editorial matters."[78] Every
issue contained two or three editorials, each a full column or column
and a half in length, a remarkable indulgence in a two-page paper.[79]

Of the fifteen to eighteen editorials appearing weekly in the *Examiner*, Daniel himself wrote only two or three, for perhaps his greatest editorial talent lay in his ability to select and encourage good writing.[80] He assembled a brilliant if wild corps of editorial writers who reflected his own cranky and sometimes perverse style of journalism and welcomed the occasional contributions of the South's best writers, such as Dr. Bagby, editor of the *Southern Literary Messenger* from 1860 to 1864. Daniel hired as associate editors such prolific writers as the fiery, pistol-packing Edward A. Pollard, anti-Davis polemicist and author of *The Lost Cause*, and the equally fiery Irish revolutionary emigre, John Mitchel, who came to the *Examiner* late in 1863 from the *Richmond Enquirer* to fill Pollard's shoes. Among others, Daniel employed as editorial assistants journalist and later judge Robert W. Hughes ("one of those who lent truculent and almost inhuman bitterness to the *Examiner*"), linguist and scholar Professor Basil Gildersleeve, and volatile Henry Rives Pollard.[81] Even anonymous contributions in the *Examiner*'s mail, if sufficiently clever, were converted by Daniel's emendations into material for his editorial columns.[82]

As proprietor and editor-in-chief, Daniel controlled absolutely the policy of the *Examiner* and thoroughly edited everything appearing in his paper.[83] "Any fault of grammar or construction, any inelegance, he detected immediately. He improved by erasure as much, or more, than by addition; but when a thought in the contributed article was at all suggestive, he seldom failed to add two or three, and sometimes ten, and even twenty lines to it."[84] At least once, Bagby failed to recognize his own article after it had received the Daniel treatment. "Sure enough," Bagby discovered, "there was an article twice as long and twice as good as the one I had written—my own ideas, but so enveloped in Daniel's fine English, and so amplified that it was hard to recognize them."[85] Daniel infused so much of his spirit and style into the editorial page that, despite the variety of contributors, the *Examiner* spoke with one voice. Even so kindred a spirit as Henry Rives Pollard, who inherited Daniel's duelling pistols, found it impossible to distinguish Daniel's editorials from those of the other able writers.[86]

By such means the *Examiner* achieved popularity as well as influence.[87] The *Richmond Examiner* correspondent of the *New Orleans Picayune* reported that most Richmond citizens read the *Examiner* not because they concurred in its strictures but because "its articles are for the most part usually racy and suggestive."[88] But John Esten Cooke remembered, "The whole country read the *Examiner*, from the chief officers of the administration to the humblest soldier in the trenches. It shaped the opinions of thousands. . . . spoke the public sentiment, uttered its views with fearless candor, and conveyed those views in words so terse, pointed, and trenchant—in such forcible and excellent English—that the thought of the writer was driven home, and remained fixed in the dullest apprehension."[89] George Cary Eggleston offered even more eloquent tribute by paying one dollar for the *Examiner* when he "might have got the Whig, Dispatch, Enquirer, or Sentinel, for half that sum."[90] With such demand and high prices—and because the *Examiner* did not spend much on news gathering—the *Examiner* became a valuable property, clearing about fifty thousand dollars for Daniel in the third year of the war and making him at last a wealthy man.[91]

In addition to wealth, Daniel earned fame—primarily as the tormentor of Jefferson Davis. Although initially supportive of the administration,[92] after First Manassas, the *Examiner* steadily lost faith in the president's ability to prosecute the war. In late 1861 it publicly rejected Davis's defensive strategy and called for an invasion of the North. By early 1862, after defeats at Roanoke Island and Fort Donelson, spasmodic opposition escalated into a full-scale attack on the administration.[93] According to historian Emory Thomas, the *Examiner* accused the Davis administration of despotism at home, sloth in the field, and favoritism in appointments. Emiline Stearns identified three chief causes of Daniel's opposition to the administration: the Davis government's failure to apply the *lex talionis*, the redundancy of the Confederate currency, and the retention in command of incompetent generals (Braxton Bragg and John C. Pemberton) coupled with the failure to use others (Joe Johnston and P.G.T. Beauregard) to their full ability.[94]

Useful as these generalizations are, they fail to cover the remarkable variety of Daniel's targets. While editorial abuse of individuals at first declined along with the political partisanship on which it thrived, it resurfaced in full force in warfare against Confederate incompetence. Accusations were legion: the Cabinet lacked brains; the Congress was altogether too subservient to the executive and was lackadaisical in performing its duties; slackers, untouched by enforcement of the conscription laws, endangered Richmond society; Deep South cotton planters harmed morale by refusing to burn their cotton.[95] The *Examiner* attacked the cavalry command—by implication J.E.B. Stuart and his staff—after Confederate horsemen were surprised and bloodied at Brandy Station, and on rare occasions it even questioned the commanders of the Army of Northern Virginia. Lee made the *Examiner* unhappy by failing to counterattack after the slaughter of the Federals on Marye's Heights at Fredericksburg.[96] Many defeats, but especially the loss of Vicksburg, were attributed to Davis; Secretary Mallory was held responsible for reverses on the seas and the Confederacy's feeble efforts to break the blockade; and Secretary Memminger was scored for runaway inflation.[97] Impressment, which farmers evaded by hiding their produce to avoid forced sales at below market prices, was deemed legalized robbery; "if Richmond starves," concluded the *Examiner*, "it will not be the fault of the enemy but the Secretary of War and impressment."[98] In the *Examiner*'s diatribes, personal references were seldom kind: Daniel's paper called Congressman William Porcher Miles "Wamba the Witless," and—parodying the legendary command of General Taylor during the Mexican War—demanded, "A little more brains, Captain Bragg."[99]

Some historians and many of Daniel's contemporaries thought that the editor lashed out irresponsibly and had not the least idea of practical measures. Hudson Strode, Davis's biographer, asserted that John Daniel heaped ridicule on the vulnerable president because "he wanted everyone to hate Jefferson Davis."[100] In truth, some editorials smacked of cynical hatred born of personal frustration; *Examiner* judgments were often absolute, uncharitable, and extreme. It was a marvel, noted Benjamin Hill, how the best generals always wound up in editorial offices.[101] One must wonder if Daniel had been isolated too long in a make-believe editorial world and the Court of Turin. Perhaps. Certainly Daniel's demand in late July 1861 for the recruitment of five hundred thousand men in six weeks, without the slightest consideration of how they were to be armed, clothed, fed, and equipped, suggests an irresponsibility both foolish and dangerous.[102]

Yet, in all of the *Examiner*'s controversial editorials and diatribes, there was only one real purpose: to advance the conduct of the war. Inspired by Southern enthusiasm after success at Fort Sumter and First Manassas, Daniel looked to the government for leadership in mobilizing the Confederacy, and the government failed him. In January 1862, he charged that it was too lenient and that it failed to grasp the revolutionary nature of the great civil upheaval.[103] A month later he wrote: "In the midst of revolution no greater calamity can befall a people than for their affairs to pass into the control of men who could not understand it in the beginning, and are incapable of appreciating the demands of the crisis as they arise."[104] Daniel tested and found wanting President Davis's ability to think and act anew to save the country (to use Lincoln's words). "The war we are waging is essentially a revolutionary one," he insisted in November 1862. "In the mental excitement with which it was inaugurated; the upheaving of the masses; the close sympathy between the army and the people; and the desperate spirit; it has all the elements which make up the historical idea of revolution."[105] ÉDaniel had preached secession unsuccessfully before Fort Sumter; now he preached revolution unsuccessfully in the midst of civil war. In fact, Daniel's polemics may have stiffened Davis's resistance to change.[106]

Nonetheless, Daniel's criticism apparently sprang more from genuine concern for the South's fate than from hatred of Davis, the desire to sell papers, or his own yearning to be the capital's center of attention.[107]

Daniel coupled an extreme editorial policy defending states' rights and constitutional safeguards with his efforts to goad Davis. He feared tendencies toward dictatorship, the specter of perpetual martial law, and Congress's acquiescence in executive rule.[108] Daniel rejected despotic presidential rule as unconstitutional, yet he also publicized his wartime credo: "To the dogs with Constitutional questions and moderation."[109] The explanation for this apparent inconsistency lies in Daniel's growing conviction of Davis's inadequacy. Daniel demanded strong governmental leadership with due respect for the separation of powers; he drew the line at dictatorial power and demanded vigorous congressional action to restore checks and balances. "If we would have a wise and efficient management of our Executive department we must demand a wise and vigorous control of our Legislative department. Universal support of the errors of the Executive is as dangerous as universal opposition to its meritorious action."[110]

A firm believer in the rights of states and individuals, Daniel nevertheless would advocate almost anything short of dictatorship to win the war. He recommended conscription in 1861, and may justifiably be credited as one of the chief authors of the first intrastate conscription on American soil.[111] The *Examiner* backed impressment, but only with just compensation, and supported legislation to require farmers to plant an amount of grain proportionate to the labor they employed.[112] Daniel decried excessive issues of paper money as a violation of contract and advocated heavier taxation to finance the war.[113] He could still write paeans to federalism, but he had adopted the maxim, "First save the country, then save the constitution."[114]

Revolutionary war meant suffering, and Daniel felt that the government must not be too squeamish. Davis's numerous calls for days of fasting and prayer smacked of weakness; Daniel wanted the government to organize the militant nation in arms.[115] Infuriated by Yankee raids and economic devastation, Daniel demanded retaliation. Southerners must wake up; chivalry was dead. "While it is not for the South to fight with any mean advantage, it is time for her to abandon those polite notions of war which she had got from Waverly novels, and to fight fire with sword." Repeatedly calling for blood and invasion of the North, he persisted, "Sentimentalism is as much out of place in destroying Yankees, as in *killing chinches!*"[116]

Daniel's attacks on the Davis administration, becoming ever more embittered and personal after 1863, exasperated contemporaries, embarrassed the government, and, according to numerous historians, fostered disunity and harmed morale.[117] Mary Boykin Chesnut declared that Daniel ought to be hanged for fomenting division and giving aid and comfort to the Yankees. "I do not see how the *Herald* or the *Tribune* could do us more injury than the *Examiner* of today," she wrote in July 1862. "A bomb from the enemy's camp exploding in the *Examiner*'s office would not have hurt the Confederate cause."[118] Of course Mary Chesnut was sensitive to Daniel's fulminations, for on occasion they hit close to home. Daniel failed to respect "even our feminine insignificance. He went for the merrymakers, the partygoers, the promoters and attenders of festivities at such a time," she wrote. Here Daniel obviously criticized with considerable perceptivity and justice, but many always believed that he and other irresponsible editors harmed the cause. Those who sacrificed for their country, grumbled William Porcher Miles, "must feel pretty flat when they read in the *Examiner* and the *Mercury* that they were done to death by their own inefficient government."[119] One Confederate official argued that the South could win in six months if all the papers would support the president but that attacks by the Richmond press prolonged the struggle by aiding and encouraging abolitionists who claimed there was a huge Unionist element in the South.[120] Even Southern journalist Thomas DeLeon thought that a gag law might have been useful.[121]

Hostility toward Daniel and the *Examiner* was very real, and demands that he moderate his tone and cease his destructive attacks grew as the *Examiner* became more rabid.[122] Daniel's convictions, his courage, and his thick skin, toughened by a lifetime of combat, made him impervious to criticism. Rumors abounded that the police would shut down his press. Army officers threatened the paper, and government employees demanded action.[123] "Red-tape has a mortal abhorrence of a free press," Daniel sneered in response to these "parasites of power."[124] He condemned proposals to remove the draft exemptions of newspaper employees as threats against press freedom. Some legislators agreed with him, and Congress—largely because it needed press support for unpopular war measures—rejected attempts to change this aspect of its conscription legislation in 1863 and 1864.[125]

The conflict between press freedom and harmful, irresponsible wartime journalism is, of course, a classic dilemma.[126] To some it would seem that Daniel's principles of press freedom were as timeless as they were self-serving; while he called for restrictions upon the rights and liberties of others for the advancement of the cause, he accepted no infringement on press freedom. The *Examiner* was not unique in this regard. Fed upon the meat of polemical ravings and scurrilous and vulgar epithets, and dedicated to the principle of press freedom, most Civil War era newspapers, North and South, saw no reason for moderating criticism of the government even when faced with the novelty of total war. Certainly those who abhorred the *Examiner*'s damaging attacks would have agreed that the *Examiner* and most of its contemporaries cherished their privileges even more than the survival of the nation.[127]

But Daniel never felt that curtailment of press freedom would help win the war, and neither did Jefferson Davis and a majority of the Confederate Congress.[128] Daniel admitted that press criticism of the government caused pain and increased tensions, but in wartime more than ever a country benefited from a free press. "All danger to the public liberty comes from military usurpation, all danger to the public morals springs from official immunity from censure; and official corruption is the usual incentive to military usurpation. Is the press, that faithful sentinel on the watch-tower of liberty, to be gagged and manacled at a time when all power is in the army and all authority in Government?"[129] Public harmony could be bought at too high a price.[130] If the people refused to inquire into the causes of disaster and demand reform, then blunder after blunder would lead them to Yankee bondage. The press did not exist "to tell the old women that all is well!"[131]

The paper's crankiness was tolerated because it vehemently advocated its society's war aims. Rather than a Southern version of the Copperhead *New York World*, which questioned the necessity for war and rejected abolition as a Northern war aim, Daniel's *Examiner* was the South's *New York Tribune*; it found its government too weak for the harsh war that had to be waged.[132] There was no significant peace party in the South. Had there been one, Davis's government might well have had to impose censorship on the press because it could give aid and comfort to a lethal enemy within.[133]

Paradoxically, the South's press was free because Southern society was closed. Within the limits of the South's overriding orthodoxy on slavery, white supremacy, Southern independence, and the superiority of Southern civilization, men like Daniel were free to honor their conscience or assert their individualism or their egos in criticizing government leadership. Only in some military districts was there official censorship; elsewhere, inhibited only by public pressure, voluntary press censorship of military information, and the absolute inability to question Southern orthodoxies, editors' vigorous and persistent wartime criticism of men and measures revealed a genuine love of first amendment freedoms in a Southern context.[134]

Traditionally, far too much attention has been given to the *Examiner*'s opposition to the government; not every editorial was a diatribe against the Davis administration or the Congress. Richard Beringer, et al., in *Why the South Lost the Civil War*, cite isolated examples of defeatism in the press and suggest that "the depressed morale of the home front communicated itself to the soldiers through the newspapers."[135] It may not be possible to prove the press's impact on morale, but the vast majority of editors and important newspapers supported the war effort and did everything possible to stimulate resistance and revolutionary austerity.

Louis T. Griffith and John E. Talmadge once summarized the stratagems of wartime propaganda: "Those most commonly employed are: (1) to establish immediately the enemy's war guilt; (2) to remind, constantly, both foe and friend that your country is bound to win; (3) to personalize your people's war hatred in the leaders of the enemy; (4) to refrain from normal political activities in the interest of unity; (5) to charge the enemy with atrocities; (6) to win allies; and (7) to foster, at all times, among your people the will for victory."[136] Using these tactics, the Southern press threw itself into the war for independence. It was, said Daniel, the soul and inspiration of the country.[137] As the Northern anaconda tightened its coils and Southerners were asked to make greater and greater sacrifices, papers like the *Examiner* bolstered morale and redefined Southern identity. *Examiner* editorials, Robert Hughes claimed, were even read at the head of regiments.[138] The *Charleston Daily Courier* praised the *Examiner* for "doing a great deal towards ferreting out the abuses and exposing the charlatanism engrafted upon Richmond by the war, and expecting reforms therein,"[139] and Catherine Ann Devereux Edmondston of North Carolina confided in her diary on February 28, 1864, that she took comfort from an *Examiner* editorial emphasizing the strength of the Confederate army and people and predicting that they would carry the cause through to success despite maladministration of the government.[140]

Ever confident of victory, the *Examiner* praised the unselfishness of Confederates in supporting the revolution and insatiably called for still more dedication,[141] but it could also attack the stay-at-homes, extortionists, shirkers, or, as in Mary Chesnut's case, the party-goers. Revolutionary austerity was a favorite *Examiner* theme. Southerners must look to themselves. Foreign aid being a delusion, only determination, self-reliance, and spirit would bring victory: "No powerful nation has ever been lost except by its cowardice. All nations that have fought for an independent existence have had to sustain terrible defeats, live through deep, though temporary distress, and endure hours of profound discouragement. But no nation was ever subdued that really determined to fight while there was an inch of ground or a solitary soldier left to defend it."[142] Victory would be theirs regardless of cost, declared the *Examiner*, for a nation such as the Confederacy would never bear disgrace. Up until the evacuation of Richmond, recalled George Cary Eggleston in his postwar memoir, papers such as the *Examiner* remained confident of victory, and though much of this optimism was whistling in the dark perhaps, Confederates tried hard to believe.[143]

If Daniel doubted eventual victory for the South, he never admitted it in print.[144] Unfailingly optimistic, the *Examiner*, like most Southern papers, could evade even the plainest inconvenient truth.[145] For instance, as shortages of food struck the capital and the desperate populace demanded relief, the *Examiner* intoned that "scarcity of provisions exists only in imagination." When a hungry Richmond mob broke open stores to take food and other goods priced out of reach by skyrocketing inflation, Daniel blamed the incident on secret agitators, probably from the North, and complained that the Northern press would exaggerate these episodes: "they will be called bread riots."[146] His treatment of the depreciation of Confederate currency offers another example of his denial of unpleasant realities. When his campaign for drastic monetary change was ignored, he resorted to wishful thinking: "That our national currency is safe from any great danger of depreciation is a proposition so plain, and so consistent from what we learn from history, that any alarm on this score must be referred to a very blind and gross ignorance."[147]

Sacrifices came easier when there was something to hate, and Daniel was always a good hater. He surpassed even his own previous standards of editorial malice in brilliant, vicious, anti-Yankee tirades. Early in the war he ridiculed Abraham Lincoln as the Yahoo president, a ludicrous hybrid of Western country lawyer and Yankee barkeeper; as the war became a brutal, bloody struggle the *Examiner*'s buffoonish Lincoln became a tyrannical, ogreish Lincoln.[148] The entire race of Yankees was vulgar and mercenary, devoid of honor, excelling only in toadyism, flunkyism, cowardice, and lying.[149] Such descriptions raised a derisive laugh; others were designed to evoke raging hatred. "The torture of famine is a Yankee invention," Daniel wrote, "and their depraved journals are quite in love with pictures of women and children huddled on the naked hearth-stone, with eyes glistening with hunger."[150] Daniel traced the differences between the two American cultures to the roots of colonial settlement: New England had been peopled by religious "refugees and schismatics chiefly from the lower classes of the English population. The Southern colonists, being true born Englishmen, brought over the distinctive instincts, sentiments and institutions of the mother country."[151] These differences, far from narrowing with time, formed the starting point for ever-widening divergence. And by 1860, of all the Yankee race, the most depraved were the abolitionists. Not content with breaking up the Union, the *Examiner* charged, they now controlled the Lincoln administration, ruled without public support, and urged Southern blacks to massacre defenseless women and children.[152] Editorials lampooned the North's confession of weakness: rich as it was in men and materiel, it must appeal to the blacks to save them by joining the army.[153]

The Grand Army of the Potomac, the *Examiner* asserted in May 1863, had never achieved a success. It had been "periodically defeated for two years, and cannot, without such lying as would hurt the conscience of a prostitute, claim a single victory. The annals of history may be searched in vain for another military organization which has been paid more, supplied more, recruited more, deserted more, moved on more, been more whipped, or which has run away such a monstrous number of times."[154] Even as Grant besieged Petersburg, Daniel dismissed him as lucky and mockingly consoled the general lest he be discouraged by Northern recrimination about his butchery and drunkenness: "Let him not resign himself to despair, nor give himself up wholly to drink. A good man struggling with adversity is a spectacle for the Gods; and although he can by no means take Petersburg, not to speak of Richmond, yet let him remember that he who ruleth his own spirit is greater than he who taketh a city."[155]

Although the *Examiner* never doubted that Confederate courage and devotion would be victorious, it occasionally varied its abuse of the Yankees by discussing the atrocities that they would inflict on the South if they should by some happenstance win. Atrocity stories appeared most commonly late in the war, when the tide of battle turned against the South. "Such articles! Mon Dieu!" exclaimed editorial assistant John Mitchel. "I point out diligently and conscientiously what is the condition of a nation which suffers itself to be conquered, draw pictures of disarmings, and disfranchisements, and civil disabilities, such as we have experienced in Ireland, and endeavor to keep our good Confederate people up to the fighting point."[156] Lurid talk of the gibbet, the headsman's axe, deportations, and the ravishing of women today suggests gross exaggeration, but given wartime hysteria such talk may well have been believed.[157] The *Examiner*'s claim that Yankees would steal all Southern property down to the last shirt and petticoat was probably even more plausible, since readers were conditioned to think of Northerners as sordid, greedy, and ruthlessly acquisitive.[158] The paper proved its case by quoting that renegade Southerner, the Yankees' vice president: "Treason must be made odious, traitors must be punished, impoverished, their property taken from them."[159] Such dire predictions of the fate of a defeated South formed a minor but persistent feature of *Examiner* propaganda.

Such scare tactics were less successful in boosting morale than positive reenforcement, especially the emphasis on fighting in a just cause. The *Examiner* interpreted American history in the decade before the war as one assault after another on the South by Northern fanatics and bigots.

The South was compelled to fight for its "honor, character, standing and reputation." The war was a struggle for political liberties, for the hallowed principles of 1776.[160] Southerners fought for the ideal of genuine federalism and the right of self-government; they would defend in blood the right of a state to resist unconstitutional assaults of the federal government.[161] The North's "cuckoo cry" of waging war to save the life of the nation was mere nonsense. Was there no Union, inquired the *Examiner*, no life for the North, without the South? Was the North then merely a parasite?[162] Desiring only its freedom, the Confederacy attacked no one and obtruded its domestic institutions on no other people.[163]

The *Examiner* extolled a Southern ideal of social order based on chattel slavery and dedicated to freedom for whites. Domination of an inferior race strengthened the character of Southern whites and sharpened their skills of leadership. Among white men, whether slaveowners or not, it encouraged self-respect and dignified deportment, since "no man likes to let himself down before his inferiors—to play harlequin before his children, or to descend to familiarity with his servants."[164] The South thus could repel the great numbers and physical advantages of the North because of its superior moral force. Pity the North, for it imposed upon itself a degrading, debased form of slavery.[165] Brutal, mongrel Northern majorities sought to coerce even individual conscience, and in the crisis of war Northerners looked to a tyrant for authority.

Daniel doubted the efficacy of majority rule even among white men blessed by the benefits of slavery. On occasion he criticized popular elections as tending to advance men who struggled for place and pay—greedy, cunning manipulators of rival factions.[166] Gentlemen of the better sort would not compete with demagogues in flattering and bribing the masses. The post-Jacksonian world of the common man and democratic rule disgusted Daniel, who longed for the world of Thomas Jefferson and the gentlemen planters who ruled by virtue of their greater success in life. No one admired aristocracy more than the self-made editor who, though blessed by a proud name and family connections, rose from poverty and obscurity by hard work and pure political partisanship. The war gave him the chance to preach the ideal of the "masters born," as opposed to the "masters-to-be," and to become rich enough to take his self-appointed place among the former.[167]

Northern and Southern papers typically interpreted the course of the war through the prism of patriotism and propaganda. Daniel, although obviously reflecting wartime bias, was nevertheless not like some editors such as John Forney, who urged his staff to treat the news of Fredericksburg as other than the major disaster it was. The morning after receiving word of the defeat Forney's paper announced gratification "beyond measure in being enabled to assure the country . . . that the wild rumors of defeat and disaster are without foundation."[168] Daniel occasionally practiced some "economies" of truth but usually did not intentionally deceive;[169] he would not suppress the facts of military setbacks though he had an amazing ability to explain such facts away. Daniel asserted that it was not *Examiner* policy to cheat the public of the news; nor would he endanger the paper's reputation for truthfulness by printing false stories planted to confuse the enemy.[170] On January 6, 1863, for example, the *Examiner* announced the chilling news of General Bragg's strategic reverse ("the causes and extent unknown") at Murfreesboro. It then added:

So far the news has come in what may be called the classical style of the Southwest. When the Southern army fights a battle, we first hear that it has gained one of the most stupendous victories on record; that regiments from Mississippi, Texas, Louisiana, Arkansas &c., have exhibited an irresistible and superhuman valor unknown in history this side of Sparta and Rome. As for the generals, they usually get all their clothes shot off, and replace them with a suit of glory. The enemy, of course, is simply annihilated. Next day more dispatches come, still very good, but not quite so good as the first. The telegrams of the third day are invariably such as to make a mist, a muddle, and a fog of the whole affair.[171]

Daniel could recognize an absurdity when he saw one, and he often rejected exaggerated rumors of Confederate victories which his more gullible colleagues printed. For example, his response to the rumors of Lee's capture of forty thousand prisoners at Gettysburg showed a rare and refreshing realism: "Forty thousand is a phrase in telegraphic language equivalent to x in algebra. It means that the reporter does not know how many."[172]

Daniel was as capable as any editor of putting a better face on military reverses. His reaction to the surrender of Vicksburg was a classic display of wartime editorializing. As the siege neared its climax, Daniel warned that Vicksburg, second in importance only to Richmond, was the key to the Mississippi and the last grip on the great empire beyond. After its surrender he blamed Davis for the loss, but coolly announced that Vicksburg was really of trivial importance. For a year the South had held the river stronghold only from pride. "We gained nothing from the Mississippi," and now the North must employ troops in garrison duty.[173]

J. Cutler Andrews concluded his study of the Southern press and the Civil War with the suggestive query "whether a policy of greater candor and realism on the part of Southern newspapers would have contributed to higher civilian morale during the latter part of the war," and the authors of *Why the South Lost the Civil War* echoed this refrain.[174] The endless flow of optimistic propaganda amid defeat and destruction may well have had its effect in enervating and disillusioning the public.[175] The message of Yankee atrocities, noble cause, stout-hearted resistance, and the glories of sacrifice and success gradually lost its effectiveness. One disillusioned North Carolinian explained why his countrymen ignored the plea of the papers: "the people do not fear their condition being worsted. The time has gone by that the people can be madened [sic] by such newspaper and pulpit slang as Yankee confiscation, appropriation of pretty women etc." A North Carolina editor received an angry blast from a plainspoken backwoodsman, who recalled bitterly that according to the newspapers "cession was to be peaceable. Cotton was to be King, and if by any possibility war should ensue, it was to be a mighty little thing. The Yankees would not fight etc., and etc."[176] Perhaps the experience of Robert Toombs was typical; he soon learned that the newspapers were "such liars I cannot rely on them."[177]

But Andrews's point is somewhat academic; candor and realism were impossible in the South. In battling free-soilers and Republicans in the 1850s, and in urging secession, Southern politicians, orators, and journalists (the Rhetts and the *Courier* editors are prime examples) had fostered illusions about Southern strengths and Northern weaknesses that could never be repudiated.[178] There could be no serious challenge to Confederate orthodoxy. Thus Daniel's *Examiner* preached the same doctrine until Appomattox, regardless of whether anybody believed it; there was nothing else to do. Under the circumstances, it is remarkable that the paper indulged in as much criticism of Davis as it did. Only Daniel's impeccable orthodoxy in the greater ideological context, self-defeating as it was, enabled him to criticize the Confederate government in detail. Whether his orthodoxy or his criticism did more damage to Southern morale in the long run is an open question.

John M. Daniel ranks among the notorious leaders of nineteenth-century personal journalism not only because of his attitude toward men and events and because of the material he believed should be included in his paper, but also because of his pyrotechnic extremes. Unlike other celebrated Southern editors, Daniel was not a respected community leader. No city father, he was more often loathed than loved, yet he turned his columns into the most talked-about paper in the state—a reflection of his lacerating wit, breadth of interests, and swaggering hotheadedness. The *Richmond Examiner* exhibited his singular personality—his "omnivorous mind" and "carnivorous disposition."[179]

But the *Examiner* showcases much more than the editor's mesmerizing eccentricity, for the journalism of John M. Daniel created and celebrated Confederate nationalism. Daniel sought to build consensus at home for a devastating war while simultaneously advancing the slave-holders' vision of a Southern way of life. Though sometimes the tormentor of Davis, he was always the champion of the cause and of Confederate identity. [180]

Personal brilliance, crankiness, and Confederate commitment aside, Daniel's *Examiner* represents well the fate of Southern journalism in wartime. While the war pushed the Northern press toward the center of national consciousness, as Michael Schudson has noted, the Southern press became by war's end another lost cause. [181] A majority of Southern newspapers had collapsed, and the survivors, with abbreviated columns, limped along with makeshift equipment and insufficient material, labor and financial resources. The crisis of wartime morale had its journalistic counterpart in a crisis of credibility; yet Southern newspapers seemed always in demand. Everyone was desperate for news—or what passed for news.

In the North wartime journals stood on the threshold of modernity as they expanded circulation and news-gathering facilities and raked in profits, but Southern papers remained provincial sheets mired in the old journalism of exhortation and diatribe. Such journalism was familiar, and not without appeal. In 1865 Southern resistance was entering a transition stage and would be in need of a daily voice rallying the people to undying opposition to all things Yankee. The cause—of the South and of the press—would not be lost for long. Reconstruction editors would blaze no new trails but would instead follow the well-worn path of the battling Southern editor.

6
Resisting
Reconstruction
John Forsyth and the
Mobile Daily Register

"The editor dies, even as the actor, and leaves no copy," mused an elderly Henry Watterson. "Editorial reputations have been as ephemeral as the publications which gave them contemporary importance."[1] Marse Henry's melancholic observation may well have been prompted not only by the oblivion to which posterity had consigned the lesser lights of the newspaper world but also by the eclipse of the reputation of *Mobile Daily Register*'s John Forsyth, regarded by contemporaries as the premier Southern editor in the period between John Daniel and Watterson himself. Praised at his death in 1877 by the *Atlanta Constitution* as a "leader of men, and during the last quarter of a century . . . as prominent in shaping the politics of the South as either Toombs, or Wise, or Rhett,"[2] the all-but-forgotten John Forsyth had a significant impact on the Reconstruction South. That impact has been interpreted variously: fellow Democrats praised his courageous and successful fight for redemption and acclaimed him a community spokesman while Republicans attacked the Southern press as one of the chief obstacles to a peaceful and effective reconstruction.[3]

Forsyth earned the right to pontificate for unreconstructed rebels after Appomattox by editorially championing the Democratic party in the 1840s and 1850s, defending the South in the prewar decade, and enthusiastically propagandizing for the Confederacy. The son of a Georgia Democrat who had been governor and then secretary of state for six and a half years in the Jackson and Van Buren administrations, Forsyth entered public life in the 1830s in Mobile, Alabama's largest city and a thriving port. Like New Orleans, Mobile experienced an annual boom and doom cycle related to the cotton harvest and the sickly season, and also like New Orleans, its greatest days were over by the time of the Civil War. When Forsyth reached the pinnacle of influence as a Reconstruction editor, he spoke from a newspaper field shrinking in size and in economic significance.[4]

He first entered journalism as co-owner and editor of the *Mobile Daily Register* in 1837. In the mid-1840s and early 1850s he edited the *Columbus* (Ga.) *Times* until returning to the *Register* in 1854. When the War broke out he merged his Democratic *Register* with its bitter rival, the Whig *Advertiser*, forming the *Mobile Daily Advertiser and Register*.[5] As a journalist Forsyth quickly became an important voice of the Southern Democracy, campaigning to popularize his party as the South's protector and the country's only national party.[6] Like most successful editors of his time, he did not trouble to see more than one side to any political question. Such myopic dedication would serve him well in his role as propagandist for the Confederacy and for home rule and white supremacy in Reconstruction Alabama, but first it helped win him a prominent place among Southern journalists as a partisan warrior.

Two great battles marked his prewar career. As editor of the *Columbus Times* he achieved a notoriety of sorts during the 1850 crisis over California and the New Mexico territory when he briefly abandoned the Democrats for a Southern Rights party led by fire-eater William Lowndes Yancey.[7] Forsyth urged armed resistance rather than compromise Southern principles. Later, after rejoining the Democrats, he explained that the sovereign state of Georgia had agreed to the compromise of 1850 over his objections and that he would bow to the will of his people.[8] This was political realism—and a lesson well learned. Later, in the battle over the 1860 presidential election (and also the 1872 Democratic presidential nomination), Forsyth would again bow to the will of his people when, against his better judgment, they chose expediency over principle.

At some point in the mid-1850s Forsyth moderated his extreme Southern rights beliefs and became increasingly attracted to the candidacy of Stephen Douglas, even coming to accept Douglas's Freeport Doctrine.[9] This remarkable turnabout may have resulted from fear concerning the rising tide of radicalism among Southern Democrats and from his conviction that only a strong national party could beat the Republicans; thus, the Northern Democrats must be appeased.

As a Douglas Democrat, Forsyth delivered some fifteen hard-hitting speeches during a successful campaign for the state legislature in 1859, but the tide state-wide turned against the Douglasites.[10] In the next year Forsyth campaigned to send Douglas delegates to the Democratic National Convention at Charleston, but the radical forces sent a Yancey delegation bent upon either defeating Douglas and endorsing a federal slave code for the territories or seceding from the party. Forsyth denounced the Yanceyites as wretches who would destroy the only power "that stands between the Constitution and the Federal ravisher."[11] Ignored at Charleston, Forsyth and other moderates organized a state meeting and sent a rival delegation to the Democratic convention, which had by now adjourned to Baltimore. Although this new delegation was seated and Douglas won the nomination, the war between the Yancey and Douglas factions had only begun. In the Alabama campaign of 1860, the Yanceyites swept to victory, but not before Forsyth had aroused a spirited opposition which attracted national attention.[12] In Mobile County, Douglas won handily—a victory universally credited to Forsyth and the *Mobile Register*.[13]

Forsyth interpreted the 1860 presidential balloting as a portent of radicalism's triumph North and South. Consequently, he suddenly altered course, announcing his support for secession since a common government with Republicans in Washington was impossible and all efforts to save the Union would be fruitless. Still unwilling to unite with the Yanceyites, he appealed to conservative men to direct the secession movement so as to avoid "the worst consequences of the inevitable revolution which must soon burst upon us."[14]

Forsyth construed the formation of a Confederate government of moderates rather than radicals as a restoration of the Constitution of 1787-89 and a rebirth of the spirit of the Founding Fathers.[15] He now dedicated himself totally to the Confederacy and the war effort. From the guns of Fort Sumter until Forsyth fled the federal invader in April 1865, Alabama's leading journalist achieved considerable stature. He served as a war correspondent, was captured and paroled in Kentucky in 1862, and was wounded while reporting the fighting at Spottsylvania in 1864. His paper became one of the most frequently quoted papers in the Confederacy as he sought to raise soldiers' morale, preached citizen support of the war effort, and consistently backed the policies of the Davis administration, although not so closely as did the *Richmond Enquirer* or the *Charleston Daily Courier*.[16] Forsyth's popularity never stood higher than it did after the war, when he and other editors made honor and resistance the sacred litany of Reconstruction. And he was soon to show, as he had done in his career prior to Appomattox, that on issues which defined the South—racial subordination and white supremacy, states' rights, and home rule—he was remarkably consistent.[17]

Ironically, the fugitive Forsyth was invited to return to Mobile soon after Appomattox by the Union occupation commander, General E.R.S. Canby. Canby recognized Forsyth's influence and perhaps recalled Forsyth's opposition to the fire-eaters and his moderation in the secession crisis of 1860-61. According to Forsyth, Canby requested that he resume publication of the *Register* in order "to reconcile the people to the new order of things." [18] When Forsyth reestablished the *Mobile Daily Advertiser and Register* in July 1865, he spoke with a voice of experience and authority; for fifteen years he had been a major factor in Alabama politics.

Initially Canby's faith in Forsyth was not misplaced. During July and August the editor generally adopted a watchful approach to Reconstruction issues. The *Register* suggested that a cordial restoration of the Union was only a matter of time and urged all Southerners, in their "Duty of the Hour," to take the presidential oath of amnesty, qualify to vote, and help in the reorganization of the state. [19] Forsyth supported most of the president's Reconstruction policies though dissenting on the repudiation of Alabama's war debt (much of which was held in Mobile). [20] "There is nothing," he wrote, "in these requirements of the Government which any Southern man who means to remain in the United States should hesitate to accept." [21]

Forsyth's politically moderate editorials impressed many contemporaries and ingratiated him with the Union military. When General Wager Swayne wanted to enforce black testimony in Mobile courts and the mayor blocked his efforts, Swayne forced Governor Parson to remove the recalcitrant mayor by threatening to declare martial law in Mobile and garrison the city with black troops. Swayne then received permission to appoint Forsyth to the office. Later, after Forsyth had emerged as a spokesman for resistance, Swayne told a farcical story about taking a tugboat down the bay to meet Forsyth at a resort to offer him the job; on the way, he spied the editor on another boat and had to chase him for miles round the bay until he could make him understand that he was not to be arrested but to be made mayor of Mobile. In his short tenure in city government, Forsyth accepted black testimony in the courts. Later, in response to charges of fostering racial change, he argued that he had pursued the only realistic course—to accept black testimony (under the jurisdiction of Alabama judges) in order to avoid martial law. [22]

Forsyth's course and the *Register*'s editorial advice probably seemed more moderate and realistic than they were. Forsyth admitted defeat and accepted the existence of a perpetual Union, and no doubt he believed that the South was loyally complying with all the demands for restoration. Still, he was fully committed to restoring the status quo ante bellum as closely as possible. Although Eric McKitrick has shown that Northern demands were never clearly delineated, the Republican majority in Congress certainly wanted substantive changes and guarantees of good behavior—the enactment of a protocol of defeat, as McKitrick has it— and these demands Forsyth neither understood nor accepted. [23] From a Northern viewpoint, defeat had not humbled the Mobile editor or altered his thinking in any significant way. [24]

Late in July Forsyth visited Montgomery for the first time since the beginning of the Union occupation. In a lengthy letter to the *Register*, he encouraged Alabamians' hopes for recovery, political influence, and an honorable place in the Union.[25] The fire-eating spirit, he began, had vanished, and the people of Montgomery were determined to make the best of the situation. "We people of the South will soon spring again into active political life, and we shall have our weight in shaping the destinies of our re-united States. The South still lives, as those short-sighted men will find out who have given themselves over to sullen despair because of present gloom. The land has been scarred and furrowed by the iron ploughshare of war, but the soil and climate are still our own, and the people with their distinctive characteristics, are still here—a sadder and wiser people." Forsyth counseled unity among all white Southerners and combination with the conservatives of the Northwest against the South's only enemies, the "political Puritan Radicals" of New England. He reminded the South: "We shall have powerful allies against these extremists in religion and politics, all over the North, for now that men begin to see clearly, under the lifting smoke of battle excitement, they discern that whatever of change has been wrought by the rough statesmanship of the last four years in the *status* of State sovereignty and the principles of self-government South, attaches with like effect to the states and their people in the North." In light of these observations, he confidently predicted the eventual triumph of "sound" principles of constitutionalism.

Southern editors resisting change were not always in agreement; by nature quarrelsome, they argued among themselves as they struggled to establish a distinctive voice in their communities, monopolize a field of journalism all too limited, and dominate policy formation in the only political party that mattered. Some editors thought the wisest course a policy of partial cooperation with more moderate Republicans; others advocated violent resistance; and still others a variety of policies falling somewhere between these alternatives. The confusion of voices, it must be emphasized, concerned tactics; the primary goals—salvaging as much of the old order as possible, particularly white supremacy and home rule—elicited fundamental agreement. In 1868 many opted to meet Radical rule halfway; to accept military reconstruction and work toward winning back home rule at the ballot box.[26] Rejecting an open resort to violence, Forsyth nevertheless emerged as a champion of the hardliners who proved triumphant in the 1870s. Resistance would be Forsyth's motto.

A policy toward the freedmen was one of the first requirements of the new era; Forsyth could contemplate only the old formula of white dominance tempered by paternalism. "We of the South must take care of these people, for their sakes and for our own sakes," he wrote. Slavery was dead, but black labor remained vital to "our tropical productions," and the physical and moral welfare of blacks was necessary to the health of all Southern communities. He warned that Northern Radicals, ignorant of the nature of the black race, must never arrogate to themselves "the discharge of the social obligations and police duties of Alabama."[27] For a brief period Forsyth opposed ratification of the Thirteenth Amendment because although he accepted—at least formally—the abrogation of slavery, he suspected that the amendment might be a cunning device to extend federal authority over state laws and displace local police jurisdiction. Faced with the continuance of military government if the amendment failed, Forsyth abandoned his opposition to ratification,[28] but this equivocal position on emancipation, the most crucial issue for any sectional agreement, did not go unnoticed, North or South.

No ambiguity blurred his position on black voting rights; the South, he declared, was unalterably opposed to black voters: *"This is a White man's government."*[29]

During the summer and early fall, Republican congressmen and Northern editors became disgusted with the South's obstinacy. The leniency of presidential amnesty was especially disturbing, and several Northern congressmen demanded the imposition of an ironclad oath of allegiance, which would exclude the vast majority of ex-Confederates from politics. Forsyth counterattacked by insisting that Southern honor was at stake and denouncing Southern fainthearts who suggested that the South nominate only men who could conscientiously take the ironclad oath. The South was doing all that anyone could legitimately demand, Forsyth maintained, by accepting the judgment of arms, complying with the president's terms for readmission, and sending its true representatives to Congress. "Let us not demean ourselves for the purpose of conciliating the radical disunionists, and thereby creep in the back door of Congress."[30]

In December a Republican Congress refused to seat Southern representatives until there were guarantees of loyalty and protection for blacks and Southern unionists. When this news reached Alabama, Forsyth at first adopted a cautious, patient attitude. The spurning of Southern delegates, he suggested, was a partisan trick which the will of the people might presently undo. The times called not for vengeance but for pacification and an end to strife.[31] Forsyth's hopeful phase ended abruptly when he at last realized that Congress was serious in repudiating presidential reconstruction. His contentious spirit could be held in check no longer; the South was again besieged by the old Yankee enemy, the vicious, unprincipled, fanatical Republicans—"one hundred and forty crazy Radical members of Congress." On December 12, Forsyth declared political war: "This day's work will long be remembered. It is a fountain from which political events of great magnitude will flow out upon the land. The Radicals have deliberately sown the wind of revolution in the Government of the fathers; let them prepare for the whirlwind."[32]

Forsyth's war against radicalism lasted from December 1865 until his death in 1877. The *Register* reported episodes of Reconstruction. In these political battles the editorial page took precedence, but, characteristically, even Forsyth's news features and headlines blared his loathing for the Republicans. A Republican memorial to Congress or state legislation concerning credit would be heralded as a "Buncombe Memorial" or "Outrageous Legislation of the Jacobins,"[33] in a logical extension—indeed, perhaps a culmination—of the partisan journalism of the 1830s and 1840s, the press's sectional warfare of the 1850s, and the Confederate newspapers' propaganda. Perhaps at no other time in American history has any significant part of the press so blindly devoted itself to a political campaign for so lengthy a period.

Forsyth waged a continuous campaign to dispel Southern apathy and cultivate a sense of outrage and a desire to fight back. If, as Forsyth believed, the traditional leaders of Alabama were silenced, then the press must preach the crusade. "Having no army in the field to defend them [Southerners], and voiceless in the councils of the nation," Forsyth wrote in November 1867, "the press of the South is the last bulwark of the People, and while they impart to it the strength to be free, outspoken and brave there is no need to despair of ultimate redemption."[34] Again and again, after each Radical "outrage," Forsyth summoned the Southern press, that "mighty engine of public opinion," to lead the resistance.[35] In November 1870, he exalted in the "inestimable service" of the Southern press: "It has stripped the enemy of his every guise of hypocrisy, and exhibited him naked in his crimes against the commonwealth, to the gaze of the people. It has advanced the standard of redemption and blazed for the people the path to victory. All honor to the free press of Alabama!"[36] Since the onset of Radical Reconstruction, Forsyth wrote in April 1871, "the key-note in the conduct of this journal has been pitched upon the mighty thought of resistance. . . . Our motto has been, 'suffer and be strong'; render to Caesar what belongs to Caesar, but death rather than deserve to be despised by the political Puritan."[37]

Defying the Radicals to do their worst, Forsyth urged Alabamians to reject Reconstruction laws and constitutional amendments; no Southern ratification should ease the Radical course.[38] In 1868 he urged his readers to refuse entry into the Union on Radical terms, and he helped lead the movement of Alabama whites to boycott the polls and thus defeat the Radical Constitution. If honor impelled Lee to order Pickett's men up the slope at Cemetery Ridge or to slug on from Spottsylvania to Cold Harbor and endure at Petersburg, no less could be expected of white Democrats in the trying political warfare of the late 1860s. "It does not become the compatriots of the living Lee, and the martyred hero, Stonewall Jackson, to be creeping into the back doors." Wait until the South is welcomed back, he advised, and on that happy day when the Democratic party vanquished the Radicals, it would cleanse the Augean stables of national politics.[39]

The *Register* belabored white and black Republicans with Forsyth's ample vocabulary of abuse. The Mobile editor seldom dignified his opponents with the name Republicans; instead, they were Radicals or Jacobins, tyrants or crazy politicians.[40] Congress was a collection of lunatics, and the Republicans in the Alabama Assembly were "the asses at Montgomery." When Congress decided to investigate Ku Klux Klan atrocities, the *Register* trumpeted the creation of a Ku Klux "smelling committee."[41] And during the campaign of 1876, Forsyth wrote, "Pinchback, the negro, Clayton, the perjurer, Chandler, the debauchee, Schenck, the gambler, Belknap, the sneak-thief, Grant, the drunkard, are violently opposing her [the South's] return to the halls of her Fathers, the halls built with the blood of the heroes of 1776."[42]

In the *Register*'s pages, the tyrants and their "pimps" were engaged in cold-blooded "villainy"; they were intent upon mongrelism and preferment for "the sacred race."[43] Alabama's two carpetbag senators were "creatures spawned by reconstruction upon a manacled commonwealth; political maggots, bred by corruption and rottenness."[44] Forsyth never tired of depicting the martyrdom of the white South:

It is one of the fruits of reconstruction, that Southern communities are simply held by the throat by the strong arm of the Federal military power, to be preyed upon, speculated upon, and kicked and abused by every "ring" of adventurers and scoundrels that have an axe to grind or a scheme of revolution to exploit. The people are nothing, because they are helpless. They are bound hand and foot, for Grant and his party stand by with a loaded blunderbuss to protect every lawless political rascal and every sneak-thief who has designs upon the peace of society, or the property of the people.[45]

A steady diet of such rhetorical abuse reinforced Southern prejudices and helped deny to the Republicans any recognition as loyal, respectable opponents who could be trusted with the reins of government.

The Radicals, Forsyth claimed, were only a minority party, and yet they had revolutionized and centralized the federal government. They, not the South, were killing the Constitution.[46] Forsyth incessantly savaged the characters and misdeeds of the carpetbaggers and scalawags.

The white cohorts of the Republican party had the gall to complain of social discrimination, he remarked in astonishment.

> They have migrated here from abroad because of the generally worthless and odious character they sustained where they came from, or they have sprung up among us, from the dregs and dung hills of society, and crept by the means of ballot-boxes, stuffed with the votes of fraud and ignorance, into places of profit and trust, that they could never have aspired to . . . under any properly-organized and well-regulated system of government. . . . And these complainers who have become a stench in the nostrils of all who discriminate between virtue and vice, between the good and the bad, between the honest man and the knave, grumble at social ostracism![47]

Even the military commanders, many of whom were originally of a conservative bent, were the "willing tools of tyranny."

According to the *Register*, President Grant was a Jacobin tyrant enthroned at Washington to the peril of free government; a "thick-skulled, coarse, uncouth person," Grant was "that idiot in regimentals who lives at the white house, when he isn't at Long Branch, or some such brandy-and-watering place."[48] The slothful Grant, the *Register* sneered, had signed without even reading the congressional bill returning Georgia to military rule in 1870; and the mendacious Grant, lusting for reelection and needing another rebellion to crush, had manufactured an insurrection in South Carolina.[49] The *Register* headlined this atrocity:

TERRORISM IN SOUTH CAROLINA

CRUEL AND INHUMAN BARBARITY OF THE SOLDIERS

NO REBELLION, NO RESISTANCE, NO COLLISIONS

GRANT'S GREAT LIE.[50]

The *Register's* course in the racial warfare of Reconstruction paralleled its route in the political turmoil of the era, passing through a brief lull of cautious moderation before launching on an odyssey of resentment and ill feeling. For a fleeting period after the onset of Radical Reconstruction Forsyth and the Democratic party had hoped to control the votes of the ex-slaves, but when this proved futile, Forsyth's bitter racial animosity burst out unchecked.[51] The *Register* never viewed the freedmen as responsible agents of Reconstruction but, rather, considered them dupes of Northern Radicals. The paper constantly lampooned or abused blacks, featuring stories, for example, about how Radicals "bamboozled the wooly heads," referring with much disgust to an "odor d' Afrique," and alluding to black U.S. Senator Hiram Revels as "that thousand dollar darkey."[52]

When Forsyth spoke of the Southern people, he included only the whites. Radical journals complained of his manner of speaking, but Forsyth was unrepentant: "Language is but a representative of thoughts and things, and until Radicalism succeeds in teaching mankind to walk upon their heads, 'the people' in this land will still remain the white people."[53]

Forsyth's bitterness against blacks grew as white Alabamians tried unsuccessfully to overturn Reconstruction. In February 1870, he confessed that once he had thought blacks sensible and amenable to the influence of white leadership, but he had seen the Negro grow into "a senseless and stolid brute, imperturbable to reason and incapable of gratitude or generosity."[54] In 1874, Alabama's year of redemption, Forsyth proclaimed that the blacks were doomed to defeat, and with heavyhanded sarcasm he surmised that "the only move left to them for defeating the will of the people is to extend the ballot to the mules, with a constitutional amendment that their drivers may vote their proxies."[55] He played up dissension between white and black Radicals, predicting an interracial struggle for Radical spoils. There was a "Coon in the Meal tub," he shouted.[56] The crime of the blacks, the editor concluded, was that they had separated themselves politically and gone against the white citizens of the state. Now, he prophesied gleefully, the game was played out; "negro worship" had gone far enough, and Grant, the carpetbaggers, and scalawags were about to leave the blacks alone and unsupported in the midst of Alabama's increasingly hostile white population.[57]

Stories ridiculing blacks or denouncing their participation in politics were surpassed in emotional intensity only by reports or editorials on black violence. The headlines of the *Register* frequently screamed such outrages as:

NEGROES IN THE PUBLIC SCHOOLS

BLACK BOY MURDERS AN INNOCENT WHITE SCHOLAR

CIVIL RIGHTS WITH A VENGEANCE [58]

Such accounts, like many of Forsyth's race stories, reflected anything but the truth. The *Register* twisted the story of the 1871 Meridian (Mississippi) Riot, in which enraged whites shot numerous blacks after the whites had provoked a courtroom shootout, into a black rampage. At Meridian, the *Register* alleged, the Radicals had incited the blacks to a fiendish attack on innocent whites.[59]

Typical *Register* headlines during the 1876 campaign in South Carolina shrieked,

THE PROSTRATE STATE
_____

NEGRO OUTRAGES IN SOUTH CAROLINA
_____

SHOOTING WHITE CITIZENS
_____

TROOPS ORDERED TO THE STATE TO PROTECT THE
BLACKS IN THEIR WORK[60]

Such tales of atrocities undoubtedly reflected a genuine fear of racial upheaval, perhaps even race war. The altered racial situation of Reconstruction had, if anything, accentuated the anxiety endemic to antebellum Southern society. Yet there was an obvious political motive behind the emphasis on black outrages and the one-sided editorializing, much of which appeared during political campaigns.[61] No other issue had such emotional impact; white voters could be stampeded to the polls by editorials such as the following, printed during a city election campaign of 1871:

People living in the suburbs and near the city know too well how common it is for drunken, vagrant negroes to make night hideous with their yells and shouts and firing of muskets, pistols, fowling pieces, and all sorts of fire-arms. They know, also, how many instances have occurred, of burglary, nocturnal assaults, and other species of violence, even to murder.

Think, if these things happen now, under comparatively favorable circumstances, what it would be with a negro sheriff and negro assistants. How the elements of disorder and crime would break forth, freed from the restraints and terrors of authority.[62]

Most Southern journals of the Reconstruction period spoke with similar accents. The *New Orleans Picayune* argued, against the prevailing style, that calm remonstrance and clear statement of fact would be far more influential in molding opinion among Northern Democrats and thus overturning Reconstruction. "Mere agitation down here by the Gulf," it concluded, "is not going to shake the wills and purposes of the voters in Maine, Nebraska and Ohio."[63] John Forsyth and most other Southern editors disagreed, apparently believing that the goal of redemption justified any journalistic excesses. In 1870 Forsyth announced, "The more the Southern press is loaded with bombs and the more determined and defiant the Southern pluck, the sooner will the tyrant relax his hold."[64] Accused by a Northerner of too frequent use of "hateful expressions," Forsyth excused himself by reference to the fury of the war and the atrocious acts of Ben Butler, Thad Stevens, and their ilk.[65] Nevertheless, his rhetorical extremism was basically a continuation of past journalistic styles, North and South, and many Radical Republican journals were equally bombastic.[66] The tone of Reconstruction papers presaged

E.W. Scripps's formula: because a daily paper must be unfailingly interesting to the masses, who were coarse and vulgar, its language must be passionate. "Therefore the blood that runs in our veins and in our newspapers must be warm." [67]

Southern editors like Forsyth coined, disseminated, and popularized the rhetoric of Reconstruction. The common (but loaded) terms surviving today—carpetbaggers, scalawags, and redeemers—are only pale reflections of the steady diet of distorted rhetoric and verbal abuse with which editors daily inflamed political passions and racist fears and hatred. Though born of crisis and something akin to hysteria, such language was knowingly used for political effect. Editors like Forsyth enshrined the Democratic party in a halo of honor and constructive statesmanship, abused as ignorant, criminal, or immoral anyone operating under the Republican label, portrayed whites alone as the Southern people, and dehumanized blacks. In so doing, editors marshaled the forces which would destroy Reconstruction. In part because of editorial rhetoric and vilification if not actual incitement to bloody deeds, the use of violence became a legitimate means for overthrowing Republican rule. The tone of racism, furthermore, changed, as "overt and vicious racism became a highly visible feature of daily life, often a source of amusement for whites." [68]

Integrally related to Forsyth's savage attacks on all things Radical was his defense of all things Southern and his denial of any Southern wrongdoing. Like John M. Daniel during the war, Forsyth in the midst of a "cold war" proclaimed the eternal rightness of Southern principles, identified them as the true basis of the American republic, and advanced a one-sided interpretation of recent history. Secession had been morally and legally right since the North had centralized the government. Southerners, in fact, had never really been rebels because they had defended the Constitution. Reconstruction was unnecessary since the South was loyal in 1865, and resistance to martial law was an essential part of American liberty, which only the South seemed interested in defending. The South had not sinned; there was no call to repent. [69]

However much the conflict of Reconstruction revolved around the issue of race, Forsyth, like many defenders of Southern independence, including Jefferson Davis and Alexander Stephens, argued that the ongoing sectional struggle was actually a conflict over federalism—a conflict rooted in the clash between Jefferson and Hamilton and unresolved by the Civil War. One philosophy might seem triumphantly ascendant, but "he who imagines that the irrepressible conflict between the two rival systems was settled at Appomattox has read history to little purpose. The mob may shout for the Suatrian to-day and behead her tomorrow. They may rush from Lafayette to Robespierre, and from Danton to Napoleon. . . . Men change; circumstances change; but principles are immortal." For a period of several weeks in 1871, Forsyth published each day a copy of the "Old Constitution," the federal Constitution minus the three war amendments.[70] And in the successful redemption campaign Forsyth relied heavily on the theme of an enduring constitutionalism extending from the Revolutionary era. "I stand by the government of our fathers," he declared, "and believe still that the divided power of local sovereignty and federal administration, with delegated powers for general and specific purposes, constitutes an autonomy by which liberty and just laws can be assured to the American people."[71] How much more attractive white supremacy looked when dressed in the principles of constitutional liberty.

Forsyth and other Southern editors scoured the Northern Radical press for prejudicial charges and indignantly rebutted them almost daily. Perhaps, they reasoned, Southern readers could be goaded into angry resistance by a sense of grievance against their hypocritical, unscrupulous accusers. Forsyth sprang to the defense of the embattled Jefferson Davis. When Northern papers described duelling as a Southern abomination, Forsyth denounced their ignorant prying into their neighbors' affairs; and for every Northern reference to Andersonville atrocities, Forsyth demanded an accounting of Johnson's Island and Camp Douglas.[72] "During this whole decade," Forsyth complained in 1872, "since the North arrayed herself in race-hostility against her Southern sisters—the men of this section have been defamed and slandered by system. They have been painted as Ku-Klux and law-breakers and hotbrained ruffians, unfit for self-government and unworthy of brotherhood in Moral Ideas."[73]

Forsyth and other Southern editors found charges of Klan violence particularly obnoxious and threatening since such allegations sustained the South's violent image and justified a continuation of Reconstruction. For these reasons Southern editors worked mightily to explain the Klan away. Some editors, such as Josiah Turner of the *Raleigh Sentinel*, Ryland Randolph of the *Tuscaloosa Monitor*, Isaac Avery of the *Atlanta Constitution*, and Randolph Shotwell of the *Rutherfordton Vindicator*, were prominent Klansmen.[74] Those, like Forsyth, who were not members, and who did not publicly encourage the Klan, were apologetic or at least silent about its depredations. The *Register* censured "the serious practical jokes perpetuated in the name of this real or mythical organization—whichever it may be." The Klan (if it existed at all) was defensive in nature and justified by political discrimination which prohibited white Southerners from operating openly. The nefarious Loyal Leagues, backed by Congress and the army, Forsyth argued, lacked any excuse, yet the Radical press said nothing about their depredations. Whereas the publications of the so-called Klan were so grotesque and extravagant as to have an air of unreality, at worst frightening only women and children, the Loyal Leagues were "quiet, silent, secret, and dark" in their movements and therefore a serious political menace.[75]

Before long Forsyth began to argue that the Klan was an invention of Radical propaganda.[76] Manufactured atrocities, he believed, were used to arouse Northern voters. "It has often been said," he wrote in 1876, "that one dead negro was worth a hundred votes in any Northern market. . . . A tale, properly told of a negro-whipping, is more effective with a New England bigot than any array of facts."[77] Yet when Forsyth reviewed Democratic prospects for 1868, he indirectly acknowledged Klan violence. "I trust," he cautioned, "'the Ku-Klux Klan' will handle their weapons with the knowledge that they possess a double edge, one for their enemies and one for their friends. Prudence, obedience to the laws, and no violence."[78] The *Register*, like other Southern journals, finally took to describing Northern urban disturbances and rowdyism as "Ku Kluxism." Wrote Forsyth self-righteously: "We had no idea—we, of the quiet South—that things had attained such a degree of lawlessness in any part of the North."[79]

Forsyth's steadfast, singleminded, but multifaceted defense of the South made his *Mobile Daily Register* Alabama's most important organ for urging Southern resistance to Radical rule and the perceived threat of racial upheaval. The *Register* announced, and perhaps helped create, the program which would lead to the redemption of Alabama in 1874. From the time when Republicans organized black voters in 1868—and from the time, it must be emphasized, when the Democrats failed to corral these black voters—Forsyth called for white unity and retribution.[80] He editorialized: "In union alone, union complete, spontaneous, and undisturbed by one single break—is there any safety."[81] In 1870, organizing Alabama editors to push the white line against those who sought to court the black vote, he heralded the beginning of a new political campaign:

A WHITE MAN'S GOVERNMENT.
A WHITE MAN'S PARTY.
A WHITE MAN'S PAPER.
WE FIGHT ON THAT LINE.
THE WHITE REPUBLIC OF WASHINGTON.
ALWAYS WHITE!
ALWAYS DEMOCRATIC!
ALWAYS CONSTITUTIONAL!
REGISTER FOR THE GREAT CAMPAIGN OF 1870[82]

To Forsyth it was axiomatic that white intelligence and character would eventually dominate Negro insolence, ignorance, and inexperience.

"Rally, then, the white people on the white man's issue of self-defense and self-assertion," he cried, "and let us see what effect a show of independence and power will have on these wayward, misguided, grown up children."[83]

There was, however, vigorous opposition to the white line campaign, especially from black belt Democrats fearful that such a tactic would boomerang into a huge black turnout which at the very least would ensure Republican control at the local level. Forsyth preached the white line from 1870 on (except for the Greeley campaign in 1872), but until 1874, the editor explained, Democratic unity and the political victories necessary to restore the old order proved elusive because of voter apathy, divisive tactics (such as the effort to woo black voters), white disfranchisement, and the sheer size of the Republican vote. Forsyth tried to dispel the atmosphere of defeat and disunity by constant appeals to white pride and fear.[84] In 1874, for example, he summoned whites to resist the civil rights bill and the threat of racially mixed schools. If this issue could not break down apathy and mold a united white opposition, nothing could. "No wonder then," he wrote, "that political friends, differing and even quarreling in the past on collateral issues of opinion or policy, should be prompted to rally to each other in a Roman phalanx of irresistible strength to shield themselves and their families against so appalling a calamity."[85]

The divisive "collateral issues" were a disturbing factor in the campaign for white unity. The *Register* pleaded with Alabamians to forget ancient asperities between Whigs and Democrats and conflicts over secession.[86] The threat to racial dominance superseded even class friction: when a malcontent complained that the circle running the Mobile Democratic party was aristocratic, Forsyth scoffed at the suggestion that the Democracy of Mobile was not controlled by "the boys" and urged all of Mobile's whites to "let us have peace."[87]

Forsyth's program of redemption called for the destruction of the Radical coalition through the separation of scalawags from blacks. According to the *Register*, much of the evil of Reconstruction—especially the inflated dreams of the blacks—was scalawag work. Damning the scalawags as traitors to the South, the *Register* during the campaign of 1874 threatened and verbally abused these white renegades in short editorial paragraphs scattered throughout the paper.[88] For example, the *Register* reported that only five white men in Tuscaloosa had voted for the blacks' candidate for city marshal—and then it listed their names.[89] "The time approaches," Forsyth intoned, "when a white man will find out that he pays too dearly for his whistle who barters the welfare of his State and the profound race susceptibilities of his own people for negro office-alms."[90] He maintained that even the whites of northern Alabama "who were seduced into the Republican party are determined no longer to act with a party which makes the Civil Rights bill the test of allegiance."[91]

The *Register* sought to split the Republicans by encouraging and then exaggerating blacks' demands for a fair share of the offices. "Mr. Darkey" is invited to vote early and often for his overseer, wrote the editor; then he is invited to celebrate the glory of free suffrage. But the notion is now "crawling through their heads" that they should have some of the offices. "We have heard that every colored delegate who came in from county beats, had a Congressional nomination on the brain."[92] Black voters were warned that whites would bide their time, and there would be a day of accounting. On one occasion the *Register* applauded those whites who had kicked some wholesome lessons into blacks who tested their civil rights, and on another it suggested that the best way to deal with the lawless blacks threatening Mobile was "to seize them at once by the throat and not waste words upon them."[93]

Forsyth also called for economic pressure to put blacks in their place. He advocated a boycott of Pullman sleeping cars because Pullman opened them to blacks, and the *Register* reported with approval an agreement signed by sixty-nine Shreveport merchants to fire any black who voted the Radical ticket.[94] In 1874 Forsyth asked Mobile's employers to reward white mechanics and laborers for their endorsement of the white man's party movement. White workers must be given preference, he argued. "Come, men of Mobile! Come, in the name of your own safety, and for the great stake that you have in the coming electoral struggle. Teach the negro that he cannot eat of your salt and stab you in the back; teach him that as he works for your political undoing, he cannot share your patronage. Give it to the white laborers who have your own blood in their veins, and your own cause in their hearts."[95]

The Democratic party was to be the instrument for the achievement of white unity and redemption, and the *Register* belonged to the Democratic party "heart and soul and intellect and principle."[96] Before every polling date the paper depicted conditions as favorable to Democratic victory, and afterwards made copious excuses for Democratic failure. Defeat was due to fraud and the voting of Negro urchins; demoralization due to carpetbagger misrule, or even, on one occasion, to a yellow fever epidemic which forced hundreds of Democrats from the city.

Constantly urging unity on Democratic principles—which it defined variously as white rule, local self-government, opposition to the Fourteenth and Fifteenth Amendments (regarded as revolutionary, null, and void), hard money, and free trade[97]—the *Register* demanded that Democrats close ranks during campaigns and speak no evil of anyone who supported the party.[98] Forsyth denounced Southerners who indulged in the luxury of dividing their vote or backing independent candidates.[99] In 1874 the *Register* commended the unanimity achieved in county nominating conventions.

[These meetings] uniformly declare that no member of the party who imperils its success by becoming an independent candidate, should receive the support of the party or any of its members. The remarkable sameness of the county meetings show how united the Conservatives are as to a platform. Nearly every meeting resolves that this government, representing the white man's love of liberty and law, was established by white men, and wisdom dictates that it should be administered by white men for the common benefit and protection of the rights and interests of all citizens, both white and black.[100]

Adhering to its own demands, the *Register*, although posing as the organ of a virtuous party battling corruption in government, publicly praised the Tammany machine as a benefactor of the poor as well as a great power in New York politics.[101] There were no Democratic sinners.

Clearly the *Mobile Daily Register* was essentially a political journal. The *Register* became a force in Alabama politics in part because it was a loyal and effective party workhorse. The daily political activities of the *Register* and its staff included all the humdrum work of party organization and management. The *Register* office served as a gathering place for local politicos. Campaigning provided such constant labor that the *Register* had once complained, "We would like to have less political talk and to turn our attention to industrial topics, but there is nothing of more absorbing interest than the grave questions which are threatening the life of society and government."[102]

The *Register* was always eager for battle. The newspaper even gave of its own family; it released its mechanical staff, which in 1868 numbered some forty-five men, to turn out the vote, and in the process had to cancel its issue for the following day for lack of workers.[103] And on one occasion, just before the polls opened, the *Register* nominated a candidate to replace a Democrat who suddenly concluded that he was ineligible for office. Forsyth opened the 1872 presidential contest in early 1871 despite the ridicule of fellow Democrats who thought he would run out of bombs before the rest of the nation knew that political war had commenced.[104]

Forsyth crammed his journal with political news and announcements,[105] placing his faith in organization and drill. "It is in politics as it is in war; the battle is not always to the biggest army, but rather to the best drilled." In order to produce a military apparatus, he proceeded to instruct party activists:

1. *Don't waste all your strength on parades . . .*
2. *Don't rely too much on public meetings.*
3. *Don't rely too much on circulars . . .*

4. *Don't waste your money on Campaign Chowder Club/or barbecues outside the seaport of Mobile!*
5. *Organize the party thoroughly by districts . . .*
6. *As soon as a Club is formed* [in each ward] *APPOINT active canvassers to visit every home . . .*
7. *Have district meetings at regular times. . . . "Never mind gatherings for bun combe, but meet often for business."*
8. *Do these things at once.*[106]

Forsyth was one of Alabama's influential politicians in his own right. Although Alabama and congressional Republicans viewed him as such a red-hot Confederate that his political disabilities were not removed until 1874 (whereupon he was immediately elected to the Alabama assembly and boomed for the governorship or U.S. Senate), throughout Reconstruction he was a power within the Democratic party. In 1866 he served as delegate to the National Union Convention in Philadelphia, and in 1868 he was elected to the State Executive Committee of the Conservative party and the Executive Committee on the Democratic National Committee. As perhaps the most authoritative spokesman for Alabama's Democrats, Forsyth often traveled north to confer with party leaders and played a major role in helping to create a reunited Democratic party.[107]

Forsyth's relations with the Democratic newspapers of the North served the party's cause in still other ways. It has seldom been recognized that the Democratic press North and South did as much as party leaders and officials to establish a dialogue concerning the course of the Democratic party, and that Northern and Southern editors played a crucial role in the reintegration of the Democratic party after the Civil War. To be sure, editors sometimes exacerbated tensions before ironing out a common political program. Some Southern journals aired the belief that Northern Democrats wanted Southern votes only to further their party's aspirations for national office and that the Northerners cared not one whit about the fate of the Old Confederacy.[108] John Forsyth quarreled with his Northern colleagues, but he also kept open the lines of communication essential to ultimate party harmony.

When editors saw eye to eye, readers could expect fulsome mutual compliments on editorial courage, wisdom, and sound political principles. In 1868, for example, the Democratic *New York World* puffed the *Register* as a doughty champion of Democratic principles for fifty years, while the *New York Day Book* praised Forsyth's fight against usurpation, mongrelism, and despotism, adding that the *Register*'s large circulation would expedite the South's rescue from the terrible curse of black Republicanism, which was transforming the region into a wilderness. In 1870 the *Register* returned this plaudit by extolling the *New York Day*

Book's fight against "mongrelism and congressional reconstruction in all its forms of deviltry." [109]

More often, however, editorial relationships ranged from a certain coolness or wariness to outright hostility. Disagreements over tactics or doubt about the goodwill of fellow Democrats from different sections of the nation often erupted in embittered exchanges of insult. The question of Southern loyalty to the Union disturbed Northern Democrats as well as Republicans, and the tension over this issue was not easily assuaged. Forsyth, for example, had to defend the South's loyalty when he visited Milwaukee in 1868 to confer with Democratic leaders. He assured Milwaukee's readers that the South was the innocent victim in the Reconstruction drama—that it had complied with Northern demands only to see the murder of self-government in ten states. [110]

The *Register* often groused about its Northern counterparts' preference for expediency over principle. It considered the Northern press too timid, too passive, and sometimes downright insensitive to Southern feelings. Appreciating the sacrifices of Northern Democrats in standing by constitutional principles during the war, Forsyth expected them to accept Southerners' devotion to constitutional rights and honorable leaders such as Jefferson Davis. Democratic colleagues to the north, he warned, must discard their air of condescension toward the former "rebels." [111]

Yet in an effort to further party harmony, Forsyth for a time acquiesced in the common assumption that Northern leaders would play a dominant role in the party. He maintained this attitude through the late 1860s but eventually grew impatient. In November 1871, he pointedly criticized the timid and unsuccessful policies of his Northern colleagues. Southern Democrats must have an equal voice in their party. "They have political experience, brains, and sagacity that have long been acknowledged. They have done themselves harm, and no good to their allies, by retiring sullen, like Achilles to his tent, from the arena of political battle. We think we ought to say, 'South to the front!' To the front, not as dictators, not as Bourbons, but as equals in the camp of faithful and honorable allies. One becomes weary of being tolerated." [112]

The presidential campaign of 1872 presented the ultimate test of Forsyth's resolve to join in bolstering party unity no matter how strained the feelings among various Democratic factions, for in that year the Democrats joined with the Liberal Republicans to support candidate Horace Greeley, whose radical social views and former abolitionism had made him anathema to the South. Having preached the white man's movement and denounced any "new departures" for more than a year before the convention, Forsyth suddenly felt himself obligated to engage in the sort of abandonment of principle for expediency which he had found contemptible in Northern counterparts. Only the Democratic party could redeem the South, and Forsyth would stick to it despite its aberrations.[113] Coming out for party unity, he announced that he would campaign for the Democratic nominee—whose name he could hardly bear to mention. Opposed as he was to Grantism and Butlerism, he could do no less and perhaps he could influence the new administration with Democratic principles.[114] Still, the Greeley campaign was traumatic. Ever afterward Forsyth had to explain and re-explain his waffling in that campaign. In 1874 he announced that he had never said Greeley once "until the Democratic Party took him up, and then he ran, not after Mr. Greeley, but after the Democratic party which he was unwilling to leave, even in its wild goose chase."[115]

Although Forsyth lived for politics and the *Register* was a weapon of political warfare, he did not ignore the South's economic development. "Our second care," he proclaimed, "will be to promote, in an especial manner, the great Agricultural, Commercial, and Industrial Interests of Alabama and Mississippi."[116] Predictably, however, even his discussion of economic questions was essentially political as he blamed economic as well as sectional turmoil on the Radicals and maintained that a "speedy restoration" was the answer to all financial trouble, national and sectional.[117]

The subordination of economic to political interests created a curious rhythm in Forsyth's journalism. A spate of articles, editorials, and letters boosting Alabama's and Mobile's prospects for economic growth followed every political defeat. For example, after the defeat in 1868 Forsyth, ostensibly proud, produced a series on economic progress, while admitting that "the restless tide of politics swept us all off in the same gulf of oblivion and discouragement." The titles of his editorials suggest his themes: "Enterprise," "The Vital Trade Interests of Mobile," "The Resources of Alabama," and "Southern Lands in Demand."[118] In April 1871, he wrote, "We wait patiently and bide our time. We till our soil, build our railroads, deep green the mounds over our dead, maintain our self-respect and dignity, and can afford to smile scornfully at the malicious fools, who, while trying to educate us into a condition for their contempt, are digging their own political graves."[119] A year later, painting a bright economic future, he reminded his readers that Radicalism could not "destroy the natural attributes of climate, of soil and ores beneath the soil. When Sherman marched to the sea the cotton bolls did not refuse to open, and the soil that trembled beneath the tramp of his legions was no less rich in mineral stores."[120]

Politics aside, however, Forsyth genuinely believed in the particular economic mission advanced by his paper, which was to make Mobile the great commercial port on the Gulf. He strove to meet the postwar exigencies of the area's image and reputation, of Mobile's commercial development, and of the South's labor needs and efforts for economic diversification.[121] Now more than ever the voice of economic progress was needed in Mobile, for new railroads and transportation patterns and the rise of interior cotton marketing towns and processing centers damaged Mobile's importance. The city in the 1870s did not merely stagnate; it declined relative to other Southern cities, and its population fell by three thousand.[122] Forsyth fought these trends. He advocated city, state, and national subsidies for regional development and opposed governmental restrictions on trade, taxes which hurt business, and obstacles to Northern or European investment in Alabama. He execrated the advocates of state debt repudiation; they not only harmed Mobile (where the largest group of bondholders lived) but also damaged the state's long-range economic growth, since no government could afford to sacrifice its credit.[123]

Working diligently to foster growth and modernization, the *Register* voiced the economic views of Mobile developers. For twenty years, Forsyth had urged the dredging of the harbor and bay to make Mobile a first-class, deep-water port. He campaigned for wharf and harbor improvements and the creation of an ocean fleet based at Mobile.[124] Mobile suffered from competition with New Orleans and Pensacola; with improved transportation facilities the city could not only survive but even achieve dominance of the region. Forsyth also devoted a good deal of energy to promoting railroads—any railroad with a terminus at Mobile, but especially a rail line to the coal and iron fields of Alabama and to a major Atlantic port.[125]

Like other Southern dailies, the *Register* was also concerned about the reliability of the postwar labor force. During Presidential Reconstruction Forsyth showed only slight interest in the attempt to replace black labor; but as the political situation deteriorated, he became more critical of the freedmen and looked elsewhere for dependable workers.[126] Under the carpetbaggers' influence, the *Register* scoffed, blacks degenerated.[127] Blacks were consumers, not producers; they were human caterpillars and bollworms—disturbers of peace, industry and property, the paper concluded.[128] Some Alabamians regarded the Chinese as an ideal substitute labor force, but the *Register* rejected them as repulsive and morally degraded. The solution, the *Register* suggested, lay with sturdy white Europeans or even Northerners, if they would leave their political ideas at home.[129]

Despite the paper's political conservatism, change was the hallmark of the *Register*'s economic policy. Forsyth deplored the Old South's dependence on cotton and looked to a new era of more diversified farming and the establishment of manufacturing in Mobile and Alabama. The

Register, like other Reconstruction papers, came to sound like the New South boosters of the 1880s. Its Agricultural and Horticultural Department, stressing the need for diversified farming and improved methods of agriculture, featured an enormous variety of articles such as "Hogs and Hog Raising in the South," "Hints on Horse Flesh," "Clover," and "Utilizing Night Soil."[130] Forsyth and various *Register* contributors criticized Alabama planters for putting too much acreage in cotton and too little in corn. Southerners should, as the saying went, "eat at home," and they certainly should reduce the size of the cotton crop in order to raise its price.[131]

The editorial page popularized the need for home industry and manufacturing of any kind but especially the construction of cotton mills. Forsyth's message was that industrial labor created wealth while purchasing goods manufactured elsewhere simply sent Mobile's money abroad.[132] In an editorial, "The Secret of Yankee Prosperity," Forsyth explained that Alabama shipped its cotton at its own expense to New England and then bought it back as cloth at inflated prices which included the cost of transport back to Alabama. "What a kind-hearted people we Southerners must be!" The secret of Yankee prosperity, he concluded, was machinery. The South, if it was to become prosperous, must set its own spindles in motion.[133] If coal and iron were essential to the rise of manufacturing, as seemed true in other Northern examples, then Mobile must tap the rich resources of central Alabama.[134] Forsyth urged his readers to learn the lesson of the Confederacy's wartime economy—that the South was capable of manufacturing; it had produced gunpowder and "cast the finest ordnance to man our forts and warsteamers; . . . built our own means of military transportation, and created trains of wagons, gun carriages, and all that was needful to move armies."[135]

Cotton had once brought prosperity to the South, but clearly cotton alone could never bring prosperity in the postwar world. New railroads, harbor improvements, factories, Forsyth wrote, were adjustments to a "different era from that of cotton sheds; these were of the petty past, the others are the foreshadowings of the immense future."[136] A letter to the editor insisted on "the absolute necessity of manufacturers, and our willingness to aid in their establishment. . . . The dry rot is upon us. . . . A handful of cotton factors, a few banks and insurance companies will be as impotent to save us as would be the attempt to dip out the Mississippi with a tea-spoon."[137]

By backing almost every development project that came along, the *Register* soon acquired plenty of enemies. Undoubtedly Forsyth's calls for change unsettled Mobile's entrenched elite, which reflected the interests and power of King Cotton.[138] When his most important projects failed, Forsyth labeled his critics croakers and barnacles, blaming them for a paralysis of will which left undeveloped Mobile's great commercial promise. Scolding these influential nay-sayers, the *Register* challenged them to support a "people's policy" and to "build a town that is worth living in."[139] In 1871 the *Register* launched a crusade to secure city support for the Mobile and Northwest Railroad, a project which, Forsyth proudly proclaimed, was conceived in the *Register* office. Volumes of *Register* publicity beat futilely against considerable opposition.[140] At last, in disgust, the *Register* decided that it had sacrificed enough in this cause.[141] With some petulance, Forsyth wrote: "A newspaper cannot afford to be treated as a beast of burden and harnessed to every loaded car that is labelled 'public good'. . . . We fought hard for the New Orleans Railroad enterprise, for the Nicolson pavement, the most valuable and, in an economical and sanitary point of view, the most useful enterprise that could be inaugurated, and for the Grand Trunk Railroad appropriation, and all this as we believed and still believe, for the 'public good.' Well the public doesn't seem to have appreciated the 'good' and rewarded us with more kicks than coppers."[142]

Despite such moments of discouragement, Forsyth continued to take up apparently profitless causes in what he perceived to be the public interest of Mobile and southern Alabama. In many ways Mobile's economy was a fabric of cotton; cotton and the cotton trade dominated the thinking of many of the city's antebellum and postbellum leaders. Nevertheless, the *Register*, despite the arguments of Jonathan Wiener, David Goldfield, and others, was not essentially a planter newspaper.[143] To be sure, the *Register* boosted agriculture, sought the prosperity of Alabama's planters and usually defended their interests, though at times it criticized their shortsighted planting methods and once even suggested that their refusal to surrender their slaves had cost the life of the Confederacy. On occasion it directly opposed them. In 1874 and 1875, for example, the *Register* broke with planter interests by campaigning against debt repudiation.[144]

Those who share Jonathan Wiener's view of the *Register* as a planter newspaper argue that it voiced the planters' fears of industrialization. Certainly the *Register* was sometimes critical of Birmingham's iron and steel industry, but not because of any ideological concern or opposition to a New South—rather because Birmingham's growth and prosperity might prove harmful to Mobile's. Such fears were not without foundation, for, in fact, as historian Don Doyle explained, "the rise of Birmingham's steel and coal industries, instead of thrusting the old seaport into new roles as a manufacturing and coal export center, only stimulated railroad development into the interior, sapping trade that formerly flowed downriver to Mobile."[145] The *Register*'s criticism of Birmingham industry was not an example of planter hostility but a typical case of urban rivalry.

The *Register*'s central economic concern was Mobile; the *Register* spoke not for the planters' interests but for Mobile's. Often their interests were complementary or identical, for the planters exported much of their cotton through Mobile. But support for planting interests did not preclude boosting railroads and factories or anything else which would benefit Mobile.

The *Register*'s course under Forsyth gives credence to those historians who have stressed the lack of conflict between planters and industrialists and the essential unity of the South's ruling class in the postwar decades.[146] Though hampered by Reconstruction turmoil, an optimistic, modernizing ethos and civic spirit emanating from the larger towns and the cities sought the prosperity of cotton planters, the improvement and diversification of farming, the expansion of commerce, and the development of industry.[147] Here was the antebellum booster spirit now dedicated to lifting the South from the ashes of war, to combating economic stagnation in the 1870s, and to catching up with a prosperous North, and none sounded this theme more consistently than editors of urban dailies. In the 1850s Forsyth's paper had puffed local industry and campaigned for railroads to save Mobile from the fate of becoming a mere outpost of New Orleans. Forsyth had fought the local croaker spirit as well as New York City's financial and commercial hegemony by demanding more local investment.[148] The Reconstruction *Register* reiterated and expanded on these themes. The *Register* and other leading Southern dailies, such as the *Memphis Daily Appeal*, the *Nashville Republican Banner*, the *Savannah Morning News*, and the *Charleston News and Courier* embraced schemes for economic advancement,[149] perceiving mills "not as the advance guard of a wrenching, disruptive industrialization but merely as adjuncts, increasingly needed, to the farm and village."[150]

Increasingly in the late nineteenth century, urban newspapers addressed a diverse audience, speaking for dominant economic interests whose goals and prosperity they believed would benefit everyone. They intended to broaden a sense of the shared community interest rather than divide the public.[151] Editors saw themselves as unifiers who knew best for the entire community. Appeals for community support and unity on economic matters came naturally to Southern editors accustomed to Reconstruction battles against Yankees and Republicans. The Southern elite—planters, merchants, and industrialists—and bourgeois elements shared beliefs in social and political stability, low taxation, cheap labor, and minimal, conservative government,[152] and the press defended their interests, interpreting them in ways palatable to the larger public. If editors served the many varied interests of this broadly based elite, they nevertheless were often its most progressive spokesmen.

Yet Reconstruction editors were rather naive, advancing simplistic solutions to nearly intractable, complex problems. From the editorial chair, prosperity was logically and easily wished into existence; a few strokes of the pen glossed over a multitude of obstacles. An infusion of investment capital would bring forth factories and railroads:[153] "The new rail systems would support the new industries which in turn would give business to the railroads. The deficiencies of the labor supply would be eliminated, editors thought, by the arrival of immigrants who would move south if the proper inducements were offered." [154] If moral exhortation and whistling Dixie could transform the South, the new era of industry and prosperity lay at the end of the next cotton row down by the river where a cotton mill was soon to be established.

The rhetoric of 1880s New South boosters and developers was rehearsed in the 1860s and 1870s, and it echoed the programs of antebellum urban boosters and advocates of Southern commercial development.

The economic message of the Reconstruction *Register*, although neither new nor especially practical, was nevertheless genuine. Given the paper's political focus and bitter partisanship, this optimistic economic message suggests a certain schizoid tone. Reaction in politics was coupled with rather progressive views on other matters, many of which reflected Forsyth's view of his paper's role. While serving as the political oracle of southern Alabama and persistent booster for growth and development, the *Register* also acted as public servant, morale booster, urban improver, public scold, and self-appointed conscience of the city. These roles had appeared in the antebellum period and continued with greater intensity during Reconstruction. In the 1850s the *Register* advocated larger appropriations for sanitation, clean streets, and public education; it campaigned for a medical school in Mobile and praised donations to the Female Benevolent Society while urging well-to-do ladies to supply employment to needy women.[155] Among its many causes the *Register* of Reconstruction supported Mobile's summer nights concert series, proclaimed the need for a city workhouse and a house of refuge for boys and girls, demanded backing for efforts to improve sanitation, criticized rowdyism in the Fire Department, urged better pay for city teachers, argued for the establishment of a first-class college in the Mobile area, and publicized complaints about filthy gutters and alleys and then applauded a successful clean-up effort.[156] The *Register* spoke with some success for the organization of an efficient, uniformed police force, drilled in the use of arms, trained to walk a beat properly, and free from political influence.[157] In a furious editorial, "Murder by Law," written after the Hudson River Railroad disaster, Forsyth indicted railroads, which he always supported editorially and financially, for placing speed above public safety, and he called on the press to investigate and expose those responsible.[158]

Forsyth emerged from the political battles of the 1860s and 1870s as Alabama's leading Democratic editor and one with proto-progressive tendencies. One of his goals, to edit and publish "the model newspaper of the South," appeared to be within reach.[159] Noting that circulation of the *Register* "[had] for some time . . . extended beyond Southern boundaries," the Mobile editor boasted, "Since the days of Thomas Ritchie and the old Richmond Enquirer, no Southern newspaper has enjoyed a national reputation and circulation. The *Register* is rapidly advancing to that position."[160]

In 1869 the *Register* claimed a circulation in excess of five thousand for its daily and twenty thousand for its weekly, making it the largest paper in the South except for the *Louisville Courier-Journal*.[161] In the 1870s it became the sole survivor of Mobile's once-numerous dailies, and in 1876, billing itself as the "Democratic Organ of the South," it claimed the largest circulation "in this section."[162] There were many signs of Forsyth's success. In 1870 the *Register* purchased a new Hoe double cylinder press to meet the demands of its increased circulation, and in 1871 it appeared in new type.[163] When in 1871 the Democrats finally recaptured Mobile, the *Register* received the city's public printing contract.[164] A personal triumph for Forsyth came in 1874 when he purchased the paper he had edited for some twenty-five years, having declined attractive offers to direct the editorial page of other well-known journals. Forsyth seemed at the peak of success just at the moment of Alabama's long-awaited liberation.[165]

But the *Register* was in serious financial trouble, and in 1876 it narrowly averted bankruptcy.[166] As Forsyth knew, the appearance of health had always belied actual financial conditions. He had constantly bemoaned the cost of publishing and the lack of public support for Alabama's best newspaper.[167] Why, then, had he purchased the *Register*? It would seem that his goal was independence and freedom to use the *Register* as he saw fit for the advancement of his causes. He despised journalism devoted to moneymaking; he once attacked the *New York Sun* as a purveyor of sensationalism, charging that it was published solely for profit, not to secure any higher purpose.[168] By the 1870s journalism was his life, and the *Register* as dear to him as his life's blood.

Money, Forsyth said, was not the purpose of journalism, but on the other hand no one could produce a quality paper without plenty of it.[169] And Southern papers labored under huge handicaps. Here, too, Forsyth sounded a refrain typical of the Southern press throughout the nineteenth century. It was bad enough that Southern towns were too small to support newspapers capable of competing with Northern urban dailies. Even worse, complained Forsyth, the South did not support its local press with the loyalty and vigor it should. All Southern publishing ventures eventually failed, in part because of "the bad taste of Southern readers in preferring everything that is not of home manufacture." "Her people are shamefully parsimonious in their contributions to their newspapers." [170]

Forsyth tried to impress his readers with the tremendous cost of publishing a daily. The expenses of the *Register*, exclusive of such incidental costs as wear and tear on the machinery, interest on capital, and outlays for three to eight paid contributors, amounted to some $2,250 a week for wages and salaries (skilled labor was one of the greatest costs of a modern daily), paper, telegraph bills, press and special dispatches, rent, gas, and 150 other items. [171] By contrast, the *New York Herald*, the nation's largest journal, spent some four to five thousand dollars daily. The key to the *Herald's* success, Forsyth concluded, was that its circulation and advertisements justified such huge outlays: "When the daily outlay of the *Herald* is greatest, its income is proportionately increased." [172] Forsyth believed that his *Register* would have had ten times its circulation were it located in one of the great cities of the North, and contrariwise, the London *Times* or the *New York Herald* would have failed within six months if removed from the great centers of population, intelligence, enterprise, and trade. [173]

The South seemed deaf to Forsyth's woeful pleas for money. While his editorial reputation and political stature grew steadily, the *Register* always reflected the parsimony of Mobilians and the limited scope of the southern-Alabama and Mississippi market. The *Register* remained only a four-page paper except for the Sunday edition. Telegraphic news, although an important page-one feature, was of limited scope, and for news, comment, and essays the *Register* relied heavily on exchanges. Mobile's leading paper could afford relatively few correspondents, although it did maintain essential services at Montgomery, Washington, and New York City. Talented journalists were scarce in the South. Forsyth lamented that "in the editorial profession in Mobile, when the front rank man falls there is absolutely no file in his rear to step into his place. Editors are not to be had in the city." [174]

The financial problems of Forsyth and the *Register* typified those of other editors and journals in the South. The upheaval of war and Reconstruction, the high cost of publication, and the Panic of 1873 killed off many Southern dailies, most of which had begun anew—from scratch— in 1865. Not until 1880 did the Mississippi press recover its 1860 circulation. In Nashville seven dailies were started after the war, but after a short time only two continued to publish.[175] Forsyth embraced the increasingly orthodox view that the South had too many papers; as he put it, it was a cutthroat game and only the fittest could and should survive.[176]

Neither the threat of bankruptcy nor occasional bouts of despondency about the editor's thankless task—"the daily and hourly annoyances, the weight of responsibility, the censure, so often undeserved, the incessant strain upon the mental faculties"—prevented Forsyth from enjoying a certain amount of national recognition.[177] By the midseventies, having helped to redeem his city and state, the *Register*'s helmsman was applauded as the South's outstanding editor by many of his Southern colleagues and much of the Northern metropolitan press as well.[178] At his death in 1877, reported the *New York Sun*, his name was recognized throughout the country. Forsyth, the *Sun* concluded, had exercised a dominance over the Southern press unequaled since the days of Thomas Ritchie.[179] R.H. Henry, in his reminiscences of great editors, recalled that Colonel John Forsyth was regarded "as the truly great editor of the South, for in Forsyth's time, Henry Watterson was just coming on the stage as the successor of George D. Prentice, and Henry Grady was unknown."[180]

Many probably agreed with the editors of the *New York Sun* and the *Philadelphia Press* that the *Register* was a journal of the fire-eaters and one of the most bitter organs of the Southern irreconcilables.[181] Some thought Forsyth notorious rather than famous. The North as well as the South knew that Forsyth considered the Republicans dogs and recommended that they be treated as such.[182] In Washington, Alabama's carpetbagger senator, George Spencer, aired the rumor that Forsyth had advocated the assassination of Republicans in the South.[183] Perhaps Forsyth's enemies were too impressed by his rhetoric. Forsyth was usually more moderate than he sounded; his journalism featured extravagant insults and militant policies but combined them with a tendency for compromise for the good of the South and the Democratic party. In comparison with other editors—Klansman Ryland Randolph of the *Tuscaloosa Monitor*, for example—Forsyth was quite tame. Randolph was a trigger-happy headhunter whose outrageous editorial describing Alabama's black legislators as animals resulted in his expulsion from the Alabama legislature. Shortly thereafter he was wounded in a rencontre with Cadet James Webster Smith, the first black appointed to West Point.[184] Other journals such as the *New Orleans Bulletin*, which for a brief time was known for "pure cussedness," were far more militant than the *Register*.[185]

In the final analysis, John Forsyth's reputation rested on his articulation of Southern feelings in a style readers found familiar, if sometimes infuriating. His was traditional personal journalism, opinionated, abrasive, and always distinctive. When Northern editors responded with personal abuse and intemperate rebuttals the Mobile editor assumed that he was doing his job well.[186]

Near the end of his career, Forsyth concluded that if the *Register* could not become a "great daily" like the *Herald*, it could always do "better political cyphering." He observed with satisfaction that the whole country knew "from the beginning *The Register* held fast to the faith, and in and out of season, uttered it, that it was the appointed mission of the Democratic party once more to save the Republic from the most fearful perils in its history. We never wavered in this belief."[187] He never wavered from the faith, and the tragedy of sectional journalism in Reconstruction was that good political cyphering translated into misunderstanding and sectional animosity. Accuracy in reporting and news gathering had little to do with Reconstruction journalism. In pursuit of resistance and Southern victory, Forsyth consistently distorted Republican intentions and misinformed Southern readers about Northern politics and attitudes.[188] Reconstruction editors like Forsyth deserve credit for much of the South's defiance; they must also share blame for much of the tragedy of Reconstruction.

Forsyth's contemporaries on the Republican side—white and black— shared this view, which was not mere politics. The press epitomized by Forsyth's *Mobile Daily Register* led the South down the road to destruction, concluded the biracial *New Orleans Tribune*, a radical daily addressed to New Orlean's Creole people of color and former slaves.[189] The *Tribune*'s editor scorned the folly of the mainstream press, a bought press whose policies were pernicious for the country's welfare: "This lying press precipitated and multiplied the problems; it ruined the planters who, had they been well advised, would have obtained an ample reimbursement for their slaves before the war. It encouraged resistance and bred anger when it was futile and all hope was lost. It drove the slaveowners from one mistake to another; these mistakes brought about a social transformation."[190]

The *New Orleans Tribune* was hardly alone in its radical critique. The closed nature of the Southern press represented by Forsyth—and its active hostility to any but the interests of the white Democracy—called into existence an alternative press of carpetbag, scalawag, and black journals. White Republican journals proved largely ephemeral, but the black political weeklies of Reconstruction, however short-lived and poorly financed, and though dependent upon a largely illiterate and isolated clientele, established a press tradition in the South that has survived until today. Black newspapers founded during Reconstruction— six appeared before the end of 1865—published what the white press would not.[191] Such papers as the *Loyal* (Augusta) *Georgian*, the *Colored*

(Nashville) *Tennessean*, the Charleston *South Carolina Leader*, and the Little Rock *Arkansas Freeman* spoke for people ignored by Forsyth and his colleagues, demanding equal rights and the suffrage (oftentimes even before the advent of Radical Reconstruction). In addition they celebrated with pride the record of black soldiers, demanded equal access to public facilities and the establishment of public schools for blacks, and announced developments and meetings important to the black community.[192] Reconstruction's black editors—politicians, ministers, teachers, and others of the black elite—were militant crusaders dedicated more to a cause than to making profits. When Tabbs Gross of the *Arkansas Freeman* attacked carpetbaggers for monopolizing political offices, he risked the loss of party support but lived up to his paper's motto, "Dedicated to the Interests of the Colored People of Arkansas."[193] When James T. Rapier established his campaign journal, the Montgomery *Republican Sentinel*, he paid for most of the cost of publication from his own pocket. He admitted that it was money well-spent: "I issue 1000 copies weekly and flatter myself that much good has been accomplished . . . as we reach a class of reader who get no other paper [the *Sentinel* was free], and knowing mine to be edited by one of their own race, have confidence in it."[194]

If black political weeklies could hardly aspire to compete with the big city dailies, one should not ignore their interesting similarities. Forsyth's journalism was heavily political; so was that of the black press. Forsyth spoke the mind of the white elite; black editors voiced the opinions of the black elite. Forsyth's editorial view was, in regard to Yankees and the federal government, strongly defensive; so too was the view of black editors regarding Southern Democrats. White editors found financial resources limited; for blacks they were practically nonexistent. If Forsyth is praised for courageous defense of his people, so should men like Tabbs Gross or James T. Rapier, who worked in an environoment even more threatening. Still, the Reconstruction newspapers of the white South and black South are best interpreted in terms of one major difference; the mainstream press represented by Forsyth, almost smothering in its influence, spoke for reaction and a closed community while the black press celebrated equality and racial justice.

In a 1983 essay, "Bourbonism, Reconstruction, and the Persistence of Southern Distinctiveness," historian George C. Rable reviewed the debate over unity and continuity in Southern history and concluded that a solid South has great validity as a cultural concept. "More than any other section of the country, the South achieved a social unity challenged by only the boldest or most foolhardy of her inhabitants. The mind of the postbellum South was in many respects the mind of the antebellum South. The survival of the proslavery argument, the growth of racist ideology, the persistence of paternalism, the resiliency of southern nationalism, the politics of personal honor, and a rigid constitutionalism that seemed to run against the tide of modern thought all gave the southern mind during Reconstruction its special character."[195] Challenges from Republican papers, black and white, were brushed aside, and these characteristics of the Southern mind appear in daily fulminations of Reconstruction newspapers, one of the most important and neglected sources of Southern intellectual history.

John Forsyth's *Register* was typical of the mid-nineteenth-century Southern press. From Old South to New South, Forsyth and other editors defended racial subordination, fought Republican and Yankee aggressors, attacked centralizers in Washington, called for Southern economic independence, and boosted the South's agricultural, commercial, and industrial resources while celebrating the superiority of a Southern way of life. Forsyth's intractability during Reconstruction embodied honor itself, the highest virtue of his section. Other editors differed from Forsyth in style and tone, but such individuality did not detract from a unity of belief and common goals. Southern journals, like the Southern mind, "could be tactically malleable but at the same time ideologically inflexible."[196] Forsyth's rage at carpetbaggers and black politicians and diatribes against all things Radical placed him in the front ranks of Reconstruction resistance; Forsyth was merely the vanguard of a united front against perceived revolutionary change. Unfortunately, Forsyth's and his editorial colleagues' single-minded dedication to the politics of resistance dwarfed the infant stirrings of progressive change.

7
Three Giants of New South Journalism
The Formative Years

The sectionalization of politics and parties and the revolutionary changes sweeping through the Northern metropolitan press during the antebellum era denied the obsessively partisan prewar Southern press a truly national voice. The war devastated the South's newspapers, and Reconstruction delayed their technical modernization while prolonging their fixation on politics. In content, temper, and style Southern journalism of Reconstruction preached only to the ex-Confederate faithful.

In the 1880s, however, a few Southern editors transcended these constricting traditions. None received more local and national acclaim than Henry Watterson of the *Louisville Courier-Journal*, Francis Warrington Dawson of the *Charleston News and Courier*, and Henry Woodfin Grady of the *Atlanta Constitution*.[1] Each inspired and eventually symbolized important transitions in Southern journalism and sectional development. Although editors continued to worship at the shrine of party and although partisanship and personality still dominated newspaper circles, new standards of independent journalism and news gathering emerged in trendsetting Northern urban journals. These changes, appearing at first largely as ideals rather than accepted practice, arrived just at the time when Southern editors fought for Redemption with all the partisanship and vindictiveness they could muster. Nevertheless, the newest concepts of journalism—"political independence" within the thrall of party loyalty and, later, in the 1880s, emphasis on the news concept of journalism, the efficacy of crusades, and sensationalism and entertainment for the masses (all of this soon to be designated as the New Journalism)—made headway in the leading journalistic centers of the South.[2]

To be sure, Watterson, Dawson, and Grady built upon legacies of the Old South (which embraced boosterism and a belief in regional development as well as backward agriculture and conservative leadership) and fought editorial battles grounded in the hatred of Reconstruction, yet they also accepted the need for change and frequently took their journalistic cue from successful Northern papers. Wherever practicable they advanced the New South and the New Journalism. They were modernizers. The "liberalism" of twentieth-century progressives and of newspaper critics in the 1920s and 1930s was preceded by and in certain essentials based upon the legendary conservatism of the late nineteenth century, the age of the Redeemers or Bourbons. Theirs was not a world apart; elements of both change and continuity were present. The best of the late-nineteenth-century Southern newspapermen looked both backward and forward. New South editors, proud of the Old South and Lost Cause, emerged as heralds of hope and a better way of life.[3] If in the final analysis they spoke for and defended a power elite of planters, industrialists and urban commercial elements, they were the most progressive leaders of a conservative coalition. As spokesmen for a new South, they shared a creed which idealized an affluent, successful, and morally innocent South based on commercial and industrial development, agricultural diversification, urban growth, and racial harmony.[4]

Even though the New York City press sometimes patronized them as second-rate and provincial, Watterson, Grady, and, to a lesser extent, Dawson reached a national audience as progressive and attractive symbols of a regenerated American South. Their readers viewed them as metropolitan and unprejudiced, an assessment which stands in distinct contrast to some recent works which sneer at boosters and condemn elite leadership as exclusively self-serving.[5] Despite widely varying attitudes toward these editors, both then and now, few would deny their importance to Southern development or, at the very least, Southern mythologizing and elite rule.

Henry Watterson had superior preparation for the editor's chair. Born in 1840, the only child of a Tennessee congressman who later edited the *Nashville Union*, Watterson grew up in an adult world and absorbed his father's cardinal faith in the Democracy and the Union. As a child he read history and biography at the Library of Congress and with his parents dined at the White House.[6] The center of an adoring world, and with a winsome personality, he "experienced at an early age the pleasant sensation that comes to those who suspect that they alone hold correct information on men and affairs."[7] An excellent education, both at home and in Philadelphia, the experience of publishing a Tennessee country weekly at age sixteen, accomplishment at the keyboard which led to a brief stint as music critic on the *New York Times*, and ready access to high social and government circles as a reporter for the *Washington States*—all featured prominently in the maturation of a remarkably precocious teenager.[8] It was well that Watterson possessed from an early time a self-confidence bordering on arrogance, for his would be a journalism of personal and partisan combat as he, like many another editor, viewed his purpose as laying bare the schemes of tricksters who would betray the people.

The Civil War destroyed Watterson's budding career in Washington. Although opposed to secession and slavery, the young newspaperman surrendered to the pressures of his social circle, kinsmen, and friends by reluctantly casting his lot with the South. After brief service in the cavalry of Nathan Bedford Forrest, Watterson found his niche as editor of the peripatetic, fanatically Confederate *Chattanooga Rebel*, the "most widely read journal of the Confederate Army."[9] Despite steadfast service to the new nation, Watterson coolly accepted (and may even have welcomed) the collapse of the Confederacy.[10] His revived unionism, his border state origins, and his vision of a new South of industry and diversified agriculture made his adaptation to a rebuilt Union and a new era of nationalism easy and comfortable.[11] Soon the North was hearing welcome words of conciliation from the whilom editor of the *Chattanooga Rebel*.

In 1868 Watterson abandoned a job in Nashville, an unhappy, wartorn city, to take a position in Louisville, a thriving, gateway city that had never known war's devastation. Louisville prospered in the postwar era: its railroad network expanded into the South, its mercantile community revived, and a rising industrial sector flexed its muscles in tobacco products, bourbon, cast-iron pipe and plows, steam engines and boilers, and coarse denim cloth. Industrial employment soared by 61 percent in the 1870s. A strong and diverse industrial and commercial base brought population growth, 30 percent in the 1880s, and with a population of 123,758 in 1880, Louisville claimed prominence as a regional metropolis.

It is significant that Watterson cast his lot with the citizens of Kentucky, for most of them had stood by the Union, and even if emancipation, Radical Reconstruction measures, a lengthy Yankee military presence, and sympathy for the South as victim and defender of a just cause converted many Kentuckians to Confederate sympathies, they were hardly the bitter-enders of the Deep South. In fact, from that geographical perspective, Louisville frequently seemed allied with Northern Philistines in Yankeeizing the South. Watterson's Confederate credentials as a cavalryman with Forrest and editor of the *Rebel* were perfectly acceptable to his new constituency.[12] Louisville offered the ideal journalistic field for interpreting one section to another—or, paradoxically, for being misunderstood in both sections.[13]

The once great *Louisville Journal*, which Watterson joined as editor in 1868, had fallen on evil days. His famous but aging predecessor, George D. Prentice, had been a Whig Unionist profoundly opposed to the Confederacy; with Kentucky's changing political sentiment the *Journal* had fallen to third place in circulation behind Walter Haldeman's *Courier* and William Harney's *Democrat*. Moreover, for any editor aspiring to regional influence, Louisville's press faced serious competition from that of Chicago, Cincinnati, and St. Louis, cities of double or triple Louisville's size.[14] Watterson accepted the challenge of rebuilding the *Journal*; with an improved reportorial staff, more foreign news and more literature, the *Journal* quickly increased its circulation. Within a year Watterson was able to negotiate a merger between his *Journal* and Haldeman's *Courier*, and together they secretly purchased the *Democrat*. Watterson received one-third of the stock of the new paper and command of the editorial page and news management while Haldeman directed the business affairs, an arrangement that prospered for some fifty years.[15]

Louisville was surprised and perturbed by the sudden collapse of its three papers and the emergence on November 8, 1868, of a new one, the *Courier-Journal*. Loyal readers of the three papers "felt they had been tricked. . . . Men were not yet accustomed, in those days of small journals expressing every shade of political thought, to one large monopolistic city press."[16] Although the *Courier-Journal* had no English-language rival for its first year, it did not flourish. Watterson and Haldeman soon concluded that their monopoly had affronted the city; Watterson later recalled, "[We] willingly accepted an offer from a proposed Republican organ for a division of the Press dispatches which we controlled. Then and there the real prosperity of the Courier-Journal began, the paper having made no money out of its monopoly."[17] The illusion of competition reconciled the citizenry to the *Courier-Journal*'s dominance, but Watterson was right in his conviction that Louisville could support only one editor of national prominence. Genuine newspaper competition in a one-party political situation would compel each editor to identify himself with a particular local faction, eliminating all hope of national stature or successful competition with papers in Cincinnati or St. Louis.[18] And, of course, Watterson and every big-city Southern editor aspired to be a nationally recognized, powerful pundit.

Watterson found a strong editorial voice in the *Courier-Journal* just in time to influence the national debate on Reconstruction. In an age of personal journalism, passion and prejudice were assets as much as were the gift of words and political knowledge, and the bitterness of Reconstruction reinforced the well-established tradition of editorial acrimony.

Watterson contributed bitter, impassioned, and irresponsible rhetoric, yet unlike most of his Reconstruction contemporaries he came down hardest on the extremists of both sections. He denounced carpetbaggery as an unmitigated curse and swindle, but he also arraigned the stiff-necked Bourbons who ignored Appomattox and the reality of the Fourteenth and Fifteenth Amendments.[19] When some diehards turned to Ku Klux violence, Watterson damned them as cruel monsters worthy of immediate execution.[20]

The crux of the continuing sectional problem, Watterson realized, was the freedman. Out of necessity the South must treat him leniently and recognize his new status imposed by federal bayonets. It was a bad but inescapable situation, the editor advised his countrymen; only a policy based upon fair play and educational opportunity rather than continual animosity would ease racial tensions and convince Northerners of the South's goodwill.[21] Between May 1869 and the spring of 1871 Watterson threw the *Courier-Journal* into a successful fight to permit blacks to testify in the state courts. His editorials contributed significantly to the victory, and their moderation and realism made Watterson a national figure for the first time.[22]

Inevitably Watterson paid a price for his success; he was excoriated by Republican Radicals, Southern Bourbons, and hostile editors in the Deep South. Watterson later recalled, "They [Kentucky Bourbons] regarded me as an impudent upstart—since I had come to Kentucky from Tennessee—as little better than a carpet-bagger; and had done their uttermost to put me down and drive me out."[23] The more conservative country press seemed chronically aggrieved at their "metropolitan contemporary," especially over his acceptance of the Fifteenth Amendment.[24] Editors in the Deep South resented his publicizing of racial troubles, Klan violence, and his remarkable admission that Southerners "need moral emancipation no less than political enfranchisement." For such statements Watterson was damned as a creature of the Freedmen's Bureau.[25] Much later he recalled that "for years the Courier-Journal, standing on the border line, was the one friend of the South which had the ear of the North, and its task was made ten times harder by the fire, which, in its resistance to proscription and malice, it was constantly encountering from the rear."[26] From Mobile, John Forsyth struck back after Watterson had criticized his call for a white man's party. The Louisville editor, the *Mobile Daily Register* argued, was ignorant of the conditions of a mongrelized and negroized state and therefore was insufficiently orthodox on race.[27] That Watterson's moderate policy was intended to rid the country of Radical rule and prevent further federal intervention, and that Radical Republican speeches warranted publication because they were newsworthy, were hardly acceptable defenses.[28]

Inevitably, Watterson sounded more liberal than he actually was, especially as he spoke for Northern as well as Southern consumption. Watterson was a Southern conservative. Paternalism, expediency, and fear of federal intervention structured his editorials far more than any abstract concern for justice. Yet in an era of Reconstruction violence, his cautious policies placed him to the left of center in the South.[29]

Inheriting the mantle of the brawling and brilliant Prentice, Watterson accepted the challenge of his era: he fought for moderation by jumping every other day into some muddy ditch for an editorial brawl.[30] He brought courage, combative gusto, and an abiding faith in union and reconciliation to his editorial columns, but he scarcely raised the tone of American journalism. Despite Watterson's catholic interests and tastes, the centrality of politics to the *Courier-Journal* was obvious; Watterson became a political journalist, or, as Henry Grady once charged, a journalistic politician.[31] How could it be otherwise? "There was in those days," Watterson later wrote, "but a single political issue for the South. Our hand was in the lion's mouth, and we could do nothing, hope for nothing, until we got it out."[32] Reconstruction extremism as well as the traditional excesses of personal journalism made Watterson devote his abilities to invective and attack. "That Watterson style," recalled the *New York Times* upon Watterson's death in 1921, "pungent, vivid, superlatively personal; those adhesive epithets, that storm of arrows, those 'razzers flyin' through the air,' the ludicrous imagination, the swift sarcasm, the free frolic of irresistible humor—it was as if the page was not written but spoke and acted before you."[33]

Watterson's reputation increased rapidly during the battles of Reconstruction. From Cincinnati his uncle, Stanley Matthews, a politician and judge, wrote that he was making "not only a good and great name in journalism and statesmanship but a great and triumphant power," and D.G. Croly, an editor on the *New York World*, told him he was "too big a man for Louisville" and urged him to come to New York.[34] In the Greeley-Grant campaign of 1872 Watterson "became acquainted . . . with some of the most powerful men in the nation: men in public office who ran the government, or editors of great newspapers who voiced and directed public opinion. Watterson's fighting ability, together with his . . . geniality and exuberance made him welcome in their company."[35] Watterson was soon on intimate terms with the leading journalists of that day—Charles A. Dana, Whitelaw Reid, Murat Halstead, and Parke Godwin, among others.[36] The *New York Herald* and the *New York Tribune* began quoting Watterson as a Southern leader of the New Departure, an honor he earned by his intellectual consistency on reconciliation if not by the number of his Southern converts.[37] By 1876 his voice reached a national audience, and when he endorsed Samuel

Tilden for President on April 25, 1876, and warned the South to abjure sectionalism if it wanted restoration, his editorial was everywhere re-published and discussed. When in the 1880s a cult of personality made "Marse" Henry Watterson a celebrity nationwide, he was so stereo-typed as a delightful, improvident, Bourbon-drinking Kentucky colonel that some newspapermen and historians exaggerated the importance of his person to the detriment of his journalistic significance. The *Courier-Journal* was noted for "the rich and expansive personality of its edi-tor."[38] In 1923, Arthur Krock, the twentieth-century's dean of American journalism and once one of "Watterson's boys," concluded that "it would be difficult to think of the emanation of any newspaper in Ameri-ca so potent in a National sense."[39]

In November 1865 a thrice-wounded ex-Confederate officer wrote his English mother: "I would wait a century patiently to have one more blow at them before I die."[40] Captain Francis Warrington Dawson would eventually win fame as a New South editor and voice of South Carolina, but at war's end he, like many others, faced a new beginning with no capital other than the honorable scars of battle.

Dawson was an outsider, born in London in 1840, the oldest son of devout Catholic parents. Reaching manhood with only meager prospects despite a superior education and the beginnings of a literary career, Daw-son fled the land of his birth in pursuit of a romantic dream of fighting for the South (and perhaps to escape family troubles). Not until 1862, after crossing the Atlantic as a seaman in a Confederate ship, did he first set foot in the South. Although promoted to Master's Mate, he resigned from the navy because of the lack of action and joined Lee's artillery. He emerged from the war a committed Southerner.[41] "Here I have a high position and a high reputation," wrote Dawson to his mother. "In Eng-land I should be less than nobody; here I have a thousand friends where in England I have none; here the whole people are linked together by suffer-ings and by perils shared in common, and by a hope for the future."[42]

Dawson never doubted the promise of the Southern future, and he, even more than his more famous colleagues Watterson and Grady, would be a self-made man. Amid the rubble of the postwar South, Dawson could rely upon a charming personality, limitless physical courage, abun-dant energy, keen intelligence, and the ability to write. Soon he was working for the venerable *Richmond Examiner* and acting as "adviser and best man" in the notoriously hotheaded Henry Rives Pollard's principal rencontres. When federal authorities suppressed the *Examiner*, Dawson found work with the *Richmond Dispatch*. He shifted from job to job, joined Richmond's social whirl, and accumulated friends and well-wishers—especially among Richmond's mothers and wives, who applauded his efforts to organize a society to care for Confederate graves.[43] Ambitious and proud, young Dawson boasted to his mother: "Think of my having been an officer in the Navy, an officer in the Army, a bookkeeper, the editor of two newspapers, and Ass't Supt. of an Express Co. in five years and succeeding in all of these."[44] When a friend obtained for him an editorial position on the *Charleston Mercury*, which was soon to make its first postwar appearance, Dawson abandoned Richmond for Charleston, once again to make his way as an outsider in Southern society.[45]

Dawson's journalistic career was deeply affected by the nature of Charleston, the citadel of rebellion and the most aristocratic city of the Old South. With a population of 48,900, roughly 53 percent of whom were blacks, Charleston was only half the size of Louisville.[46] Whereas Watterson's Louisville prospered during and after the war and Grady's Atlanta would rise like the phoenix to preeminence in the New South, Dawson's Charleston stagnated in the 1870s and entered a long period of decline in the 1880s. Charleston suffered from a host of problems— among them ruined railroads, competition from booming urban rivals, a shallow harbor unsuited to deep draft vessels, a federal government unresponsive to the needs of the Cradle of the Confederacy, and the crushing inertia of Reconstruction debts. Not the least of the city's burdens was the lingering influence of aristocratic families unwilling to surrender an ideology based upon tradition, nostalgia for King Cotton, and hostility to the progressive reforms of capital. Whereas Atlantans celebrated the success of the self-made man and glorified material success, Charlestonians remained transfixed by "genealogy, manners, cultural refinement, old homes, and a shared, precious past as the basis of honor and authority within the community."[47] Although Dawson's journalistic efforts addressed Charleston's problems and may have helped to slow the decline, he could not reverse an inexorable trend. Moreover, from the journalistic perspective in the 1870s, Charleston's most significant characteristic was the extraordinary bitterness of its political strife. Political passions set very narrow limits to journalistic maneuverability, but Dawson made the most of Charleston's limited opportunities.

For a time, Dawson tried to adopt a moderate policy on Reconstruction. Of course he denounced Radical Republicans, but his remarks on the results of emancipation were often more elegiac than inflammatory. To his mother he lamented, "George Washington if he now lived would be less than a negro; and Gen. Lee has less political power at the polls than the negro boy who blacks his boots. It is a sad tumble."[48] Soon he was urging his boss and editor, the ferocious Colonel Robert Barnwell Rhett, Jr., to support the ratification of the Fourteenth Amendment in order to save the South from the frightful misery of forced Reconstruction. He also proposed that blacks be placed on the municipal ticket in Charleston.[49] He certainly did not reject white supremacy or mitigate his hatred for Radicals. He simply concluded that compliance was the best course. Like Watterson in Kentucky, he urged a moderate policy in an abrasive rhetorical style, and also like Watterson he censured the violence of extremists of all kinds.

Dawson was searching for a paper of his own within a year of his arrival in Charleston. In 1867 he and Benjamin Riordan, an old Richmond friend and fellow Catholic, bought the moribund *Charleston News*.[50] While Riordan (and later, General Rudolph Siegling) directed business affairs, Dawson made decisions on the news and issued orders on editorial matter at a noon conference every day, reserving the important subjects for himself. Working fourteen to sixteen hours a day, he drove himself, his staff, and a growing corps of able correspondents stationed in South Carolina's major towns. One reporter referred to him occasionally as the "tyrant" or the "Grand Mogul," and to himself as "Dawson's darkey."[51] Dawson's resemblance to an austere, conservative, burgher-businessman in manner and dress only heightened this image.

When the rival *Charleston Courier*, the South's oldest daily, was sold at public auction in 1873, Dawson and Riordan secretly bought it at a bargain price of $7,100. The consolidated *News and Courier* had a virtual newspaper monopoly in Charleston (the *Mercury* went under in 1868) and lorded it over the country journals. Dawson "controlled the flow of information, the character of public discussion, and the notoriety of public officials," concludes E. Culpepper Clark in his fine biography of Dawson and South Carolina politics.[52]

Dawson was a New South trailblazer long before anyone heard of Henry Grady; but although Dawson and Riordan found time and made space to encourage new industries, new commercial opportunities, diversified farming, and immigration, politics was the primary business of the Reconstruction *News and Courier*. As an owner-editor, Dawson exemplified the old-fashioned style of personal journalism in his slashing Reconstruction editorials.[53] Daniel H. Chamberlain, a carpetbag Republican successively attorney general and governor of South Carolina, once wrote ruefully that Dawson's editorials were "like surgery to me— painful but necessary! I wish I could add, healthful!"[54] Historian Robert H. Woody summarizes Dawson's position in the mid-1870s:

Not as defiant or sarcastic as the elder Rhett of the *Mercury*, there was in Dawson less bombast and more logic; his editorials cited volume and page and preserved sufficient saneness to give them weight. It is probable that the *News and Courier* did a great deal to determine the tone of the country papers generally, and most surely it, more than any other, was considered representative by outsiders. Denouncing, arguing, demanding reform, in season and out, Dawson's pen was persuasive and eloquent. . . . It is probable that in all the Southland there was no pen than his more unmerciful in its relentless, caustic, and eternal attacks upon carpet-baggers, scalawags, and all that went with 'Radical' rule. There was no viewing a question from two sides. . . . One may hesitate to assert it dogmatically, but the writer thinks that never in South Carolina's turbulent history has a single paper so dominated the thought of the state.[55]

Woody's picture is accurate up to a point, but it underestimates Dawson's advocacy of a moderate South Carolina response to Reconstruction. Dawson had first essayed a realistic, practical course, and from time to time after 1870 he had flirted with cooperationist-fusion politics in order to divide the Republicans and ensure the triumph of Democratic principles. But in 1876 a similar advocacy of moderation nearly brought him to ruin. In the struggle to redeem South Carolina in the centennial year, Dawson fought the political battle of his life, one eventually involving the very survival of his paper. Dawson broke with white majority sentiment in South Carolina by urging a policy of moderation and fusion with the better Republican element, rather than a resort to intimidation and violence, in order to put South Carolina once again in the Democratic column. After the so-called Hamburg riot, in which disarmed black militia were shot down by white rifle clubs, racial passion obsessed the state. Dawson attacked the perpetrators of this atrocity— white Democrats all—and demanded prosecution. Using many of the standard epithets usually directed at carpetbaggers, he denounced the Democratic extremist leaders (called Straight-outs) who all along had rejected fusion and who would now use the Hamburg tragedy as an excuse to terrorize blacks and wipe out the 30,000-vote black majority. Of course Dawson favored a Democratic victory and white supremacy, but any resort to violence, he believed, would damage South Carolina's image in the nation, retard Charleston's business development, possibly lead to renewed federal intervention, and perhaps touch off a racial war in the low country, where blacks outnumbered whites.[56]

Dawson went well beyond his community's limits of dissent. His enemies, now legion, established a rival paper, the *Journal of Commerce*, and installed the pugnacious Colonel Rhett as editor, with license to eviscerate Dawson and the *News and Courier*. The *Journal of Commerce* almost succeeded, even though it was a trashy sheet—all editorial blast and bluster, without adequate news coverage or any other redeeming quality.[57] In 1876 South Carolinians cared hardly a whit for Dawson's progressive journalism. "Bushel baskets full of new subscriptions came to the *Journal*; challenges to duels came to Dawson in a number almost equal to stop orders for his paper."[58] The circulation of the *News and Courier* collapsed almost overnight, and Dawson narrowly escaped bloody encounters with Rhett, Jr., and an ex-Confederate cavalry general who led the Edgefield County Straight-out faction. Faced with the destruction of his paper, his influence, and his position in society, Dawson succumbed after four weeks: he got right on race and politics by completely reversing his stand. He rejected fusion with the honest Republicans, damned the black "insurrectionists" at Hamburg, and praised the Straight-out Democrats who had been trying to ruin him. In the fall campaign and in the final push for Redemption after the disputed state election, the weight of the *News and Courier* proved crucial to Democratic triumph.[59] For the rest of his life Dawson would criticize his state and its citizens on many issues, but never again would he experiment with unorthodoxy on the essential tenets of Southern faith: race, Democratic solidarity, and home rule.

In the North, Dawson's stand against violence had won him a reputation for courage, moderation, and progressive journalism, but it was this part of his past that he had to live down in Charleston. For many years, despite the *News and Courier*'s contributions to victory in 1876, many white South Carolinians remembered that he had been "soft on Radicalism," and they would not fully accept the English Catholic who had dared to oppose majority white sentiment on an issue of race and political power.[60] "If I had been born in South Carolina," Dawson wrote in 1888, "I should not have had as much difficulty in making myself and my actions understood."[61] Gradually, however, Dawson and likeminded conservatives got a grip on the state Democratic party and isolated the Straight-outs, while the *News and Courier* reconquered Charleston journalism.[62] In July 1878 Rhett's *Journal of Commerce* collapsed. A creature of crisis, it could not survive in a normal climate. Dawson complacently penned its epitaph, arguing that personal antagonism was not enough to sustain a new journal:

With newspapers, as in the animal kingdom, the survival of the fittest is the inexorable law. The *Journal of Commerce* was not, we may say without egotism, nearly as good a newspaper in any respect, as *The News and Courier*. . . . Such a city as Charleston must choose between one newspaper of high grade, or two, or more, puny sheets, half-starved, and equally unsatisfactory to their owners and to the public. This is the experience of Augusta, Savannah and Macon, also, where the effort to keep alive two daily newspapers of merit and ability has signally failed. When there is but one journal, the publishers can afford to continue to spend money lavishly, without embarrassment, in collecting and publishing news. They make a newspaper which is a credit to the city. By its newspapers, away from home, the standing of a city is estimated and judged.[63]

After 1878 Dawson's *News and Courier* bestrode the state like a colossus, dominating the home areas of such dailies as the *Columbia Daily Register* and the *Greenville News*.[64] It was resented and feared as well as respected and praised. By 1880 the *News and Courier*'s daily circulation surpassed that of all other Southern papers except the *Louisville Courier-Journal* and two New Orleans journals.[65]

Henry Grady was only thirty-six years old in 1886 when his New South oration before the New England Society of New York made him a national sensation.[66] Henry Watterson and Francis Warrington Dawson, both ten years his senior, had preceded Grady in advocating New South principles, but perhaps they were too closely associated with the rebel South and too tainted by Reconstruction bitterness ever to serve as national symbols of a new era.

While Watterson and Dawson laboriously rose to national editorial prominence in the 1860s and 1870s, Grady was growing up at home, attending the University of Georgia and the University of Virginia, and breaking in as novice reporter and editor. Raised in an upper-middle-class businessman's family in Athens, Georgia, Grady, unlike the destitute ex-soldiers Watterson and Dawson, never knew poverty. With family money he secured the college education denied Watterson and Dawson, and with family money he financed several journalistic ventures between 1869 and 1876. Despite his father's death in 1864 from wounds received near Petersburg, there is little evidence that the war intruded upon his world so as to thrust him along unwelcome and unexpected paths.[67] Similarly, the Reconstruction experience seems to have left no permanent mark on him. Although Grady was not so young as to avoid the political battles raging in Georgia, these battles seem never to have been the focal point of his life as they were for Watterson and Dawson. Later one of Grady's allies would be Atlanta developer Hannibal Kimbal, formerly a notorious Georgia carpetbagger.[68]

Character, even more than youthfulness, may explain the minimal impact of the war and Reconstruction on the rising editor. Grady was a born optimist, a self-confident and engaging glad-hander. By nature a joiner, a booster, and an enchanting conversationalist, wherever he went he made friends and won followers. His enthusiasm and his zest for life were infectious.[69] "He had, even when a child," wrote his friend Joel Chandler Harris, "all those qualifications that draw attention and win approval. It is easy to believe that he was a somewhat boisterous boy. Even after he had a family of his own, and when he was supposed (as the phrase is) to have settled down, he still remained a boy to all intents and purposes. His vitality was inexhaustible, and his flow of animal spirits unceasing."[70]

But Grady was not simply a shallow and brainless boon companion; he believed deeply in mankind and showed a constant (though not always well-informed) sympathy for the poor and downtrodden. Moved by the tales of Bret Harte and the novels of Charles Dickens, Grady savored human interest stories which mingled humor, sentiment, pathos, and whimsicality.[71] Harris, writing shortly after Grady's death and admittedly seeing only his friend's saintliness, remarked that his humor was seldom sharp or biting but gentle and genial like that of Charles Lamb, as he could not bear the thought of distressing or harming anyone.[72] His characteristic sentimentality, which twentieth-century readers often find maudlin and annoying, met an affectionate welcome from contemporaries. Nor did Grady hesitate to put his religious beliefs into his editorials; he had "the simple faith of a child," and believed that "God had a hand in everything."[73]

Perhaps no character could be so simple and disarming as Grady's seemed. It may be that Grady was much more complex, that as author and coworker I. W. Avery believed, his personality ran to contradictions. Avery called him a human antithesis: having a perfervid temperament, Grady revealed to his readers a steady and reflective conservatism; naturally impulsive, he was remarkably poised; full of imagination and passion, he was discreet and self-controlled even in the most trying times.[74]

In 1869 Grady made his debut in Georgia journalism with a series of columns for the *Atlanta Constitution*. His articles were a sensation. Breaking from gloomy routine, they were "full of that racy humor," audacious, sparkling, fresh, and irresistible.[75] Grady presently found permanent employment as associate editor of the triweekly *Rome Courier*, and then, after a quarrel with the proprietor about exposing a politicians' ring, purchased the triweekly *Rome Commercial* to launch his thwarted antiring crusade. As a novice editor in Rome, a town of three thousand, Grady practiced a breezy, enterprising journalism; he was indefatigable in pursuing advertising support. Here, as later in Atlanta, he threw his enormous energy into capturing the big, newsmaking event, the sensation. The daily drudgery of newspaper management bored him, so he avoided it. Occasionally overcome by the tedium of slow days, he altogether ignored his paper, which was then put together by his print shop foreman.[76]

The *Rome Commercial* was a success despite numerous periods of financial hardship. Grady emphasized politics—especially the fight against the carpetbag Governor Rufus Bullock.[77] Although disdaining the crude hatchet work of typical partisan editors, he uncharacteristically indulged in several minor journalistic quarrels which partly belie the saintly image conveyed by Harris and others. But Grady's youthful fights never degenerated into the deadly and embittered brawls common in contemporary Southern journalism. Moreover, Grady shortly had his fill of this strife, and he trumpeted his own "new departure" by promising to ignore future editorial quarrels.[78] When in 1872 he got a chance to perform in the larger field of Atlanta, he left the *Commercial*, as he told his subscribers, "one of the best circulated, best patronized, and handsomest papers in Georgia."[79]

The Atlanta to which Grady migrated had long ago stuck out a welcome mat to new men on the make, even to Yankees. Business superceded politics in bustling Atlanta; Yankee developers and capitalists were eagerly recruited for new enterprises if not always invited home for dinner. Grady would eventually join an economic elite of upwardly mobile, new men who, though having roots in the rural South, embraced city-building ideals. Their Atlanta, a self-confident city, would enjoy two decades of vigorous growth as a rail center and an inland commercial depot for the accumulation and export of staple crops and the wholesale distribution of manufactured goods. "The addition of processing and manufacturing industries, along with administrative services beginning in 1868 as Atlanta became the state capital, fortified the startling growth stimulated by the railroads."[80] A street railway came to Atlanta in 1871, and a cotton factory, among many new businesses, was built in 1875. The 1880s were even better. The "elegant eighties"—when Grady's *Constitution* cut a swath across Southern journalism—saw the "transformation of Atlanta from an unpaved, gas-lit and largely wooden town into an electric lighted, partially paved brick city." In the 1890s Atlanta was the hub of no less than ten railroad lines radiating like spokes from the city. With a population of sixty-five thousand by 1889, Atlanta was the most optimistic, enthusiastic place in the South; it was made for Henry Grady, and he for it.[81] Or so Grady's account—and the account certainly emblazoned in the popular imagination—would have it.

Nevertheless, Atlanta faced serious problems, dependent as it was upon a backward hinterland burdened by sharecropping. Perhaps in comparison with decaying seaport cities Atlanta boomed, but as David Goldfield reminds us, Atlanta in 1900 was still, in most statistical and physical aspects if not in its booster, ideological spirit, little more than a large country town, a walking city not far removed from the antebellum era. No wonder Grady and his papers launched boom after boom; much remained to be accomplished.[82]

But Atlanta and Grady were on the rise. With a loan from his mother, in late 1872 Grady became part owner and business manager of the *Atlanta Herald* of Colonel Robert Alston and Alexander St. Clair-Abrams. The former was a fiery South Carolinian and the latter was an even more fiery Creole with delusions of journalistic grandeur from a recent stint on the sensation-seeking *New York Herald*.[83] It is doubtful whether Atlanta—despite its spirit—was quite prepared for this expensive experiment in metropolitan journalism. Featuring eye-popping headlines of sex crimes and murders, campaigning against corrupt local ring rule and addressing political problems in a strident blare, the *Herald* made its challenge to the

Constitution for hometown supremacy. The three editors attempted to put out the newsiest paper, rented costly special locomotives to beat the *Constitution* into rural Georgia (dispensing champagne to all the country editors on the initial run), and waged special promotional giveaways to increase *Herald* subscriptions.[84] Nobody paid much attention to the business office, where Grady was ludicrously miscast as business manager. "The principal idea," Joel Chandler Harris fondly recalled, "was to print the best newspaper in the South, and for a time this scheme was carried out in a magnificent way that could not last."[85]

When Abrams left the *Herald* in 1873, the twenty-three-year-old Grady became managing editor.[86] He continued the paper's enterprising search for news and headline-grabbing stories but now altered the *Herald*'s policies to conform more closely to New South principles and to foster his New Departure political stance. The ideas for which Grady became famous in the 1880s emerged in the mid-1870s but do not seem to have created much stir. Moderating the *Herald*'s political tone was easy enough; home rule had been achieved in 1871, and white Georgians were steadily gaining a sense of security. Grady never encountered the fearful political pressure which finally broke Francis Dawson. Financial problems were another matter, however. Atlanta in the early 1870s was still too small to sustain two morning dailies of the ambition and caliber of the *Herald* and the *Constitution*. The *Herald* borrowed heavily, continually lost money, and early in 1876, when funds ran out and creditors became importunate, it closed its doors and sold its equipment and goodwill to the *Constitution*.[87]

Rebounding from the collapse of the *Herald*, Grady threw his money and himself into two other journalistic ventures, both of which failed within a few months. Broke at last, and thrown upon his own resources for the first time, Grady remained undaunted. He cheerfully hunted for jobs and was hired in rapid succession as special Georgia correspondent by the *New York Herald* and as editorial reporter by the *Atlanta Constitution*. He was an immediate success in free-lance journalism and by 1878 was writing for at least six journals including Watterson's, which, one supposes, made him one of "Watterson's boys."[88] "I have written more about the South, I suppose, than any ten men living," he claimed in 1881.[89]

Spending much of his time on trains, rushing to and fro to report the news, Grady acquired a firsthand view of a changing South. In 1876 Grady reported the Ellenton riots in South Carolina and scooped his rivals in covering the Florida election frauds, winning by this last coup a prominent display in the *New York Herald* and in the *Constitution*. Between 1876 and 1880 he conducted interviews with famous Americans, reported the South's every forward economic stride, and wrote numerous human interest stories—all of which required a versatility beyond the ken of the specialized political reporter.[90]

At last, in 1880 Henry W. Grady secured an important editorial position when he purchased a quarter interest in the *Atlanta Constitution* by means of a timely loan from New York manufacturer and financier Cyrus Field. As managing editor, controlling all of the news and editorial departments, Grady found himself perfectly suited to an expanding and prosperous Atlanta. Fortunately the *Constitution* had a strong business manager in Captain Evan Howell, Confederate veteran, politician, and businessman. The partnership of Grady, Howell, and Joel Chandler Harris, all extraordinarily able men in their complementary fields, catalyzed the creation of "the South's standard newspaper," the *Atlanta Constitution*.[91]

By 1880 Watterson, Dawson, and Grady had learned their craft in the hard-fought battles of recent years and had established their credentials as authoritative city and state thunderers who represented their communities and had access to the established powers in their region. Ahead lay annual campaigns to develop the South, struggles to overcome regional lethargy, daily vigilance in defense of their cities against the encroachments and claims of Southern rivals, yearly contests to ensure the triumph of the only political party that mattered, constant efforts to monitor North-South relations and rebut Yankee aspersions, never-ending editorial concern for an improved and harmonious racial climate (which would leave political, economic, and social relations essentially unchanged), and, overall, an intense commitment to moving their region toward the twentieth century. Massive poverty, virulent racism, and limited journalistic opportunities, however, placed constraints on their progressive tendencies. How could their battles be won? New South editors aspired to be all things to all people. They would unify Southern leadership and please dominant economic and political groups, present themselves as the articulate voice of the enlightened middle and upper classes seeking prosperity for all, and essentially monopolize their respective states' daily journalism in an effort to rank close to the metropolitan giants to the north. In this way they developed the clout which would make up for the lack of mass circulation. Fervent boosterism, editorial jeremiads, and fully developed, accurate news stories impressed readers even if they sometimes failed to modernize Southern thinking. In 1880 Watterson, Dawson, and Grady stood on the threshold of their most productive years; by the end of the decade they were the preeminent New South spokesmen and harbingers of the New Journalism.

8
Three Giants of the New South
Triumph in the Eighties

For long periods in the 1870s and 1880s Henry Watterson's *Louisville Courier-Journal*, Francis Warrington Dawson's *Charleston News and Courier*, and Henry Grady's *Atlanta Constitution* were the only significant morning dailies in their respective cities. No other Southern editor would have as much national influence as Watterson and Grady, at least until the rise of the *Atlanta Constitution*'s Ralph McGill in the mid-twentieth century. Ideologically Watterson, Dawson, and Grady seemed to be all of a piece, as each accepted, though in varying degrees, the importance of the New South gospel and the New Journalism. Nevertheless each editor had his own journalistic style, and each fashioned a unique newspaper expressing his own personality and reflecting the opportunities and nature of his journalistic field.

From time to time successful editors have essayed to enlighten the public on the guiding principles of their profession or to instruct their rivals or employees upon the duties of an editor. Henry Watterson, Francis Warrington Dawson, and Henry Grady occasionally spoke in this avuncular fashion, and if their papers did not always come up to their noble journalistic ideals, these ideals nevertheless were significant, reflecting honest intentions and the extent to which these editors grasped some of the modern trends sweeping American journalism.

The journalistic ideals of Watterson and Dawson were quite similar. Both visualized the editor as a great lord, ruling his newspaper and commanding the respect and even the deference of his readers. The great editor was more than a mere writer; intimately familiar with every aspect of the newspaper business, exerting undisputed editorial authority, he stamped his unique personality and style upon every paragraph of his paper.[1] Editing a modern urban journal was not a job but a calling, one far more influential for good or evil than political office, the bar, or the pulpit. Never known to reject the moral high ground, editors of urban dailies in the 1880s portrayed themselves as objective professionals above grubby factionalism—as dedicated servants educating the people and guarding them against all enemies.[2] A journalist of any kind had to be wholly devoted to his work. Dawson, criticizing his *News and Courier* reporters who abandoned their work during Charleston's great earthquake of 1886, huffed, "Perhaps I ought not to call it cowardice, but they thought more of running after their families than of sticking to their posts."[3]

Although the era of personal journalism had begun to wane when Dawson and Watterson rose to prominence in the 1870s, personalism would remain a factor throughout the century, and the leadership of the daily press exhibited a mix of "curmudgeons, civic uplifters, and ballyhoo experts."[4] Both Watterson and Dawson thought of themselves as redeeming the personal style from the ignorant, abusive pettiness of their predecessors. Watterson once described the old-fashioned editor as "a mere player, strutting and fretting his hour upon the stage, acting a part by command of his liege lord, the party leader." These primitives, he recalled, "wrote fierce nonsense, and fought duels, and hickuped Fourth of July orations every day of the year in exceeding bad grammar. Journalism in those days was a sort of inebrious knight-errantry; a big joke, considerably drunken and blood-stained."[5] Watterson believed that wit rather than savagery should inspire the personal exchanges and criticisms that added spice to newspaper stories. If an editor had to accuse or arraign an individual, he should apply the laws of courtroom evidence.[6] In reviewing his editorial career, Watterson thought that he had rejected the worst aspect of personal journalism, filth, and had toned down vindictive quarrels while maintaining the prime benefit of personalism which he described as "character"—a clearly identifiable and accountable voice.[7]

For much of his later career, Francis Dawson offered a good example of the more positive aspects of personal journalism, which he idealized for its outspokenness and crusading qualities. But both Dawson and Grady, unlike Watterson, found the quarrels which invariably enveloped a forthright editor most unpleasant and annoying. Once entrenched at the top of South Carolina's press, Dawson avoided needlessly provocative writing, even in the most censorious of his editorials.[8] He lectured his star reporter against the use of bad-tempered and querulous (though basically truthful) descriptions which involved the paper in needless controversy, ordered employees to "kill anything that can possibly be considered libellous," and went to great lengths to avoid offending members of white minorities.[9] On one occasion he red-penciled "Christian morality" for fear of angering Jews, and on another occasion struck out a reference to German laxity in deference to the sensitivities of one of Charleston's more important political pressure groups.[10] His rejection of certain aspects of personalism is all the more notable when contrasted with his hard-hitting style during Reconstruction. Some Northern observers, however, interpreted avoidance of personal quarrels (which sometimes included the rejection of an independent, critical course) as an indication of a more modern style of journalism.

Perhaps no ideal of journalism concerned Watterson and Dawson more than independence from party domination. As Dawson had learned in 1876, dedication to truthful news and honest analysis was sometimes irreconcilable with performance of personal service for partisan success.[11] Although both the *Courier-Journal* and the *News and Courier* were good Southern Democratic papers, their editors frequently proclaimed their independent stance. Northern journals occasionally scoffed. The *Kalamazoo* (Michigan) *Herald* cynically remarked: "Hypocrisy is the homage that vice pays to virtue, and the fact that partisan newspapers assume the name of 'independent' proves an important proposition, viz.: It shows that there is a large and increasing class of citizens who prefer political independence in their newspapers and these pretended 'independent' journals assume the name to secure their patronage."[12] Undoubtedly there was much truth in the *Herald*'s statement. Nevertheless the ideal of independence was very real for Watterson and Dawson. They believed that advocacy of a party's cause on the editorial pages did not preclude impartial news reporting and analysis, and they asserted their right to criticize Democratic candidates and policies. Moreover, a firm rule for both editors, broken only once, briefly, by Watterson, was the avoidance of political office-seeking or any other outside entanglement which might sully the editor's reputation for impartiality.[13] "The soul of journalism," Watterson thundered, "is disinterestedness," an ideal which he thought his *Courier-Journal* had pioneered in Kentucky: "Anterior to its coming, the newspapers of Louisville had largely looked to Main street for their business, to Frankfort [the capital] for their party orders. None of them was strong enough to stand upon its merits and its rights, and to go its own gait, regardless of the merchants and the politicians. The Courier-Journal flew the flag of freedom from the first. It proposed to be its own master—to do its own leading—and, if die it must, to die fighting."[14]

The editorial page was, of course, the heart of the paper. The nation marveled at Watterson's profuse outpourings for Democratic principles, his "Star-eyed Goddess of Tariff Reform," his blistering anathemas, and whimsical sallies. The lengthy, erudite constitutional essay, typical of Thomas Ritchie's day, had no place in this journalism.[15]

Dawson used his editorial page frequently as a forum to enlighten South Carolinians, for abuses which escaped public notice often caught the journalistic eye. "It is his [the editor's] duty to remonstrate, to rebuke, and to condemn when pernicious plans are afoot."[16] The editor must be a man of courage. Long after his 1876 debacle, Dawson mused, "In buying a newspaper the public do not buy men's souls. Yet it is expected, many a time, that the newspaper shall bow obsequiously to the demands of its readers, and, right or wrong, echo their complaints. Of what worth is such a newspaper—a journalistic chameleon that takes the hue of what it feeds on?"[17] Dawson hoped that the better sentiment of the community would prevail, that society would tolerate the editor's honest differences of opinion.[18] On race, Democratic solidarity, and home rule Dawson learned otherwise, but on other issues he did encounter sufficient tolerance to maintain his independence.

Although the editorial department was their chief concern, neither Watterson nor Dawson neglected the news pages, which many journalists by the 1870s considered the key to success. "The daily journal must be above everything else," affirmed Watterson, "a newspaper."[19] He supposedly once remarked that journalism was the art of knowing where hell was going to break loose and having a man there to cover it, yet he also specifically rejected sensationalism, scandal, and "many things not fit to be told that amuse or disgust the public."[20] Late in life he proudly declared the South the last bastion of chastity in journalism.[21] Watterson defined the news as "trustworthy information, of some use, interest, and import, recent enough to be given to the public for the first time; and if commented upon, to be fairly commented upon"—a definition which Dawson would have accepted.[22]

As more and more journals modernized by augmenting their reportorial staffs and news budgets and as technology made news gathering easier yet more sophisticated, the front page set the pace and standard of journalism.[23] What then of the editorial page? For Dawson and Watterson its function and importance did not change, and on this matter they clung to a traditional and increasingly obsolescent view. After the exhilaration, the distractions, and the excitement of the news pages, wrote Watterson, the editorial ought "to be as a raised dais in the center of a great hall, a seat of power and charm; an elevation to survey the passing show" and expose its deeper meaning.[24]

Such ideals never had much attraction for Henry Grady. The younger man first won fame as a peripatetic freelance reporter. Even as a nationally famous editor, Grady still thought the reporter the aristocrat of journalism and perceived the "elevation" of a good reporter to an editorial chair as a loss to the profession.[25] "News is the feature and opinions are of secondary importance," he wrote in the 1880s. "If I see a dog fight and think I can hit if off to suit the reader, I'm going to do it."[26] The new journalist needed a flair for showmanship. One of Grady's favorite books, predictably, was P.T. Barnum's autobiography,[27] but Grady unlike Barnum, used his showman's talents for the promotion of public enterprises.

Different from Watterson and Dawson in many ways, Grady agreed with them at least in arguing that journalism needed a distinctively personal quality. If ever a journalist should have succeeded, Grady once wrote, it was his former colleague, Alexander St. Clair-Abrams. Unfortunately, Abrams wrote as if editing the London *Times*, which made for stellar metropolitan journalism but a cold and unsympathetic paper for Atlanta's readers. "In small cities," Grady concluded, "there must be provincial touches in the journal—concessions that the journalist must make to circumstances."[28] Grady knew that the reading public wanted to see the man behind the pen, so he threw his engaging personality into the *Constitution*.

Like Watterson and Dawson, Grady had no use for the officeholding editor, and he refused to run for office though a congressional seat was almost a certainty. One of his editorials repudiating a political career in favor of journalism drew favorable comment from over one hundred editors throughout the country.[29] Grady and Dawson, unlike Watterson, disdained the trappings and glory of a national or regional political power broker, which for the first half of the nineteenth century had been the standard gauge of journalistic stardom.[30] Influence in state politics and state economic development attracted the Georgian and the South Carolinian. If, as Joel Chandler Harris said, an editor must have a mission, Grady found his mission in the promotion of Atlanta and the New South, and the *Atlanta Constitution* became an outstanding booster paper.[31]

By the 1880s Henry Watterson occupied a secure place in the front rank of America's journalists. Ballard Smith, a New York editor and former coworker, concluded that the editorial page of the *Courier-Journal* dictated the politics of Kentucky and the South.[32] Superintending all news coverage of the *Courier-Journal*, and making the editorial page his own preserve, Watterson became the *Courier-Journal's* "best advertisement, its best source of news, its reason for being a national instead of a small provincial paper."[33] Flattered by national and international attention, "he came to regard himself as something of a dean of journalism."[34]

The *Courier-Journal* excelled in reporting national and international political news, but its editorial page was its greatest asset.[35] Challenging, vibrant, and informative as well as fearless and independent, the editorial page sparked controversy and debate. If Watterson's choice of sides in the conflicts perpetually swirling around him was frequently unexpected, people at least considered him honest; that perception helped to ensure a large readership throughout the nation.[36] Kentuckian Isaac Marcosson, author and interviewer, recalled that in his boyhood days men did not ask each other, "'What is in the paper to-day?' The daily query was, 'What does Watterson say this morning?'"[37] And what he said was sometimes as unconventional as it was unpredictable. When taken to task for breaking with Grover Cleveland, the first Democratic president in twenty-five years, Watterson answered by asserting that he spoke the truth as he saw it, and concluded, "Things have come to a hell of a pass when a man can't wallop his own jackass."[38]

Watterson was a brilliant if not always welcome critic of his own party, but he also stood for positive policies: he campaigned in season and out for honest, efficient, decentralized government, sound money, and tariff reform. He wrote these goals into the party platforms of 1876, 1884, and 1888, and coined slogans and phrases evocative of Democratic beliefs, such as a "tariff for revenue only" and the "Star-eyed Goddess of Tariff Reform."[39]

Until the meteoric rise of Henry Grady, Watterson stood unchallenged as the nation's New South advocate. Pioneering the theme of reconciliation in the 1870s, Watterson—heralded rather extravagantly as "the evangel of healing and the apostle of brotherhood"—defused the partisan use of sectionalism and seemingly sought justice for the black man.[40] On race he was more liberal than Grady,[41] and despite Grady's eventual near monopoly of the industrial issue, Watterson pioneered in that area also. He steadily encouraged his readers to emulate Yankee energy, industry, and thrift, boomed the coming of railroads and cotton mills, praised Southern efforts at crop diversification, and rolled out the welcome mat for Northern investors, who quickly learned that when the lines were drawn between labor and capital, the latter could always count on the *Courier-Journal* for support.[42]

Despite his New South endeavors, Watterson devoted surprisingly little attention to the daily activities associated with Louisville's development. Dawson and Grady, in contrast, gravitated to every booster activity in their towns. The great enthusiasm Atlanta exhibited for Grady found no parallel in Louisville and Watterson,[43] perhaps because Watterson focused on issues of national importance, many of which appeared more attractive to Northern audiences than realistic or practical to Southern industrialists, farmers, and workers. Watterson's New South credentials were justly earned, but they were the result of a national dream and were not translated immediately into a Louisville or Kentucky renaissance.

Gifted with the rare ability to enliven even the dullest subjects, Watterson created an editorial page that struck the nation's fancy.[44] Such topics as greenbackism and the tariff, soporific stuff in other newspapers, metamorphosed into a grand drama of the people against the insidious Rag Baby or the Money Devil.[45] He could use the rapier as well as the bludgeon. The Grant administration, he quietly remarked, "was not long in becoming an affair of horses and dogs supplemented by the companionship of spirits congenial to the enjoyment of these luxuries."[46] Visiting the nation's capital, Watterson sweetly reported, "It occurred to me that Washington would be a nice, quiet place to get a good night's rest. And, sure enough, I find it as reposeful as a drowsy sermon or a dose of chloral. Intellectually it was always the sleepiest city in America. They only excite their bodies here. They rarely think, and never tire their minds."[47] Sometimes, rather unpredictably, he chose the bludgeon. Irritated by the extravagance of New York society women, he discarded the Kentucky charm and scribbled a blistering indictment headlined "A Flock of Unclean Birds," and for weeks thereafter his editorial was the subject of a roiling debate. When the Louisville editor had something to say, he wanted it read and remembered.[48]

Watterson thrived on jousting with the knaves and fools of the world.[49] The *Courier-Journal* pictured a Manichean world, with Watterson's innocent and virtuous journal under attack from the forces of darkness. "Always has it [the *Courier-Journal*] been subjected to the enmity of the vicious and the venal—to organized misrepresentation, constant, unscrupulous, and methodical—the tribute that envy pays to success."[50] Some imbroglios were matters of high policy; others were petty and trivial; all were colorful. Watterson explained his quarrel with President Cleveland with characteristic energy: "The people are not a huddle of children playing at hide-and-seek, nor the press a dark closet for the concealment of dirty linen, nor the President a sacred beast to be slicked over each morning with a bit of pickled pork. The more light there is, the more truth; the less blind servility to power."[51] The young Mark Sullivan, blundering into a Watterson controversy, was dismissed as a wharf rat who had crept unnoticed into a respectable journal, clutching his editorial pencil—"an irresponsible bit of lead at one end and a fool at the other."[52]

"He was at his best while attacking,"[53] one scholar has concluded. But despite almost constant quarreling, sometimes with as many as four editors at once, Watterson made amazingly few enemies. Most of his editorial quarrels involved horseplay rather than enmity, and his editorial colleagues forgave him much because they found him a warm-hearted, sympathetic friend. They looked upon him "as too genial to be heroic, too humane to be a headsman, too fundamentally broadminded to be the hide-bound partizan his editorials" professed. As he aged, myth embellished reality and he became "Marse Henry," the prototypical, bourbon-drinking, improvident Kentucky colonel.[54] Watterson looked the part and on occasion drank plenty of beer or champagne and indulged his fondness for poker (which, incidentally, he played poorly).[55] The *New York Times* affectionately described a reception for Marse Henry in 1887: "As many members of the Press Club as the clubrooms would hold gathered yesterday to welcome the blue grass editor, Col. Henry Watterson. Kentucky horses, whisky, beauty, and editors, as well as the 'star-eyed goddess,' were battered about like tennis balls by a dozen clever tongues."[56] From time to time Watterson expressed annoyance at the "Marse Henry" stereotype; yet he liked it well enough to use "Marse Henry" as the title for his autobiography, and he often went out of his way to play the role. His lecture on "Money and Morals" began: "I am going to talk to you about money and morals. I am well equipped for I have neither."[57] Actually he had both, but he knew what his public expected to hear.

Watterson "more than any other," concluded Elmer Clarke of the *Arkansas Democrat* in 1919, "has stood in the eyes of the world for Kentucky and the Old South, the land of work and play and joy-in-life, and of 'the fair fight and no gouging.'"[58] Useful as such an image may have been both in replacing the Ku Klux Klan reputation of the South and in advancing Watterson's career, it obscured much of Watterson's real achievement in journalism. That the public, for the most part, accepted the lovable Kentucky colonel image in the 1880s and forgot about the rabble-rousing wartime editor of the *Rebel* serves as an indication of the nation's success at reconciliation. Unfortunately for Watterson, however, the "Marse Henry" image was so prevalent that some readers refused to take him seriously. "In spite of his talents, brilliancy, and services," Joseph Rogers concluded, "his name ever provokes a smile . . . his genial personality stands out in such marked contrast to his preachments that the people read and say: 'Go it, Marse Henry,' and then laugh."[59]

Even more troublesome for any complete assessment of Watterson's journalism is the suspicion of irresponsibility. Watterson so loved political quarrels and the success of his extravagant style that he sometimes forgot about everything—including his own principles about the application of courtroom rules of evidence—except the next bit of repartee in the *Courier-Journal*.[60] The page-one events of the day, though fully reported, too often appeared to the *Courier-Journal's* public through the prism of "the little Pope of Democracy." His headlines often exhibited bias, as when he wrote "Congress Votes to Grind into the Dust the Honest Yeomanry of the Land."[61] Francis Warrington Dawson found Watterson erratic and altogether too likely to surrender to his penchant for the smart saying.[62] Even the irrepressible Henry Grady thought his editorials too flippant and his reputation warped by his well-known whims and fancies.[63] *The Journalist*, one of Watterson's few real enemies, lampooned his ludicrous "Star-eyed Goddess of Tariff Reform," declaring that he was getting to be a "howling maniac on the subject of stars."[64]

The charges of irresponsibility went back at least to Reconstruction when Watterson had once briefly crusaded for a third term and military dictatorship for Grant. But the incident most damaging to his reputation was the "100,000 demonstrators" episode. At the peak of the sectional crisis over the disputed presidential election of 1876,[65] in a letter from Washington, Watterson counseled peace in such belligerent but ambiguous tones that he was thought to be advocating mob action. Many citizens, wrote a friend, "saw visions of a hundred thousand Kentucky colonels, their white mustaches quivering with anger, advancing upon the national capital with horse-pistols and mint juleps."[66] Overblown style obscured his serious message about the right of peaceful petition. Watterson complained that his words had been misunderstood, but Henry Pringle shrewdly concluded, "This was a confession of sin, although it was true. Marse Henry would have dismissed an editorial writer who had similarly failed to make himself clear."[67] A Thomas Nast cartoon of the time depicted Watterson puffing clouds of steam while the editor of the *Cincinnati Commercial* poured ice water on his head.[68]

Thereafter, anyone who disagreed with Watterson found it easy to label him irresponsible. A good example appears in Watterson's break with President Cleveland, who—because of his devotion to limited government and honest, efficient administration and his interest in tariff reform—could have expected Watterson's support. Few could fathom Watterson's criticism of Cleveland; many attributed it to pure perversity. Perhaps Watterson took umbrage at the president because he considered him a tariff reformer *manqué*. He certainly thought Cleveland a "bull in a china shop."[69] Historian Allan Nevins simply concluded that Watterson was "brilliant, hotheaded and irresponsible," an assessment many exasperated Democratic editors would surely have accepted.[70]

Francis Warrington Dawson of the *Charleston News and Courier* was a much less colorful figure than Henry Watterson, and he addressed a much smaller constituency. Nevertheless Dawson made his paper one of the South's most important journals in the 1880s. As co-owner of the *News and Courier* and after 1882 as president of the News and Courier

Company, Dawson commanded every aspect of his paper from setting its national policy to choosing the kind of packing thread used.[71] The editorial page, interpreting the political and business world in terms of Democratic doctrine, remained Dawson's first love, as it was Watterson's, but Dawson spoke to South Carolina in clear, serious, eminently logical editorials and rejected as far as possible unnecessary rhetorical flourishes. Dawson preferred to limit daily editorial matter to two carefully crafted and uncrowded columns; he abhorred the cluttered style of the smaller papers' editorial pages, whose overworked staffs disfigured the issues of most Southern dailies.[72] He avoided personal controversy, even making it standard *News and Courier* policy never to mention his own name unnecessarily. Like Grady, but in contrast to Watterson, Dawson made a favorable impression as a public servant and city father, organizing charities, serving as harbor commissioner, and joining the Charleston Chamber of Commerce and the Hibernian Society. Such community activities and nonpolitical offices built goodwill and kept Dawson on top of city developments. Both the *News and Courier* and the *Atlanta Constitution* contained better local coverage than the *Louisville Courier-Journal*.

Dawson tried to strike a happy medium between the narrowly focused political sheets of an earlier era and the contemporary rage for newspapers of sensationalism, literature, and illustrations. Newspapers, he advised, were not to take the place of histories, novels, essays, and art publications.[73] To report all the news accurately and comment on it fairly—to be like the *New York Times* rather than Joseph Pulitzer's vulgar *New York World*—was his ideal, although he made many concessions to popular journalism:

Be careful [he instructed his employees] to avoid running too heavily on crimes. Unless the circumstances are particularly striking or novel, it is not necessary to say much more about them. We can't afford to make The News and Courier in any sense a "Newgate Calendar." Every day we ought to have some light reading matter and something funny. Remember also that the womenfolk are a power, and that they ought to be pleased, as far as possible. They like fashions, society talk, and innocent scandal. On the fifth page we should have about two columns each day entirely outside of politics. Literary matter is always good for these purposes and so is scientific news.[74]

With no real competition in South Carolina between 1878 and 1888, the *News and Courier* returned lucrative profits for its owners. "The paper is making barrels of money," wrote its star reporter, Narciso Gener Gonzales, in 1882. "This year the net profits are 50 per cent or $50,000. A dividend of 25 per cent has been distributed and the rest devoted to improvements."[75] In the mid-1880s the *News and Courier* opened bureaus in Washington, D.C., Augusta, Georgia, and Columbia, South Carolina, hired correspondents for other key South Carolina locations, and maintained an exclusive Associated Press franchise.[76] In 1884 it expanded from four to eight pages and acquired a new, much superior press (a "Web-Perfecting Type-Revolving and Folding Machine") which could print, paste, cut, and fold at the rate of twelve thousand papers an hour. In 1887 the paper went to sixteen pages and two editions, and in that year the *News and Courier* earned a thirty-thousand-dollar profit on a capital valuation of three hundred thousand dollars.[77]

Firm boundaries, however, circumscribed the *News and Courier*'s potential growth. The limited journalistic field of Charleston and South Carolina narrowed the paper's financial support from advertising and subscriptions and thus constricted its news-gathering potential. The excellent reportorial and editorial staff—as large as any in the state even as late as the 1930s—was much smaller than the huge forces mustered by metropolitan journals, and it was simply overworked. Lacking funds to hire many reporters and correspondents outside the state, unable to pay for a great number of special reports or letters, Dawson still relied heavily on old-fashioned newspaper exchanges and the editorial scissors, reading some five hundred Southern daily and seventy-five state weekly exchanges.[78] For national news the *News and Courier* depended on the *New York Times, New York Herald, Philadelphia Times,* and *Baltimore Sun.*[79] By comparison with the great journals growing in the urban centers of America, Dawson's *News and Courier* was a shoestring operation.

Fortunately, the *News and Courier* depended more on Dawson's political power than on its out-of-state news coverage. After flirting with heresy in 1876, Dawson threw himself into the day-to-day operation of the Democratic party and the local and state governments. During the 1880s he served on the Democratic subcommittee for the South Atlantic states.[80] Within South Carolina, Dawson wielded the party whip. He had championed Democrats against Republican wrong-doers in Reconstruction and driven out many an enemy. A prominent Georgia Republican wrote, "Liberty of the press in South Carolina! There is none. The metropolitan Thunderer, the *News and Courier*, issues its Jovian mandate, and the country newspapers croak, 'Me, too; Me, too; Me, too,' like the little, slender frogs in the pond when some huge amphibian makes general proclamation."[81] When Narciso Gonzales crowed that "The News and Courier is the greatest power in the State," he made no idle boast, as B.W. Edwards, an aspirant for office, knew.[82] Edwards confidentially sought Dawson's assurance of fair treatment, since "that canvass will be, so far as the people will ever know, very much what the News and Courier sets it down."[83] In the South Carolina of the 1880s Dawson could not possibly live up to his ideals of independence and impartiality. "Everyone is entitled to fair play, of course," he wrote to Gonzales, "but to our friends we must always be especially kind."[84] For political enemies there was usually silence, occasionally fair coverage, and from time to time the bludgeon.[85]

Although Dawson spoke his mind and could never be considered as simply the mouthpiece of a statehouse ring, ultimately his *News and Courier* must be read as the organ of the conservative regime entrenched since 1877. Always the friend of textile mill owners and developers, Dawson defended and encouraged long hours of labor for millworkers and the employment of women and children, which he viewed as an opportunity for wealth, mobility, and social improvement via mill village schools and churches. He spoke always for agricultural improvement, scientific farming, and a more profitable mix of corn over cotton, but his concern was largely for modernization and the commercial success of South Carolina and Charleston rather than for the plight of the state's poorest farmers and croppers. On matters of capital and labor, business development, and honest, efficient, low-tax government, Dawson stood shoulder to shoulder with the ruling group.[86] By the late 1880s Dawson so dominated the Palmetto State that Ben Tillman and the forces of agrarian unrest "would seek power, not by attacking an elected official but rather the editor of the *Charleston News and Courier*."[87]

The *News and Courier* has attracted historical attention as much for its New South boosterism as for its political power, and indeed these features were often inextricably intertwined. In the 1880s Dawson joined Watterson, Grady, and a host of other Southern publicists in proclaiming that "the South had buried its resentments and had entered a new era of good feeling based upon an integration of material interests."[88] Good feelings were expressed especially for the benefit of Northern developers, but there was often plenty of resentment directed at urban or state rivals. When Grady received the lion's share of the acclaim for the economic rebirth phenomenon with his 1886 New South speech and thus obscured Dawson's pioneering role, Dawson grew jealous, peevishly lashing out at Georgia and Grady in the columns of the *News and Courier*. Grady's success hurt all the more because Dawson believed that South Carolina never received its due for its agricultural and industrial progress, but the quarrel antedated Grady's New South apotheosis. Three years before Grady's famous New South speech Dawson publicly recognized a South Carolina–Georgia rivalry and announced South Carolina's intention to surpass Georgia in industrial development. He also sniped at Georgia's factional politics. Fuel was added to the simmering dispute when Grady criticized the South Carolina phosphate industry (a *News and Courier* darling) for its tendency to encourage cotton over corn. There seemed to be an infinite variety of subjects about which Grady could rile Dawson: Grady referred to Charleston, accurately enough, as the citadel of the old regime, Grady's Yankee protectionism offended Dawson's low-tariff principles, and Grady's scoop of the *News and Courier* in national coverage of Charleston's earthquake in September 1886 drove Dawson nearly to distraction.[89]

Since the two shared most of the same goals, Dawson picked his quarrel on a point of Southern pride rather than of policy. Grady, Dawson complained, was too apologetic and forgetful of Southern principles, too free with confessions of Southern errors before a New York and New England audience in his famous address. "It is not for the sons to apologize for their fathers whose homes and honors they inherit. They need no apology; they require no excuse or defense for the lives they lived, the principles they upheld, the long hopeless struggle they made."[90] Dawson, the scarred veteran of war and Reconstruction, found Grady's optimism exasperating. He wrote almost enviously about those who were too young "to have had any connection with the war, and free from the prejudices which, more or less, affect the feelings of those who shared the glory and sorrow of the men who wore the grey."[91] From this level the editorial insults descended to petty banter about Grady's looks (handsome he was not) and Dawson's silk socks and underwear (which Dawson said were better than none).[92]

Happily, the editors were soon on cordial terms again. In February 1887, Dawson made two speeches to garner a share of the New South glory. He confessed to his wife that he was an awful orator, but since "I had been amongst the first to sow, I thought it advisable to keep to the front myself."[93] In New York he addressed the subject of free trade and in Baltimore spoke about the soul of the Confederacy, "Our Women in the War."[94]

An estrangement between Dawson and Grady seemed almost unavoidable. Dawson belonged to the war generation which was in honor bound to revere the sacrifices of the men in grey, and among Dawson's many disagreements with the younger man was his objection to Grady's admission that slavery was a root cause of the war. The political temper of Charleston, furthermore, necessitated caution in making aspersions about the Old South, a sensibility of which Dawson the outsider was acutely aware. Finally, the differences between Atlanta, with an ebullience born of urban growth and industrial boom, and Charleston, the city of memories and a quaint past, enhanced Grady's optimism and made Dawson's task much more difficult.[95]

Dawson deserved and actually won much acclaim for his New South stand. As early as January 1868, he had written that the lessons of the past "taught the Southern planter that he cannot live by cotton alone," and for years prior to Grady's success he elaborated a creed of hard work, development of manufactures, growth of cities, extension of railroads, and gradual education of the people.[96] But the life of the pioneer is not easy. In portraying a new Southern ideal so soon after the war, he implied—however unintentionally—dissatisfaction with the Old South, and in voicing moderation during the dark days of Reconstruction he drew upon himself the wrath of the embittered resisters. Moreover, Charleston suffered from more serious obstacles to economic development than did Atlanta or Louisville.

Yet Dawson became, in the words of Narciso Gonzales, Charleston's herald of hope. He campaigned for harbor development, improved port facilities, and rail outlets to the west, but failed in all three endeavors largely because of Charleston's heavy debt, lack of capital, and the inertia and despair of a decayed planter and commercial elite. With considerable temerity, given his sometimes insecure status, the editor grumbled about old fogeyism and bemoaned his city's lack of ambition and talent: "the importation of about five hundred Yankees of the right stripe would put a new face on affairs, and make the whole place throb with life and vivid force." After the collapse of efforts to construct a tourist hotel in Charleston, Dawson suggested that a new hotel could be built on Mars with less difficulty than in Charleston.[97] When the causes of Charleston's difficulties were discussed, Dawson called for retrenchment yet paradoxically still spread the booster spirit.[98] Charleston might well have declined much farther had there been no powerful journal to lift morale and inspire hope.

Had Dawson's *News and Courier* always remained a loyal party workhorse and New South booster it would have been a good but unexceptional Southern paper. Dawson, however, saw too clearly the backwardness of his state and the excesses of the South Carolina character. A tradition of social criticism had never developed in Southern journalism,[99] but in Charleston, the least hospitable location, Dawson's *News and Courier* became in the 1880s a gadfly on society. Almost as if it were Boston or New York City, there suddenly emerged in Charleston a voice for liberal reform—a Southern-style mugwump.

Despite the harrowing experience of 1876, his desire to avoid controversy, and his position as spokesman for a conservative regime, Dawson proved to be an enlightened and courageous critic. His earlier inclination toward fusion with Republicans was somewhat analogous to the genuine political independence of Northern mugwumps, although true independence from parties was impossible for an editor of a powerful Southern urban daily. Dawson exhibited a penchant for political mugwumpery in other ways: he fought political corruption with civil service reform and suffrage restriction (but was willing to buy votes in extreme situations to prevent worse evils, or so he implied), argued for low tariffs (with some protection for Southern industry), and supported a strong, independent regulatory commission for South Carolina railroads. In modest ways he saw the need to ease the burden of the unfortunate and to expand opportunities for the less successful members of society: he advocated women's rights, spoke in favor of reformatories to segregate youthful offenders from hardened criminals, "resisted efforts to restrict immigration, resented any discrimination based on a man's religion, rebuked the nation for its shabby treatment of the Indian, fought zealously for Irish home rule, and felt that labor often got a raw deal." [100]

Dawson became a celebrated critic of South Carolina's violence and mob law. He waged a crusade against pistols, whiskey, and gambling. Demanding that on duelling South Carolina choose between civilization and barbarism, he was largely successful in driving the custom from the state. [101] Nor would the editor hide the evils of the chain gang. "Criminals are sent to the Penitentiary in punishment for their offences against the law," he wrote, "and not to be put to death by slow torture, for economic or any other reasons." In the best tradition of the latter-day muckrakers, he dramatized the system's inhumanity by exposing one gang in which 17 percent of the convicts had died within six weeks. [102] Not infrequently, editorial appeals to justice and morality accompanied his criticisms. After an outbreak of mob violence in Allendale, South Carolina, the *News and Courier* demanded an acknowledgment of the supremacy of the law over community spirit or community action. "There is no other way than this, that we know of, in which South Carolina can secure and maintain a reputation as a law-abiding State, and in which the rights and interests of all of us shall be adequately protected. We may not prevent the violation of the law. We do not desire to [keep] any citizen from protecting his own life. But we insist that, when blood has been shed, the Courts, and not newspapers or citizens, shall decide, upon a fair trial by an impartial jury, what is the measure of personal responsibility and where it rests." [103]

In regard to race, Dawson was a paternalistic white supremacist; his moderate policies and somewhat contradictory editorials suggest that he recognized that blacks were fellow human beings with rights which could not be ignored. Nevertheless, blacks must be restrained so that they would not become the proverbial millstone to drag down South Carolina's whites. White control and philanthropy and black self-help were keys to modest uplift and more harmonious race relations. Victorious in the racial battles of Reconstruction, Dawson in the 1880s envisioned a permanent black presence in politics, but not necessarily in the Republican party and certainly not controlling the state. His paper on many occasions provided impartial coverage of events in Charleston's black community, spoke favorably of black education, and ridiculed the idea of segregated railroad cars. With such stories the *News and Courier* attempted to make real its verbal welcome of black subscribers while simultaneously disparaging "Cuffee's" aspirations for genuine equality. Showcasing rhetoric rather than real achievement, Dawson's approach to black South Carolina offered minimal hope; still, he could have done nothing, or he could have actively fought any post-Reconstruction advancement of blacks. If not the black man's friend, he was not his worst enemy; after Dawson's death, *News and Courier* policy hardened toward blacks.[104]

Northern editors viewed the *News and Courier* as the Bible of South Carolina's affairs and recognized Dawson's special role in Southern life. For example, the *New York Herald* applauded the *News and Courier*'s editor when in 1888, after the defeat of the Democratic presidential candidate, he reassured Southerners that there would be no return to the politics of the color line, that Radicalism had been tried and had failed, and that the nation's mutual economic progress and the millions of Northern and Western capital invested in the South precluded any resort to coercive legislation.[105] Most Northern editors appreciated and applauded Dawson's agitation for a new South, and many were even more impressed by his campaign against violence and his defense of the law.[106] When South Carolina banned duelling, the nation's press rang with praise for the man most responsible, Francis Warrington Dawson. The *New Haven* (Connecticut) *News* paid him a glowing tribute:

We do not understand why the influence of Mr. Dawson (lately knighted by the Pope), of the Charleston *News and Courier*, should not be more generally recognized. He divides the sway of Southern political ideas with Mr. Watterson only, and is more distinctly Southern than he. He is Southern without being sectional, and his views are as broad as they are elevated. As a writer, he is also calmer, clearer and more logical than Watterson. His journal has undoubtedly done more to mold the real Southern opinion of the day than any other. By his persistent labors he has won his own State away from many of her old and injurious prejudices, and induced her citizens to absorb much of the political sentiment of their fellow-citizens, North, West, and East. South Carolina can no longer be reproached with the dense provincialism which affected her so long after the war. To Dawson, and other editors of an enlightened and energetic spirit in the South, all honor is due for their conservative liberalism, and it is fully time that the North recognized the fact.[107]

Tragically, Dawson's career ended not in an hour of triumph but at a moment when the newspaper he had built seemed on the verge of dissolution. Its financial resources, though respectable, had never been lavish, and the *News and Courier* had grown soft with easy success in South Carolina. When a serious rival, the *Charleston World*, and two other lesser Charleston newcomers at last challenged the *News and Courier* in 1887 and

1888, and another opposition daily in Columbia offered combat, the fragile prosperity of South Carolina's giant suddenly vanished.[108] The *News and Courier* lost advertising, subscriptions, and staff to the *World*, and Dawson pared all unessential expenses in order to add new features and purchase a partial service of a competing press franchise.[109] Perhaps worse, rail schedules were altered so that the *News and Courier* lost much of its circulation in the part of the state north of Columbia. The crisis left Dawson despondent. The newspaper "fight waxes hotter, but there is no way of telling what the end will be," he warned his wife. "It does not follow here that the fittest will survive, or that I am the fittest." Within a year Dawson was dead and the *News and Courier* near collapse with only forty-seven dollars to its credit in the bank, worn-out equipment, and securities inflated far beyond their earning capacity. Although the rival *World* collapsed within two years and the *News and Courier* went on to a long, illustrious career as South Carolina's outstanding paper, the future of the *News and Courier* in 1889 looked bleak.[110]

Why had the *News and Courier* come so near to ruin? Dawson had defended the rise of the monopolistic press as the only possible hope of superior journalism in a provincial city, but the crisis of 1888-89 revealed the reverse side of the story. The *News and Courier*, a one-man press in a one-paper city and state, had become a flabby giant grown hesitant, conservative, and arrogant through lack of competition. Complacent and perhaps consuming too much of its limited profits as dividends rather than reinvesting in news-gathering facilities, the *News and Courier* failed to keep pace with more aggressive, more modern journals.

Henry Grady's *Atlanta Constitution* developed a more modern style than did Dawson's *News and Courier* or Watterson's *Courier-Journal*. News features and New South boosterism rather than political commentary and editorial fulminations made Grady's *Constitution* memorable. The *Constitution* did not aspire to national political leadership as did the *Courier-Journal*; instead, it offered a balanced variety of news spiced with sensationalism and sought successfully the role of political-power broker within Georgia. Grady acquired considerable leverage by backing the triumvirate of John Gordon, Alfred Colquitt, and Joe Brown.[111] Emphasis on state politics and Southern development, coupled with renowned talent in local-color humor and weak coverage of international affairs, lent the paper its strong regional flavor.

Between 1876 and 1883 the *Constitution*, facing little or no competition, established a firm hold on the affections of Atlanta's readers. Daily circulation grew from 5,200 in 1880 to 12,000 in 1890. Strong advertising support played an equally important part in enabling the *Constitution* to expand and spend lavishly for new equipment, news gathering, and writing.[112] In 1881, shortly after Grady assumed the duties of managing editor, he expanded the paper from four to eight pages to make room for enlarged news coverage and gave it a new, attractive type dress and, a year later, a new format.[113] With a new perfecting press costing $27,500, the *Constitution* claimed the most advanced printing equipment south of Chicago and Philadelphia and paid itself a handsome compliment by emphasizing that the *New York Herald* had just ordered presses like the *Constitution*'s.

About this same time the *Constitution* boasted that its telegraphic bill for gathering news was "as much as that for every other paper in six Southern states combined."[114] With an exclusive Associated Press franchise, the *Constitution* obtained national news usually within twenty-four hours of the event. Grady's *Constitution* had a daily Washington correspondent, a special feature matched by no other Southern paper except Watterson's *Courier-Journal*.[115] Grady sought out able writers and business administrators; Evan Howell and Joel Chandler Harris contributed editorials and special features, and W.A. Hemphill directed the business office from 1868 until 1902.[116] In 1886 the *Journalist* selected the *Constitution*'s Frank Richardson (Washington correspondent), Josiah Carter (city editor), and E.C. Bruffy (head of local matter) for special recognition.[117]

Bruffy praised Grady's role in the *Constitution*'s surge toward modern journalism:

It was his ability to tell where the news was, and how to get it, that Henry W. Grady stood pre-eminent among his workers on the press. By an instinct which cannot be explained, he was current with the event. . . .

Nothing stood in his way when he wanted to weave the threads of an event into a story. Money was nothing and work was a pleasure. With himself, he never knew what it meant to grow tired, and those he trained and sent forth into the journalistic world became inoculated with his energy.

Hiring special engines and chartering telegraph lines were common events in the work with which he electrified the world.

None of these ventures was a response to reader demand. Grady's innovations, according to Bruffy, appalled Southern readers, who "could see no sense in his lavish expenditure of money."[118] Grady had to modernize not only the Southern press but also the Southern reader.

In the 1880s the *Constitution* contained special columns of state and regional news: "Georgia Gossip," "Georgia by Wire," and "The States Around." The *Constitution* possessed many of the qualities of the country press, yet the urban scene received thorough coverage. Six reporters wrote up all the local news of interest to Atlantans, from state politics to baseball. Grady himself interviewed important industrialists, politicians, and former Southern generals, even though some newsmen still doubted the ethics of "keyhole journalism."[119] Stonewall Jackson's widow would have agreed with them after her encounter with a smooth-talking interviewer, one Henry Grady. He "came unexpectedly to me, sought an interview, and being a southern man of kind and pleasant manners, and professing to have come for the purpose of encouraging and assisting me in the selection of popular items, I was incautiously led into answering too fully the multitude of questions with which I was plied."[120]

But enterprising and lively journalism helped place Grady's paper in an unrivalled position in the deep South by the late 1880s. "The Constitution was such an accepted institution in this community," economist H.C. Nixon jokingly recalled, "that I once thought it was started by a convention in 1787."[121] Even more phenomenal was the sudden rage for the *Constitution*'s weekly edition, Grady's compilation of the best daily news and features of the week.[122] On February 20, 1887, the *Weekly Constitution*'s circulation topped 100,000, and by 1890 it approached 144,000, making it unquestionably the leading organ of Southern opinion and sentiment.[123] "It reaches, allowing the usual rate of five readers for each paper, more than 500,000 people. It goes into every state in the union. . . . As each copy of the paper contains as much reading matter as a good-sized book it is like scattering an enormous library through the homes of the people."[124] When new subscriptions for the weekly swamped the *Constitution* staff and the *Constitution* displaced the *New York Tribune* as the out-of-state paper with the largest circulation in Iowa, it seemed to Grady's staffers that there was nothing to prevent the *Weekly Constitution* from becoming the new colossus of the West as well as the South.[125]

The *Constitution*'s success cannot be attributed solely to the paper's superior news-gathering ability. Promotional gimmicks, such as Christmas drawings and wholesale prices on watches and sewing machines for new subscribers and the fact that Atlanta was a rail center offering quick access to outlying towns, played no small role in the circulation increases.

Important also was the paper's tone. Grady accepted the modern journalistic rule of publishing what would please the public.[126] A *Constitution* editorial summed up the formula for success: "We print a southern newspaper, that is southern to the core, but that is American in the best and broadest sense. We print a cheerful, clean and newsy paper, reliable in its relation and in its counsel. We are spreading the gospel of cheerfulness, liberality, frankness and hope throughout the entire nation."[127] Grady, Howell, and Harris were not afraid of sentiment, and they enjoyed dwelling on Horatio Alger stories mirroring their own phenomenal rise. And if they headlined murders and executions, they always found a moral lesson to redeem the sordidness of bloody episodes.

The *Constitution* had all the late-nineteenth-century passion for monitoring ethical conduct,[128] but as if to ease the strain of such heavy handed moralizing, the *Constitution* featured light, humorous material such as the tall stories and sayings of Bill Arp (Major Charles H. Smith), Old Si (Samuel W. Small), Betsey Hamilton (Mrs. E.B. Ploughman), and best-known of all, Uncle Remus (Joel Chandler Harris). The Dixie humorists constituted one of the paper's strongest and most enduring departments.[129]

Preferring the front-page feature story to the editorial, Grady lent his special touch to the widest variety of topics. Late in the 1880s he devoted more attention to the editorial page, writing short, effective paragraphs which won the praise of no less a journalistic master than Charles A. Dana of the *New York Sun*. Sometimes he wrote the entire editorial page for the Sunday edition.[130] Generally Grady concentrated on subjects with a human interest or promotional angle and left the articles on national and international affairs to Harris and editorial writer N.P.T. Finch.[131] Whether in exciting news stories, informal essays, or human interest tales—on industrial fairs, Florida oranges versus Georgia peaches, buxom women, poor Mortimer Pitts the ragpicker, or surf bathing—Grady's descriptive powers, homely illustrations, and wit captured a vast audience.[132] He wrote about the big and small business of living and dying.[133] When Grady reported a hanging, his readers could hear the victim's neck snap. "The terrible thud of the gallows drop still sounds in my ears as I write," ran one of his lead sentences.[134] His report on the trial of James Garfield's assassin offers an example of Grady's inimitable style.

I do not know how the ladies stand the spicy details which Guiteau throws into the proceedings on occasions, but I suppose the old ones are too wise to be giddy and the young ones too innocent to blush. . . .

That he [Guiteau] should be hung there is no doubt. That he will be there is scarcely less. But I could not help pitying him as I witnessed his unequal and hopeless struggle. And back of this what a hard unloved life was his, with its shabby makeshifts—with its hungry nights and days of disappointments—its mortifying beggary, its looming ambition and wretched performance.[135]

Although Grady intended to please and divert his readers, journalism was not to be mere entertainment. Even in the most frivolous of stories on Florida oranges or poor Mortimer Pitts the ragpicker, there was always a lesson to be learned or a moral to be taken to heart.[136] Undoubtedly Grady agreed completely with one journalist's dictum that "the editor who will pleasantly convince a thousand women to throw away frying-pans and get gridirons will do as much good as he who advises a thousand men to vote for Paddy Teufelsdroch for alderman."[137]

The single unifying theme of the *Constitution* in the 1880s was the development of Atlanta. Grady heralded every forward stride of the New South and labored assiduously for regional development, but his real passion was for his adopted hometown, now bristling with a vigorous rail traffic and endlessly hopeful of developing a major industrial sector. Grady boomed "Busy Atlanta" daily in his columns, but the realization of his city's triumph sometimes necessitated the derogation of rivals like Charleston or his Georgia competitors, Macon, Savannah, and Augusta. Concerning the latter, for example, Grady bluntly wrote of business conducted in worm-eaten buildings, of unpaved streets and irregular sidewalks, and of a muddy and unreliable water supply. But optimism, boosterism, and building up were far more typical of the *Constitution's* spirit.[138]

Grady launched one crusade after another to raise his city's civic consciousness and promote its industrial growth. He campaigned for paved streets, artesian water, a modern sewage system, a new cotton factory, and a new YMCA building.[139] He helped bring organized baseball and a world cotton exposition to Atlanta and established a Piedmont Chautauqua and a Confederate Home. Atlanta boomed, and Joel Chandler Harris concluded that "there is hardly a public enterprise in Georgia or in Atlanta—begun and completed since 1880—that does not bear witness to . . . [Grady's] ability, his energy, and his unselfishness." Grady became Atlanta's favorite son in the 1880s, and he enjoyed the social amenities of such status, residing among the elite on Peachtree Street and securing membership in the exclusive Capital City Club and Gentlemen's Driving Club.[140]

But Grady did not forget the unfortunate in his city. When he learned of the suffering of the poor during the hard winter of 1884, he immediately announced a drive to "warm up the whole town" and formed a committee to put fifty wagons in the streets collecting provisions for the needy. "The members of the committee . . . never knew of their appointments until they saw their names in the paper. It was Sunday, when stores were closed, drivers scattered, clerks gone, and partners separated. In spite of this, two hours after The Constitution appeared, there were men and wagons, wood and clothes, money and provisions in profusion. All that was wanted was furnished and more too."[141] "Up one side and down the other," crowed Grady, "Atlanta is the best town on the top of this earth."[142] Grady won praise for his labors in behalf of the needy, but his efforts were designed to stimulate private charity. He and other late-nineteenth-century developers and city leaders neglected social welfare services and focused instead on urban growth and amenities for the central city rather than outlying or working class neighborhoods. In Atlanta, as elsewhere, "the expansion of physical welfare services during the 1880s generally and not unexpectedly followed the residential movement of white-collar whites."[143]

Henry Grady was the New South's prophet if not its pioneer. The popular orations which gave him national fame encapsulated the notions that permeated the feature stories and editorial columns of the *Constitution*. The age of the Southern statesman was past; the means of regional influence and uplift lay no longer in politics but, rather, in economic boosterism.[144] When Grady rejected a political career for himself, he sketched his dream for a prosperous South.

I shall be satisfied with the labors of my life if, when those labors are over, my son, . . . [can look] abroad upon a better and grander Georgia—a Georgia that has filled the destiny God intended her for—when her towns and cities are hives of industry and her country-side the exhaustless fields from which their stores are drawn—when every stream dances on its way to the music of spindles, and every forest echoes back the roar of the passing train—when her valleys smile with abundant harvests and from her hill-sides come the tinkling bells as her herds and flocks go forth from their folds.[145]

Joel Chandler Harris spoke for many Georgians when he concluded, "It is due to his unique methods of advertising that the material resources of the two states [Georgia and Florida] are in their present state of development."[146] More recently historian Don Doyle has echoed Harris's views by emphasizing the role of community enterprise and organizational skills—Grady strong points—in enabling Atlanta to capitalize on advantages of geography and shifting patterns of trade and industry.[147]

Grady was not, however, without his critics—then or now. Some disagreed with his policies and the interests he backed, others with his journalism. No doubt Grady's devotion to his New South mission was inconsistent with his own ideal of editorial independence, disinterestedness and objectivity. New South fanaticism could warp editorial judgment just as much as could old-style partisan politics. Those incessant economic statistics in the *Constitution*, too good to be true, took their toll: among rival editors, friendly and otherwise, "Grady's facts" became a mirthful byword. A few recent writers, similarly, argue that his eloquent speeches bore little relationship to reality. Grady's vision of a New South shone too brightly "to be examined critically as a social philosophy, but rather [it was] to be accepted almost as a religion."[148]

Grady's competitive drive to scoop his rivals sometimes cost him his sense of proportion and accuracy. His constant hyperbole exasperated many of his contemporaries. Francis Dawson once ridiculed Grady's exaggerated description of a high wind which unroofed an Atlanta church, dubbing it "Grady's hurricane."[149] Moreover, the Dickensian world featured in some of Grady's stories—appealing, sentimental, and pathetic— was often more imaginary than real. He launched a press crusade to free poor Sallie, an unfortunate young white girl sentenced inexplicably to a Georgia chain gang. The mounting public frenzy of gullible readers quickly secured her release to the Benevolent Home, whereupon this not-so-young, hardened streetwalker promptly resumed her interrupted career.[150] Finally, some critics thought Grady too frivolous about serious subjects, especially hangings. "The Aerial Waltz," "Nicked in the Neck," "Hemped Hence," and "Terrible Twist" suggested a note of levity not quite proper in civilized society.[151]

The archetype of the great editor is the social reformer attacking the greatest moral evils of the age—a Horace Greeley, attacking slavery. Grady does not fit this mold. He lacked a critical awareness of the problems of the new industrial era and of his region's social injustices; no profound problems invaded Grady's vision of the South.[152] Unlike Watterson and Dawson, Grady praised and promoted; he did not inquire critically except where he found backward agricultural methods obstructing his industrial renaissance. In short, Grady was unquestioningly, enthusiastically orthodox—and forever disappointing to liberal historians. "A snake-oil salesman," an "insufferably ingratiating Pollyanna," are two recent characterizations.[153]

Nowhere was Grady's optimism more obvious than in his role as defender of the racial status quo and propagandist for racial harmony. Grady grew almost lyrical in describing the white South's fondness for the "old timey Negro" (he spoke often of his love for his black mammy) and the loyalty of blacks in guarding white families during the war. He spread similar visions via editorials and news columns for the exchanges, essays in popular monthly magazines, and speeches before Northern audiences. Of course behind his fine phrases on racial peace and progress lay his dedication to white supremacy; thus it is not surprising that from time to time the facade of harmony was fractured by tales of evil-minded, ignorant, riotous, or lazy blacks. Such stories were something of an embarrassment for Grady, and he soon learned to couple any negativism with a comparison favorable to his section. Racial violence sometimes occurred in the South, he was forced to confess, but no more often than in the North. He argued that the $45 million worth of cotton raised in a single year was not the product of an oppressed race but of black workers who were as well off as their Northern brethren in character, prosperity, and legal protection. In the South, blacks were voters, citizens, and welcome workers, and they were there to stay. "The southern people have no prejudice against the negro."[154]

Grady's views, reflecting both prejudice and a rather myopic sense of goodwill, were common among well-meaning whites in that age. Certainly he had no truck with racial extremism, probably on principle, but also because extremism had a negative effect on Northern opinion and thus had to be denounced. On one occasion he fired a *Constitution* employee who had joined a white mob attacking blacks. Like Booker T. Washington, he fashioned a program which would placate diverse constituencies: whites, Northerners, and blacks. It "was awkward and seldom in balance," explains Harold E. Davis, "and it always had him on edge, but it was the best he could do." But sometimes the best wasn't good enough, as when white Georgians denounced his protest of white vigilante action, or when a black editor hooted in derision at his description of the fair treatment of black train passengers.[155]

Nevertheless, Grady's successes outnumbered his failures. Daily Grady surveyed his world and found it good. He even reported favorably on the convict lease system and the chain gang, although admitting to some problems. Horrors by the column, he said, were only to be expected from other newspapers, since "the wild-eyed correspondent is abroad in the land. . . . The fact that the penitentiaries under fire are filled mainly with negroes lends an old-time zest to the crusade of the philanthropists."[156] Other busybodies like the Salvation Army also drew his wrath. They should throw away their tambourines and go to work; the South's organized church system, its missionary labor, its evangelists, and its great body of the religious people of the South, made the Salvation Army unnecessary.[157]

Grady was comfortable with the dominant Protestantism of his land and with the Southern social order. He backed Georgia's ruling class and was consulted by it. Other journalists in the 1880s might charge Georgia's governors with ring rule and corruption. Grady, despite mounting evidence, denied such charges and insisted that Georgia was never so prosperous and so efficient; taxes and expenses had been reduced and the credit of the state improved.[158] With all the innocence and concern of a dedicated civic leader, Grady pleaded for Democratic unity as the best way to overcome factionalism in state politics (and, conveniently, to strengthen the hand of Georgia's ruling elite). He warned the public—and especially his Macon rivals—of the danger of political cliques: "The people of this state cannot be bulldozed or driven, and whipped in and out of ranks at the dictation of a few inflamed 'reformers.'" The alleged Atlanta "ring," he noted, was really the people of Georgia, and he predicted a heavy frost in August if ever the *Constitution*, which would fight ring rule wherever it was found, and the people of the state could be found at odds.[159]

Grady never would admit that he was in fact master of an Atlanta ring of businessmen, industrialists, and promoters who, in alliance with Georgia's black-belt planters, ruled the state behind the leadership of Joe Brown, Alfred Colquitt, and John Gordon. Grady, a power behind this Bourbon triumvirate, manipulated politics to boost Atlanta and make it the railroad hub of the southeast, to limit the opportunities of rival Georgia cities, and to keep Atlantans in the governor's chair and other key offices of the state. Grady's behind-the-scenes machinations stand in stark contrast to his public, nonpolitical, Sunday-school morality. An acute awareness of Grady's hypocrisy, in addition to his self-promotion, tedious ebullience, and groundless optimism, has fueled recent criticism.[160]

All of this does not make Grady a reactionary, as is sometimes thought, for he exemplifies a progressive model of a leading industrial developer and civic improver who would bring a new era of prosperity and happiness to the Georgia folk and who cared for the deserving poor by stimulating private, voluntary charity.[161] The deficiencies of his public policies and journalism, criticized by historians, were common enough in his own time. Possessing a secret, self-serving quality as well as a constructive public presence, Grady fit perfectly into an age of business boosterism and promotion; he also reflected a typical editorial stance of simplicity and naivete in the face of longstanding problems. If he did not rise above his era as a social critic, at least he did not sink beneath it. He was accepted by his contemporaries as a progressive, a modernizer, a builder who fought poverty, harmful agriculture, and backwardness in all its forms. He led successful battles to extend urban amenities and mobilize capital and entrepreneurs to benefit Atlanta and the South. Even before his New South speech of December 1886, he had marched to the front ranks in Southern journalism, a triumph acknowledged by the *Philadelphia Press* in 1882.[162] In May 1886, the *New York Sun* praised him as the editor of the most progressive newspaper in the New South: "Few men deserve more credit for earnest, sensible work in building up the town where he lives, the region wherein his paper circulates, and the spirit of manly good faith with which the reconstructed States have wrought out of disaster a wonderful prosperity."[163] For a man who did not live to see his fortieth year, his achievement was extraordinary.

The nineteenth-century editor's chair was not easily filled. It required a superior understanding of men and affairs, an exceptional breadth of knowledge, a mastery of writing, and abundant courage and self-confidence. By the late nineteenth century American journalism was in a transitory state. The emerging journalist sought to break from the traditional role of party hack and began to recognize different standards and principles—including accuracy in reporting, critical assessment of men and events, news-gathering instinct, and perhaps even social responsibility. Some saw the disappearance of personal journalism as a key factor in late nineteenth-century journalism; others the decline in prominence of the editorial as emphasis shifted to news and entertainment. Most recognized the extent to which journalism in major cities had become a big business, affected overwhelmingly by the high costs of news gathering and the new techniques of printing. Standardization increased as press association dispatches and syndication, which amplified and standardized the old newspaper exchange system, reduced regional differences on the news pages.[164]

Still, there was as yet no single model of journalistic excellence. For example, New York City in the 1880s witnessed the phenomenal rise of Joseph Pulitzer's *World*, a sensation-seeking, reform-minded titan, while the *New York Times* still provided a brilliant example of conservative journalism which would not truckle to unseemly innovations. At least until the end of the 1890s—when, according to Michael Schudson, the *New York Times* set the standard for modern mass circulation journalism— variety was a hallmark of American journalism.[165] It is not surprising that the leading New South journalists differed from one another in many essentials. But there are unifying themes: all were *Southern* journalists sensitive to Northern slights and Yankee criticism, all spoke for a dominant Southern elite, and each in his own way moved toward a more modern journalism and championed a respectable press.

Though the pall of Reconstruction lifted in the 1880s, shadows of sectional antagonism still clouded the South when Watterson, Dawson, and Grady reached the peak of their fame and began preaching sectional reconciliation. As spokesmen for their region they could not ignore what Southerners saw as persistent Yankee arrogance and hostility in whatever form it appeared—condescension, taunts, outright attacks, discriminatory legislation, and so forth. Quick to answer sneer with sneer, insult with insult, accusation with accusation, New South editors eagerly jumped into combat with Yankee antagonists while simultaneously courting Northern businessmen and investors. Reconciliation, they believed, had been achieved in business circles and even among most politicians, but some had not surrendered old passions or bad habits. Consequently, Watterson, Dawson, and Grady wrote defensively; they guarded Confederate memories, justified the South, and bolstered Southern egos.

Northern condescension elicited immediate rebuttals both sarcastic and scathing. Watterson preferred the latter. Grady's *Constitution*, urging readers simply to ignore unfavorable remarks, as they made no real difference to anyone, did not practice what it preached. Perceived Reconstruction-style attacks provoked *News and Courier* headlines such as "The Enemies of the South" and "A Political Murder" (how government officers bulldozed blacks to testify falsely), under which Dawson bitterly denounced continuing federal prosecutions and recalled for South Carolinians memories of the old Yankee "outrage mill." Such grievances made it natural for Southern journalists to celebrate with glee the hope and the increasing ability of Southern mills to compete with, if not threaten, New England textiles. "Northern Mills Alarmed" and "Northern Drygoods Men Driven to the Wall" indicated that political antagonism had in part given way to economic competition. Despite talk of reconciliation, "vanquished rebels hailed the erection of each new cotton factory as a victory over the hated Yankee."[166]

The enduring Northern assumption of a pervasive and deadening backwardness below the Mason and Dixon line rankled the Southern press. In 1883, for example, crime was the focus of this North-South clash. Dawson rejected Northern aspersions about Southern criminality by citing census figures showing that the percentage of prisoners among the Southern white population was less than half that reported among New England's white population. Grady observed with mock wonder that there existed no crime in the North, although an occasional criminal was "swung up in Massachusetts as a lesson to criminals in the South and other foreign lands." Watterson chortled with glee at the discovery of a murder wave in the center of moral leadership in Pittsburgh.[167]

Always careful to defend the old Southern verities, New South editors were apologists and traditionalists as well as advocates of economic change and social improvement. They wrote vigorously on all sorts of subjects and took pains not to alienate their reading public. If they sometimes adopted a critical approach to the problems of their respective cities and states, as did Dawson, they operated within the limitations imposed by Southern orthodoxy. If their proposed solutions to economic and social problems were frequently naive and simplistic, such were the vices of editors who had learned, sometimes through bitter experience, that boosting paid and knocking did not.[168]

Reaching beyond their cities into the hinterland, editors like Watterson, Dawson, and Grady—aspiring mass mediators—were of necessity harmonizers and unifiers. They sought to downplay division and disharmony and to encourage every enterprise productive of growth and development. Around these goals they sought to create a sense of community. "The newspaper reflects the region, and the region reflects the newspaper," Jack Claiborne recently wrote of the *Charlotte Observer*, a paper typical of the New South press. "Through the *Observer*, the region gives and receives an image of itself and becomes a community. Its people gained a shared experience that builds a common bond. . . . [the paper] highlights both accomplishments and shortcomings, inspires hope and satisfaction, records disappointment and defeat. It reinforces tradition and stimulates change. And the rhythm of its publication, morning after morning, year after year, builds a sense of direction and continuity." [169]

New South editors were the spokesmen for the political-social-economic system of a ruling elite that gave them power and prestige. The sense of community they created rested upon the values and interests of the most powerful. None was alienated from his society or its conservative regimes; none questioned—and certainly none crusaded against—the reigning Southern orthodoxies on race, politics, religion, or labor. None was like Walter Hines Page, formerly of the *Raleigh State Chronicle*, whose attacks on Southern problems and prejudices made more enemies than converts and earned their author opprobrium as a traitor to the South.

Though widely quoted, Page had lasted but a year and a half in Raleigh. He violated Southern sensibilities on racial matters, expressing kind words for blacks in an editorial "Our Brothers in Black" and capitalizing the word "Negro," but his real problem arose from frustration over his inability to publish a truly metropolitan journal. His expenses were too high; he spurned political patronage which would have strengthened his paper financially; and he failed to provide those necessary touches—gossip, sports, and household topics—to a people more accustomed to rural than urban ways.

Page's heterodoxy emerged fully only after he left Raleigh, when his New York City "mummy" letter denounced the state's most influential leaders as incompetents who were blocking progress. That letter effectively destroyed any chance of his returning to North Carolina, supposing he had wanted to do so. He had become a prophet without honor in his state.[170]

In the twentieth century a handful of Southern editors would build upon the tradition of Page, and a score would win acclaim (and Pulitzer Prizes) for exposing a benighted South. Such was impossible in the late nineteenth century. New South editors sometimes spoke against rival editors, the economic interests of rival cities and states, Yankee self-righteousness, labor unions, unruly blacks, or, in the mugwumps' view, the dangerous classes seething with unrest. Rarely did they speak against industrial developers, planters, progressive farmers, commercial interests, hard-working mechanics, Confederate veterans, Southern womanhood, or the Lost Cause. Big city editors in the South directed establishment papers, and in the postwar period they would add industry and urban development to agriculture and commerce as a driving force in their journalism. They sought always to broaden their appeal, to be custodians of the public's interests. And it was in the public's interest to maintain unity in the Democratic party—to combat factionalism and to unify planter, industrialist, and merchant. The editors' cities, after all, were adjuncts to the countryside.

Because none viewed the interests of agriculture, industry, and commerce as mutually exclusive, it was natural for editors to celebrate the accomplishments and future glories of all and to rally planters and capitalists to a common program of conservatism on taxes, labor, and social services. Democratic leaders who challenged the economic program of the Reconstruction and post-Reconstruction Republican party would promise to deliver to the Southern people shops and factories set amid rich farms and plantations. In particular states one element of the Democratic coalition might have been more prominent than another, but urban editors sought to avoid conflict and division by boosting all economic enterprises almost indiscriminately. Even the weekly country press, which far more than urban dailies represented a farm people, took up the cudgels for industrial progress and progressive change.[171]

Historians continue to debate the nature of post-Civil War Southern leadership—whether the South's Democratic elite and builders of a New South reflected planter persistence or the rise of new men. The literature on this theme is voluminous.[172] The "planter dominance" interpretation was the conventional wisdom of the first half of the twentieth century. Among the more recent works supporting this thesis is Jonathan Wiener's *Social Origins of the New South: Alabama, 1860-1885*. C. Vann Woodward's seminal work, *Origins of the New South* (1951), popularized the revisionist "new men" interpretation, emphasizing the emergence of a new middle class of aggressive businessmen centering in the booming cities. More recently David L. Carlton and Lacy K. Ford have identified a new class of merchants, professionals, and boosters in the thriving towns of the upcountry as the builders of a new South.[173]

John J. Beck in a recent article on Rowan County, North Carolina, argued that synthesis of this plethora of interpretation is possible.[174] James C. Cobb took a major step in this direction in his essay "Beyond Planters and Industrialists," arguing that planter influence did not impose significant restrictions on development strategy, that in fact planter policies often appealed to industrialists. Cobb writes: "In the South a lingering dependence on labor-intensive agriculture and the courtship by default of industries highly sensitive to labor, tax, and material costs helped to shape a society whose leaders saw social control as a better, less expensive investment than social uplift. Regardless of who ruled the late nineteenth-century South, the prevailing core of reactionary, socially insensitive policies that characterized the era was far more likely to please than to put off the industrialists who were choosing Southern locations."[175]

The situation in Georgia illustrates the potential for planter-industri-

alist cooperation, and it may prove typical of the strengths and weaknesses of this alliance. Planters, the dominant element in Georgia because of their control of the general assembly and the state Democratic
party, allied themselves with the Atlanta Ring of businessmen and industrialists led by Grady. This informal truce ended only with the death
of Grady and the rise of the Farmers' Alliance. On the whole, planters
were not anti-industrial in their feelings; widely shared values perhaps
explain why in virtually every election in the 1870s and 1880s "the majority of urban votes were cast for the same candidates as those supported by planters in the Old Black Belt."[176]

Grady worked assiduously for Atlanta; but the welfare of Georgia's
farmers was essential to Atlanta, and rural votes vastly outnumbered
urban votes. So he boasted incessantly of Georgia's farms and campaigned for more balance in local agriculture and the cultivation of more
food and foodstuffs so that farmers could feed themselves and their
livestock. He urged farmers to save money by relying more on barnyard
fertilizer and less on the commercial product. The future of Georgia
farming lay in truck farming rather than cotton, he proclaimed.[177]

Grady and the *Constitution* probably believed, at first, that their farm
program would work, Harold E. Davis observes. "They wanted capital-
ist/managers on the farms to make common cause with capitalist/man-
agers in the cities. By 1887, however, most Georgians knew the program
was successful only for a few people. It was then that Grady and the
Constitution began to use their plan as a calculated ticket to continued
influence."[178] Though Grady's farm efforts failed, they stand as strong
evidence of a policy that was operative for most of the 1880s, and they
also reveal the faith of New South editors that a working alliance between planters and industrialists could and should be maintained.
When that alliance failed, it was seldom followed by warfare—at least
not among former allies. Advocates of the New South sought change,
not destruction of the plantations. Such destruction, indeed, would
have served no purpose, for "whatever hopes the planters may have
entertained of controlling or limiting urban and industrial development," concludes historian Don H. Doyle, "they posed no obstacle to
the multitude of towns and factories that flourished in the New South.
Indeed, the urban press never seemed concerned with the planters as
opponents of the new order. They were treated as remnants of the past;
the future of the South belonged to the cities."[179]

Although New South editors arrogated to themselves the right and
duty to speak for all Southerners, in practice they seldom spoke for all
Southerners equally. In the final analysis, they spoke for the reigning
conservative elite. Yet Watterson, Dawson, and Grady were not quite
defenders of the way things were, but rather advocates of improve-

ments in the way things were. This distinction is crucial. They represented the best in the conservative tradition: they advocated sectional reconciliation and industrial development, encouraged scientific farming, and sought to encourage racial harmony while maintaining black subordination. Most New South editors criticized the worst abuses and problems of the New South while defending the basic integrity of Southern society. Perhaps in the 1880s the lessening of sectional animosity and a calmer interlude in race relations (calmer than the violence of Reconstruction or the upheaval associated with Populism) were due in part to the smothering leadership of New South editors and other elite spokesmen. But apathy in race relations bore a high price for future generations, and all recognize the tremendous gap between rhetoric and reality in New South advocates' rhapsodies on the glories of a resurrected South in industry and scientific agriculture. Yet the urban press of the late nineteenth century fostered conditions which contributed to the growth of industry and a new vitality in the towns and cities as evidenced in new textile mills, railroads, iron and steel mills, waterworks, sewer services, streetcars, bridges, city halls, schools, market houses, and paved streets. By inculcating middle-class urban values and encouraging modernization, newspapers helped create the New South era, which was a prelude to progressivism.[180]

As a journalist, Henry Watterson, the most backward-looking of the three New South editors discussed here, can be viewed as a transitional figure in the rise of modern journalism.[181] The Kentucky editor continued the tradition of personal, autocratic, editorializing journalism, but Watterson spoke his own mind and exhibited an independence which distinguished him from party hack editors. He welcomed the able business management of the Haldemans, father and son, and the *Courier-Journal* had the most modern press equipment outside of New York City and a large, specialized staff—both hallmarks of the New Journalism.[182] With such a base, Watterson made his editorial page nationally famous, so famous that it is easy to forget that the *Courier-Journal*'s news coverage was first-rate.[183] The *Courier-Journal* surpassed all Southern rivals in coverage of foreign affairs, Congress, and national politics and in expressing the political views of the Southern Democratic leadership. In time, apprenticeship on Watterson's *Courier-Journal*, being one of "Watterson's boys," made a newspaperman's reputation and provided immediate entree onto the metropolitan papers of the Northeast.[184]

Francis Warrington Dawson—abjuring as much as possible personal quarrels, though still committed to the traditional emphasis on politics and the editorial page—brought to South Carolina journalism a critical, progressive spirit.[185] Representing the reformist wing of the conservative regime, he opposed violence, lawlessness, and backward agricultural and business practices and spoke for industrial development and modernized farming. Whether it was the need for a stock law, improved public roads, textile mills, rail connections to the west, or South Carolina's presence at a Boston industrial exhibit, the *News and Courier* set the daily agenda for public consideration of useful projects. Though New South editors, addicted to partisanship and industrial development, could not in the fullest sense be mugwumps, a strain of middle-class mugwumpery nevertheless coursed through Dawson's paper (and to a lesser extent Watterson's and Grady's as well).

In victory or defeat, the *News and Courier* spoke for—in Dawson's words—"all progressive South Carolinians."[186] His small but excellent staff, modern presses, telegraphic news service, and South Carolina correspondents were the finest his state had ever seen. Dawson, said one friend with some exaggeration, had established a new standard of Southern journalism which would inspire editors all over the South.[187] Still, Charleston's dimensions were too small to support a paper worthy of national ranking. Consequently Dawson's fame north of the Mason-Dixon line, unlike that of Grady and Watterson, grew from editorial acclaim rather than widespread popular acceptance.

Unscathed by the war and Reconstruction, young Henry Grady took advantage of the opportunities afforded by Atlanta's growth, and there was nothing transitional about his enterprising journalism. A broad concept of the news, a commitment to the primacy of news over editorials, the elaborate and expensive news-gathering facilities financed by solid advertising patronage as well as large circulation, the quest for sensational and human interest stories, aggressive promotional policies to build readership—all featured prominently in placing Grady in the front ranks of the New Journalism along with Edward W. Scripps in Cleveland and Cincinnati, Melville Stone and Victor Lawson in Chicago, William Rockhill Nelson in Kansas City, and Joseph Pulitzer in St. Louis and New York City.[188] In some ways, the *Constitution* of the 1880s is reminiscent of the style of Pulitzer's *World*. "Consciously or not," concluded Louis T. Griffith and John E. Talmadge in their study of Georgia journalism, "Grady successfully employed the most basic of Pulitzer's policies: to attract the readers by sensational news and then preach to them through high-minded, liberal editorials. The newspaper resulting from such a program might appear incongruous, but it was one which attracted large audiences for both editors."[189]

Grady and Dawson both died in their prime in 1889. Stunned, many country editors devoted as much space to their passing as they did to that of Robert E. Lee, Jefferson Davis, Alexander Stephens, or James Garfield. "Their passing," historian Thomas Clark noted, "was as that of prophets, because they had set the progressive theme for a large portion of the editorial fraternity."[190] Charleston was especially shocked by the manner of Dawson's death—murdered by a coward who, with utter ineptitude, tried to hide evidence of the crime. South Carolina mourned, and the nation's editors recognized the loss of a major figure. The *New York Times* praised Dawson's devotion to progress and the new opportunities of a more modern postwar era.[191] To the *Nation* he represented one of the South's most prominent editorial forces over the past twenty years: "In politics Captain Dawson stood for all progressive impulses, and his paper never hesitated to defy prevailing sentiment when the editor thought that the populace was wrong."[192]

The many glowing editorial eulogies for Henry Grady reflected his nationwide popularity.[193] Colonel John A. Cockerill, former managing editor of Pulitzer's *World*, praised Grady's creative brilliance;[194] but of all those who paid tribute to the man and his career, the often critical *Journalist* most aptly assessed his role: "From his efforts he created not a sect, but immediate results, and those results are to be found to-day in every newspaper office in the South. He showed how a newspaper could be made clean, bright and newsy, and how it could be read—in short, he introduced, if he did not found, progress and enterprise among the ranks of his people. For ten years the Atlanta Constitution has been the model newspaper, not only of Georgia, but of the Southern States."[195] His journalistic triumph enabled him to become the herald of the New South.

Henry Watterson survived his colleagues by thirty-two years, all the while maintaining his position as a Southerner and one of the leading editorial figures in the nation. "For fifty years," summarized fellow Kentuckian Young E. Allison, "Mr. Watterson has been more than the Editor of the *Courier-Journal*. He has been the auxiliary editor of and inspiration to countless newspapers."[196] When in 1919 the nation's editors and publishers contributed articles to a special *Courier-Journal* edition honoring Watterson's seventy-ninth birthday, he clearly ranked with James Gordon Bennett, Horace Greeley, and Charles A. Dana as one of the giants of the nineteenth century.

9

Conclusion

Southern Journalism, From Old South to New South

Any historical conclusions from this study of a handful of outstanding editors must of necessity be tentative. Much more research, including investigations of the less well-known dailies, the black press, and back-country papers, as well as dissenting and often transient editors, is necessary before historians can grasp the general history of Southern journalism. The foregoing essays suggest some provisional interpretations and possible directions for further study.

Political issues and political parties dominated Southern journalism throughout most of the nineteenth century. The parties virtually created the papers, provided much of the readership, awarded profitable public printing contracts and, in the absence of news-gathering facilities, gave editors much of the material they needed to fill their columns. The transition that the Northern penny press made from a journalism of party patronage to a journalism of mass readership and lucrative advertising was considerably complicated and inhibited in the South by the social and economic problems of the area and also by an obsession with defensive politics that lasted into the 1870s and beyond.

In circulation and readership, staff size and press equipment, news-gathering ability and financial support, Southern newspapers fell far short of Northern metropolitan giants. The *Picayune* of the 1840s was an exception largely because of the nature of New Orleans. Editors' dreams might be unlimited, but the demands of the business office restored reality on a regular basis. Costs had to be kept to a minimum. In 1883 there were, for example, only five steam-driven presses in all of Mississippi (where there were 123 journals of all kinds) and five in North Carolina (with 142 journals).[1] Because limited means kept staffs too small to allow for much division of labor, it was easy for strong editors to dominate most departments, thus strengthening the hold of personal journalism in the South.

Lacking a huge readership concentrated in urban centers, Southern editors of urban dailies aggressively sought readers among a relatively small, dispersed population in the towns and rural areas, and editors emerged as spokesmen of state interests rather than of an exclusively urban clientele. Much of the Southern readership, furthermore, consisted of recently transplanted farm people; nineteenth-century Southern dailies, even the New South organs, never completely abandoned the personal quality of country papers. Contrary to Gunther Barth's thesis about the metropolitan press as an urban institution, the Southern daily press did not reflect a need to explain a bewildering metropolis to a diverse population of newcomers and make diversity acceptable.[2] Rather, Southern dailies aimed to rally the people politically, defend their interests, encourage development, and keep city folk informed about village affairs as well as affairs of state.

Disadvantages of size and scant financial backing, sometimes minor nuisances, at other times nearly lethal handicaps, shaped Southern journalism. These problems were more prevalent in Thomas Ritchie's day than in the New South era, when publishing was big business and earnings and expenses were commensurately larger. Parties and governing bodies subsidized the papers of the 1820s and 1830s. These papers circulated largely among a limited group of "influentials"; reporters were not a large item of expense since rhetoric and reasoning overshadowed news and sensationalism and since what passed for news could be extracted from the exchanges, which were free. Southern political papers were always hard pressed for cash, but at this stage they were still competitive. In political cyphering for an elite, Southern editors suffered no disadvantages. Nevertheless, the lack of public support for the political press, especially in contrast to the riches of the Northern press, irritated the Rhetts, John Forsyth, and others.[3]

Yet if the journalism of the pre-Civil War era appealed to a rather limited section of the population, its high level of intellectual and literary quality gave it a compensating advantage. Thomas Ritchie's lengthy essays on constitutional and legal issues, embellished with a profusion of learned allusions, would be impossible for an editor of a popular paper of later times. The nickname his younger colleagues bestowed on Ritchie, Old Nous Verrons, was in part an allusion to his use of a rich and varied vocabulary. Simple thoughts simply expressed were not the style of the nineteenth century; Ritchie, Daniel, Watterson, and others loved editorial essays of maximum rhetorical elaboration. Perhaps some of the habitual bellicosity of Southern journalism may be attributed to the common assumption that great editors must express themselves in memorable philippics.

Regardless of their locale or political commitment, virtually all these spokesmen found themselves, at one time or another, seriously alienated from powerful Southerners whose support made newspapers possible; and all of them had to recant their errors in order to survive.

Extremist fanatics like the Rhetts came into their own at the peak of crisis, such as in 1850, but as the political temperature dropped they became isolated and embittered. The Rhetts, often thought typical of the Southern style, chose, in the late 1850s, to dissemble their true convictions in order to stave off bankruptcy. The Rhetts' rivals, Aaron Willington, William King, and Richard Yeadon of the *Charleston Daily Courier*, mirrored the Rhetts' actions—producing an identical but reversed pattern by surrendering against their better judgment to political extremism in the heat of sectional conflict and then comfortably enjoying the more temperate periods between crises.

John Daniel's flirtation with transcendentalism split him from his readership and threatened his career until he capitulated. Daniel's savage criticism of Jefferson Davis during the war indicates that it was acceptable to be more Southern than the president, whereas it was never tolerable to be less than Southern on an essential issue.

Francis Warrington Dawson best exemplifies the importance of timing and political touch in Southern editorship. Dawson was grossly premature in urging Southern reconciliation to the loss of the war and ratification of the Fourteenth Amendment, and his condemnation of the more barbaric white supremacist outrages in South Carolina's redemption campaign nearly put an end to his career and his paper. He survived by reversing his stand on every major issue.

Even John Forsyth, stiff-necked champion of Southern interests and implacable enemy of Radical Reconstruction, flirted with disaster early in his career. First, he broke with the Democrats by urging armed resistance to the Compromise of 1850, and second, in 1860 he opposed the rising tide of militancy by supporting highly unpopular Stephen Douglas. He eventually had to repudiate his own editorials and toe the line. He and other editors invariably found it impossible to stretch the acceptable range of opinion in the South.

In the three decades before the war entrepreneurs of the penny press pioneered journals which surpassed their more limited predecessors in general news and coverage of economics and politics. The South could not support mass circulation papers outside New Orleans or Baltimore, and the scale of operations of the South's few penny papers such as the early *Picayune* was much smaller than that of the Northern giants. The new journals in the North, reliant on mass readership and financially independent of political patronage, could choose their own issues and campaign in the name of the general public. An aggressive Northern press could virtually set a political agenda, especially on the local or state level.

The old journalism of party patronage, on the other hand, had awaited the initiatives of the political leaders and then tried to impose the leaders' chosen political issues and positions on the public. This distinction explains why Southern journalism seemed so old-fashioned in the postwar period. Southern journals fell farther behind just as sectional confrontation reinforced and deepened the worst elements of political journalism. Southern journalism degenerated into sectional journalism, which at its worst was an uninterrupted partisan snarl and a factor in enduring animosity. Papers like the *Mercury* were propaganda sheets which rejected tolerance, openness, and newspaper and party competition. Until the oppressive weight of Reconstruction diminished, the old-fashioned papers remained suitable for single-issue politics.

The Northern stereotype of Southern journalism reduced the spectrum of Southern editors to a single, unpleasant image: a Yankee-hating, trigger-happy, ranting, incompetent alcoholic. In the 1880s a commentator in the *Journalist* found Southern papers pathetically weak in everything except dramatic exaggeration, which was, he said, "as strong as defiance of grammatical rules and an utter ignorance of everything pertaining to dramatic art can make it."[4] Two years later another *Journalist* "authority" sneered: "In the old days, newspapermen in the South were fond of braggadocio, and many an hour have I spent listening to their gasconading regarding the superiority of Southern climate, its people and institutions over those of the North. They were fond of saying "By Gawd, sir" . . . while they merely checked the flow of their fierce eloquence to say 'The same as before' to the barkeeper."[5]

Perhaps a little of this prejudice sprang from a persistent Northern belief that the Civil War had been a product of thirty years of Southern ignorance, carefully nurtured by the Southern press.[6] Evidence of low esteem for the Southern press also appeared abroad. A London literary journal, *Macmillan's Magazine*, popularized the view that liquor fueled a Southern press which appealed to feelings more than intellect: "The fervid language, jocose familiarity, and political vituperation . . . have gained them the unqualified censure of the more dignified Press of the old world."[7] Such views fostered a disinclination to recognize the modernity of some Southern papers edited by men like Dawson and Grady. Above all, however, the stereotype ignored the high quality of the best antebellum Southern journalism as judged by the standards of its own time.

In the great years of the *Richmond Enquirer*, before giant dailies began to modernize journalism, no editor—North or South—surpassed Thomas Ritchie as a journalist. From the early years of the nation to the 1850s, Ritchie was an editor of power and conscience and a serious political journalist, concerned with constitutionalism, national policy, candidates, platforms, and party success. Although the *Enquirer* sometimes lapsed into crude editorial brawling, Ritchie set an example far ahead of his time in opening his columns to his opponents. Almost no scurrility and only the barest hint of extremism touched his pages.

Another fine prewar Southern paper often conveniently forgotten was the *New Orleans Daily Picayune* of Kendall, Lumsden, and Holbrook. It was as new and fresh and independent as anything in American journalism at the end of the 1830s. By the end of the 1840s the *Picayune's* news coverage, foreign reporting, entertainment, and cautious editorializing as well as sound business management placed it in the front ranks of American papers. Unfortunately New Orleans's uniqueness precluded replication of Kendall and Lumsden's efforts elsewhere in the South of the late 1830s and 1840s.

The few Northerners who acknowledged the existence of extremists in their own ranks dismissed their excesses by arguing that theirs was a worthy cause. More to the point, the fire-eating style never monopolized Northern journalism of the middle period, and Northern pluralism encouraged editorial diversity and a greater toleration of differing points of view. Northern editors were profiting from boom times rather than struggling with wartime devastation and the uncertainties of a slave-plantation economy in transition. By contrast, the typical Southern editor, laboring with inadequate resources to keep his four-page journal afloat, had to devote practically his entire working life to the battle for Southern survival and home rule. Thus, the editorial pages of Daniel, the Rhetts, and Forsyth—though the products of different times, personalities, and localities—were variations on the theme of resistance to tyranny. Little wonder then that the daily fulminations of many a Southern editor both enhanced his local reputation for community service and high-minded leadership and excited the contempt of his Northern colleagues.

Only late in the century did some of the most successful Southern editors escape the Northern stereotype. The end of military occupation and the North's decreasing concern for the rights of blacks resulted in a decline of Southern "frontal attack-stink bomb" diatribes, permitting New South journalists to focus on issues other than North-South combat.[8] Henry Grady's perpetual optimism would have strained his readers' patience in the dark days of the past, while Dawson's campaigns against duelling and chain gangs might well have been regarded as inexcusable diversions from the main issues. Henry Watterson was singularly fortunate in the postwar world: service with Forrest and editorship of the *Chattanooga Rebel* gave him impeccable credentials as a Southerner, while his border-state location gave him far greater latitude to denounce Southern extremism and make gestures toward the welfare of the freedmen. The remarkable fondness of Northern journalists in later years for "Marse Henry" suggests a waning interest in the old concerns; how many quintessential Southern "Colonels" would have been lionized in the days when slavery and the rights of freedmen were crucial national concerns?

To Northern observers New South journalism was vastly different—vastly better—than Old South journalism. The real change, however, had been not so much in the Southern press as in the general climate of opinion. Actually, considerable continuity characterized nineteenth-century Southern journalism across the great divide of the Civil War. A study of one editor's career, extending from the age of Ritchie to the age of Grady, highlights important similarities.

William Tappan Thompson edited a Savannah daily newspaper for thirty-two years, from 1850 to his death in 1882.[9] Though born and raised in the North, Thompson first gained fame as the author of *Major Jones' Courtship*, a volume of humorous tales of life and customs among Georgia's "crackers." But despite the popularity of his Major Jones stories, his literary career failed and he turned to journalism. In 1850 he established the *Savannah Morning News*, a penny paper neutral in politics and devoted to general news for the entire community. Thompson soon became an honored city father, community booster and sometimes scold, advocate of home manufactures for economic self-sufficiency, and noted authority on politics. His *Savannah Morning News*, however, did not long remain a penny paper, for sectional discord and passion for politics destroyed Thompson's independence and drove him into the Democratic party. The *Morning News* became another Southern political paper, a weapon its editor wielded to attack Northern and Republican hegemony, whether political, economic, or intellectual.

In the crisis of the Union Thompson demanded Southern unity in support of secession, and in no time his daily efforts focused completely on the Confederate cause. With defeat, Thompson's call for resistance to Northern military might transformed into resistance to Northern political might. White supremacy, home rule, and Democratic triumph eventually excluded other topics from the editorial page.

The angry, combative style of the late fifties grew worse in the seventies; Thompson's editorial billingsgate was unusually vitriolic even for a period when newspaper language was least inhibited by good taste.

Emphasizing that Georgia had been betrayed, persecuted, and given over to the atrocities of a savage race, Thompson despised anything suggesting appeasement, demanding instead unity within the Democratic party to outlast the vicious radicals to the north.

With Redemption, editor Thompson at last felt sufficiently secure to reemphasize themes he had developed earlier but downplayed in the turmoil of Reconstruction. He again romanticized the future glory and prosperity of Savannah and of Georgia's farms, lobbied for new factories, and surprisingly wrote occasional editorials welcoming Northern capital. Thompson recalled the heroic struggles of Confederate armies and appropriately praised the holy work of decorating Confederate graves. The past was not forgotten, but his journalism no longer centered on the theme of resistance.

By the end of the seventies Thompson was a distinguished Savannah civic booster and spokesman for the conservative, business-and-planter-oriented, upper-middle-class Democrats who would dominate Georgia politics into the 1890s. When insurgency threatened the security of all that had been won by Redemption, his *Savannah Morning News* launched salvo after salvo in something akin to the old extremist style against those who would wreck the racial and political harmony of the state—or challenge elitist control. As I have argued elsewhere, the editorial life of William Tappan Thompson "reveals the Old South roots of the New South. It illustrates an essential continuity of nineteenth-century Southern history, especially the continuity in the world outlook of Southerners molded in the antebellum and Civil War era. Despite the upheavals of the Civil War, emancipation, and Reconstruction, William Tappan Thompson voiced throughout his long life the essence of editorial policies on race, politics, economic development, and the North set forth daily in the 1850s."[10]

Unity and continuity prevailed in nineteenth-century Southern journalism as in other aspects of Southern history. Daily newspapers below the Mason-Dixon line contained similar features, many of them distinctively Southern, and these appear in both antebellum and postbellum journalism. Though representative of different styles of journalism at different times and in different places, the editors covered in this study share certain characteristics. Most obviously, all of these editors were Southern spokesmen—except perhaps for Lumsden and Kendall in their early years (and they are exceptions which prove the rule). The intensity and tenor of their message, whether low-key (as in the case of Ritchie, Lumsden, Yeadon, or Dawson, for example) or passionate, defensive, or aggressive (as in the case of the Rhetts, Daniel, Forsyth, or sometimes even Watterson), reflected their perception of the South's needs and the seriousness of outside threats as well as their own personal journalistic style. Despite the limits to dissent, a large area remained open for personal controversy and public discussion.

Southern defensiveness in journalism matched defensiveness in politics. To a Southern Whig paper in the early 1840s journalism amounted to publishing the speeches of Henry Clay; by the end of that decade the press was a chief means of protecting slavery and advancing Southern interests in the territories and in the nation's capital. The career of Democrat Thomas Ritchie reflects this transformation. Sectional tensions curtailed his effectiveness in state and national politics and helped ruin his last years in journalism. As a siege mentality descended upon the South, a Southern editor had to be first and foremost a defender of his section, not an advocate of compromising political discourse or an ally of Northern politicos. Sectional diatribes replaced partisan combat; editors adopted a stance of intractability; and the press became a major bulwark in the intellectual blockade designed to keep the South pure. Grievances were legion. Of course the Southern press engaged in deadly combat with anything that smacked of abolitionism, but it also attacked government aggrandizement, Yankee arrogance, Northern commercial domination and cultural pretenses, women's rights, spiritualism, and what it perceived as the irrational nature of many Yankee reforms which (in the South's opinion) weakened society's stability and lowered its moral tone.[11] Whether controlled or hysterical, editorial brag and bluster, expressed publicly, reflected honorably upon the South's daily defenders: "What northern observers saw as brazenness and braggadocio southern conservatives perceived as the highest virtue."[12] Editors raged through war and Reconstruction, and even in the days of reconciliation, New South editors seldom missed an opportunity to set Northern critics right. Nineteenth-century Southern editors, as Fred Hobson has put it, were defenders, apologists, and traditionalists. Real critics and iconoclasts like Walter Hines Page were shunned and silenced, and many left the South.[13]

From Old South to New South, nineteenth-century Southern editors shared a common ideology. They defended and justified slavery until Appomattox and advanced the white South's gloss on race relations afterward. They took their stand for strict constitutionalism. The view northward was often dark, foreboding, defensive, and pessimistic; for the homefolk it was optimistic and encouraging. These editors exhibited for home consumption much the same enthusiasm, exaggeration, and romantic hope for progress as others in the editorial fraternity to the north, proclaiming the virtues of struggle and upward mobility and revealing nineteenth-century bourgeois values in their admiration for hard work, success, and wealth. For Southern editors, promoting was a natural and astute policy, but it also became a sectional mission:

the South had to be prepared to withstand Northern economic aggression in the 1850s or to modernize in order to catch up with national standards in the 1880s.

Identified with the promotion of Southern industry, economic development, and building of railroads on a large scale, New South editors were preaching what responsible Southern editors had endorsed since the 1840s. Southern editors had always spoken as boosters and cheerleaders for growth—not merely urban growth but any growth beneficial to their newspaper fields. Boosting, praising, unifying, mollifying, but above all developing their region's economic potential and building readership—this was what most editors did both before and after the Civil War. "In 1886," notes David Goldfield, "New South prophet Henry W. Grady assured members of the New England Society in New York that the South has 'sowed towns and cities in the place of theories, and put business above politics.' More than a generation earlier, the Richmond *Daily Dispatch* had informed a much less select group that 'a new and brighter era is evidently at hand. . . . The man of business is substituted for the political theorist.'"[14] It now seems clear that postwar Southern developers—and chief among them were newspapermen— had antebellum roots. Historian James Michael Russell concludes that "the rhetoric and behavior of post-Civil War Atlanta boosters were natural extensions of antebellum tendencies," while Laurence Shore, in emphasizing the continuity of the South's ruling elite and its capitalistic message, sagely notes that "the postbellum South's Northern-style work ethic and ideology of Northern-style economic development do not qualify as one of history's virgin births."[15] Even the Rhetts, who were as singlemindedly political and "Old Southern" as anyone, at least paid lip service to certain "New South" economic ideals thirty years before the coming of the name.

Charleston's papers were typical of the editorial efforts to sponsor urban growth and regional prosperity and security in the 1850s. Two traditional themes of the Southern press—urban commercial boosterism and Southern economic nationalism—merged in the *Mercury* and *Courier* and in countless other papers.[16] Rhett, with his rice plantations, and Yeadon, with his orchards and farm, understood the problems and opportunities of Southern agriculture and were its obvious enthusiasts. Nevertheless, their papers, published in the most planter-dominated state in the South, continually argued that the patriotic duty of the planters and townfolk was to support Southern efforts to develop shipping, railroads, retailing and manufacturing (as well as literature, education and, of course, the defense of Southern rights). Both papers supported the commercial convention movement; publicized the activities of railroad promoters, directors, and stockholders; advocated the development of Southern industry for regional security and self-sufficiency; and campaigned for direct trade between Charleston and European ports.[17]

Given these elements of substantive continuity, it is not the content of the New South message that justifies the use of the term so much as the absence of political obsession and a dwindling of the paranoid style in Southern journalism. To be sure, Southern defensiveness persisted, but New South journalists reflected their society's increasing sense of security in a Union no longer eager to enforce a social revolution by demanding black advancement. Without doubt, Marse Henry Watterson was vastly more congenial than the snarling, fanatical Forsyth, and certainly Grady was a more appealing and sympathetic person than the embittered Rhett; but all agreed on the economics of the New South program. Grady saw economic development as a path to prosperity and sectional reconciliation while Rhett saw it as a program for self-sufficiency and separation. Still, it bears repeating that differences in ultimate goals and in style should not obscure their essential agreement on the issues of Southern economic development.

But nineteenth-century editors showed little awareness of the ways in which commercial or industrial development would affect their society. From Southern economic nationalists in the 1840s and 1850s to Grady in the 1880s, editorial prescriptions for industrialization reflected an almost romantic reverie colored by booming commerce and smoking factories yet utterly innocent of practical obstacles or an awareness of social turmoil and labor strife usually associated with rapid industrial change.

Southern editors spoke for the interests of a conservative elite that held sway throughout the nineteenth century. Regardless of these editors' origins, they became respected members of a civic elite, and some also became influential politicians. From Ritchie, Kendall, and Lumsden to Dawson and Grady, these editors were honored city fathers. One exception was the misanthropic John M. Daniel, who inspired fear rather than respect. As community leaders they were, again except for Daniel, urban and regional boosters.

The unity of the Southern press as it marched in lockstep with the dominant elite on issues of major significance was remarkable. No Southern press except the early *Picayune* rose to fame by mocking the elite as did the *New York Herald*; no Southern daily shocked and titillated an eager reading public as did the *Chicago Times*; and no Southern journal could exhibit the independence of the *New York Evening Post* when it pursued its own course in the 1872 and 1876 presidential elections.[18] The South fostered little variety of opinion, no tradition of criticism, no clash of ideas, and no significant alternative clientele for the irreverent and enterprising editor. That humorous gadfly of the late 1830s and early 1840s, the *New Orleans Picayune*, was unique, and it soon metamorphosed into a rather staid, conservative Whiggish daily.

There was, however, an alternative weekly press in the nineteenth-century South—a press important in and by itself. The mainstream press can be understood by examining what it was not. That press was never the advocate of iconoclastic reform and never the spokesman for the black community. A brief foray into the South's alternative press in the late-nineteenth century highlights the major failing of the South's dominant press—its one-dimensional nature.

In the 1880s and 1890s Alliance and Populist weekly newspapers challenged the dominant journalism. Hard-hitting editorials in dozens of county seat weeklies and organs of state Farmers' Alliances scored telling points as they railed against the policies of Bourbon politicos, railroad owners, and bankers. They proclaimed the farmer and not the Bourbon senator the heart and soul of democratic politics. In contrast to the mainstream dailies, which celebrated the way things were in the South, the reform press found nothing right and everything wrong. Every news article was an editorial. Alliance and Populist editors attacked the crop-lien system and crusaded for the sub-treasury scheme. In the course of a relatively brief existence they introduced elements of economic realism and a genuine humanitarian concern for the rural poor lacking in the dominant press.[19]

With a clientele too poor to buy newspapers and major advertisers hostile to anything but subserviency to the Democracy, reform editors defied economic logic by their ability to maintain their existence, however brief. They were celebrated for their zeal and dedication; they sought influence, not profits. The most famous Populist weekly, Tom Watson's *People's Party Paper*, had at its peak a circulation of twenty thousand, but fewer than five hundred were paid subscribers.[20] Courage as well as principled dedication to a cause distinguished these editors, for many suffered persistent intimidation and not a few met violence at the hands of conservative Democrats.[21]

If the Bourbon establishment damned and then drove under most Populist journals, it usually ignored the black press. Also ignored were the activities and interests of the black community; hence the necessity for a special press. During Reconstruction black editors had focused on the political struggle, advancing the cause of the Republican party and fighting for equality and universal suffrage. In the 1880s, with hopes of equality and political influence dwindling, a conservative trend swept across black journalism in the South. Angry, militant, political journalism was increasingly rare. It simply was too risky, and more than one editor was driven from town, lucky to escape with his life, for uttering his opinions fearlessly. The most forthright defenders of Southern racial injustice published in Northern cities, where greater tolerance and concentrated black populations with greater financial resources and higher rates of literacy offered more opportunity and greater reward. A few black Southern editors were militant crusaders, such as John Mitchell, Jr., of the *Richmond Planet*, but most were compromising and accommodating and worked cautiously against discrimination, violence, and lynching.[22]

Politics still presented the prospect of employment and influence, but black editors now broadened the scope of their papers. The press of the 1880s placed the needs of the black community ahead of those of the Republican party or any other political organization. These editors were more than mere journalists. Many an aspiring black professional saw the press as a springboard to renown and community leadership. Black editors provided the community with examples of middle class mobility and success; they in turn boosted black achievements, featured self-help stories and tales of economic advancement, and worked to instill a sense of community among their readers. Establishing a forum for the articulation of black ideology, they protested racial injustice and offered wise counsel in times of distress. Probably most papers contained a mixture of militancy and conservatism, but their tone was dignified and their policies circumscribed.[23]

Publishing a black weekly was a haphazard venture at best. The high rate of illiteracy, the lack of advertising, the general poverty and isolation of most blacks limited the economic potential of every newspaper venture. Black journalists were excluded from white news-gathering facilities, and to obtain national and international news readers had to purchase the white press. While New South editors expanded their operations and modernized their plant and equipment, black journalists relied almost exclusively on scissors and paste.[24] Nor were they unchallenged in their own bailiwicks. Perhaps because of their militance, Northern black journalists such as T. Thomas Fortune of the *New York Globe* (and later the *Freeman* and the *Age*), Edward Cooper of the *Indianapolis Freeman*, and Calvin Chase of the *Washington Bee* sold well in the South, offering unwanted competition to their Southern counterparts. It is understandable that many a Southern editor earned his livelihood outside journalism and published a weekly more as an avocation than a business venture. Such difficulties underscore the achievements of black newspapermen, which should be measured not by newspaper longevity, but by influence, courageous leadership in a time of increasing oppression, and a readership which far exceeded subscriptions.[25]

The black press survived in a nether world unknown to whites; the combative rural reform press disappeared after a brief heyday as Bourbons reunited the South under the banner of white solidarity and white supremacy. The Populist fling was the exception which proves the rule. The Southern newspaper tradition, which is the focus of these essays, was that of the political journals and big city dailies, and they voiced the views of an elite. But what kind of an elite?

Before the war the values, interests, and ideology of a planter-merchant-professional class filled the columns of the major urban dailies. This was not a planter press *per se*, for its interests were anything but narrowly-focused. If there was a planter press at all, it most likely coalesced in the weekly rural press, where a small group of powerful planters could dominate a weak, divided opposition. After the war the dominant group in the South, the Redeemers or Bourbons, might best be viewed as a planter-merchant-professional-businessman-industrialist elite. If businessman-industrialist interests had more clout than planters in the big-city press after the war, it was because of the relatively greater size and ideological vigor of the expanding postwar cities compared with prewar cities.[26]

Despite the increased significance of New South urban business leaders and their newspaper allies, New South editors reached out to the most powerful groups in the countryside as well. In so doing, New South editors (unconsciously) emulated Old South editors. The *Courier* and *Mercury* on the eve of the war envisioned a Southern Republic strong in industry and trade as well as agriculture. Later Dawson, constant advocate of textile mill development, would be eulogized as the herald of practical, progressive agriculture in his state.[27] Henry Grady, the darling of industrialists and architect of Atlanta's rise from the ashes, campaigned for an agricultural renaissance and prefaced nearly every speech and promotional article with his love for the Old South. The needs and ideology of the Southern elite of the 1880s showed little difference from those of the Southern elite in the 1840s; even defenders of the Lost Cause and romanticizers of the Old South, such as Charles Colcock Jones and Thomas Nelson Page, anticipated in the 1880s a favorable reception in Southern newspapers because they espoused the official position of laudatory obeisance to the South and its causes, lost and enduring.[28]

Paradoxically, most Old South editors of the 1840s and 1850s and New South editors of the 1880s were among the most progressive elements of the Southern elite, for they promoted an ideological framework which enabled them to link economic development with social improvements and to present their interests as those of the South at large. As Tennant McWilliams has argued, "contemporary readers perceived the dynamic New South editors as 'metropolitan' and 'unprejudiced,'" but in the 1830s and 1840s Southern unionists also advocated "progressive

Southern change," striving to blunt ideas about secession and in varying degrees urging economic diversification.[29] In the intervening decades of war and Reconstruction progressive elements receded as editors rallied Southerners to an unyielding standard of resistance.

By the 1870s and 1880s the palpable lag in Southern journalism offered to many another example of Southern backwardness, but rather than a function of time, this lag reflected the sectional focus of the Southern world and the South's restricted newspaper field—lack of cities, a small, dispersed readership, a relatively high rate of illiteracy, limited capital resources, and a black population intentionally excluded from the realm of white newspapers. In the 1880s, however, sectionalism abated, and new technology and newspaper consolidation enabled the outstanding New South editors to overcome some of the worst handicaps and to excel and secure recognition as regional spokesmen. New South editors took advantage of the new climate and opportunities; they developed a sense of professionalism and studied closely the latest developments in the press world. Watterson, Dawson, Grady, and others spent time in New York City and other large Northern cities, visiting and observing the best metropolitan papers. Journalists of the 1880s had to be more cosmopolitan, looking for news stories, potential employees, and all the latest gossip of their profession.[30] Increasingly the dominance of New York and the eastern seaboard was challenged by a score of strong, nationally recognized newspapers far from the old centers of journalism. In the South, as elsewhere, the telegraph speedily brought the latest news and lessened dependence on slow-traveling mail and newspaper exchanges,[31] while hiring reporters and paying for the expensive but essential Associated Press dispatches raised dramatically the cost of keeping up with "the journalistic Joneses."

Earlier than elsewhere the number of major dailies decreased sharply in the South as a host of papers weakened by war and Reconstruction and by the costs of the latest news-gathering techniques sought through peaceful merger or bloody combat to eliminate rivals.[32] Too many poorly financed papers became an impediment to survival, to say nothing of prosperity.[33] Consolidation seemed the only answer. In postwar Richmond the *Enquirer* and the *Examiner* combined briefly before final collapse, and in New Orleans the *Picayune* was the only English-language daily to survive the war. By the 1870s the daily newspaper landscape in the South had been altered drastically: in Milledgeville, Georgia, the story of newspapering was summarized by the rivalry of the *Southern Recorder* and the *Federal Union*, which ended in consolidation in 1872;[34] in Charleston, the *Mercury* and the *Sentinel* disappeared and Dawson and Riordan joined the *News* and the *Courier*; and, in Louisville, Watterson presided at the marriage of the *Courier* and the *Journal* while the old *Democrat* went under. Among other postbellum papers born of combinations of well-known antebellum dailies were the *Augusta Chronicle and Constitutionalist, Columbus Enquirer-Sun,* and *Macon Telegraph and Messenger.* In the 1880s Alabama had only two or three major daily papers whose circulation, long tradition, and lack of competition made them a major force: the *Mobile Register, Montgomery Advertiser,* and perhaps the *Selma Times.* Atlanta in the early 1880s was essentially a one-paper town, but in 1886 two new dailies arose to compete for the evening market left open by the morning *Constitution.*[35]

Suspensions and mergers in the Southern press in the 1870s and 1880s proved the correctness of Dawson's dictum: "There is not room for two first-rate newspapers in any of the Southern cities, excepting New Orleans."[36] The *New York Express* commented on "Southern Journalism" in 1877: "Where it is not suspension, it is consolidation. . . . The South before the war, with not so many readers in proportion to the population, had more newspapers than the North, and journalism there in the olden time was intensely personal. Gales and Seaton, Ritchie and Daniels [sic], Rhett and Kendall and Holbrook were alike either leaders of the press or of the parties. This has been much less true since the war closed than before, and the effect of reducing the number has been to make journalism less personal, more liberal and far better as newspapers."[37]

The Solid South's support of one political party accelerated movement toward monopoly, though factionalism sometimes produced or sustained competing organs.[38] This phenomenon represented a major change from antebellum journalism, which had featured rival Democratic and Whig presses in all the major cities.[39] The Southern cities that supported two dailies, like Atlanta after 1883, usually had a morning Democratic and an evening Democratic paper, with the evening paper increasingly prominent because of the fuller flow of news from press services, improvements in home lighting, shorter working hours and more leisure time. In the North newspaper competition was far more significant not only because of a larger, concentrated readership, easier tolerance of conflicting opinions, and greater class, ethnic, and religious pluralism, but also because of a stronger two-party system. In Cincinnati, for example, two distinguished Republican journals combined in 1883 to stave off bankruptcy, but in so doing they still maintained a strong Republican voice to compete against the city's powerful Democratic *Enquirer.* Northern political editors gradually realized that partisan ranting shut them off from a huge readership among the opposition, and the abatement of partisanship signaled an interest in expanding circulation and increasing advertising revenues. In the South daily newspapers of any significance were Democratic and closed off from a large potential readership—the black community.[40]

A small group of New South editors, especially Watterson, Dawson, and Grady, championed modernization in the Southern press in the 1880s and came to dominate their newspaper fields if they did not drive out competition altogether. In 1882 the *Independent*, setting aside traditional stereotypes, declared that "the politicians who are fond of quoting the Oklaloona States (now named, if I remember right, The Solid South) should learn that this pestilent sheet is detested at the South no less cordially than the paper is here. . . . The press of the South is far above the grade usually assigned by vanity and ignorance by our Northern popular opinion. It is in the large cities exceptionally independent and allies itself with religion and philanthropy."[41] Even the *Journalist*, for once complimentary in regard to Southern enterprise, recognized a new stirring, acknowledging that the "befo the wah" style had been revolutionized by the lively innovations of the *Memphis Commercial*, "the 'phenomenon' of the Mississippi Valley."[42] In a special article on "The Southern Press," the *New York Evening Post* cited the national reputation of the *Atlanta Constitution* and praised its success in breaking down prejudices and in arousing the Southern people to the gospel of work. The *Evening Post*, applauding the *News and Courier*'s victories over violence, concluded: "The men who represent 'the new South' in the press have done good, honest, patriotic work. . . . They have made the press what it was designed to be—the leader and guide of readers."[43]

Notes

Introduction

1. Jean Folkerts, "Functions of the Reform Press," *Journalism History* 12 (Spring 1985): 22-25.

2. Ritchie is the only editor covered in this study who did not edit a Southern daily—his *Richmond Enquirer* appeared twice or thrice weekly.

3. Quoted in Billy Bowles and Remer Tyson, *They Love a Man in the Country: Saints and Sinners in the South* (Atlanta: Peachtree, 1989), 283.

4. James Bryce, *The American Commonwealth*, new ed. (New York: Macmillan, 1910), 2: 275; Edward Dicey, *Spectator of America*, edited and with an introduction by Herbert Mitgang (1863; reprint ed., Chicago: Quadrangle, 1971), 19-20; Waldo W. Braden, ed., *Oratory in the New South* (Baton Rouge: Louisiana State University Press, 1979), 11.

1. The World of the Southern Editor

1. Donald W. Curl, *Murat Halstead and the "Cincinnati Commercial"* (Boca Raton: University Presses of Florida, 1980), 140-43; Isaac F. Marcosson, *"Marse Henry": A Biography of Henry Watterson* (Westport, Conn.: Greenwood, 1951), 54, 55; J. Cutler Andrews, *Pittsburgh's Post-Gazette: "The First Newspaper West of the Alleghenies"* (Boston: Chapman and Grimes, 1936), 72; William J. Thorn, "Hudson's History of Journalism Criticized by His Contemporaries," *Journalism Quarterly* 57 (Spring 1980): 102; Harriet A. Weed, ed., *Autobiography of Thurlow Weed* (Boston: Houghton, Mifflin, 1884), 1: 411-12.

2. John Calhoun Ellen, Jr., "Political Newspapers of the Piedmont Carolinas in the 1850's" (Ph.D. diss., University of South Carolina, 1958), 119-21. Evidently the newspaper exchanges spread far and wide the analogy of editors with mules and starving anacondas. See *New Hampshire Patriot and State Gazette*, 26 March 1846.

3. Frank Luther Mott, *American Journalism; A History: 1690-1960*, 3rd ed. (New York: Macmillan, 1962), 113-14, 153.

4. Bert Marsh Mutersbaugh, "Jeffersonian Journalist: Thomas Ritchie and the 'Richmond Enquirer,' 1804-1820" (Ph.D. diss., University of Missouri-Columbia, 1973), 28-31.

5. *Charleston Mercury*, 16 August 1860.

6. Thad Stem, Jr., *The Tar Heel Press* (Charlotte: North Carolina Press Association, 1973), 26.

7. Bernard A. Weisberger, *The American Newspaperman* (Chicago: University of Chicago Press, 1961), 47; Mott, *American Journalism*, 146.

8. Ibid., 146-47; Clarence S. Brigham, *Journals and Journeymen* (Philadelphia: University of Pennsylvania Press, 1950), 68-69.

9. John Tebbel, *The Compact History of the American Newspaper*, rev. ed. (New York: Hawthorne, 1969), 73.

10. *American Journalism*, chap. 9 and pp. 124, 143, 167; Elwyn B. Robinson, "The Dynamics of American Journalism from 1787 to 1865," *Pennsylvania Magazine of History and Biography* 61 (July 1937): 435.

11. Beman Brockway, *Fifty Years in Journalism* (Watertown, N.Y.: Dailey Times Printing and Publishing House, 1891), 414. See also Mott, *American Journalism*, chaps. 9, 10, 14.

12. John Russell Young, *Men and Memories* (New York: F. Tennyson Neely, 1901), 1: 3.

13. *The Journalist*, 2 August 1884, 6; Weisberger, *American Newspaperman*, 78-84; Tebbel, *Compact History*, 80; Brockway, *Fifty Years*, 423, 425; Edwin Emery and Michael Emery, *The Press and America*, 4th ed. (Englewood Cliffs, N.J.: Prentice Hall, 1978), 108; William E. Smith, "Francis P. Blair, Pen-Executive of Andrew Jackson," in Edwin Ford and Edwin Emery, eds., *Highlights in the History of the American Press* (Minneapolis: University of Minnesota Press, 1954), 142-43.

14. J. Mills Thornton III, *Politics and Power in a Slave Society: Alabama, 1800-1860* (Baton Rouge: Louisiana State University Press, 1978), 128-29.

15. Weisberger, *American Newspaperman*, 9; Marvin Davis Evans, "The Richmond Press on the Eve of the Civil War," *The John P. Branch Historical Papers of Randolph-Macon College*, New Series, 1 (January 1951): 14; Mott, *American Journalism*, 198-204.

16. Francis J. Grund, *Aristocracy in America*, ed. G.E. Probst (1839; reprint ed., New York: Harper and Row, 1959), 193; Julius Wilcox, "Journalism as a Profession," *The Galaxy* 4 (November 1867): 801.

17. *Memphis Daily Appeal*, 18 September 1847.

18. Allan R. Pred, *Urban Growth and the Circulation of Information: The United States System of Cities, 1790-1840* (Cambridge, Mass.: Harvard University Press, 1973), 57.

19. Robinson, "Dynamics of American Journalism," 440.

20. William David Sloan, "The Early Party Press: The Newspaper Role in American Politics, 1788-1812," *Journalism History* 9 (Spring 1982): 18-19; William Cullen Bryant, "William Leggett," *The United States Magazine and Democratic Review* 6 (July 1839): 19.

21. David Macrae, *The Americans at Home* (1871; reprint ed., New York: Dutton, 1952), 583; Weed, ed., *Autobiography of Thurlow Weed*, 1: 8, 97; Edwin A. Miles, "The Mississippi Press in the Jackson Era, 1824-1841," *Journal of Mississip-*

pi History 19 (January 1957): 13; Guion Griffis Johnson, *Ante-Bellum North Carolina* (Chapel Hill: University of North Carolina Press, 1937), 788; W. Stanley Hoole, *Alias Simon Suggs: The Life and Times of Johnson Jones Hooper* (1952; reprint ed., Westport, Conn.: Greenwood, 1970), 107.

22. Thomas Harrison Baker, *The Memphis Commercial Appeal* (Baton Rouge: Louisiana State University Press, 1971), 43-44. By way of illustration, when the *New Orleans Picayune*'s office burned down, the paper's rivals offered the *Picayune* the use of their full resources until it could get on its feet again. *Charleston Daily Courier*, 22 January 1858.

23. Isaac Clark Pray, *Memoirs of James Gordon Bennett* (New York: Stringer and Townsend, 1855), 44. Patrician New Yorker Philip Hone made the same point in his diary in 1837: "Everybody wonders how people can buy these receptacles of scandal, the penny papers, and yet everybody does encourage them; and the very man who blames his neighbors for setting so bad an example, occasionally puts one in his pocket to carry home to his family for their and his own edification," quoted in Gunther Barth, *City People: The Rise of Modern City Culture in Nineteenth-Century America* (New York: Oxford University Press, 1980), 73.

24. James Silk Buckingham, *America* (London: Fisher, Son, 1841), 3: 412-13.

25. Brockway, *Fifty Years*, 425.

26. Quoted in Bernard A. Weisberger, *Reporters for the Union* (Boston: Little, Brown, 1953), 15.

27. Weisberger, *Reporters*, 16. Of course Dickens might have found targets closer to home. "In 1829 John Stuart Mill claimed that 'more affectation and hypocrisy are necessary for the trade of literature, and especially the newspapers, than for a brothel-keeper.'" Alan J. Lee, *The Origins of the Popular Press in England, 1855-1914* (London: Croom Helm, 1976), 24.

28. See, e.g., *Charleston Mercury*, 18 July 1860; *Charleston Daily Courier*, 25, 28 January 1858; 6 February 1858; 5 April 1858; 27 September 1858; 22 April 1859; 27 September 1860; 22 October 1860; 16 November 1860.

29. Justin E. Walsh, *To Print the News and Raise Hell!* (Chapel Hill: University of North Carolina Press, 1968), 18, 22-23, 44, 93, 100-101, 122, 125, 127, 129.

30. James G. Harrison, "Nineteenth Century Novels on American Journalism: I," *Journalism Quarterly* 22 (September 1945): 217.

31. John Pendleton Kennedy, *Quodlibet* (1840; reprint ed., Upper Saddle River, N.J.: Literature House/Gregg Press, 1970), 79.

32. Ibid., 79-81.

33. Quoted in Hodding Carter, *Their Words Were Bullets* (Athens: University of Georgia Press, 1969), 10.

34. Lambert A. Wilmer's *Our Press Gang: A Complete Exposure of the Corruptions and Crimes of American Newspapers* (Philadelphia: J.T. Lloyd, 1859) was the antebellum era's most thorough antipress diatribe. Wilmer was a former editor. See also Charles T. Congdon, *Reminiscences of a Journalist* (Boston: James R. Osgood, 1880), 268; Wilcox, "Journalism as a Profession," 801, 802; Buckingham, *America*, 2: 35-37, 333-35.

35. *Charleston Daily Courier*, 16 March 1860; Isaac F. Marcosson, *Adventures in Interviewing* (London: John Lane, 1919), 59-60.

36. Congdon, *Reminiscenses*, 254. See also Wilcox, "Journalism as a Profession," 804.

37. *Charleston Daily Courier*, 19 July 1858.

38. Bryant, "Leggett," 18. William Cullen Bryant's friends jeered at him for exchanging the dignified profession of law for a "vulgar newspaper calling." See Allan Nevins, *The Evening Post: A Century of Journalism* (New York: Boni and Liveright, 1922), 362.

39. Quoted in John Stanford Coussons, "Thirty Years with Calhoun, Rhett, and the Charleston Mercury; A Chapter in South Carolina Politics," (Ph.D. diss., Louisiana State University and Agricultural and Mechanical College, 1971), 230.

40. David R. Goldfield, "Pursuing the American Dream: Cities in the Old South," in Blaine A. Brownell and David R. Goldfield, eds., *The City in Southern History* (Port Washington, N.Y.: Kennikat, 1977), 59-60.

41. Lawrence T. McDonnell, "Struggle Against Suicide: James Henry Hammond and the Secession of South Carolina," *Southern Studies* 22 (Summer 1983): 123.

42. Bertram Wyatt-Brown, *Southern Honor; Ethics and Behavior in the Old South* (New York: Oxford University Press, 1982), 356.

43. *Vengeance and Justice: Crime and Punishment in the Nineteenth-Century American South* (New York: Oxford University Press, 1984), 13, 17.

44. Drew Gilpin Faust, *James Henry Hammond and the Old South: A Design for Mastery* (Baton Rouge: Louisiana State University Press, 1982), 50-51.

45. Charles F. Wingate, ed., *Views and Interviews on Journalism* (New York: F.B. Patterson, 1875), 46; Andrews, *Pittsburgh's Post-Gazette*, 133.

46. Leonard W. Levy, *Jefferson and Civil Liberties: The Darker Side* (Cambridge, Mass.: Belknap Press of Harvard University Press, 1963), 68; William E. Ames, *A History of the National Intelligencer* (Chapel Hill: University of North Carolina Press, 1972), 339-45; Nevins, *Evening Post*; Weed, ed., *Autobiography of Thurlow Weed*, 1: 180. In the 1860s, when the old journalism of politics and constitutionalism— however partisan or bitter—was rapidly giving way to sensationalism, scandal, and the hyped-up news story, the elderly William S. Seaton still believed a paper should "furnish facts and arguments to the studious and thoughtful rather than the superficial 'skimmings' and impressions designed for those who 'have no use for them except for the casual conversation of the day.'" See Ames, *History of the National Intelligencer*, 324.

47. William E. Ames and Dwight L. Teeter, "Politics, Economics, and Mass Media," in Ronald T. Farrar and John D. Stevens, eds., *Mass Media and the National Experience* (New York: Harper and Row, 1971), 56; Gerald J. Baldasty, "The Charleston, South Carolina, Press and National News, 1808-47," *Journalism Quarterly* 55 (1978): 526.

48. Weisberger, *American Newspaperman*, 73; Emery and Emery, *Press*, chaps. 10, 11; Mott, *American Journalism*, chap. 13; Michael Schudson, *Discovering the News: A Social History of American Newspapers* (New York: Basic Books, 1978), 14-58 *passim*; Dan Schiller, *Objectivity and the News: The Public and the Rise of Commercial Journalism* (Philadelphia: University of Pennsylvania Press, 1981), chaps. 1, 2.

49. Douglas Fermer, *James Gordon Bennett and the New York Herald: A Study of Editorial Opinion in the Civil War Era, 1854-1867* (Woodbridge, England: Royal Historical Society and The Boydell Press; New York: St. Martin's, 1986), 18-19; James L. Crouthamel, *Bennett's New York Herald and the Rise of the Popular Press* (Syracuse: Syracuse University Press, 1989), 24, 79, 94, 98-99, 158-61.

50. Weisberger, *American Newspaperman*, 96-97, 101, 112, 118; idem, *Reporters*, 305-6; Louis M. Starr, *Reporting the Civil War: The Bohemian Brigade in Action, 1861-65*, with a new introduction by Allan Nevins (New York: Collier, 1962), 8; Walsh, *To Print the News*, 15; Tebbel, *Compact History*, 97-98; Schudson, *Discovering the News*, 66; Barth, *City People*, 64; James L. Crouthamel, *James Watson Webb, A Biography* (Middletown, Conn.: Wesleyan University Press, 1969), 152, 155.

51. Henry King, "Pay and Rank of Journalists," *Forum* 18 (January 1895): 594.

52. Wyatt-Brown, *Southern Honor*, 176-77.

53. David R. Goldfield, *Cotton Fields and Skyscrapers: Southern City and Region, 1607-1980* (Baton Rouge: Louisiana State University Press, 1982), chap. 2.

54. In 1850 the *Picayune*'s daily circulation stood at 7,000 while the *New York Sun*'s was 55,000 and the *Philadelphia Public Ledger*'s was 44,000. J.C.G. Kennedy, "Catalogue of the Newspapers and Periodicals Published in the United States . . . " in John Livingston, *Livingston's Law Register for 1852* (New York, 1852), 14, 29, 44; King, "Pay and Rank of Journalists," 594.

55. Pred, *Urban Growth*, 27-50 *passim*; Donald L. Shaw and John W. Slater, "In the Eye of the Beholder? Sensationalism in American Press News, 1820-1860," *Journalism History* 12 (Autumn-Winter 1985): 86.

56. Quoted in Starr, *Reporting the Civil War*, 8. See also George Henry Payne, *History of Journalism in the United States* (New York: D. Appleton, 1926), 301; Johnson, *Ante-Bellum North Carolina*, 785.

57. There may be something of "the chicken and the egg" puzzle here. In addition to a high rate of illiteracy, perhaps slaves, freedmen, poor whites, etc., did not buy newspapers because they were not addressed to them. Nevertheless, the fact is that throughout most of the nineteenth century, the South's daily press did not consider these groups a part of the public that counted.

2. Between Nationalism and Nullification

1. 4 July 1854.

2. Lyon G. Tyler, *The Letters and Times of the Tylers* (1884; reprint ed., New York: Da Capo, 1970), 2: 358; Francis R. Wayland, *Andrew Stevenson: Democrat and Diplomat, 1785-1857* (Philadelphia: University of Pennsylvania Press, 1949), 234; Charles H. Ambler, *Thomas Ritchie: A Study in Virginia Politics* (Richmond: Bell Book and Stationery, 1913), 112-13; Charles T. Thrift, "Thomas Ritchie," *John P. Branch Historical Papers of Randolph-Macon College* 1 (June 1902): 172; Frederic Hudson, *Journalism in the United States from 1690 to 1872* (New York: Harper and Brothers, 1873), 270; *Richmond Enquirer*, 26 June 1827.

3. Thrift, "Thomas Ritchie," 173.

4. John A. Parker, *The Missing Link* (Washington, D.C.: Gray and Clarkson, 1886), 23-24.

5. William C. Rives to Thomas Walker Gilmer, 13 November 1828, in *Tyler's Quarterly Historical and Genealogical Magazine* 6 (October 1924): 98.

6. John Spencer Bassett, ed., *Correspondence of Andrew Jackson* (Washington, D.C.: Carnegie Institution, 1929), 4: 18; *Daily Albany* (New York) *Argus*, 6 July 1854.

7. Andrew Jackson to James K. Polk, 13 December 1844, in Tyler, *Letters*

and Times of the Tylers 3: 155-56; John Randolph to Andrew Jackson, 1832, in Bassett, *Jackson*, 4: 410, 420.

8. *Richmond Enquirer*, 4 July 1854. Hereafter the title of Ritchie's paper will be shortened to *Enquirer*.

9. Thomas C. Leonard, *The Power of the Press: The Birth of American Political Reporting* (New York: Oxford University Press, 1986), 133, 167.

10. Bert Marsh Mutersbaugh, "Jeffersonian Journalist: Thomas Ritchie and the Richmond *Enquirer*, 1804-1820" (Ph.D. diss., University of Missouri-Columbia, 1973), 21-22; *Enquirer*, 25 July 1854. The *Enquirer* was published three times weekly when the legislature was in session.

11. For Ritchie's early life and preparation for journalism, see Ambler, *Ritchie*, 10-12; Mutersbaugh, "Jeffersonian Journalist," 15-19; Richard B. Davis, *Intellectual Life in Jefferson's Virginia, 1790-1830* (Chapel Hill: University of North Carolina Press, 1964), 80-81; *Dictionary of American Biography*, 8: 628.

12. Mutersbaugh, "Jeffersonian Journalist," 32-56, 82; Ambler, *Ritchie*, 18, 19, 28, 157; Culver Smith, *The Press, Politics, and Patronage* (Athens: University of Georgia Press, 1977), 43. Ritchie had attempted to secure the state's official patronage, but after unsuccessful attempts in 1804 and 1805, he refused to contest the issue for fear of dividing the Virginia Republicans (and perhaps receiving another rejection).

13. Mutersbaugh, "Jeffersonian Journalist," 64-67; Ambler, *Ritchie*, 19; *Enquirer*, 1804.

14. Mutersbaugh, "Jeffersonian Journalist," 133, 134.

15. Ibid., 452.

16. *Enquirer*, 7, 25 July 1854; Ritchie to Andrew Stevenson, 4 March 1839, Stevenson Family Papers, Library of Congress, Washington, D.C.; Samuel Mordecai, *Virginia, Especially Richmond in By-Gone Days*, 2nd ed. (Richmond: West and Johnson Publishers, 1860), 235; Robert W. Hughes, *Editors of the Past* (Richmond: William Ellis Jones, 1897), 10; Mutersbaugh, "Jeffersonian Journalist," 64, 109.

17. John P. Heiss to Ritchie, 15 September 1846, Thomas Ritchie Mss., Library of Congress.

18. Ambler, *Ritchie*, 296; *New Orleans Daily Picayune*, 11 February 1838; 10 December 1842; C.W. Gooch to Col. David Campbell, 20 January 1820, Campbell Family Papers, Perkins Library, Duke University. See also Ritchie's appeal for the payment of annual subscriptions, in *Enquirer*, 4 November 1831.

19. Thomas Green to Ritchie, 6 April 1845, Ritchie Mss.; Ritchie to William C. Rives, 17 September 1836, Rives Mss., Library of Congress; C.W. Gooch to Col. George Thompson, 29 August 1828, Gooch Family Papers, Accession No. 3921-a, Box 1, Alderman Library, University of Virginia; Thomas Ritchie to Archibald Ritchie, 8 June 1830, and 28 December 1830, in "Letters of Thomas Ritchie—Glimpses of the Year 1830," *The John P. Branch Historical Papers of Randolph-Macon College* 2 (June 1902): 147-54; Jonathan Campbell to Col. David Campbell, 2 April 1822, Campbell Family Papers; *New Orleans Daily Picayune*, 10 December 1842.

20. Alison Goodyear Freehling, *Drift Toward Dissolution; The Virginia Slavery Debate of 1831-1832* (Baton Rouge: Louisiana State University Press, 1982), 34.

21. David R. Goldfield, "Urban-Rural Relations in the Old South: The Example of Virginia," *Journal of Urban History* 2 (February 1976): 148-49; idem, *Urban Growth in the Age of Sectionalism: Virginia, 1847-1861* (Baton Rouge: Louisiana State University Press, 1977), 29-31, 36, 39.

22. *Enquirer*, 25 July 1854; *New York Herald*, 4 July 1854; Ritchie to W.C. Rives, 22 March 1837, Rives Mss.; Parker, *Missing Link*, 24-25; Mutersbaugh, "Jeffersonian Journalist," 210. See, for example, *Enquirer*, 16 November 1824; 21 December 1824; 26 October 1838.

23. *New York Times*, 4 July 1854.

24. *Enquirer*, 26 June 1838.

25. See, e.g., the *Enquirer*, 10 April 1810, and early January 1838.

26. Ritchie to W.C. Rives, 5 June [1835?], in "Unpublished Letters of Thomas Ritchie," *The John P. Branch Historical Papers of Randolph-Macon College* 3 (June 1911): 221; *Enquirer*, 26 January 1843.

27. *Enquirer*, 20 June 1817.

28. Ritchie to Robert T. Hubbard, 8 April 1844, Hubbard Family Papers, Accession No. 8039, Box 2, Alderman Library, University of Virginia; F.W. Randolph to Ritchie, 29 January 1837, Randolph Family Papers, Accession No. 8937-b, Box 4, Alderman Library, University of Virginia.

29. *Enquirer*, 17 February 1838; 25 July 1854.

30. Milo Milton Quaife, ed., *The Diary of James K. Polk*, with an introduction by Andrew C. McLaughlin (Chicago: A.C. McClurg, 1910), 4: 216.

31. Wayland, *Stevenson*, 34, 72.

32. Ambler, *Ritchie*, 294; Mutersbaugh, "Jeffersonian Journalist," 250, 252; *Enquirer*, 31 January 1824; 25 July 1854.

33. Jonathan Daniels, *They Will Be Heard* (New York: McGraw-Hill, 1965), 95-96; Ambler, *Ritchie*, 40, 294; Wayland, *Stevenson*, 198; Mutersbaugh, "Jeffersonian Journalist," 15, 184; *Enquirer*, 24 July 1854; Marvin Duke and Daniel P. Jordan, eds., *A Richmond Reader, 1773-1983* (Chapel Hill: University of North Carolina Press, 1983), 347-48; Goldfield, *Urban Growth in the Age of Sectionalism*, 59; John Niven, *Martin Van Buren: The Romantic Age of American Politics* (New York: Oxford University Press, 1983), 120.

34. See, e.g., *Enquirer*, 20 September 1815; Mutersbaugh, "Jeffersonian Journalist," 87, 370-85, 396.

35. *Enquirer*, 6 November 1832; 3 April 1838; 9 November 1838; 22 November 1842; Ambler, *Ritchie*, 64-65; Norma Lois Peterson, *Littleton Waller Tazewell* (Charlottesville: University Press of Virginia, 1983), 166; Davis, *Intellectual Life*, 32-33; Virginius Dabney, *Liberalism in the South* (Chapel Hill: University of North Carolina Press, 1932), 89-90.

36. Davis, *Intellectual Life*, 75.

37. Mutersbaugh, "Jeffersonian Journalist," 363. See, e.g., *Enquirer*, 5, 12 November 1824. Editorials on foreign affairs were minimal in the 1820s and 1830s.

38. James Buchanan to Edmund Burke, 31 August 1849, Edmund Burke Papers, Library of Congress.

39. Ritchie to Charles Campbell, 6 April 1842, in "Unpublished Letters of Thomas Ritchie," *The John P. Branch Historical Papers of Randolph-Macon College* 3 (June 1911): 248. By contrast, the *Enquirer* showed little interest in the presidential election of 1820 since there was no real contest. See *Enquirer*, 7 November 1820.

40. *Enquirer*, 21 May 1824; 6 November 1832; 2 January 1838; Mutersbaugh, "Jeffersonian Journalist," 62.

41. *Enquirer*, 2 April 1833.

42. Ibid., 7 November 1806.

43. Ibid., 23 January 1838; 9 May 1845; Ambler, *Ritchie*, 257. A small elite in the editorial corps shared his views. William Cullen Bryant, for example, echoed Ritchie's sentiments: "The influence of the journalist is even greater than that of the orator, inasmuch as it is constant and perpetual, at the same time that it is more widely diffused—he is the daily counsellor of his reader, and of thousands of readers." See *Washington Daily Union*, 27 June 1850 (hereafter cited as *Daily Union*); William Cullen Bryant, "William Leggett," *The United States Magazine and Democratic Review* 6 (July 1839): 25.

44. *Enquirer*, 15 August 1806; 7 November 1828; Mutersbaugh, "Jeffersonian Journalist," 142.

45. *Enquirer*, 7 November 1806; 15 January 1824; 23 January 1838; 4 November 1842.

46. Marvin Davis Evans, "The Richmond Press on the Eve of the Civil War," *The John P. Branch Historical Papers of Randolph-Macon College*, New Series, 1 (January 1951): 17.

47. *Enquirer*, 7 September 1832; 26 March 1833; 17 January 1843.

48. Mutersbaugh, "Jeffersonian Journalist," 221.

49. *A Pamphlet containing a Series of Letters, written by Colonel John Taylor, of Caroline, to Thomas Ritchie, Editor of the "Enquirer" . . . Richmond* (Richmond: E.C. Stanard, 1809), 4; *Enquirer*, 17 January 1845.

50. *Enquirer*, 27 April 1824.

51. Ibid., 7 November 1806; 15 July 1842; 4 November 1842; *Daily Union*, 15 April 1851.

52. *Enquirer*, 23 January 1838. It seems that the convention's primary purpose was to address the problem of delinquent subscribers and to standardize advertising rates. Editors elsewhere also supported press conventions aimed at reducing editorial abuse and dealing with delinquent subscribers. See Guion Griffis Johnson, *Ante-Bellum North Carolina* (Chapel Hill: University of North Carolina Press, 1937), 793.

53. Mordecai, *Virginia*, 236.

54. Lester J. Cappon, *Virginia Newspapers, 1821-1935* (New York: D. Appleton-Century, 1936), 11; *Enquirer*, 2 March 1838; F.N. Boney, "Rivers of Ink, A Stream of Blood: The Tragic Career of John Hampden Pleasants," *Virginia Cavalcade* 18 (1968-69): 39; Barbara J. Griffin, ed., "Thomas Ritchie and the Code Duello," *The Virginia Magazine of History and Biography* 92 (January 1984): 72; Peterson, *Tazewell*, 240.

55. Cappon, *Virginia Newspapers*, 11; *Enquirer*, 6 September 1842. The relationship was not always one of combat or mortal enmity. Journalistic courtesy was occasionally evident. Once, for example, the *Whig* permitted the *Enquirer* to see its proof sheets so that the Democratic paper could include President Jackson's message to Congress in its current issue. Of course, at this time both the *Enquirer* and the *Whig* were fighting nullification. See *Enquirer*, 6 December 1832.

56. *Enquirer*, 12 August 1842, in "An Editorial from the Richmond Enquirer, 1842," *The John P. Branch Historical Papers of Randolph-Macon College* 3 (June 1911): 271.

57. *Enquirer*, 24 January 1843.

58. Carl R. Osthaus, "An Affair of Honor—Not an Honorable Affair: The Ritchie-Pleasants Duel and the Press," *Virginia Cavalcade* 26 (Winter 1977):

110-23. My interpretation differs from that of Barbara Griffin ("Thomas Ritchie and the Code Duello"). She maintains that Ritchie's letters in 1843 and 1846 indicate that though he never fought a duel, he was, on duelling, very much a man of his time and place, and that his role in these incidents was not a restraining one. My reading of the evidence is that Ritchie was a proud father defending his sons' reputation, which made him seem to endorse Thomas Jr.'s actions in the duel. See *Enquirer*, 2 March 1838; Ritchie to William C. Rives, 23 August 1834, *The John P. Branch Historical Papers of Randolph-Macon College* 3 (June 1911): 218.

59. *Enquirer*, 15 August 1806; 5 October 1806; 14 September 1832; Mutersbaugh, "Jeffersonian Journalist," 144.

60. Mutersbaugh, "Jeffersonian Journalist," 124. See, e.g., *Enquirer*, 5 October 1806; 9 July 1819; 16 April 1824; 19 October 1824; 4 January 1838; 17 February 1838.

61. Harry Ammon, *James Monroe: The Quest for National Identity* (New York: McGraw-Hill, 1971), 274-75.

62. *Enquirer*, 3 August 1832; November-December 1832; January 1833.

63. See, e.g., *Enquirer*, 1 April 1830.

64. *Enquirer*, 2 April 1830; Dickson B. Bruce, *The Rhetoric of Conservatism: The Virginia Convention of 1829-30 and the Conservative Tradition in the South* (San Marino, Calif.: Huntington Library, 1982), 31-34.

65. *Enquirer*, 15 August 1837; J.L. Martin to Van Buren, 19 September 1843, Martin Van Buren Mss., Library of Congress; James R. Sharp, *The Jacksonians versus the Banks: Politics in the States After the Panic of 1837* (New York: Columbia University Press, 1970), chap. 9.

66. The *New Orleans Daily Picayune* (10 February 1838) observed how Ritchie never would be caught in a minority.

67. Ammon, *Monroe*, 430; Mutersbaugh, "Jeffersonian Journalist," 422-31.

68. Smith, *Press, Politics, and Patronage*, 93.

69. *Enquirer*, 25 May 1838; Ritchie to Andrew Stevenson, 4 August 1839, Stevenson Family Papers; Amos Kendell to Col. C.W. Gooch [1837?], Gooch Family Papers, Accession No. 3921-a, Alderman Library, University of Virginia; Andrew Jackson to Martin Van Buren, 18 December 1838, Van Buren Mss.; John Letcher to Martin Van Buren, n.d., Van Buren Mss.; Sharp, *Jacksonians versus the Banks*, chap. 9.

70. James Buchanan to Martin Van Buren, 11 May 1839, Van Buren Mss.

71. Andrew Jackson to James K. Polk, 13 December 1844, in Tyler, *Letters and Times*, 3: 156; "Letter of C.W. Gooch to Martin Van Buren, 1835," *The John P. Branch Historical Papers of Randolph-Macon College* 3 (June 1911): 255; W.C. Rives to Governor Campbell, 22 June 1839, Campbell Family Papers.

72. See, e.g., *Enquirer*, 6 July 1838; Joseph W. Jackson to Ritchie, 1 April 1852, Ritchie Mss.; Alfred Balch to Ritchie, 20 February 1847, ibid.

73. See the comment from the *Richmond Examiner* in the *Enquirer*, 11 July 1854.

74. Ambler, *Ritchie*, 25.

75. Ibid., 165-67; Clement Eaton, *The Freedom-of-Thought Struggle in the Old South*, rev. ed. (New York: Harper and Row, Harper Torchbooks, 1964), 167; *Enquirer*, 6 July 1832. During the Missouri Crisis, Ritchie had referred to slavery as a stain (24 October 1820). The Nat Turner uprising sparked considerable criti-

cism of slavery and free blacks (13 September 1831; 18, 21 October 1831; 4, 8 November 1831).

76. *Enquirer*, 7, 12, 19 January 1832.

77. Freehling, *Drift Toward Dissolution*, xii, xiii. While I have profitted from Alison Freehling's 1982 study of the Virginia slavery debate, I still see Virginia, in regard to slavery, as a closed society. The 1831-32 debates were exceptional. John Hampden Pleasants maintained his "liberalism" on slavery longer than Ritchie, but Pleasants's position was impossible to sustain and he abandoned it. See Robert Hume Tomlinson, "The Origins and Editorial Policies of the Richmond Whig and Public Advertiser, 1824-1865," (Ph.D. diss., Michigan State University, 1971), 84, 85.

78. *Enquirer*, 4 February 1832.

79. Ibid., 12 January 1832; 4 February 1832.

80. Quoted in William W. Freehling, *Prelude to Civil War: The Nullification Controversy in South Carolina, 1816-1838* (New York: Harper and Row, Harper Torchbooks, 1965), 83.

81. Freehling, *Drift Toward Dissolution*, 201; Tomlinson, "The Origins and the Editorial Policies of the Richmond Whig . . . ," 83; *Enquirer*, April 1832; Joseph Clarke Robert, *The Road From Monticello: A Study of the Virginia Slavery Debate of 1832* (1941; reprint ed., New York: AMS Press, 1970), 43-45.

82. Boney, "Rivers of Ink," 35-37.

83. *Enquirer*, 17, 24 August 1824; 7 November 1828; 2 March 1843; 25 July 1854.

84. Merrill D. Peterson, *The Jefferson Image in the American Mind* (New York: Oxford University Press, 1962), 38.

85. Ambler, *Ritchie*, 42-45, 58; Mutersbaugh, "Jeffersonian Journalist," 129, chap. 3 *passim*; Thrift, "Thomas Ritchie," 176.

86. Ambler, *Ritchie*, 72-74, 78-81; Peterson, *Jefferson Image*, 38-39.

87. Glover Moore, *The Missouri Controversy, 1819-1821* (Lexington: University of Kentucky Press, 1966), 242, 243; Daniel P. Jordan, *Political Leadership in Jefferson's Virginia* (Charlottesville: University Press of Virginia, 1983), 32-33.

88. Moore, *Missouri Controversy*, 233-34, 250; C.W. Gooch to Col. David Campbell, 16 February 1820, Campbell Family Papers.

89. *Enquirer*, 14 May 1819; 21 December 1819; Moore, *Missouri Controversy*, 232, 233; Ambler, *Ritchie*, 78.

90. *Enquirer*, 8 February 1820; Tyler, *Letters and Times*, 1: 325; Moore, *Missouri Controversy*, 233, 236.

91. Peterson, *Jefferson Image*, 38-39; Ambler, *Ritchie*, 81; Mutersbaugh, "Jefferson Journalist," 450; Robert Shalhope, *John Taylor of Caroline, Pastoral Republican* (Columbia: University of South Carolina Press, 1980), 193.

92. *Enquirer*, 7 March 1820; Moore, *Missouri Controversy*, 239.

93. *Enquirer*, 3 June 1817; 14 December 1824; 25 July 1854; *Daily Union*, 15 January 1846; Mutersbaugh, "Jeffersonian Journalist," 455.

94. Jordan, *Political Leadership*, 32-33.

95. Cappon, *Virginia Newspapers*, 4.

96. Joseph H. Harrison, Jr., "Oligarchs and Democrats: The Richmond Junto," *Virginia Magazine of History and Biography* 78 (1970): 188.

97. Harrison, "Oligarchs and Democrats," 188.

98. The Junto's controlling influence within Virginia can be gauged by an

incident in the vice-presidential balloting in 1824. At the last minute, after the collapse of a political deal, Virginia's electors cast all twenty-four electoral ballots for a surprise candidate, Nathaniel Macon, whose sole electoral support came from Virginia. Harry Ammon notes that "the only indication that he [Macon] was to be the choice of Virginia was in the form of a brief article published in the *Enquirer* shortly before the electors assembled pointing him out for their consideration. Ritchie's word seems to have been quite sufficient notice." See Harry Ammon, "The Richmond Junto, 1800-1824," *Virginia Magazine of History and Biography* 61 (1953): 395, 397.

99. Ibid; Harrison, "Oligarchs and Democrats," 187,189; Jordan, *Political Leadership*, 76-79.

100. Davis, *Intellectual Life*, 430; Harrison, "Oligarchs and Democrats," 188, 190; Jordan, *Political Leadership*, 24.

101. Harrison, "Oligarchs and Democrats," *passim*; Ammon, "Richmond Junto," *passim*; Mutersbaugh, "Jeffersonian Journalist," 182.

102. Ammon, "Richmond Junto," 408-9.

103. Ibid., 401; Harrison, "Oligarchs and Democrats," 190, 195; Mutersbaugh, "Jeffersonian Journalist," 56-58, 175, 201.

104. Ammon, "Richmond Junto," 395, 398; Harrison, "Oligarchs and Democrats," 186.

105. *Enquirer*, 21 September 1824; 26 June 1827; 30 October 1832.

106. Jordan, *Political Leadership*, 25-26.

107. *Enquirer*, 25 July 1854; McCormick, *Second American Party System*, 184, 188; Harrison, "Oligarchs and Democrats," 187; Ammon, "Richmond Junto," 405-6; Mutersbaugh, "Jeffersonian Journalist," 254; Jordan, *Political Leadership*, 206-10; John P. Frank, *Justice Daniel Dissenting: A Biography of Peter V. Daniel, 1784-1860* (Cambridge, Mass.: Harvard University Press, 1964), 77-78.

108. William J. Cooper, Jr., *The South and the Politics of Slavery, 1828-1856* (Baton Rouge: Louisiana State University Press, 1978), 12; Peterson, *Tazewell*, 144.

109. Harrison, "Oligarchs and Democrats," 197.

110. Ambler, *Ritchie*, 120, 122-23; Ammon, "Richmond Junto," 397, 418; Mutersbaugh, "Jeffersonian Journalist," 453; *Enquirer*, 1 February 1817; Davis, *Intellectual Life*, 410. Eventually the constitution of 1851, which granted universal manhood suffrage, stripped the legislature of power to elect state officials and made the county courts subject to popular elections, thus destroying the basis of the Junto's power.

111. Hudson, *Journalism in the United States*, 269.

112. *Enquirer*, 20 January 1824; 2, 26 March 1824; 30 July 1824; 29 December 1824; Ambler, *Ritchie*, 293. For the fears expressed by the *Enquirer's* readers, see the letters of C.W. Gooch in the 1820s in the Alderman Library, University of Virginia.

113. Martin Van Buren, *Inquiry into the Origins and Course of Political Parties in the United States* (New York: Hurd and Houghton, 1867), 322.

114. *Enquirer*, 22 June 1824; Ritchie to L.W. Tazewell, 28 February 1827, Tazewell Papers, Virginia State Library, Richmond; Ambler, *Ritchie*, 108; Charles Wiltse, *John C. Calhoun* (Indianapolis: Bobbs-Merrill, 1949), 2: 348-49; Richard E. Ellis, *The Union at Risk: Jacksonian Democracy, States Rights, and the Nullification Crisis* (New York: Oxford University Press, 1987), 14.

115. *Enquirer*, 22 April 1828; 27 July 1832; Smith, *Press, Politics, and Patronage*, 66-67; McCormick, *Second American Party System*, 189.

116. *Enquirer*, 7 November 1828; 17 January 1845.

117. Richard H. Brown, "The Missouri Crisis, Slavery, and the Politics of Jacksonianism," *South Atlantic Quarterly* 65 (1966): 55-72.

118. Gales and Seaton to Ritchie, 17 October 1824, Gooch Family Papers, Accession No. 3921-a.

119. William C. Rives to Thomas Walker Gilmer, 13 November 1828, *Tyler's Quarterly Historical and Genealogical Magazine* 6 (October 1924): 98.

120. Ambler, *Ritchie*, 184-85. Before his break with Ritchie, Van Buren voiced the political debt he owed to the Virginia editor. See John C. Fitzpatrick, ed., *The Autobiography of Martin Van Buren* (Annual Report of the American Historical Association for the year 1918; Washington, D.C.: Government Printing Office, 1920), 2: 385.

121. *Enquirer*, 4 May 1838; 12 July 1842; 17 January 1843; 4 March 1843; Wiltse, *Calhoun*, 2: 135.

122. Silas Wright to Van Buren, 1 April 1844, Van Buren Papers; Ambler, *Ritchie*, 228-45.

123. 68 (10 May 1845): 153.

124. This was a constant theme for over twenty years. See *Enquirer*, 2 March 1824; Ambler, *Ritchie*, 124, 218.

125. *Daily Union*, 2 June 1848; Brown, "Missouri Crisis," 55-72.

126. *Enquirer*, 4 December 1832; 25 July 1854.

127. Cooper, *South and the Politics of Slavery*, 113, 115; Ellis, *Union at Risk*, 139.

128. *Enquirer*, 30 November 1832; 22, 24 January 1833; Cooper, *South and the Politics of Slavery*, 45; Ambler, *Ritchie*, 152; Ellis, *Union at Risk*, 131.

129. *Enquirer*, 5 October 1832; Ambler, *Ritchie*, 153.

130. *Enquirer*, 7 May 1833.

131. Ritchie to William C. Rives, 6 January 1833, Rives Mss.; Cooper, *South and the Politics of Slavery*, 47; Wiltse, *Calhoun*, 2: 139; Ellis, *Union at Risk*, 72, 128-29, 138; Merrill D. Peterson, *Olive Branch and Sword—the Compromise of 1833* (Baton Rouge: Louisiana State University, 1982), 58-59.

132. *Enquirer*, 8 October 1832; 30 November 1832; 19 February 1833.

133. Ibid., 8 January 1833; 2 February 1833.

134. Ibid., 30 November 1832; 20 December 1832; 9 March 1833.

135. Ibid., 12 March 1833. In fact, the Jackson administration had privately requested Virginia's mediation (Wiltse, *Calhoun*, 2: 139).

136. *Enquirer*, 28 August 1832; 26 October 1832.

137. See, e.g., ibid., 11, 14 September 1832; 9 February 1833; 5, 7 March 1833.

138. Ibid., 20 December 1832; 15 March 1833. On November 1, 1831, Ritchie had listed the steps necessary before the final remedy of secession could be employed: appeal to public opinion through the press, appeal to "our sister states" for cooperation, appeal to Congress and the president, and call a convention to revise the Constitution.

139. *Enquirer*, 26 January 1833; 16, 21 February 1833; Cooper, *South and the Politics of Slavery*, 47-48; Ellis, *Union at Risk*, 172-73; Richard B. Latner, "The Nullification Crisis and Republican Subversion," *Journal of Southern History* 43 (February 1977): 34-36; Ellis, *Union at Risk*, 173.

140. *Enquirer*, 12 April 1833; 14 May 1833.

141. Ibid., 15 March 1833; 24 September 1833; Peterson, *Olive Branch and Sword*, 93.

142. *Enquirer*, 8 January 1833.

143. William E. Ames and Dwight L. Teeter, "Politics, Economics, and the Mass Media" in Ronald T. Farrar and John D. Stevens, eds., *Mass Media and the National Experience* (New York: Harper and Row, 1971), 54-56.

144. There is almost universal agreement among Ritchie's contemporaries that his editorship of the *Union* was an unfortunate concluding chapter to a productive career. See, e.g., *Daily Picayune*, 6 July 1854; *New York Times*, 4 July 1854; Hudson, *Journalism in the United States*, 271.

145. Quoted in *Niles' Weekly Register* 68 (10 May 1845): 153.

146. President James K. Polk to Andrew Jackson, 17 March 1845, in Bassett, ed., *Jackson*, 6: 382-83; Thomas Ritchie, "Refutation of John C. Rives's Statements Concerning Public Printing," 55-56, *et passim*, Virginia State Library; Hudson, *Journalism in the United States*, 242-43; John W. Forney, *Anecdotes of Public Men* (New York: Harper and Brothers, 1873), 1: 106; J. George Harris to George Bancroft, 13 September 1887, in *Tyler's Quarterly Historical and Genealogical Magazine* 7 (July 1925): 15; Smith, *Press, Politics, and Patronage*, 161-73; Thomas Green to Ritchie, 6 April 1845, Ritchie Mss.; F.B. Marbut, *News from the Capital* (Carbondale: Southern Illinois University Press, 1971), 68; Ambler, *Ritchie*, 252-53. Perhaps other money was involved also, since promises were made to Ritchie that sufficient funds would be available to pay off the *Enquirer*'s debts so that Ritchie could move to Washington.

147. Ritchie, "Refutation," 65-68; Ritchie to "My Dearest Bell," 8 April 1845, Ritchie Mss.; F.P. Blair to Ritchie, 5 April 1845, ibid.; W.D. Wallach to Ritchie, 1 February 1845, ibid.; Parker, *Missing Link*, 30-31; Ambler, *Ritchie*, 252-53; Charles Sellers, *James K. Polk, Continentalist, 1843-1846* (Princeton: Princeton University Press, 1966), 277. Despite Ritchie's considerate treatment, Blair always resented the way he was forced out. Quarrels over the terms of the contract to purchase the *Globe* arose shortly and led to a long, public controversy between Ritchie and John Rives.

148. Smith, *Press, Politics, and Patronage*, 212-13; John A. Dix to Martin Van Buren, 1 August 1846, Van Buren Mss.; J. Rutherfourd to Ritchie, 19 June 1845, Ritchie Mss.; John P. Heiss to Ritchie, 1 October 1846, ibid.; Sellers, *Polk*, 280; Frederick B. Marbut, "Decline of the Official Press in Washington," *Journalism Quarterly* 33 (1956): 336.

149. Forney, *Anecdotes*, 1: 105.

150. *Daily Union*, 10 August 1846; 16 March 1851; Ritchie to Thomas Green, March 1851, in "Ritchie Letters," *The John P. Branch Historical Papers of Randolph-Macon College* 4 (June 1916): 414; Ambler, *Ritchie*, 284; Smith, *Press, Politics, and Patronage*, 212-14.

151. *Daily Union*, 1 May 1845.

152. Letter, 4 March 1845, Ritchie Mss.

153. Ambler, *Ritchie*, 259-60; Smith, *Press, Politics, and Patronage*, 163.

154. Forney, *Anecdotes*, 1: 106-7.

155. Ambler, *Ritchie*, 258.

156. James Buchanan to Edmund Burke, 31 August 1849, Burke Papers.

Extensive arrangements for a full and correct report of the proceedings of both houses of Congress were announced in the *Union* (1 January 1846) with the comment: "We are ambitious of publishing a paper that is worthy of the Union."

157. Bernard A. Weisberger, *Reporters for the Union* (Boston: Little, Brown, 1953), 21.

158. *Daily Picayune*, 21 October 1847.

159. In the *Union* of June 6, 1850, Ritchie claimed to welcome temperate expressions by his opponents, but I failed to find any critical appraisal of the Polk administration in the *Union*'s columns.

160. James E. Pollard, *The Presidents and the Press* (New York: Macmillan, 1947), 161-62, 241.

161. *Daily Union*, 16 March 1846.

162. Ibid., 15 May 1846.

163. See, e.g., *Daily Union*, 4 March 1846, and also *Daily Picayune*, 2 November 1847.

164. Forney, *Anecdotes*, 1: 108.

165. *Daily Union*, 11 March 1846; 3 October 1846.

166. Ibid., 9 March 1848; 13 May 1848; 9 March 1850; 21 April 1850.

167. Ritchie to "My dear Sir," 14 August 1829, Campbell Family Papers.

168. Charles A. McCoy, *Polk and the Presidency* (Austin: University of Texas Press, 1960), 185; Sellers, *Polk*, 448.

169. Quaife, *Diary of James K. Polk*, 3: 237; Pollard, *Presidents and the Press*, 231.

170. Parker, *Missing Link*, 31.

171. *Daily Union*, 24 June 1846.

172. *Daily Union*, 3 March 1846; *Daily Picayune*, 21 February 1847; Quaife, *Diary of James K. Polk*, 2: 377-78; McCoy, *Polk*, 190; Nathan Sargent, *Public Men and Events* (Phildelphia: J.B. Lippincott, 1875), 2: 311; Alfred Balch to Ritchie, 20 February 1847, Ritchie Mss.; Arthur Campbell to James Campbell, 16 May 1846, Campbell Family Papers. Ritchie's strictures against anti-administration senators had been harsh, but expulsion was an overreaction reflecting political and sectional antagonism, and it won for Ritchie considerable public sympathy. For Calhoun's opposition, see John S. Coussons, "Thirty Years with Calhoun, Rhett, and the Charleston Mercury: A Chapter in South Carolina Politics" (Ph.D. diss., Louisiana State University and Agricultural and Mechanical College, 1971), 238, 245, 249, 250.

173. Simon Cameron to Edmund Burke, 15 June 1849, Burke Papers; Francis P. Blair to Martin Van Buren, 24 March 1850, Van Buren Papers; Ambler, *Ritchie*, 276-77; Pollard, *Presidents and the Press*, 244-45.

174. *Daily Union*, 6 May 1846; Arthur Campbell to "Dear brother," 16 May 1846, Campbell Family Papers.

175. Quaife, *Diary of James K. Polk*, 1: 351-52, 358; 2: 170; 3: 237; Forney, *Anecdotes*, 1: 108-9; Ritchie to John P. Heiss, 13 April 1845, James K. Polk Mss., Library of Congress; *Daily Union*, 24 April 1846.

176. Forney, *Anecdotes*, 1: 108; L.A. Gobright, *Recollections of Men and Things at Washington* (Philadelphia: Claxton, Remsen and Haffelfinger, 1869), 70; *Niles' Weekly Register* 68 (10 May 1845): 153; Arthur Campbell to James Campbell, 23 September 1845, Campbell Family Papers. A Ritchie letter of 1852 reveals an

acute mind and good recall of public events forty years earlier (Ritchie to "My Dear W [George Wythe Munford], 11 November 1852, Munford-Ellis Family Papers, Perkins Library, Duke University).

177. Sellers, *Polk*, 448.

178. *Daily Union*, 24 March 1850. See also ibid., 21 April 1848; 29 June 1850.

179. Cooper, *South and the Politics of Slavery*, 302-3; Parker, *Missing Link*, 11; "Thomas Ritchie's Letter Containing Reminiscences of Henry Clay and the Compromise," n.d., Ritchie Papers; *Daily Union*, January-June, 1850. See specifically issues of 1 February, 5 May, 7 May 1850.

180. *Daily Union*, 4 January 1850; 12 March 1850.

181. Ibid., 21 February 1850.

182. Edmund Burke to Ritchie, 14 February 1850, Burke Papers; Ritchie to Burke, [14 February 1850?], Burke Papers; Ritchie to Burke, 12 March 1850, Burke Papers; *Daily Union*, 5 June 1850.

183. *Daily Union*, 25 April 1850; 21 May 1850.

184. Ibid., 21 May 1850.

185. Ibid., 14 May 1850.

186. Ibid., 16 May 1850.

187. Ibid., 18 June 1850; 12 April 1851; Gobright, *Recollections of Men and Things*, 111; John Barnwell, *Love of Order: South Carolina's First Secession Crisis* (Chapel Hill: University of North Carolina Press, 1982), 115, 172; Helen Kohn Hennig, "Edwin DeLeon" (M.A. thesis, University of South Carolina, 1928), 20-22; David Campbell to "My dear nephew," 15 November 1850, Campbell Family Papers. The best source on the *Southern Press* is Howard C. Perkins, "A Neglected Phase of the Movement for Southern Unity, 1847-1852," *Journal of Southern History* 12 (May 1946): 153-203.

188. Perkins, "Neglected Phase," 198.

189. Ibid., 181, 183-87, 191, 199-200; *New Orleans Daily Picayune*, 19 October 1850.

190. Perkins, "Neglected Phase," 198.

191. Marbut, "Decline of the Official Press," 336; *New Orleans Daily Picayune*, 8 October 1850.

192. Amos and Teeter, "Politics, Economics, and the Mass Media," 53, 54, 56; Marbut, "Decline of the Official Press," 337-39; Donald Lewis Shaw, "At the Crossroads: Change and Continuity in American Press News 1820-1860," *Journalism History* 8 (Summer 1981): 41, 43.

193. Leonard, *Power of the Press*, 92; Marbut, "Decline of the Official Press," 338.

194. Edmund Burke to Ritchie, 14 February 1850, Burke Papers; Ritchie to Burke, [14 February 1850?], Burke Papers; Smith, *Press, Politics, and Patronage*, 213-14; *New Orleans Daily Picayune*, 8 October 1850.

195. *Daily Union*, 15 April 1851.

196. Ibid.

197. Ambler, *Ritchie*, 293.

198. Ames and Teeter, "Politics, Economics, and the Mass Media," 62; Robert W. Hughes, *Editors of the Past* (Richmond, Va.: William Ellis Jones, 1897), 4; William David Sloan, "The Early Party Press: The Newspaper Press in American Politics, 1788-1812," *Journalism History* 9 (Spring 1982): 19.

199. Alfred Balch to Ritchie, 20 February 1847, Ritchie Mss.

200. *New Orleans Daily Picayune*, 6 July 1854.
201. Clement Eaton, *A History of the Old South*, 3rd ed. (N.Y.: Macmillan, 1975), 444.

3. The Rise of a Metropolitan Giant

1. *Times-Picayune*, 25 January 1917 (80th Anniversary Issue); Fayette Copeland, *Kendall of the Picayune* (Norman: University of Oklahoma Press, 1943), 22; John S. Kendall, "George Wilkins Kendall and the Founding of the New Orleans 'Picayune,'" *Louisiana Historical Quarterly* 11 (April 1928): 266; Harry James Brown, ed., *Letters from a Texas Sheep Ranch, written in the years 1860 and 1867 by George Wilkins Kendall to Henry Stephens Randall* (Urbana: University of Illinois Press, 1959), 123. George Kendall recalls that the *Picayune* was begun with $75 capital, but other sources put the figure at $400.
2. Copeland, *Kendall*, 22; Thomas Ewing Dabney, *One Hundred Great Years; the Story of the Times-Picayune from Its Founding to 1940* (Baton Rouge: Louisiana State University Press, 1944), 15-16.
3. Quoted in J.S. Kendall, "George Wilkins Kendall," 266-67.
4. *New Orleans Picayune*, 25-28 January 1837; *Times-Picayune*, 25 January 1917; Copeland, *Kendall*, 22. (Hereafter, the *New Orleans Picayune* or *New Orleans Daily Picayune* will be cited as *Picayune*. The paper added "Daily" to its name on November 2, 1837.)
5. For the penny press, see Frank Luther Mott, *American Journalism; A History: 1690-1960*, 3rd ed. (New York: Macmillan, 1962), chaps. 12, 13; Edwin Emery and Michael Emery, *The Press and America*, 4th ed. (Englewood Cliffs, N.J.: Prentice-Hall, 1978), chap. 10; Dan Schiller, *Objectivity and the News: The Public and the Rise of Commercial Journalism* (Philadelphia: University of Pennsylvania Press, 1981), chap. 1, 2; Michael Schudson, *Discovering the News: A Social History of American Newspapers* (New York: Basic Books, 1978), 14-58; Thomas C. Leonard, *The Power of the Press: The Birth of American Political Reporting* (New York: Oxford University Press, 1986), 150-51; Alexander Saxton, "Problems of Class and Race in the Origins of the Mass Circulation Press," *American Quarterly* 36 (Summer 1984): 216-19. For a recent account of the founding of another Southern penny paper see Harold A. Williams, "Light for All: Arunah S. Abell and the Rise of the Baltimore *Sun*," *Maryland Historical Magazine* 82 (Fall 1987): 197-213.
6. *Picayune*, 17 November 1842; 16 December 1842; 2 February 1845.
7. There is disagreement over the intended market of the penny press. Mott and the Emerys stress the common man; Schudson the middle class; and Schiller the urban tradesmen and artisans. Saxton suggests that artisan printers of the early penny press courted the working man, endorsing their interests, their racism and their desire for expansionism. In *City People: The Rise of Modern City Culture in Nineteenth-Century America* (New York: Oxford University Press), chap. 3, Gunther Barth argues that the rise of the metropolitan press (which originated in the penny press) reflects in large part the longing of urban masses for identity. There is no agreement even concerning the large circulation of the nation's most successful penny paper, the *New York Herald*. According to James L. Crouthamel, the most recent authority on the *Herald*, "The best that can be

concluded about the audience is that Bennett's paper had a large circulation and that its contents had a wide and diverse appeal." See note 5 above and James L. Crouthamel, *Bennett's New York Herald and the Rise of the Popular Press* (Syracuse: Syracuse University Press, 1989), 161.

8. *Picayune*, 7 October 1838.

9. Dabney, *Great Years*, 17; Schiller, *Objectivity*, 13, 48; Saxton, "Problems of Class and Race," 216-19; Louis Dudek, *Literature and the Press* (Toronto: Ryerson, 1960), 59-77.

10. Dabney, *Great Years*, 4-5; Gerald M. Capers, *Occupied City: New Orleans under the Federals, 1862-1865* (Lexington: University of Kentucky Press, 1965), 1; Lyle Saxon, *Fabulous New Orleans* (New York: Century, 1923), 249; David R. Goldfield, "Pursuing the American Dream: Cities in the Old South," in Blaine A. Brownell and David R. Goldfield, eds., *The City in Southern History* (Port Washington, N.Y.: Kennikat, 1977), 57.

11. Dabney, *Great Years*, 4-5; Robert C. Reinders, *End of an Era: New Orleans, 1850-1860* (New Orleans: Pelican, 1964), 36-40, 46-49; Terence P. Smith, "The First of 125 Great Years," *Dixie* 21 January 1962, 6-9; Capers, *Occupied City*, 2-5; Saxon, *Fabulous New Orleans*, 250; James E. Winston, "Notes on the Economic History of New Orleans," *Mississippi Valley Historical Review* 11 (1924-25): 200-209; R.S. Cotterill, "Southern Railroads, 1850-1860," *Mississippi Valley Historical Review* 10 (March 1924): 328-29.

12. Reinders, *End of an Era*, 9-20; Capers, *Occupied City*, 6-7, 9, 16. Another distinctive feature, largely ignored by the white newspapers, was the large free black population, including many French-speaking *gens de couleur*.

13. Dabney, *Great Years*, 5; Capers, *Occupied City*, 94-95; Reinders, *End of an Era*, 92-93. Even in normal times the death list averaged 3,800 per year, and the New Orleans mortality rate was always higher than that of equally large Northern cities. Constance McLaughlin Green, *American Cities in the Growth of the Nation* (London: John Degraff, 1957), 75.

14. Capers, *Occupied City*, 18.

15. Ibid., 12-13, 18; Saxon, *Fabulous New Orleans*, 247; Dabney, *Great Years*, 8.

16. Capers, *Occupied City*, 10-11, 15-16; Reinders, *End of an Era*, 33; Copeland, *Kendall*, 17; Smith, "First of 125 Great Years," 7; Merl E. Reed, *New Orleans and the Railroad: The Struggle for Commercial Empire, 1830-1860* (Baton Rouge: Louisiana State University Press for the Louisiana Historical Association, 1966), 5-6.

17. Copeland, *Kendall*, 10-16; J.S. Kendall, "George Wilkins Kendall," 263. Curiously, all of the new penny papers had been founded by printers.

18. Smith, "First of 125 Great Years," 7; Copeland, *Kendall*, 7.

19. Mott, *American Journalism*, 249-50; *Cincinnati Daily Columbian* (4 November 1853) in Copeland, *Kendall*, 265. There is a county in central Texas named after Kendall.

20. *Picayune*, 16 September 1860; 9 October 1860; *Charleston Daily Courier*, 12, 17, 22 September 1860; *Times-Picayune*, 5 September 1937.

21. *Picayune*, 1 March 1837.

22. Ibid., 31 August 1837; 17 October 1837; 17 November 1842; Dabney, *Great Years*, 24.

23. *Picayune*, 9 February 1838.

24. Ibid., 7 September 1839.

25. Ibid., 22 August 1837; 3 October 1838.

26. See, e.g., the following: Smith, "First of 125 Great Years," 8; *Picayune*, 26 March 1837; 8 August 1839; 16 April 1840; 7 August 1842; 17, 23 November 1842; 23 April 1843; 27 May 1843; 25 October 1845. On the humorous Recorder's Court scenes, see E. Merton Coulter, ed., *The Other Half of Old New Orleans* (Baton Rouge: Louisiana State University Press, 1939).

27. *Picayune*, 21, 23 October 1838; 10 September 1842.

28. Ibid., 25 March 1837.

29. Ibid., 25 January 1837.

30. Ibid., 21 August 1839.

31. Ibid., 6 April 1837; 4 April 1843; 17 April 1844.

32. Dabney, *Great Years*, 54.

33. *Picayune*, 31 January 1837; 2 March 1837; 6 October 1837; 19 October 1838; 9 August 1839; 15 September 1839; 13, 27 October 1840.

34. Ibid., 3, 9, 10 February 1837; 20 November 1842; Copeland, *Kendall*, 25, 27.

35. *Picayune*, 9 April 1839; Smith, "First of 125 Great Years," 8.

36. *Picayune*, 27 June 1837.

37. Ibid., 4 March 1837.

38. Ibid., 18 July 1837; 6 January 1838; 27 March 1839.

39. Ibid., May-October 1837; Dabney, *Great Years*, 23.

40. *Picayune*, 20 September 1837; 16 October 1837; 5 October 1842; 9 November 1842.

41. Ibid., 20 June 1843 (similarly 1 October 1840; 22 April 1843).

42. Ibid., 14 September 1842.

43. Ibid., 5 October 1842. See, e.g., the assessment of the *Picayune* in George F. Mellen, "New England Editors in the South," in Edwin H. Ford, ed., *Readings in the History of American Journalism* (Minneapolis: University of Minnesota Press, 1939), 245.

44. Dabney, *Great Years*, 28; *Picayune*, 27 April 1837; 27 September 1837.

45. *Picayune*, 22 October 1839.

46. Ibid., 5, 18 August 1837; 7 October 1837.

47. Ibid., 13, 17, 19, 22 August 1837.

48. Ibid., 4 February 1837; 2 March 1837; 28 April 1844; F. Lauriston Bullard, *Famous War Correspondents* (Boston: Little, Brown, 1914), 356; Thomas William Reilly, "American Reporters and the Mexican War, 1846-1848," (Ph.D. diss., University of Minnesota, 1975), 1: 58, 63.

49. The *Picayune* frequently complained of plagiarism (see 12 May 1837; 14 April 1840; 2 July 1842).

50. Dabney, *Great Years*, 25.

51. *Picayune*, 26 November 1841.

52. Quoted in Copeland, *Kendall*, 38.

53. *Picayune*, 4 October 1838.

54. Ibid., 29 January 1837; 3 October 1837; 22 August 1839; 27 October 1840; Copeland, *Kendall*, 14, 295.

55. *Picayune*, 23 June 1837; 20 July 1837; 22 August 1839; 15 September 1839; 29 July 1842.

56. Ibid., 2 February 1837; 3 October 1837; 1 April 1840; 23 October 1840.

57. Ibid., 25 January 1837; 23 February 1838; 22 August 1839; 4 April 1840; 24 March 1841; 9 November 1842; 26 January 1850.

58. Ibid., 21 December 1847.

59. Ibid., 9 November 1842; 22 October 1844. See also *Picayune*, 4 June 1837 and 14 September 1849. The *Picayune* made only brief mention of the news that A.C. Bullitt, who joined the *Picayune's* editorial staff in 1844, and Lumsden were elected to the state legislature.

60. *Picayune*, 9 October 1840.

61. *Times-Picayune*, 25 January 1917.

62. *Picayune*, 29 March 1837; 5 March 1843; 27 January 1847; Smith, "First of 125 Great Years," 8.

63. *Picayune*, 8 May 1845.

64. Ibid., 27 September 1842.

65. Ibid., 1, 5, 12 February 1837; 5, 9 March 1837; 27, 29 April 1837; 1 March 1841; 1, 7, 21 March 1850; 20 September 1850.

66. *Picayune*, 8 March 1837; 3 October 1838; 1 April 1840; 18 October 1842; 30 September 1849.

67. Ibid., 20 April 1844.

68. Dabney, *Great Years*, 40; *Picayune*, 12 July 1837; 9 December 1842.

69. Dabney, *Great Years*, 45; *Picayune*, 8 March 1839; 21, 28 September 1839; 2 April 1840.

70. Ibid., 16 March 1837.

71. Dabney, *Great Years*, 39; *Picayune*, 8 January 1843; 9 March 1843; 22 February 1845; 20 July 1847.

72. Ibid., 27 January 1837.

73. Ibid., 19 July 1837.

74. See, e.g., *Picayune*, 3, 23, 24 October 1837; 16 November 1837; 28 April 1839; 10 March 1843; 11 April 1844; 9, 17 May 1844; 13 August 1847.

75. Ibid., 19, 30 July 1837.

76. Ibid., 19, 21 July 1837.

77. Ibid., 21 July 1837; 7 December 1845.

78. Ibid., 19 July 1837.

79. Ibid., 28 February 1845; 7 December 1845.

80. Ibid., 26 July 1837.

81. Ibid., 23 July 1837; 6 April 1844.

82. Ibid., 9 August 1837.

83. Ibid., 30 July 1837.

84. Ibid., 11 August 1837.

85. Schiller, *Objectivity and the News*, chap. 2. Saxton has stressed the penny press's ridicule of the dominant culture ("Problems of Class and Race," 224).

86. *Picayune*, 23 February 1837.

87. *Picayune*, 26 September 1839.

88. Ibid., 28 February 1843; 5 March 1850; 11 April 1850.

89. Ibid., 3 February 1850. Concerning New Orleans's lethargy in railroad development, see Winston, "Notes on the Economic History of New Orleans," 225; Cotterill, "Southern Railroads"; and Reed, *New Orleans and the Railroad*.

90. *Picayune*, 3 October 1849; 19, 21 March 1850; 5 April 1850; 8 September 1850; 2, 12 October 1850; Dabney, *Great Years*, 96, 97; Reed, *New Orleans and the Railroad*, 8, 9, 20-23. The *New Orleans Bee* had presented the case for action much earlier than the *Picayune*.

91. Dabney, *Great Years*, 89.

92. Harold Sinclair, *The Port of New Orleans* (Garden City, N.Y.: Doubleday, Doran, 1942), 210.

93. Goldfield, "Pursuing the American Dream," 71-77; Reinders, *End of an Era*, 96; Sinclair, *Port of New Orleans*, 212; *Picayune*, 3 September 1839; *Charleston Daily Courier*, August-November, 1858; *Charleston Mercury*, August-November, 1858. The transiency of much of the city's natural leadership class, in conjunction with the ignorance of disease, the high cost of civic improvement and a certain amount of complacency, accounts in large part for the failure to meet the challenge of epidemic disease. For the *Picayune*'s treatment of the great yellow fever epidemics of 1837, 1842, and 1847 see the issues from August through October in each of these years. See also *Picayune*, 16 October 1845.

94. Goldfield, "Pursuing the American Dream," 70-72; M. Foster Farley, "The Mighty Monarch of the South: Yellow Fever in Charleston and Savannah," *Georgia Review* 27 (Spring 1973): 56-70; Jo Ann Carrigan, "Yellow Fever in New Orleans 1853: Abstractions and Realities," *Journal of Southern History* 25 (August 1959): 343.

95. *Picayune*, 16 August 1839.

96. Ibid., 11 April 1850; 20 December 1850.

97. Ibid., 23 June 1837. The reference to "languishing and dying" was figurative rather than literal.

98. Ibid., 1 February 1837; 4, 21 April 1837; 12 May 1837; 23 June 1837; 6 September 1837; 12 August 1842; 10 April 1844; 1 May 1846; 19 August 1847. The mail frequently failed near Charleston (*Picayune*, 6, 11 December 1842; 1 January 1843; 5 March 1843).

99. Ibid., 3 May 1845.

100. Ibid., 20 September 1850.

101. Ibid., 13 September 1849; *Times-Picayune* clipping, 22 August 1964, in Louisiana Collection, Tulane University Library, New Orleans, Louisiana. For examples of Kendall's articles, see *Picayune*, 6, 8 October 1844; 9 October 1849.

102. *Picayune*, 8 March 1843. *Picayune* writers offered daily evidence of their ability to pare verbatim reports down to brief news items. See, e.g., reports on the activities of the city council (26 October 1842), the state legislature (9 February 1843), and Congress (3 September 1842). Not even an important presidential message would be permitted to choke the paper's limited space but instead was boiled down to its essentials (18 August 1842; 18 December 1842). For yet another example, on 11 February 1842, the *Picayune* summarized material from the following papers: *St. Louis Reveille*, *St. Louis New Era*, *St. Louis Union*, *Louisville Journal*, *Raleigh Register*, *Baltimore American*, *Journal of Commerce* (N.Y.), *New York Sun*, and *New York Commercial*.

103. *Picayune*, 3 November 1850.

104. Copeland, *Kendall*, 140-42; J.S. Kendall, "George Wilkins Kendall," 272-73.

105. *New York Times*, 8 May 1862; Dabney, *Great Years*, 56; Copeland, *Kendall*, 33.

106. *Picayune*, 23 June 1837; 27 October 1837; 5 September 1847; Copeland, *Kendall*, 34-35.

107. *Picayune*, 7 February 1838; Reilly, "American Reporters," 55. See, e.g., "Twenty-Four Hours Ahead of the Mail: Express News by the Picayune's Private Express" (*Picayune*, 8 January 1850).

108. *Picayune*, 17 October 1848; 9 April 1850; 7 June 1850.

109. Lumsden (and perhaps Kendall, too) had been a Whig ever since he became tall enough to reach the ballot box. *Picayune*, 4 April 1840; 14 February 1847; 23 May 1847; 21 December 1847; 24 October 1848; Copeland, *Kendall*, 123, 239; Dabney, *Great Years*, 57; J. Cutler Andrews, *The South Reports the Civil War* (Princeton: Princeton University Press, 1970), 35.

110. For a long time Kendall publicized what on the surface appeared to be a trading enterprise but in fact turned out to be a filibustering expedition. J.S. Kendall, "George Wilkins Kendall," 273; Copeland, *Kendall*, 47.

111. *Picayune*, 6 April 1844; 8 May 1844; Reilly, "American Reporters," 55, 57. For international actions concerning Texas see, e.g., *Picayune*, 22, 26 July 1842; 15 November 1842; 23 April 1843. For the *Picayune*'s interest in annexation, see April 1844 and the following: 7, 25 May 1844; 6, 7 February 1845; 12 April 1846. Even after the Mexican War, Mexico and California were very much the special interests of the *Picayune*. In *One Hundred Great Years* (p. 69), the house history of the *Picayune*, Dabney claimed that the paper was never jingoistic. *Picayune* editorials, however, tell a different tale, perhaps reflecting what Copeland (*Kendall*, 95) described as Kendall's "burning hatred of all things Mexican."

112. Dabney, *Great Years*, 25. See also *Picayune*, 13 April 1837.

113. Copeland, *Kendall*, 111, 121; Dabney, *Great Years*, 55; Reilly, "American Reporters," 57.

114. *Picayune*, 2 April 1846; 10 January 1847; 19, 21 March 1847; 6 April 1847; 15, 16 June 1847; 16 July 1847; Reilly, "American Reporters," 474.

115. Reilly, "American Reporters," 474; Bullard, *Correspondents*, 351-52. Strangely, Phillip Knightley ignores the importance of Mexican War reporting in his history of war journalism. Knightley begins with the Civil War. See *The First Casualty* (New York: Harcourt Brace Jovanovich, 1975).

116. *Picayune*, 15 October 1847; J.S. Kendall, "George Wilkins Kendall," 278, 280-81; Bullard, *Correspondents*, 363; Reilly, "American Reporters," 340. For examples of Kendall's reporting, see *Picayune*, 6, 7 May 1847. Kendall was wounded slightly at the battle of Chapultepec.

117. See, e.g., *Picayune*, 26 June 1846; 8, 16 July 1846.

118. Reilly, "American Reporters," 475-76; Bullard, *Correspondents*, 373; Dabney, *Great Years*, 74-76. Among the many papers that relied heavily on the *Picayune* were the *National Intelligencer* (see, e.g., the following 1847 issues: 28 August; 11, 14, 16, 17, 21 September; 23, 26 October) and the *Daily Union* (see, e.g., the following 1847 issues: 21 April; 28 June; 10, 14, 15, 18, 21, 28 September).

119. *Picayune*, 7, 8 August 1847; J.S. Kendall, "George Wilkins Kendall," 278-79; Robert Anderson, *An Artillery Officer in the Mexican War 1846-7; Letters of Robert Anderson* (New York: G.P. Putnam's Sons, 1911), 305, 307.

120. J.S. Kendall, "George Wilkins Kendall," 276-77; Bullard, *Correspondents*, 354-55, 370-71; Dabney, *Great Years*, 72; Reilly, "American Reporters," 36-37, 55, 472; Copeland, *Kendall*, 164.

121. Otis Singletary, *The Mexican War* (Chicago: University of Chicago Press, 1960), 3.

122. *Picayune*, 1 March 1848; J.S. Kendall, "George Wilkins Kendall," 281-83; Bullard, *Correspondents*, 364-65, 372-73.

123. *Picayune*, 3 January 1847; Copeland, *Kendall*, 179-80, 212; Reilly, "American Reporters," 15-17.

124. Ibid., 343.

125. *Picayune*, 10 April 1846; 3, 5 May 1846; Justin H. Smith, *The War with Mexico* (New York: Macmillan, 1910), 1: 119-20.

126. *Picayune*, 17 May 1846. See also ibid., 5 May 1846.

127. Ibid., 21 June 1843; 28 May 1844; 2, 8 March 1845; 10, 11 May 1845; 25 November 1845; 28 December 1845; 4 April 1846; 21 May 1846.

128. Ibid., 26 July 1842; 15 November 1842; 10 June 1843. The *Picayune* at least once referred to the "imbecile Mexicans" and "hordes of predatory savages" (4 July 1847).

129. Frederick Merk, *Manifest Destiny and Mission in American History* (New York: Random House, Vintage Books, 1966), 154-55.

130. *Picayune*, 29 June 1847.

131. Ibid., 2, 8 July 1847; *Washington Daily Union*, 23 September 1847; Reilly, "American Reporters," 325-26; Copeland, *Kendall*, 228-29.

132. *American Star*, quoted in *Picayune*, 6 November 1847; *New Orleans National*, quoted in Copeland, *Kendall*, 232; Reilly, "American Reporters," 346-49. Copeland maintains there was some unintentional bias in Kendall's reporting since he naturally publicized the achievements that he witnessed while slighting those not personally observed.

133. *Picayune*, 25 November 1847; *Daily Union*, 23 September 1847.

134. Dabney, *Great Years*, 81; Copeland, *Kendall*, 240, 243. See *Picayune*, October 1848, for examples of Kendall's European articles.

135. *Picayune*, 12 March 1837; 15 July 1837; 5 October 1838; 4 April 1840; 3 November 1841; 17, 18 April 1847; 11 December 1847; 7 March 1848; 17 October 1848; Capers, *Occupied City*, 176; Copeland, *Kendall*, 37, 143; Dabney, *Great Years*, 59, 83, 85; J.C.G. Kennedy, "Catalogue of the Newspapers and Periodicals Published in the United States . . . ," in John Livingston, *Livingston's Law Register for 1852* (New York, 1852), 14.

136. Copeland, *Kendall*, 143-44.

137. *Picayune*, 3 November 1850.

138. See, e.g., *Picayune*, 23 December 1845; 22 December 1847.

139. *Picayune*, 10 October 1838; 15 November 1850.

140. Ibid., 1, 3 March 1837; 10 April 1840; 17 October 1840.

141. Ibid., 4, 22 January 1850; 9, 15 February 1850; 17, 28 March 1850; 19, 24 October 1850.

142. Ibid., 15, 22 March 1850; 27 September 1850.

143. Ibid., 1 February 1850; 29 June 1850; 11 September 1850.

144. Ibid., 15, 18, 24 September 1850; 7, 24, 27 November 1850.

145. Donald L. Shaw, "At the Crossroads: Change and Continuity in American Press News 1820-1860," *Journalism History* 8 (Summer 1981): 43. Allan Pred has stressed New York City's dominance of the flow of news in the 1840s. See *Urban Growth and the Circulation of Information: The United States System of Cities, 1790-1840* (Cambridge: Harvard University Press, 1973), 46-51.

146. S.N.D. North, *History and Present Condition of the Newspapers and Periodical Press of the United States* (Washington, D.C., 1884), 90-91. Closer to home, the *Savannah Morning News* abandoned its penny press focus of the early 1850s to become a Democratic party organ and defender of Southern rights late in the decade. See Louis Turner Griffith and John Erwin Talmadge, *Georgia Journalism, 1763-1950* (Athens: University of Georgia Press, 1951), 47, 48.

147. Copeland, *Kendall*, 246, 247. For comments on this point see Gunther Barth, *City People: The Rise of Modern City Culture in Nineteenth-Century America* (New York: Oxford University Press), 65, 106-9.

148. In 1862 the *New York Times* viewed the *Picayune* as a dignified, conservative journal. (*New York Times*, 8 May 1862.)

149. Dabney, *Great Years, passim*; Copeland, *Kendall*, 313.

150. Lamar W. Bridges, "Eliza Jane Nicholson of the 'Picayune,'" *Journalism Quarterly* 2 (Winter 1975-76): 110.

151. John Wilds, *Afternoon Story: A Century of the New Orleans "States-Item"* (Baton Rouge: Louisiana State University Press, 1976), 65.

4. The Triumph of Sectional Journalism

1. Quoted in *Charleston Mercury*, 27 March 1860. (Hereafter the *Charleston Mercury* will be cited as *Mercury*.)

2. See, e.g., Ollinger Crenshaw, *The Slave States in the Presidential Election of 1860* (1945; reprint ed., Gloucester, Mass.: Peter Smith, 1969), 47; Virginius Dabney, *Liberalism in the South* (1932; reprint ed., New York: AMS Press, 1970), 142; Dwight Lowell Dumond, *Southern Editorials on Secession* (1931; reprint ed., Gloucester, Mass.: Peter Smith, 1964), vii; Donald E. Reynolds, *Editors Make War* (Nashville: Vanderbilt University Press, 1966), 40-41; William J. Cooper, *Liberty and Slavery: Southern Politics to 1860* (New York: Knopf, 1983), 269; *Mercury*, 26 January 1858; 28 April 1859; 2 April 1860; 1 September 1860; 6 November 1860.

3. *Mercury*, 15 October 1860.

4. William Francis Guess, *South Carolina; Annals of Pride and Protest* (New York: Harper and Row, 1957), 207-8; William H. and Jane H. Pease, *The Web of Progress: Private Values and Public Styles in Boston and Charleston, 1828-1843* (New York: Oxford University Press, 1985), 14-15, 55, 224.

5. As William and Jane Pease have concluded, "the city lacked the critical mass to sustain those institutions that elsewhere promoted intellectual life," and with a declining or static population it offered "fewer attractions to professionals, little employment to scientists, and less readership for writers." See "Intellectual Life in the 1830s: The Institutional Framework and the Charleston Style," in Michael O'Brien and David Moltke-Hansen, eds., *Intellectual Life in Antebellum Charleston* (Knoxville: University of Tennessee Press, 1986), 251, 253.

6. Rosser H. Taylor, *Ante-Bellum South Carolina: A Social and Cultural History* (Chapel Hill: University of North Carolina Press, 1942), 33-34; *Charleston Daily Courier*, 30 June 1853. (Hereafter the *Charleston Daily Courier* will be cited as *Courier*.)

7. Taylor, *Ante-Bellum South Carolina*, 23.

8. James Banner, "The Problem of South Carolina," in Stanley Elkins and Eric McKitrick, eds., *The Hofstadter Aegis: A Memorial* (New York: Knopf, 1974), 72-73; Steven A. Channing, *Crisis of Fear: Secession in South Carolina* (New York: Norton, 1974), 257, 258; Michael P. Johnson, "Planters and Patriarchy: Charleston, 1800-1860," *Journal of Southern History* 46 (February 1980): 47.

9. William W. Freehling, *Prelude to Civil War: The Nullification Controversy in South Carolina, 1816-1836* (New York: Harper and Row, 1965), 15.

10. During the nullification crisis, two out of three state representatives

from Charleston were planters or professionals, not merchants and business-men. See Pease and Pease, *Web of Progress*, 88-89.

11. James Brewer Stewart, "'A Great Talking and Eating Machine': Patri-archy, Mobilization and the Dynamics of Nullification in South Carolina," *Civil War History* 27 (September 1981): 215. For a study that stresses political democra-cy among white South Carolinian males, see Lacy K. Ford, *Origins of Southern Radicalism: The South Carolina Upcountry, 1800-1860* (New York: Oxford Univer-sity Press, 1988).

12. Banner, "The Problem of South Carolina," 60-90, *passim*; Harold S. Schultz, *Nationalism and Sectionalism in South Carolina, 1852-1860* (Durham: Duke University Press, 1950), 9; George C. Rogers, *Charleston in the Age of the Pinckneys* (Norman: University of Oklahoma Press, 1969), *passim*.

13. Roy Franklin Nichols, *The Disruption of American Democracy* (New York: Macmillan, 1962), 288.

14. *Courier*, 6 May 1862.

15. William L. King, *The Newspaper Press of Charleston* (Charleston: Lucas and Richardson, 1882), 90. Upon Willington's death the *Courier* stressed that Willington had severed his last ties to the North late in the secession crisis. *Courier*, 3 February 1862.

16. "Centennial Edition," *News and Courier*, 1903, 7; Lillian A. Kibler, *Ben-jamin F. Perry: South Carolina Unionist* (Durham: Duke University Press, 1946), 268-69; Fletcher M. Green, *The Role of the Yankee in the Old South* (Athens: Univer-sity of Georgia Press, 1972); George F. Mellen, "New England Editors in the South," in Edwin H. Ford, ed., *Readings in the History of American Journalism* (Minneapolis: University of Minnesota Press, 1939), 234-47.

17. George A. Gordon to "Dear Krilla," 25 September 1858, George A. Gor-don Papers, Perkins Library, Duke University.

18. *Courier*, 3 February 1862; King, *Newspaper Press*, 105; Herbert Ravenel Sass, *Outspoken: 150 Years of the News and Courier* (Columbia: University of South Carolina Press, 1953), 20.

19. Sass, *Outspoken*, 12-13; King, *Newspaper Press*, 103.

20. Sass, *Outspoken*, 4-5, 11, 21, 23 *et passim*.

21. King, *Newspaper Press*, 128, 131; John C. Ellen, Jr., "Public Life of Rich-ard Yeadon" (M.A. thesis, University of South Carolina, 1953), 8-10, 13.

22. King, *Newspaper Press*, 131; Sass, *Outspoken*, 14.

23. Ellen, "Richard Yeadon," 14, 15.

24. Ibid., 1.

25. *The True Carolinian* (Anderson, S.C.), 7 May 1857, quoted in Yeadon Scrapbook, 1857, 51, South Caroliniana Library, University of South Carolina.

26. Ellen, "Richard Yeadon," 3-5, 43-48, 72; Sass, *Outspoken*, 11; Benjamin F. Perry, *Reminiscences of Public Life* (Philadelphia: John D. Avil, 1883), 306; William L.T. Crocker, "Richard Yeadon" (M.A. thesis, University of South Carolina, 1927), 18; Mary C. Simms Oliphant et al., eds., *The Letters of William Gilmore Simms* (Columbia: University of South Carolina Press), 1: cxlvii.

27. "Memoir of Richard Yeadon, Esq.," *American Whig Review* (May 1850): 478-85; Ellen, "Richard Yeadon," 1, 16, 28.

28. *Courier*, 4 November 1844.

29. Sass, *Outspoken*, 25; King, *Newspaper Press*, 135-36.

30. *Courier*, 4 November 1844.

31. Sass, *Outspoken*, 25-26.

32. Kibler, *Perry*, 247.

33. Richard Yeadon to Benjamin F. Perry, 6 January 1850 [actually, 1851], Benjamin F. Perry Papers, Department of Archives and History, State of Alabama.

34. Yeadon to Perry, 4 June 1850, Perry Papers.

35. Perry, *Reminiscences*, 310.

36. *Courier*, 10 January 1853.

37. Alexander Carroll died in 1856, Henry M. Cushman in 1857, and James Lewis Hatch in 1858. William Buchanan Carlisle then assumed editorial duties, aided in 1860 and afterward by Col. A.O. Andrews and the Reverend Urban Sinclair Bird. (M.F. Kennedy, "Recollections of an Old 'Courier' Printer," in "Centennial Edition," *News and Courier*, 1903, 24, *et passim*; *Courier*, 3 February 1862.)

38. Ellen, "Richard Yeadon," 40, 72; Yeadon to Perry, 4 June 1850, Perry Papers.

39. Ellen, "Richard Yeadon," 41; newspaper clippings in Richard Yeadon Scrapbook, 107ff., South Caroliniana Library.

40. See Yeadon Scrapbook, 1857-1858, *passim*, South Caroliniana Library; *Courier*, 29 March 1858; 8 April 1858; C.S. Boucher, "South Carolina and the South on the Eve of Secession 1852-1860," *Washington University Studies, Humanistic Series* 6 (1919): 118-19.

41. *Courier*, 5 April 1858. See also 31 January 1858; 2 May 1860; 4 July 1860.

42. *Courier*, 2 April 1859; *Mercury*, 4, 6 April 1859.

43. See both the *Courier* and *Mercury*, August-November, 1858.

44. Sass, *Outspoken*, 16.

45. In 1860 the *Courier* backed Breckinridge and Lane and excoriated Douglas and popular sovereignty; yet it opened its columns to the defense of Douglas's territorial views, which were overwhelmingly anathema in South Carolina, commenting that "our opinions shall not prevent a fair hearing of both sides, or a proper presentation of any opinions and agreements on grave subjects of general attention." (*Courier*, 10 May 1860, and similarly 21, 26 July 1860). When the *Courier* began to advocate disunion it nevertheless published Benjamin Perry's biting attacks on South Carolina secessionists: "Disunion . . . is now in the mouth of every flippant politician, certain newspaper editors, half-educated schoolboys, and unthinking mortals. It is the high road to office and popularity, and he who dares repeat the dying behest of the Father of his country is branded a traitor" (*Courier*, 20 August 1860). There are other examples of the *Courier*'s openness on a variety of issues. The editors acknowledged the arguments in favor of reopening the African slave trade although they had led the opposition to such a drastic proposal (*Courier*, 17, 22 December 1858).

46. Donald L. Shaw, "At the Crossroads: Change and Continuity in American Press News 1820-1860," *Journalism History* 8 (Summer 1981): 49.

47. *The Advertiser* (Edgefield, S.C.), 3 February 1858, in Yeadon Scrapbook, 109, South Caroliniana Library; I.W. Hayne to James J. Hammond, 21 April 1858, Hammond Papers (microfilm), Library of Congress; Robert Barnwell Rhett, Jr., "A Farewell to the Subscribers of the Charleston Mercury" (Charleston: Daily Courier Job Press, 1869); Sass, *Outspoken*, 32; *Courier*, 25 October 1858.

48. See, e.g., *Courier*, 9 October 1858; 17 April 1860; 28 July 1860; 8 August 1860; 2 October 1860.

49. *Courier*, 9 October 1858; Ellen, "Richard Yeadon," 42, 55-56; Perry, *Reminiscences, passim*; "Memoir of Richard Yeadon," *passim*; Crocker, "Richard Yeadon," 26; William Kaufman Scarborough, ed., *The Diary of Edmund Ruffin* (Baton Rouge: Louisiana State University Press, 1972), 1: 72.

50. Charles E. Cauthen, *South Carolina Goes to War, 1860-1865* (Chapel Hill: University of North Carolina Press, 1950), 10; Ellen, "Richard Yeadon," 42.

51. *Courier*, 14, 19 November 1856.

52. John Stanford Coussons, "Thirty Years with Calhoun, Rhett and the Charleston Mercury: A Chapter in South Carolina Politics" (Ph.D. diss., Louisiana State University and Agricultural and Mechanical College, 1971), 1, 2, 184.

53. Ibid., iv, 2, 46, 50, 155, 311, *et passim*; King, *Newspaper Press*; Laura A. White, *Robert Barnwell Rhett: Father of Secession* (1931; reprint ed., Gloucester, Mass.: Peter Smith, 1965), 12.

54. John B. Edmunds, Jr., *Francis W. Pickens and the Politics of Destruction* (Chapel Hill: University of North Carolina Press, 1986), 52, 54, 103.

55. Coussons, "Thirty Years," 7, 8, 189; Dabney, *Liberalism in the South*, 88-89.

56. Coussons, "Thirty Years," iv-v, 182, 185, 221, 229, 345; Ellen, "Richard Yeadon," 26; White, *Rhett*, 39 and chap. 5; Schultz, *Nationalism and Sectionalism*, 11.

57. William Barney, *The Road to Secession* (New York: Praeger, 1972), 93-94; White, *Rhett*, 18; *Dictionary of American Biography*, 8: 526-27; Plantation Account Book, 1853-1874, Robert Barnwell Rhett Papers, Perkins Library, Duke University.

58. White, *Rhett*, 10, 47; Barney, *Road to Secession*, 95; Henry Hardy Perritt, "Robert Barnwell Rhett: South Carolina Secession Spokesman" (Ph.D. diss., University of Florida, 1954), 374; Perry, *Reminiscences*, 131-32; Robert Barnwell Rhett to "My Dear Son," 27 February 1852, Rhett Papers, South Caroliniana Library.

59. Lorenzo Sabine, *Notes on Duels and Dueling* (Boston: Crosby, Nichols, 1855), 329; Perritt, "Robert Barnwell Rhett," 370; John Barnwell, *Love of Order: South Carolina's First Secession Crisis* (Chapel Hill: University of North Carolina Press, 1982), 185.

60. Daniel Wallace, "The Political Life and Services of the Hon. R. Barnwell Rhett, of South Carolina . . . and also, His Speech at Grahamville, S.C., July 4, 1859," 28, [pamphlet], South Caroliniana Library; White, *Rhett*, 34; *Mercury*, 27 November 1857; 16 February 1861.

61. White, *Rhett*, 10-11, 14; Coussons, "Thirty Years," 112, 343, 344; Kibler, *Perry*, 156; William Gilmore Simms to Nathaniel Beverly Tucker, 2 March [1851], in *Letters of Simms*, 3: 94.

62. Barney, *Road to Secession*, 95; Schultz, *Nationalism and Sectionalism*, 9.

63. Wallace, "Political Life and Services," 29; White, *Rhett*, 16; Schultz, *Nationalism and Sectionalism*, 9; *Mercury*, 25 April 1859.

64. White, *Rhett*, 106.

65. Ibid., 108-9, 117; Cauthen, *South Carolina Goes to War*, 4; Barnwell, *Love of Order*, 126.

66. Simms to Nathaniel Beverly Tucker, 7 April [1851], *Letters of Simms*, 3: 108; White, *Rhett*, 117.

67. Barnwell, *Love of Order*, 111, 164, 169, 172, 173.

68. A.P. Aldrich to Hammond, 10, 11 November 1851, Hammond Papers; J. Cunningham to Hammond, 10 November 1851, Hammond Papers; White, *Rhett*, 123-24.

69. White, *Rhett*, 135; Wallace, "Political Life and Services," 26.

70. White, *Rhett*, 125-28.

71. Ibid., 133-35.

72. Ibid., 142; King, *Newspaper Press*, 154-55; Schultz, *Nationalism and Sectionalism*, 14; Coussons, "Thirty Years," 3 n.2.

73. Boucher, "South Carolina and the South," 113.

74. R.B. Rhett, Jr., to Edmund Rhett [n.d.], Rhett Papers, South Caroliniana Library.

75. "South Carolina and the South," 113.

76. *Mercury*, 5 February 1857; 29 April 1859; J. Cutler Andrews, *The South Reports the Civil War* (Princeton: Princeton University Press, 1970), 36; T.A. DeLand and A. Davis Smith, *Northern Alabama, Historical and Biographical* (Birmingham, 1888), 257-58.

77. Simms to James Henry Hammond, 12 April 1858, *Letters of Simms*, 4: 49.

78. *Mercury*, 30 May 1860. The *Mercury* on occasion worked hard to avoid quarrels (see, e.g., *Mercury*, 12 April 1858). Rhett's gentle treatment of South Carolinians is not necessarily evidence for what William and Jane Pease have identified as Charleston's penchant for social cohesion, the suppression of public controversy, and "rounded edges." Of Charleston in the 1830s they write: "Fearful of acrimonious debate as the prelude to blunt confrontation, Charlestonians of power and influence perfected a language and a bearing that dulled sharp differences; when those devices failed, they resorted to behind-the-scenes mediation to reduce and obscure difference or, at the very least, to muffle fractious public debate until passions had cooled." The *Courier* and the *Mercury* were constantly engaged in controversy and political battle, and journalistic passion was but a reflection of political passion. For the views of the Peases, see *The Web of Progress: Private Values and Public Styles in Boston and Charleston, 1828-1843* (New York: Oxford University Press, 1985) and "Intellectual Life in the 1830s: The Institutional Framework and the Charleston Style," in Michael O'Brien and David Moltke-Hansen, eds., *Intellectual Life in Antebellum Charleston* (Knoxville: University of Tennessee Press, 1986), 234, *et passim*.

79. *Mercury*, 1 January 1858; 23 March 1858; 21 June 1858; 2 September 1859; 14 October 1859; 11 December 1860.

80. Ibid., 11 December 1860.

81. In fairness it should be recalled that many other partisan papers practiced a similar, one-sided journalism.

82. *Mercury*, 20 October 1860; "The Mercury's Course, and the Right of Free Discussion" (Charleston: Walker, Evans, 1857), 8.

83. "The Mercury's Course," 12.

84. Scarborough, ed., *Ruffin*, 1: 477; R.B. Rhett to Edmund Rhett, Jr., 22 October 1857, Rhett Papers, Southern Historical Collection, University of North Carolina, Chapel Hill; Andrews, *South Reports*, 37-38.

85. Edmund Rhett to Robert Barnwell Rhett, n.d., quoted in Andrews, *South Reports*, 37-38.

86. *Mercury* financial statement in R.B. Rhett, Jr., to Major M.C.M. Hammond, 6 January 1858, Hammond Papers; J.C.G. Kennedy, "Catalogue of the

Newspapers and Periodicals Published in the United States. . . ," in John Livingston, *Livingston's Law Register for 1852* (New York, 1852), 46.

87. *Mercury*, 26 October 1860.

88. *Mercury* financial statement in Rhett, Jr., to Major Hammond, 6 January 1858, Hammond Papers; White, *Rhett*, 145; Hayne to Hammond, 17, 21 April 1858, Hammond Papers; A.P. Aldrich to James Hammond, 22 April 1858, Hammond Papers; Simms to William Porcher Miles, 27 March 1858, *Letters of Simms*, 4:44 n.112, 46-47; S.G. Tupper to Miles, 19 April 1858, William Porcher Miles Papers, Southern Historical Collection.

89. Quoted in Aldrich to Hammond, 22 April 1858, Hammond Papers.

90. Hammond to Simms, 24 March 1858, Hammond Papers.

91. Hayne to Hammond, 18 December 1857, and 25 March 1858, Hammond Papers. Of these critics, Hayne clearly was personally opposed to the Rhetts. Simms, however, enjoyed friendly relations with them, and Hammond felt kindly toward Rhett, Jr. See, e.g., *Letters of Simms*, 1: cxxxiii.

92. *Mercury*, 27 March 1858.

93. *New York Times*, 11 November 1856; see also, *Courier*, 14, 17, 19 November 1856.

94. Schultz, *Nationalism and Sectionalism*, 147.

95. Hammond to Simms, 3 April 1860, Hammond Papers.

96. *Mercury*, 2 July 1858. Hammond and the other cooperationist backers of Heart probably let the Rhetts have the *Mercury* on the assumption that they would fail and the *Mercury* could be obtained at little expense (White, *Rhett*, 145-46).

97. Hayne to Hammond, 17 April 1858, Hammond Papers; Gordon to "Dear Krilla," 20 July 1858, Gordon Papers.

98. *Mercury*, 5, 15 July 1858.

99. Gordon to "Dear Krilla," 20 July 1858, Gordon Papers.

100. *Mercury*, 27 November 1858; 2 January 1860; 18 February 1861; Andrews, *South Reports*, 36. On November 10, 1860, the *New York Daily Tribune* reported that "the Mercury had a daily circulation of about 550—300 in the city and 250 sent to exchanges. Of course, it is very extensively copied out of State, though not much read in it." The *Tribune*'s source was its Charleston correspondent, but apparently that individual, like the paper that employed him, had an axe to grind and gave credence to circulation figures accurate for 1858 but hardly close in the secession crisis of 1860. Not surprisingly, since there are few documented circulation figures, historians have repeated the *Tribune*'s clever but inaccurate assessment.

101. This is the most extensively developed story in the *Mercury* of 1858.

102. *Mercury*, 20 August 1858.

103. *Mercury*, 21, 30 June 1858; 20 July 1858; 6 August 1858; 8 September 1858; 3 November 1858; 12, 16 April 1860; 23 October 1860; Cauthen, *South Carolina Goes to War*, 14.

104. *Mercury*, 1 April 1859; 21 January 1861.

105. Ibid., 18 October 1859.

106. Rhett, Jr., to Miles, 29 January 1860, Miles Papers.

107. Channing, *Crisis of Fear*, 160; Cauthen, *South Carolina Goes to War*, 29; Reynolds, *Editors Make War*, 86; White, *Rhett*, 154; Wallace, "Political Life and Services," 47; *Mercury*, 1860, *passim*.

108. *Mercury*, 31 October 1859; 17 July 1860; 29 August 1860; 24 November 1860.

109. Ibid., 19 May 1858; 9 July 1858; 22 September 1858; 8 November 1860; Reynolds, *Editors Make War*, 93; David R. Goldfield, "Pursuing the American Dream: Cities in the Old South," in Blaine A. Brownell and David R. Goldfield, eds., *The City in Southern History* (Port Washington, N.Y.: Kennikat, 1977), 89.

110. *Mercury*, 23 February 1860; 22 March 1860.

111. Ibid., 26 March 1860.

112. Ibid., 4 January 1858; White, *Rhett*, 146-50.

113. *Mercury*, 11 January 1858; 4 January 1860.

114. Ibid., 6 August 1858; Simms to Hammond, 2 March [1859], *Letters of Simms*, 4: 130.

115. Rhett, Jr., to Hammond, 25 July and 2 August 1858, Hammond Papers; *Mercury*, 19 November 1858. Perhaps the Rhetts' caution was beneficial: J.D. Ashmore wrote Hammond that "I have tried to avoid discussing it [separate state secession] taking the grounds of the Charleston Mercury, once in my life, that there is no such issue before us & its discussion is premature and ill-advised" (30 August 1860, Hammond Papers).

116. *Mercury*, 9 September 1858.

117. Ibid., 10 August 1860.

118. Ibid., 3 November 1860.

119. White, *Rhett*, 150.

120. *Mercury*, 24 July 1858.

121. White, *Rhett*, 163; Hammond to Hayne, 19 September 1860, Hammond Papers.

122. *Mercury*, 14 August 1858; 6 April 1859; 1 November 1859; Wallace, "Political Life and Services," 44.

123. Hayne to Hammond, 3 June 1860, Hammond Papers; Arney R. Childs, ed., *The Private Journal of Henry William Ravenel, 1859-1887* (Columbia: University of South Carolina Press, 1947), 20.

124. White, *Rhett*, 115-68; Cauthen, *South Carolina Goes to War*, 23, 24; Kibler, *Perry*, 320-21.

125. Hammond to Simms, 10 July 1860, Hammond Papers.

126. *Mercury*, 9 November 1860.

127. Channing, *Crisis of Fear*, 248.

128. *Mercury*, 13, 15, 28 November 1860.

129. Ibid., 3, 8 December 1860; *Courier*, 4, 5 December 1860; John R. Horsey to Miles, 10 December 1860, Miles Papers; Cauthen, *South Carolina Goes to War*, 65-66.

130. *Mercury*, 27 March 1858; 27 January 1860; 13 April 1860; 18 May 1860; Scarbourough, ed., *Ruffin*, 1: 66; Rhett, Jr., to Miles, 29 January 1860, Miles Papers.

131. Quoted in Cauthen, *South Carolina Goes to War*, 52.

132. *Mercury*, 5 October 1860. See also *Mercury*, 8, 9 August 1860; *et passim*, November, December, 1860.

133. Quoted in Perritt, "Robert Barnwell Rhett," 322.

134. *Mercury*, 2 October 1860.

135. Ibid., 29 March 1858; 5, 25 October 1860; 17 December 1860.

136. For example, in one small North Carolina town in 1859 and 1860, over

half the periodicals originated out of state, the vast majority of these being from the North. Helen R. Watson, "A Journalistic Medley: Newspapers and Periodicals in a Small North Carolina Community, 1859-1860," *North Carolina Historical Review* 60 (October 1983): 481, 484; Edwin A. Miles, "The Mississippi Press in the Jackson Era, 1822-1841," *Journal of Mississippi History* 19 (January 1957): 7; Guion Griffis Johnson, *Ante-Bellum North Carolina* (Chapel Hill: University of North Carolina Press, 1937), 785; *Mercury*, 23 September 1859; William H. and Jane H. Pease, "Intellectual Life in the 1830s," 253-54.

137. David R. Goldfield, *Urban Growth in the Age of Sectionalism: Virginia, 1847-1861* (Baton Rouge: Louisiana State University Press, 1977), chap. 6; idem, "Pursuing the American Dream," 89-90; idem, *Cotton Fields and Skyscrapers: Southern City and Region, 1607-1980* (Baton Rouge: Louisiana State University Press, 1982), 62, 64, 70, 78; Lawrence H. Larsen, *The Rise of the Urban South* (Lexington: University Press of Kentucky, 1985), 4, 60; Patrick J. Hearden, *Independence and Empire: The New South's Cotton Mill Campaign, 1865-1901* (DeKalb: Northern Illinois University Press, 1982), 15.

138. *Mercury*, 21 April 1860. See also ibid., 12 January 1860.

139. Perritt, "Robert Barnwell Rhett," 375; *Mercury*, 16 January 1860; 9 July 1860.

140. Cauthen, *South Carolina Goes to War*, 33; *Mercury*, 23 March 1858; 11, 13 October 1860; *et passim*, October, November, December, 1860.

141. Ibid., 3, 8, 10 September 1860; 5 October 1860.

142. Ibid., 17 September 1860.

143. Ibid., 17 December 1860.

144. *Courier*, 11 October 1860.

145. *Mercury*, 8 November 1860; 21 December 1860; Hammond to Ashmore, 8 April 1861, Hammond Papers; White, *Rhett*, 181.

146. See, e.g., the *Courier's* attack on Charles Sumner (7 June 1860), its defense of law and order in the South (7 October 1858), and defense of slavery (1 February 1858). See also *Courier*, 28 January 1858, and Richard Yeadon, "An Address, delivered before the Euphemian and Philomathean Literary Societies of Erskine College . . . ," (Due-West, S.C.: Office of the Due-West Telescope, 1857).

147. Yeadon Scrapbook [May 1857], 53, South Caroliniana Library.

148. *Courier*, 1 May 1858; Ellen, "Richard Yeadon," 51.

149. *Courier*, 21 July 1858.

150. Ibid., 1 October 1858; 3, 11 February 1860; 30 April 1860.

151. Ibid., 2 August 1858.

152. Ibid., 11 March 1858. See also ibid., 27 March 1858.

153. Ibid., 2, 12, 16, 21 May 1860; Cauthen, *South Carolina Goes to War*, 20.

154. *Courier*, 20 September 1860.

155. Ibid., 25 June 1860; 20 August 1860; 3 February 1862.

156. *Mercury*, 28 August 1860.

157. See, e.g., *Courier*, 16, 27 October; 12, 13 November 1860. For the conservative letters, see ibid., 3, 7 November 1860.

158. *Courier*, 7 November 1860.

159. Ibid., 20 November 1860; 13 December 1860.

160. Reynolds, *Editors Make War*, 162; "Centennial Edition," *News and Courier*, 1903.

161. Fred Hobson, *Tell About the South: The Southern Rage to Explain* (Baton Rouge: Louisiana State University Press, 1983), 27; Reynolds, *Editors Make War*, 213-17.

162. Reynolds, *Editors Make War*, 51, 72-73, 76, 117.

163. Tennant S. McWilliams has observed a Whig-progressive tradition identified as New South journalism present in some Southern papers of the antebellum era and late nineteenth and early twentieth centuries. See *The New South Faces the World: Foreign Affairs and the Southern Sense of Self, 1877-1950* (Baton Rouge: Louisiana State University Press, 1988).

164. White, *Rhett*, 207, 208-11, 224; *Letters of Simms*, 1: cxxxiii; Nathanial Stephenson, *The Day of the Confederacy* (New Haven: Yale University Press, 1919), 26.

165. C.C. Pinkney et al., to the Editor of the *Mercury*, 13 August 1861, Rhett Papers, Southern Historical Collection; Childs, ed., *Private Journal*, 91, 206; Cauthen, *South Carolina Goes to War*, 213; Ellen, "Richard Yeadon," 60.

166. White, *Rhett*, 219-23, 234; Stephenson, *Day of the Confederacy*, 88.

167. White, *Rhett*, 218; Ellen, "Richard Yeadon," 61-62; Henry Thompson Malone, "The Charleston Daily Courier: Standard-Bearer of the Confederacy," *Journalism Quarterly* 29 (Summer 1952): 307-15.

168. White, *Rhett*, 227-28; Cauthen, *South Carolina Goes to War*, 159; Ellen, "Richard Yeadon," 63-64.

169. "Comments of the Press," in Rhett, Jr., "A Farewell"; *New York Herald*, 21 June 1868.

170. Rhett, Jr., "A Farewell," 4.

5. A Study of Wartime Journalism

1. Harrison A. Trexler, "The Davis Administration and the Richmond Press, 1861-1865," *Journal of Southern History* 16 (May 1950): 181, 195; John Moncure, "John Moncure Daniel: The Editor of the Examiner," *Sewanee Review* 15 (July 1907): 269; Clement Eaton, *A History of the Southern Confederacy* (New York: The Free Press, 1954), 222; J. Cutler Andrews, "The Confederate Press and Public Morale," *Journal of Southern History* 32 (November 1966): 455; Emiline L. Stearns, "John M. Daniel and the Confederacy" (M.A. thesis, University of Chicago, 1928), 68; Paul D. Escott, *After Secession: Jefferson Davis and the Failure of Confederate Nationalism* (Baton Rouge: Louisiana State University Press, 1978), 256.

2. See, for example, C. Vann Woodward, ed., *Mary Chesnut's Civil War* (New Haven: Yale University Press, 1981), 438-40; Horace Edwin Hayden, *Virginia Genealogies* (Wilkes-Barre, Pa.: E. B. Yordy, Printer, 1891), 317.

3. Stearns, "Daniel," 70.

4. John Esten Cooke, *Mohun: Or the Last Days of Lee and His Paladins* (1869; reprint ed., Ridgewood, N.J.: Gregg, 1968), 168.

5. Henry T. Malone, "The Charleston Daily Courier: Standard-Bearer of the Confederacy," *Journalism Quarterly* 29 (Summer 1952).

6. J. Cutler Andrews, *The South Reports the Civil War* (Princeton: Princeton University Press, 1970), 29.

7. *Dictionary of American Biography* (*DAB*), 3: 67; *Appleton's Cyclopedia of American Biography*, 2: 75.

8. George W. Bagby, *John M. Daniel's Latch-Key, a Memoir of the Late Editor of*

the Richmond Examiner (1868); reprint entitled *The Old Virginia Gentleman and other Sketches* (New York: Charles Scribner's Sons, 1910), 173; Woodward, *Chesnut*, 438-40.

9. Moncure D. Conway, "Fredericksburg First and Last," *Magazine of American History* 17 (June 1887): 450; idem, *Autobiography; Memories and Experiences* (Boston: Houghton, Mifflin, 1905), 1: 79.

10. Conway, *Autobiography*, 1: 80-81.

11. Moncure, "Daniel: Editor," 262; Bagby, *Daniel's Latch-Key*, 174; Edward A. Pollard, *The Lost Cause Regained* (1868; reprint ed., Freeport, N.Y.: Books for Libraries Press, 1970), 43; Andrew Newton Wilkinson, "John Moncure Daniel," *Richmond College Historical Papers* 1, no. 1 (1915): 94; George F. Mellen, "Famous Southern Editors: John Moncure Daniel," *Methodist Review* (July-August 1897), 395.

12. Trexler, "Davis," 181.

13. Stearns, "Daniel," 74-75; Cooke, *Mohun*, 166; Conway, *Autobiography*, 2: 259; William Dillon, *Life of John Mitchel* (London: Kegan Paul Trench, 1888), 2: 199.

14. Bagby, *Daniel's Latch-Key*, 183.

15. Moncure, "Daniel: Editor," 268; Andrews, *South Reports*, 31.

16. Wilkinson, "John Moncure Daniel," 94; Mellen, "Famous Southern Editors," 395.

17. Moncure, "Daniel: Editor," 262.

18. Bagby, *Daniel's Latch-Key*, 210.

19. Ibid., 178; Cooke, *Mohun*, 302; Robert W. Hughes, *Editors of the Past* (Richmond: William Ellis Jones, 1897), 27-28; John M. Daniel, *The Richmond Examiner during the War; or, The Writings of John M. Daniel, with a Memoir of His Life, by His Brother, Frederick S. Daniel* (1868; reprint ed., New York: Arno, 1970), 53. Hereafter, references to the memoir portion of this work will be cited as *Examiner during the War . . . Memoir*; in the case of articles and editorials cited from this volume, the citation will be *Examiner during the War* plus the date.

20. Bagby, *Daniel's Latch-Key*, 202.

21. Alfred Hoyt Bill, *The Beleaguered City: Richmond, 1861-1865* (New York: Knopf, 1946), 228-29; Mellen, "Famous Southern Editors," 386.

22. Stearns, "Daniel," 77.

23. Hughes, *Editors*, 25; Bagby, *Daniel's Latch-Key*, 173; Andrews, *South Reports*, 186-87; James I. Robertson, Jr., *General A.P. Hill: The Story of a Confederate Warrior* (New York: Random, 1987), 95.

24. Lester J. Cappon, *Virginia Newspapers, 1821-1935* (New York: D. Appleton-Century, 1936), 7.

25. *Examiner during the War . . . Memoir*, 219; *DAB*, 3: 67; *Appleton's*, 2: 74.

26. Hughes, *Editors*, 20; Bagby, *Daniel's Latch-Key*, 176-77; Cappon, *Virginia Newspapers*, 12; Marvin Davis Evans, "The Richmond Press on the Eve of the Civil War," *John P. Branch Historical Papers of Randolph-Macon College*, New Series, 1 (January 1951): 22.

27. Evans, "Richmond Press," 22.

28. *Richmond Semi-Weekly Examiner*, 8 June 1848.

29. Oscar Penn Fitzgerald, "John M. Daniel and Some of His Contemporaries," *South Atlantic Quarterly* 4 (1905): 13.

30. Conway, *Autobiography*, 2: 61.

31. Evans, "Richmond Press," 10; Cooke, *Mohun*, 166-67; *Examiner during the War . . . Memoir*, 219.

32. Cooke, *Mohun*, 166.

33. Ibid., 24 December 1850.

34. Bagby, *Daniel's Latch-Key*, 202.

35. Dillon, *Mitchel*, 2: 197.

36. Cappon, *Virginia Newspapers*, 7.

37. Ibid., 12; *Richmond Semi-Weekly Examiner*, 16 April 1850.

38. John M. Daniel to R.M.T. Hunter, 27 November [1852], R.M.T. Hunter Papers, Virginia Historical Society (microfilm), Richmond, Va.

39. Ibid.

40. *Examiner during the War . . . Memoir*, 221.

41. Ibid., 223; Moncure, "Daniel: Editor," 264.

42. Daniel to William W. Crump, 22 January 1856, Daniel Letters, Virginia Historical Society; John Bartow Breckinridge to Judge W.W. Crump, 21 October 1854, Daniel-Moncure Papers, 1853-1855, Accession No. 4802, Alderman Library, University of Virginia. Daniel, or an *Examiner* editorialist, had written that "the public and press of the Southern states cannot be too often warned by [about] yankee agents for yankee books, maps and engravings. If they will take it as a social axiom that every proffer and offer which is made to them from the North, is a trap for their fleeces, and that every man who crosses Mason and Dixons line is a swindler and rogue until he has given proof to the contrary, they will save much vexation, and a considerable amount of hard earned money." (Quoted in "Circuit Court of the United States, Southern District of New York," in Daniel-Moncure Papers, 1853-1855.)

43. Daniel to Crump, 15 March 1854, Daniel Letters, Virginia Historical Society; *Examiner during the War . . . Memoir*, 224.

44. *Examiner during the War . . . Memoir*, 225.

45. Daniel to Crump, 15 March 1854, Daniel Letters, Virginia Historical Society.

46. Ibid., 22 January 1856.

47. *Examiner during the War . . . Memoir*, 228-29.

48. Daniel returned to become editor and co-owner of the *Examiner*. In the fall of 1861, when the partnership was ended and the paper sold at public auction, Daniel purchased it at a low price over the protest of his former partner, William Lloyd, who was serving in the army. Lloyd claimed that the notice of auction was too brief and that he was being pushed out by Daniel, who had seen the chance to become sole proprietor on advantageous terms. (See Daniel-Moncure Papers, 1852-1862, Accession No. 4802, Alderman Library, University of Virginia.)

49. Quoted in *Charleston Mercury*, 16 August 1858.

50. Robert Hughes (*Editors of the Past*) and John Moncure ("Daniel: Editor," 266) believed Daniel had doubts, but George Bagby (*Daniel's Latch-Key*) thought Daniel was always a genuine secessionist.

51. Harry T. Shanks, *The Secession Movement in Virginia, 1847-1861* (Richmond: Garrett and Massie, 1934), 184.

52. Stearns, "Daniel," 16-17.

53. Emory M. Thomas, *The Confederate State of Richmond* (Austin: University of Texas Press, 1971), 8.

54. Bagby, *Daniel's Latch-Key*, 170; *Examiner during the War* (19 March 1861), 7-13.

55. Stearns, "Daniel," 30-31; Hughes, *Editors*, 21, 22.

56. Stearns, "Daniel," 42-43; Bagby, *Daniel's Latch-Key*, 173; *Examiner during the War* (8 May 1861), 14, 15; (2 November 1861), 25.

57. Disappointments and increasing hopelessness aggravated Daniel's bitterness. The level of personal invective escalated in August 1863 and again in mid-1864. See, for example, Stearns, "Daniel," 56; John B. Jones, *A Rebel War Clerk's Diary*, ed. Earl Schenck Miers (New York: A.S. Barnes, Perpetua Books, 1961), 253, 259; *Examiner during the War* (5 August 1863), 109; (16, 18 June 1864).

58. *Richmond Examiner*, 15 January 1863.

59. John Esten Cooke's observation that Daniel's wartime invective was less violent supports my own conclusions. (See Cooke, *Mohun*, 167.)

60. Bill, *Beleaguered City*, 76; *Richmond Examiner*, 9 July 1861; 9 April 1863; *Examiner during the War* (29 August 1861), 22.

61. *Richmond Examiner*, 9 April 1863; 28 May 1863.

62. Ibid., 11 February 1863.

63. Allan Nevins, *The Evening Post: A Century of Journalism* (New York: Boni and Liveright, 1922), chap. 12; Lloyd Wendt, *Chicago Tribune: The Rise of a Great American Newspaper* (Chicago: Rand McNally, 1979), 181, *et passim*; J. Cutler Andrews, "The Pennsylvania Press During the Civil War," *Pennsylvania History* 9 (January 1942): 27, 28.

64. As in antebellum days, commercial notices, market prices, and financial news took up a major share of the paper. Surprisingly, local news occupied less than half a column and expanded not at all from antebellum levels despite enormous social and economic changes in wartime Richmond.

65. Stearns, "Daniel," 86.

66. Oliver Wendell Holmes, "Bread and the Newspaper," *Atlantic Monthly* 8 (September 1861): 346-48; Forney quoted in Louis M. Starr, *Reporting the Civil War: The Bohemian Brigade in Action, 1861-65*, new introduction by Allan Nevins (New York: Collier Books, 1962), 26.

67. Henry W. Baehr, Jr., *The New York Tribune Since the Civil War* (New York: Dodd, Mead, 1936), 22.

68. Nevins, *Evening Post*, 359; Wendt, *Chicago Tribune*, 145, 156, 171, 197; Andrews, "Pennsylvania Press," 36.

69. Starr, *Reporting the Civil War*, 6, 24, 25; J. Cutler Andrews, *The North Reports the Civil War* (Pittsburgh: University of Pittsburgh Press, 1955), 6-34; Michael Schudson, *Discovering the News: A Social History of American Newspapers* (New York: Basic Books, 1978), 66-67. The reporter's emergence as an essential part of the newspaper was a result of the Civil War. See Bernard A. Weisberger, *Reporters for the Union* (Boston: Little, Brown, 1953).

70. Cappon, *Virginia Newspapers*, 17-18, 23; Andrews, *South Reports*, 513; Thomas Cooper DeLeon, *Four Years in Rebel Capitals* (Mobile: Gossip Printing, 1890), 290; Starr, *Reporting the Civil War*, viii; Clement Eaton, *Jefferson Davis* (New York: Free Press, 1977), 234; Wendell Holmes Stephenson and E. Merton Coulter, gen. eds., *A History of the South* (Baton Rouge: Louisiana State University Press, 1950), vol. 7: *The Confederate States of America, 1861-1865*, by E. Merton Coulter, 493-95 (hereafter cited as Coulter, *Confederate States*); John Calhoun Ellen, Jr., "Political Newspapers of the Piedmont Carolinas in the 1850s" (Ph.D.

diss., University of South Carolina, 1958), 124; Ellen, Jr., "The Public Life of Richard Yeadon," (M.A. thesis, University of South Carolina, 1953), 67; Catherine Patricia Oliver, "Problems of South Carolina Editors Who Reported the Civil War," (M.A. thesis, University of South Carolina, 1970), 86, *et passim*; *Charleston Daily Courier*, 3 February 1862.

71. *Charleston Daily Courier*, 3 February 1862; Richard Aubrey McLemore, ed., *A History of Mississippi* (Jackson: University and College Press of Mississippi, 1973), 1: 573.

72. Cappon, *Virginia Newspapers*, 18; Coulter, *Confederate States*, 493.

73. Cappon, *Virginia Newspapers*, 10.

74. Ibid., 19.

75. See, for example, *Richmond Examiner*, 13 June 1863.

76. Ibid., 16 February 1863; 28 February 1863.

77. Bagby, *Daniel's Latch-Key*, 187; Cappon, *Virginia Newspapers*, 19.

78. Bagby, *Daniel's Latch-Key*, 186-87.

79. Ibid., 187, 189; Hughes, *Editors*, 28.

80. Hughes, *Editors*, 28.

81. Mellen, "Famous Southern Editors," 387-88; Bagby, *Daniel's Latch-Key*, 204; Andrews, *South Reports*, 31; Jones, *Rebel War Clerk's Diary*, 451; Michael Houston, "Edward Alfred Pollard and the Richmond *Examiner*: A Study of Journalistic Opposition in Wartime" (M.A. thesis, American University, 1963), 63-65; Jack P. Maddex, Jr., *The Reconstruction of Edward A. Pollard* (Chapel Hill: University of North Carolina Press, 1974), 5; Frederick Hudson, *Journalism in the United States from 1690 to 1872* (New York: Harper and Brothers, 1873), 767; Woodward, ed., *Chesnut*, 591 n.9.

82. Hughes, *Editors*, 20.

83. Ibid., 28; Stearns, "Daniel," 31-32 n.2.

84. Bagby, *Daniel's Latch-Key*, 188.

85. Ibid., 177.

86. *Southern Opinion* (Richmond), 29 February 1868; 8 August 1868; Stearns, "Daniel," 31-32 n.2; Bagby, *Daniel's Latch-Key*, 177.

87. Moncure, "Daniel: Editor," 258; Andrews, *South Reports*, 132; Frank H. Alfriend, *The Life of Jefferson Davis* (Cincinnati: Claxton Publishing House, 1868), 328.

88. *New Orleans Daily Picayune*, 19 October 1861.

89. Cooke, *Mohun*, 168.

90. George Cary Eggleston, *A Rebel's Recollections* (New York: Hurd and Houston; Cambridge, Mass.: Riverside Press, 1875), 84.

91. Bagby, *Daniel's Latch-Key*, 190, 210; Hughes, *Editors*, 25; Receipts and Expenditures of the *Richmond Examiner*, Daniel-Moncure Papers, Accession No. 4802, Alderman Library, University of Virginia.

92. Stearns, "Daniel," 68; Bell Irvin Wiley, *The Road to Appomattox* (1956; reprint ed., New York: Atheneum, 1968), 54-55; Strode, *Davis*, 3: 163.

93. *Examiner during the War* (27 September 1861), 23-24; (8 January 1862), 32; (16 January 1862), 35; Stearns, "Daniel," 46-47; Eaton, *Davis*, 235; Wiley, *Road to Appomattox*, 54-55.

94. Thomas, *Confederate State*, 142; Stearns, "Daniel," 53, 60; Andrews, *South Reports*, 253; *Richmond Examiner*, 2 January 1863.

95. *Richmond Examiner*, 3 January 1863; 16 January 1863; 23 April 1863; 13

June 1863; *Examiner during the War* (24 February 1862) 41-42; (6 March 1862), 44; (21 July 1863), 101; (7, 11 August 1863), 110-11; (1 December 1863), 147; Stearns, "Daniel," 67; Jones, *Rebel War Clerk's Diary*, 375.

96. *Richmond Examiner*, 3 January 1863; 12 June 1863.

97. Ibid., 9 January 1863; 1 July 1863; 18 June 1864; *Examiner during the War* (10 July 1863), 93; (10 December 1863), 152; Stearns, "Daniel," 49, 67; Cappon, *Virginia Newspapers*, 20.

98. *Richmond Examiner*, 14 March 1863; 24 March 1863; and ibid., 19 September 1864, quoted in Thomas, *Confederate State*, 185.

99. Woodward, *Chesnut*, 536, 596. At Buena Vista, Taylor allegedly ordered artillery Captain Braxton Bragg to "give them a little more grape, Mr. Bragg."

100. *Jefferson Davis*, vol. 3: *Tragic Hero* (New York: Harcourt Brace and World, 1964), 14.

101. Coulter, *Confederate States*, 502.

102. Bill, *Beleaguered City*, 74; *Examiner during the War* (24 July 1861), 18. This statement places Daniel at odds with his earlier view about Virginia's lack of preparedness; on April 17, 1861, the *Examiner* had declared that "the public means of resistance are simply *nil*."

103. *Richmond Examiner*, 2 January 1862; *Examiner during the War* (26 February 1862), 43.

104. *Examiner during the War* (4 February 1862), 38.

105. Ibid. (25 November 1862), 62.

106. Bagby, *Daniel's Latch-Key*, 195; Stearns, "Daniel," 71-73.

107. See below.

108. *Richmond Examiner*, 4 October 1862; Jones, *Rebel War Clerk's Diary*, 242, 318; *Examiner during the War* (10 December 1863), 153.

109. *Examiner during the War* (26 February 1862), 43; (20 February 1864), 173.

110. *Richmond Examiner*, 4 October 1862.

111. *Examiner during the War* (29 November 1861), 31; Stearns, "Daniel," 40-41; Hughes, *Editors*, 24; Edward A. Pollard, *The Life of Jefferson Davis, with a Secret History of the Southern Confederacy* (Philadelphia: National Publishing Co., 1869), 202.

112. *Richmond Examiner*, 23 January 1863; 10 March 1863.

113. Ibid., 10 January 1863; *Examiner during the War* (12 November 1863), 136, 137; Stearns, "Daniel," 57, 58.

114. *Richmond Examiner*, 6 February 1863.

115. *Examiner during the War* (19 May 1862), 53-54. Daniel ridiculed the attempt to represent cotton, corn, tobacco, etc., on the national coat of arms; it was a scheme offensive to principles of heraldry as well as common sense. "The vegetables which are proposed for the shield of the Confederacy are undoubtedly valuable; so are carrots and turnips; but they are not the figures likely to recur in imagination excited by patriotism, nor to be associated with the dignity of the country or its powers of defense or punishment." [*Examiner during the War*, (29 March 1862), 46.]

116. *Richmond Examiner*, 12 May 1863; *Examiner during the War* (8 April 1864), 185; Pollard, *Lost Cause Regained*, 43.

117. Andrews, "Confederate Press," 453; Trexler, "Davis," 181, 184, 191, 195; Hayden, *Virginia Genealogies*, 317; Eaton, *Davis*, 234; Coulter, *Confederate*

States, 503, 505; Escott, *After Secession*, 256; Emory M. Thomas, *The Confederate Nation: 1861-1865* (New York: Harper and Row, 1979), 142-43; Edward Younger, ed., *Inside the Confederate Government: The Diary of Robert Garlick Hill Kean* (New York: Oxford University Press, 1959), 103.

118. Woodward, *Chesnut*, 163, 219-20, 418, 439-40.

119. Ibid., 219-20, 535.

120. S.C. Hayes to Jefferson Davis, 6 January 1864, *The War of the Rebellion: A Compilation of the Official Records of the Union and Confederate Armies* (Washington, 1880-1901), Series 4, 3: 6. (Hereafter references to this series will be cited as *Official Records*.)

121. DeLeon, *Four Years*, 289.

122. Robert Neil Mathis, "Freedom of the Press in the Confederacy: A Reality," *Historian* 37 (August 1975): 633, 638.

123. *Richmond Examiner*, 28 August 1862, in Stearns, "Daniel," 71; Jones, *Rebel War Clerk's Diary*, 70-71.

124. *Examiner during the War* (3 February 1862), 35.

125. *Richmond Examiner*, 7 March 1863; ibid., 19 September 1862, in Stearns, "Daniel," 71; Jones, *Rebel War Clerk's Diary*, 330, 338; Mathis, "Freedom of the Press," 636-37.

126. See John F. Marszalek, *Sherman's Other War* (Memphis: Memphis State University Press, 1981), chap. 1.

127. Robert Hume Tomlinson, "The Origins and Editorial Policies of the Richmond Whig and Public Advertiser, 1824-1865" (Ph.D. diss., Michigan State University, 1971), 215, 218, 230; Oliver, "Problems of Editors," 12; Younger, *Inside the Confederate Government*, 103; Coulter, *Confederate States*, 501, 502.

128. Coulter, *Confederate States*, 503.

129. *Richmond Examiner*, 3 February 1862.

130. Ibid.; *Examiner during the War* (21 December 1864), 216.

131. *Examiner during the War* (12 December 1863), 154.

132. Benjamin Butler erroneously believed the *Examiner* to be the *New York World* of the Confederacy (see Cappon, *Virginia Newspapers*, 20). In fact, the *Examiner* imitated the North's most rabid war advocates, the abolitionists, when on July 4, 1861, it called for a lengthy war to transform Southern society and purge all Yankeeisms, just like the abolitionists who welcomed a lengthy war in order to purge slavery.

133. Mathis, "Freedom of the Press," 646-47.

134. The major features of the Confederate debate on press freedom are found in the works cited herein by J. Cutler Andrews and Robert Neil Mathis and the following: John Paul Jones, "The Confederate Press and the Government," *Americana* 37 (January 1943): 7-27; Quintus Charles Wilson, "Voluntary Press Censorship during the Civil War," *Journalism Quarterly* 19 (September 1942): 251-61; Oliver, "Problems of Editors," 9-16.

135. Richard E. Beringer, Herman Hathaway, Archer Jones, William N. Still, Jr., *Why the South Lost the Civil War* (Athens: University of Georgia Press, 1986), 275, 277, 390, 433.

136. *Georgia Journalism, 1763-1950* (Athens: University of Georgia Press, 1951), 66.

137. *Richmond Examiner*, 19 September 1862, quoted in Stearns, "Daniel," 71. See also Oliver, "Problems of Editors," 5.

138. Hughes, *Editors*, 24.

139. *Charleston Daily Courier*, 12 February 1862.

140. Beth G. Crabtree and James Patton, eds., *"Journal of a Secesh Lady": The Diary of Catherine Ann Devereux Edmondston 1860-1866* (Raleigh: Division of Archives and History, Department of Cultural Resources, 1979), 532.

141. *Richmond Examiner*, 20 May 1863.

142. *Examiner during the War* (7 August 1861), 19; (19 February 1862), 40.

143. Ibid. (26 March 1864), 181; Eggleston, *Rebel's Recollections*, 232-35.

144. *Richmond Examiner*, 6 June 1864. Both Hughes and John Moncure felt that Daniel privately lost faith in Confederate victory in 1864 or earlier. See Moncure, "Daniel: Editor," 267; Hughes, *Editors*, 29.

145. For a similar editorial course, see the account of the *Richmond Whig* in Tomlinson, "Origins and Editorial Policies of the Richmond Whig," 237, 244-45, 248.

146. *Richmond Examiner*, 3, 4 April 1862. For a good account of these bread riots, which were occasioned by scarcity of food but soon degenerated into general looting, see Thomas, *Confederate State of Richmond*, 119-22.

147. *Richmond Examiner*, 20 October 1862. See also 18 June 1863.

148. *Examiner during the War* (4 March 1861), 6; (7 September 1863), 116-17; *Richmond Examiner*, 26 May 1863.

149. *Examiner during the War* (23 August 1861), 21; (26 January 1863), 66.

150. *Richmond Examiner*, 19 May 1863.

151. Ibid., 20 June 1863.

152. Ibid., 11 October 1862; 7 January 1863; 18 February 1863.

153. *Examiner during the War* (9 February 1863), 72.

154. *Richmond Examiner*, 9 May 1863.

155. Quoted in Thomas, *Confederate State*, 176.

156. Dillon, *Mitchel*, 2: 199; James W. Silver, "Propaganda in the Confederacy," *Journal of Southern History* 11 (November, 1945): 500-501.

157. Bagby, *Daniel's Latch-Key*, 199; *Examiner during the War* (2 December 1863), 148; Silver, "Propaganda in the Confederacy," 500.

158. *Examiner during the War* (28 July 1863), 105.

159. *Richmond Examiner*, 30 June 1864.

160. Ibid., 16 July 1861; *Examiner during the War* (17 September 1863), 119; (1 January 1864), 158.

161. *Examiner during the War* (11 September 1862), 58.

162. *Richmond Examiner*, 20 May 1863.

163. *Examiner during the War* (17 September 1863), 119.

164. Ibid. (8 July 1861), 17.

165. *Richmond Examiner*, 14 March 1863.

166. Ibid., 31 March 1863.

167. Ibid., 31 March 1863; 20 April 1863.

168. Andrews, "Pennsylvania Press," 32; Silver, "Propaganda in the Confederacy," 499.

169. Daniel's universal portrayal of Yankees in the blackest colors was merely a gross exaggeration of a basic truth which he believed. (See Pollard, *Lost Cause Regained*, 43.)

170. *Richmond Examiner*, 23 June 1862, in Andrews, *South Reports*, 528; *Richmond Examiner*, 9 October 1862.

171. Quoted in John A. Dix to Abraham Lincoln, 7 January 1863, in *Official Records*, Series 1, 20 (pt. 2): 308.

172. *Richmond Examiner*, 8 July 1863; Andrews, *South Reports*, 274-75, 338.

173. Ibid., 29 January 1863; 2 March 1863; *Examiner during the War* (16 July 1863), 98. In this last issue the editor wrote: "The Confederacy has lately received two 'facers.' It has a bloody nose and a black eye—but it was never sounder in wind and limb than it is at this moment."

174. Andrews, "Confederate Press and Public Morale," 464; Beringer et al., *Why the South Lost*, 278.

175. Tomlinson, "Origins and Editorial Policies of the Richmond Whig," 216.

176. Quoted in Paul D. Escott, *Many Excellent People: Power and Privilege in North Carolina, 1850-1900* (Chapel Hill: Univerity of North Carolina Press, 1985), 76, 82. James Silver has suggested a different explanation: the Confederacy, a rural society, did not have the means to reach the masses. This suggestion would appear to be incorrect; it was not the medium but the message which was ineffective. (See Silver, "Propaganda in the Confederacy," 503.)

177. Robert Toombs to Alexander H. Stephens, 22 September 1861, in U.B. Phillips, ed., "The Correspondence of Robert Toombs, Alexander H. Stephens, and Howell Cobb," *Annual Report of the American Historical Association for the Year 1911* (Washington, D.C.), 2: 576.

178. Andrews, "Confederate Press and Public Morale," 465.

179. John d'Entremont, *Southern Emancipator: Moncure Conway, The American Years 1832-1865* (New York: Oxford University Press, 1987), 36.

180. Drew Gilpin Faust, *The Creation of Confederate Nationalism: Ideology and Identity in the Civil War South* (Baton Rouge: Louisiana State University Press, 1988), 7-8, 15.

181. Schudson, *Discovering the News*, 67.

6. Resisting Reconstruction

1. Henry Watterson, *"Marse Henry"* (New York: George H. Doran Co., 1919), 2: 225.

2. *Atlanta Constitution*, 4 May 1877.

3. Malcolm Cook McMillan, *Constitutional Development in Alabama, 1798-1901: A Study in Politics, the Negro, and Sectionalism*, James Sprunt Studies in History and Political Science, vol. 37 (Chapel Hill: University of North Carolina Press, 1955), 156.

4. *Mobile Daily Register*, 3 May 1877; J. Cutler Andrews, *The South Reports the Civil War* (Princeton: Princeton University Press, 1970), 39; David R. Chesnutt, "John Forsyth: A Southern Partisan (1865-1867)" (M.A. thesis, Auburn University, 1967), 6-7; *National Cyclopedia of American Biography* s.v. "Forsyth, John"; Don H. Doyle, *New Men, New Cities, New South: Atlanta, Nashville, Charleston, Mobile, 1860-1910* (Chapel Hill: University of North Carolina Press, 1990), 69ff.

5. *Mobile Daily Register*, 3 May 1877; *National Cyclopedia of American Biography*, s.v. "Forsyth, John"; *Mobile Daily Register*, 75th Anniversary Issue, 31 January 1895; and *Mobile Daily Register*, 100th Anniversary, 1814-1914, Alabama State Department of Archives and History, Montgomery, Alabama. The *Mobile Daily*

Register went through many name changes during the years of Forsyth's direction. When he first became associated with the *Register*, its official title was the *Mobile Daily Commercial Register and Patriot*. Among the several name alterations between 1837 and 1877, two are important: from 1861 to 1868 the words "Advertiser and Register" were in the title in some form; and from February 1868 until December 1877 the title was *Mobile Daily Register*. See Winifred Gregory, ed., *American Newspapers, 1921-1936: A Union List of Files Available in the United States and Canada* (1937; reprint ed., New York: Kraus Reprint Corp., 1967). Hereafter, the *Mobile Daily Register* will be abbreviated as *MDR*.

Forsyth was editor and part-owner of his Mobile paper until 1868, when he sold his interest to Colonel William D. Mann. Afterwards he remained as editor, for his services were by then in even greater demand.

6. Luther N. Steward, Jr., "John Forsyth," *Alabama Review* 14 (April 1961): 99; John Kent Folmar, "Reaction to Reconstruction: John Forsyth and the Mobile *Advertiser and Register*, 1865-1867," *Alabama Historical Quarterly* 37 (Winter 1975): 245.

7. Chesnutt, "John Forsyth," 8; Richard Harrison Shryock, *Georgia and the Union in 1850* (1926; reprint ed., New York: AMS, 1968), 310, 322.

8. Chesnutt, "John Forsyth," 9.

9. George Fort Milton, *The Eve of Conflict* (1934; reprint ed., New York: Octagon, 1963), 378; J.E.D. Yonge, "The Conservative Party in Alabama, 1848-1860," *Alabama Historical Society Publications* 4: 508.

10. Milton, *Eve of Conflict*, 384.

11. Ibid., 404; Yonge, "Conservative Party," 509.

12. Yonge, "Conservative Party," 517, 518; Milton, *Eve of Conflict*, 412, 499.

13. Charles G. Summersell, *Mobile: History of a Seaport Town* (University: University of Alabama Press, 1949), 13.

14. *Charleston Daily Courier*, 19 November 1860.

15. Chesnutt, "John Forsyth," 29.

16. Andrews, *South Reports*, 242, 395, chap. 8; Clement Eaton, *A History of the Southern Confederacy* (1954: paperback ed., New York: Free Press, 1965), 221-22.

17. For a similar editorial career, see Carl R. Osthaus, "From the Old South to the New South: The Editorial Career of William Tappan Thompson of the *Savannah Morning News*," *Southern Quarterly* 14 (April 1976): 237-60.

18. Folmar, "Reaction to Reconstruction," 246-47. Forsyth later claimed that he delayed his return to Mobile until learning that the Confederacy had no hope of recovery. (See Chesnutt, "John Forsyth," 32.)

19. *Mobile Daily Advertiser and Register*, 21, 28 July 1865; Chesnutt, "John Forsyth," 32; Steward, "John Forsyth," 120. Hereafter the *Mobile Daily Advertiser and Register* will be abbreviated as *MDA&R*.

20. Folmar, "Reaction to Reconstruction," 248.

21. Quoted in Steward, "John Forsyth," 210.

22. *MDR*, 19 January 1870; Folmar, "Reaction to Reconstruction," 3; Chesnutt, "John Forsyth," 74; Walter L. Fleming, *Civil War and Reconstruction in Alabama* (New York: Columbia University Press, 1905), 430.

23. Eric L. McKitrick, *Andrew Johnson and Reconstruction* (Chicago: University of Chicago Press, 1960), chap. 2.

24. *MDA&R*, 18, 19, 20 July 1865.

25. Ibid., 1 August 1865.

26. Charles F. Ritter, "The Press in Florida, Louisiana, and South Carolina and the End of Reconstruction, 1865-1877: Southern Men and Northern Interests" (Ph.D. diss., Catholic University, 1976), 3-4, 21, 93, 118-23.

27. *MDA&R*, 19 July 1865.

28. Chesnutt, "John Forsyth," 44-45.

29. *MDA&R*, 20 July 1865.

30. Quoted in Chesnutt, "John Forsyth," 47-48.

31. Chesnutt, "John Forsyth," 51-52; *MDA&R*, 7 December 1865.

32. *MDA&R*, 12 December 1865. For similar statements, see the issues of 21, 24, and 30 December.

33. *MDR*, 1 February 1870; Fayette Copeland, "The New Orleans Press and Reconstruction," *The Louisiana Historical Quarterly* 30 (January 1947): 183. In describing the *Register* for 1872, Forsyth listed the news department as third in importance (*MDR*, 31 December 1871).

34. *MDA&R*, 22 November 1867; *MDR*, 3 December 1871.

35. *MDR*, 14, 30 January 1874.

36. *MDR*, 2 November 1870.

37. *MDR*, 30 April 1871.

38. Fleming, *Civil War and Reconstruction in Alabama*, 394; Folmar, "Reaction to Reconstruction," 254; Chesnutt, "John Forsyth," 72.

39. *MDA&R*, 13 November 1867; 1 January 1868.

40. *MDR*, 21 April 1868.

41. *MDR*, 29 November 1868; 25 January 1870; 24, 25 January 1871; 14 February 1871; 28 July 1874; Chesnutt, "John Forsyth," 104.

42. *MDR*, 5 October 1876.

43. See, for example, *MDR*, 7 January 1870; 16 March 1871.

44. *MDR*, 20 January 1871.

45. *MDR*, 25 April 1874.

46. *MDA&R*, 19 November 1867; Folmar, "Reaction to Reconstruction," 258.

47. *MDR*, 1 May 1874; 4 June 1874.

48. *MDR*, 29 July 1870; 9 December 1871; Paul H. Buck, *The Road to Reunion* (Boston: Little, Brown, 1937), 76.

49. *MDR*, 6 January 1870; 10 December 1871; 30 May 1874.

50. *MDR*, 8 November 1871.

51. Without the threat of carpetbag and black domination Forsyth might have become known as a great paternalist. See, for example, his kindly sentiments on black education and black-white relations in his review of a speech by a black woman, Mrs. F.E.W. Harper (*MDR*, 1 July 1871).

52. *MDA&R*, 10 November 1867; *MDR*, 15 January 1870; 24 February 1870; 5 June 1874.

53. *MDR*, 8 December 1868.

54. *MDR*, 22 February 1870.

55. *MDR*, 15 October 1874.

56. *MDR*, 17 December 1874.

57. *MDR*, 4 June 1874.

58. *MDR*, 9 July 1874.

59. *MDR*, 8 March 1871; Vernon Lane Wharton, *The Negro in Mississippi, 1865-1890* (New York: Harper and Row, Harper Torchbooks, 1965), 188-90.

60. *MDR*, 20 October 1876.

61. See, for example, the *Register*'s front pages for 9 and 12 October 1868 and 22 July 1874. With the Mobile city election scheduled for December 22, 1874, the *Register* published on the front page of the December 15 issue one full column on Negro rape.

62. *MDR*, 5 November 1871.

63. Copeland, "New Orleans Press and Reconstruction," 225.

64. *MDR*, 13 July 1870.

65. *MDR*, 12 February 1871.

66. The language some Republican editors used against one another, suggests Eric Foner, was vitriolic even by nineteenth-century standards. Georgia editor J. Clarke Swayze described a white Republican rival as "an unprincipled hermaphrodite bastard" and a black Republican rival as "the Reverend blackguard, whoremaster, forger and passer of counterfeit money." [Eric Foner, *Reconstruction: America's Unfinished Revolution, 1863-1877* (New York: Harper and Row, 1988), 348.]

67. Quoted in Alfred McClung Lee, *The Daily Newspaper in America* (New York: Macmillan, 1937), 10.

68. Paul D. Escott, *Many Excellent People: Power and Privilege in North Carolina, 1850-1900* (Chapel Hill: University of North Carolina Press, 1985), 185; Foner, *Reconstruction*, 434; Cal M. Logue, "Racist Reporting During Reconstruction," *Journal of Black Studies* 9 (March 1979): 335-49.

69. *MDR*, 12 February 1870, 12 April 1871; 5 July 1874.

70. *MDR*, May-July 1871; see also 12 February 1870; 6 March 1870; Chesnutt, "John Forsyth," 102.

71. *MDR*, 100th Anniversary, 11.

72. *MDR*, 14 April 1868; 1 February 1871; 15 April 1871; 7 June 1871; 7 June 1874. In response to criticism of duelling Forsyth advised readers to do what was honorable, truthful, and just, and to forget about public opinion (*MDR*, 10 July 1870).

73. *MDR*, 6 November 1872.

74. Foner, *Reconstruction*, 432-33.

75. *MDR*, 8 April 1868.

76. *MDR*, 23 July 1870; 17 May 1871.

77. *MDR*, 17 October 1876.

78. *MDR*, 15 April 1868.

79. *MDR*, 6 May 1871.

80. *MDR*, 19 July 1874.

81. *MDA&R*, 6 November 1867; *MDR*, 9 October 1868; 5 January 1871; 10 February 1871.

82. *MDR*, 9 July 1870; Michael Perman, *The Road to Redemption: Southern Politics, 1869-1879* (Chapel Hill: University of North Carolina Press, 1984), 78.

83. *MDR*, 1 April 1871.

84. See, for example, *MDR*, 9, 30 October 1868; 30 January 1870; 7 March 1871; 25 April 1874; Perman, *Road to Redemption*, 156-57.

85. *MDR*, 6 May 1874; 2 July 1874.

86. *MDR*, 25 August 1872.

87. *MDR*, 15 November 1871.

88. *MDR*, 6 May 1874.

89. *MDR*, 5 July 1874.

90. *MDR*, 1 July 1874.

91. *MDR*, 5 July 1874.

92. *MDR*, 4 June 1874.

93. *MDR*, 3, 4 June 1874; 3, 10 July 1874; 6 October 1874; 5 December 1874.

94. *MDR*, 25 October 1874; 9 April 1875.

95. *MDR*, 25 June 1874.

96. *MDR*, 3 June 1874.

97. *MDR*, 12 October 1868; 12 November 1870; 5 December 1872.

98. *MDR*, 19 March 1871; 9 May 1871; 6 June 1874.

99. *MDR*, 2 February 1870; 16 February 1871.

100. *MDR*, 11 July 1874.

101. *MDR*, 15 April 1871; 25, 30 November 1871.

102. *MDR*, 17 November 1876. Forsyth also added: "We have entirely too much politics. Here in Alabama we had a State election in 1874, an election for a Convention and a Constitution in 1875, a State election in August, 1876, a Presidential election in November, 1876. Here in Mobile we will have a county election in August, 1877. Then we will have a State election in August, 1878, and a Congressional struggle in November, 1878. Then in 1879, blessed year, we will have a respite."

103. *MDR*, 29 October 1868; 7 December 1870; 15 January 1871.

104. *MDR*, 20 July 1871.

105. *MDR*, 3 October 1871. See, for example, 8 October 1868; 1 November 1868; July and December 1874.

106. Quoted in Perman, *Road to Redemption*, 128.

107. *MDA&R*, 3, 5 January 1868; 1 February 1868; *MDR*, 26 February 1874; 6 December 1874; Chesnutt, "John Forsyth," 64; *National Cyclopedia of American Biography*, s.v. "Forsyth, John"; John Witherspoon DuBose, *Alabama's Tragic Decade; Ten Years of Alabama, 1865-1874*, ed. James K. Greer (Birmingham: Webb Book, 1940), 210; Charles H. Coleman, *The Election of 1868* (1933; reprint ed., New York: Octagon, 1971), 293.

108. Ritter, "Press in Florida, Louisiana, and South Carolina," 254-55.

109. *MDR*, 2, 12 October 1868; 21 January 1870.

110. *MDR*, 14 October 1868; Jean Baker, *Affairs of Party: The Political Culture of the Northern Democrats in the Mid-Nineteenth Century* (Ithaca, N.Y.: Cornell University Press, 1983), 349-52.

111. *MDR*, 22 April 1868; 23, 24 June 1871.

112. *MDR*, 25 November 1871.

113. *MDR*, 5 May 1871.

114. *MDR*, 26 March 1871; 3, 9, 11, 12 July 1872.

115. *MDR*, 29 July 1874.

116. *MDR*, 16 July 1874.

117. Chesnutt, "John Forsyth," 73, 88.

118. *MDR*, 5, 11, 13, 19, 20 November 1868.

119. *MDR*, 30 April 1871.

120. *MDR*, 8 December 1872.

121. *MDR*, 15 December 1871; Steward, "John Forsyth," 118.

122. Don Harrison Doyle, "Urbanization and Southern Culture: Economic Elites in Four New South Cities (Atlanta, Nashville, Charleston, Mobile), c.

1865-1910," in Orville Vernon Burton and Robert C. McMath, Jr., eds., *Toward a New South? Studies in Post-Civil War Southern Communities* (Westport, Conn.: Greenwood, 1982); idem, *New Men, New Cities, New South*, 69ff.; David R. Goldfield, *Cotton Fields and Skyscrapers: Southern City and Region, 1607-1980* (Baton Rouge: Louisiana State University Press, 1982), 87-88; Howard N. Rabinowitz, "Continuity and Change: Southern Urban Development, 1860-1900," in Blaine A. Brownell and David R. Goldfield, eds., *The City in Southern History: The Growth of Urban Civilization in the South* (Port Washington, N.Y.: National University Publications, Kennikat Press, 1977), 92-95.

123. *MDR*, 14 July 1872; 22 October 1872; 29 March 1874; 7 May 1874; 5, 14 March 1875; Chesnutt, "John Forsyth," 40-41.

124. *MDR*, 5, 11 November 1868; 5 March 1875; 3 October 1876.

125. *MDR*, 30 July 1870; 28 January 1871; 8 June 1871; 11 July 1874; 4, 16 March 1875; Summersell, *Mobile*, 23-24.

126. Chesnutt, "John Forsyth," 79.

127. *MDR*, 2 March 1870; Jonathan Wiener, *Social Origins of the New South: Alabama 1860-1885* (Baton Rouge: Louisiana State University Press, 1978), 86.

128. *MDR*, 13 January 1870.

129. *MDR*, 2 March 1870; 7 May 1874.

130. *MDR*, 15 January 1871; 3, 5 February 1871.

131. *MDA&R*, 28 November 1867; *MDR*, 10, 20 January 1871; 21 December 1871.

132. *MDR*, 4 February 1871; 29 July 1871; 21 December 1871.

133. *MDR*, 6 July 1872.

134. *MDR*, 25 January 1871; 9 April 1871; 14 March 1875.

135. *MDR*, 21 December 1871.

136. *MDR*, 20 June 1871.

137. *MDR*, 4 February 1871.

138. Doyle, "Urbanization and Southern Culture," in Burton and McMath, *Toward a New South?*, 15-18.

139. *MDR*, 2 March 1871; 20 April 1871; 6 October 1871.

140. *MDR*, 2 June 1871; see also, *MDR*, 12 February 1871; 24 October 1871.

141. Forsyth's attitude did not prevent him from continuing to push the cause of the Mobile and Northwest Railroad. (See *MDR*, 24 October 1871.)

142. *MDR*, 2 June 1871.

143. Wiener, *Social Origins of the New South*, Part III; Goldfield, *Cotton Fields and Skyscrapers*, 90-91; DuBose and Greer, *Alabama's Tragic Decade*, 99; Don H. Doyle, "Leadership and Decline in Postwar Charleston, 1865-1910" in Walter J. Fraser, Jr., and Winfred B. Moore, Jr., eds., *From the Old South to the New: Essays on the Transitional South* (Westport, Conn.: Greenwood, 1981), 95.

144. *MDR*, 26 January 1871; 29 March 1874; Wiener, *Social Origins of the New South*, 154-55; Allen Going, *Bourbon Democracy in Alabama, 1874-1890* (University: University of Alabama Press, 1951), 67, 68.

145. Doyle, "Urbanization and Southern Culture," in Burton and McMath, *Toward a New South?*, 14.

146. See, for example, James C. Cobb, "Beyond Planters and Industrialists: A New Perspective on the New South," *Journal of Southern History* 54 (February 1988): 45-68; idem, *Industrialization and Southern Society, 1877-1984* (Lexington: University Press of Kentucky, 1984), 15-17, 23; Perman, *Road to Redemption*,

234-35; Patrick J. Hearden, *Independence and Empire: The New South's Cotton Mill Campaign, 1865-1901* (DeKalb: Northern Illinois University Press, 1982), chap. 5; John W. Cell, *The Highest Stage of White Supremacy* (Cambridge: Cambridge University Press, 1982), 167-69. The final word on this debate is not in, but the motives and interests of planters and industrialists would seem to be less narrowly focused than as presented in Wiener, *Social Origins of the New South*, or Dwight B. Billings, Jr., *Planters and the Making of a "New South": Class, Politics, and Development in North Carolina, 1865-1900* (Chapel Hill: University of North Carolina Press, 1979). See, for example, Dan T. Carter, "From the Old South to the New: Another Look at the Theme of Change and Continuity," in Fraser and Moore, *From the Old South to the New.*

147. David Carlton, "'Builders of a New South'—The Town Classes and Early Industrialization of South Carolina, 1880-1907," in Fraser and Moore, *From the Old South to the New*, 56-57; Lacy K. Ford, "Rednecks and Merchants: Economic Development and Social Tensions in the South Carolina Upcountry, 1865-1900," *Journal of American History* 71 (September 1984).

148. Harriet E. Amos, *Cotton City: Urban Development in Antebellum Mobile* (University: University of Alabama Press, 1985), 194-222, 230-31, 239. Advocacy of economic development before the Civil War was not at all unusual. See Amos, *Cotton City*, chap. 4. See also William Barney, "The Ambivalence of Change: From Old South to New in the Alabama Black Belt, 1850-1870," in Fraser and Moore, *From the Old South to the New*, 35-36. Barney identifies antebellum development with the Whig press, but Democratic journals were also active in this cause.

149. *Selma Daily Messenger*, 25 September 1866; Ritter, "Press in Florida, Louisiana, and South Carolina," 19-20; Going, *Bourbon Democracy*, 113; Thomas H. Baker, *The Memphis Commercial Appeal* (Baton Rouge: Louisiana State University Press, 1971), 56-59; James Summerville, "Albert Roberts, Journalist of the New South, Part I," *Tennessee Historical Quarterly* 42 (Spring 1983); Osthaus, "Editorial Career of William Tappan Thompson."

150. Perman, *Road to Redemption*, 235.

151. David Paul Nord, "The Business Values of American Newspapers: The 19th Century Watershed in Chicago," *Journalism Quarterly* 61 (Summer 1984).

152. Cobb, "Beyond Planters and Industrialists," 56.

153. Dan Carter, *When the War Was Over: The Failure of Self-Reconstruction in the South, 1865-1867* (Baton Rouge: Louisiana State University Press, 1985), 130, 146; Barney, "Ambivalence of Change" in Fraser and Moore, *From the Old South to the New*, 39; MDR, 5 March 1875.

154. Ritter, "Press in Florida, Louisiana, and South Carolina," 58.

155. Amos, *Cotton City*, 139, 145, 155, 172, 179, 188, 218-19.

156. *MDR*, 1 February 1871; 11 July 1872; 20 January 1874; June 1874; 3 March 1875; 1 October 1876.

157. *MDR*, 5 February 1871.

158. *MDR*, 11 February 1871.

159. *MDR*, 22 December 1872.

160. *MDR*, 18 June 1871; 20 January 1874; 5 June 1874; 4 May 1877. The *Register* claimed Mississippi as part of its bailiwick because readers there were almost as numerous as in southern Alabama (*MDR*, 20 June 1871).

161. *Geo. P. Rowell and Co.'s American Newspaper Directory* (New York: Geo. P. Rowell and Co., 1869), 8, 171, 178.

162. *MDR*, 1 October 1876.

163. *MDR*, 8 February 1870; 5 April 1871.

164. *MDR*, 7 January 1871; 7 February 1871; 15 April 1875.

165. *MDR*, 27, 31 March 1874.

166. *MDR*, 1 July 1876.

167. *MDR*, 27, 31 March 1874.

168. *MDR*, 1 March 1871.

169. *MDR*, 5 April 1871; 15 April 1875.

170. *MDR*, 10 December 1871.

171. *MDR*, 29 October 1868; 5 April 1871.

172. *MDR*, 27 October 1868.

173. *MDR*, 10 December 1871; 5 April 1874.

174. *MDR*, 25 October 1870.

175. See also the upheaval in New Orleans's press. Copeland, "New Orleans Press and Reconstruction," 291, 310. See also Richard Aubrey McLemore, ed., *A History of Mississippi* (Jackson: University and College Press of Mississippi, 1973), 1: 539; James Summerville, "Albert Roberts, Journalist of the New South, Part II," *Tennessee Historical Quarterly* 42 (Summer 1983): 179.

176. *MDR*, 26 March 1874.

177. *MDR*, 26 April 1871.

178. *MDR*, 5 April 1871; 18 October 1871; 20 January 1874; 5 June 1874; 21 July 1874; 4 May 1877; Raymond B. Nixon, *Henry W. Grady: Spokesman of the New South* (New York: Knopf, 1943), 158; Russell Franklin Terrell, *A Study of the Early Journalistic Writings of Henry W. Grady* (1926; reprint ed., New York: Beekman, 1974), 129; "John Forsyth—By B.F. Riley," newspaper clipping, Forsyth Papers, Alabama Department of Archives and History, Montgomery.

179. *New York Sun*, 3 May 1877.

180. R.H. Henry, *Editors I Have Known Since the Civil War* (Jackson, Miss.: Jackson Clarion-Ledger, 1922), 263.

181. *MDR*, 18 May 1871; 30 July 1871.

182. *MDA&R*, 4 January 1868; *MDR*, 19 October 1868.

183. *MDR*, 30 June 1874.

184. *MDR*, 5, 20 February 1870; 19 July 1870.

185. Copeland, "New Orleans Press and Reconstruction," 293, 295.

186. *MDA&R*, 4 January 1868.

187. *MDR*, 2 December 1874.

188. Foner, *Reconstruction*, 268.

189. Some might conclude that the *New Orleans Tribune* was not a black newspaper since it was edited by a white Belgian, Jean-Charles Houzeau, who passed for a colored Creole. Editorial policies also reflected the influence of some white radicals, especially Thomas J. Durant. Nevertheless, the paper was owned and published by Dr. Louis Charles Roudanez, a free-born, French-speaking mulatto and leader of New Orleans's *gens de couleur*. Under the direction of Roudanez, Houzeau, and others, the *Tribune* emphasized an English language section and sought to represent the interests of both freedmen and free-born men of color. See William P. Connor, "Reconstruction Rebels: The *New*

Orleans Tribune in Post-War Louisiana," *Louisiana History* 21 (Spring 1980): 159-81; Jean-Charles Houzeau, *My Passage at the "New Orleans Tribune": A Memoir of the Civil War*, edited with an introduction by David C. Rankin, translated by Gerard F. Denault (Baton Rouge: Louisiana State University Press, 1984); Roland E. Wolseley, *The Black Press, U.S.A.*, 2nd ed., with a foreword by Robert E. Johnson (Ames: Iowa State University Press, 1990), 3-5.

190. Houzeau, *My Passage*, 88.

191. Wolseley, *Black Press*, 38; Henry Lewis Suggs, ed., *The Black Press in the South, 1865-1979* (Westport, Conn.: Greenwood, 1983), xi, 289, 294; Julius E. Thompson, *The Black Press in Mississippi, 1865-1985* (Gainesville: The University Press of Florida, 1993), chap. 1.

192. For a selection of the writings of black editors during Reconstruction and the 1880s, see Martin E. Dann, ed., *The Black Press, 1827-1890: The Quest for National Identity*, with an introduction by Martin E. Dann (New York: Putnam's, 1971; Capricorn Books, 1972).

193. *The Arkansas Freeman*, 5 October 1869; Daniel F. Littlefield, Jr., and Patricia Washington McGraw, "*The Arkansas Freeman*, 1869-1870: Birth of the Black Press in Arkansas," *Phylon* 40 (1979): 75-85; Suggs, *Black Press*, 26.

194. Loren Schweninger, *James T. Rapier and Reconstruction* (Chicago: The University of Chicago Press, 1978), 107, 112.

195. George C. Rable, "Bourbonism, Reconstruction, and the Persistence of Southern Distinctiveness," *Civil War History* 29 (June 1983): 152-53.

196. Ibid., 152.

7. Three Giants of New South Journalism

1. C. Vann Woodward, *Origins of the New South, 1877-1913*, (Baton Rouge: Louisiana State University Press, 1951), 145-46.

2. Donald W. Curl, *Murat Halstead and the "Cincinnati Commercial"* (Boca Raton: University Presses of Florida, 1980), 38, 140-43; S.N.D. North, *History and Present Condition of the Newspapers and Periodical Press of the United States* (Washington, D.C.: Government Printing Office, 1884), 97; Bernard A. Weisberger, *The American Newspaperman* (Chicago: University of Chicago Press, 1961), 126; Marion T. Marzolf, "American 'New Journalism' Takes Root in Europe at End of 19th Century," *Journalism Quarterly* 61 (Autumn 1984): 529; Keith Ian Polakoff, *The Politics of Inertia: The Election of 1876 and the End of Reconstruction* (Baton Rouge: Louisiana State University Press, 1973), 6-7.

3. This point has been suggested in studies by Peter Wallenstein, Foster M. Gaines, and others. See, respectively, the "Epilogue" in *From Slave South to New South: Public Policy in Nineteenth-Century Georgia* (Chapel Hill: University of North Carolina Press, 1987), and *Ghosts of the Confederacy: Defeat, the Lost Cause, and the Emergence of the New South 1865 to 1913* (New York: Oxford University Press, 1987), 80.

4. Paul M. Gaston, *The New South Creed* (New York: Knopf, 1970).

5. Tennant S. McWilliams, *The New South Faces the World: Foreign Affairs and the Southern Sense of Self, 1877-1950* (Baton Rouge: Louisiana State University Press, 1988), 48; David R. Goldfield, *Promised Land: The South Since 1945* (Arlington Heights, Ill.: Harlan Davidson, 1987), 21; Charles L. Flynn, Jr., *White*

Land, Black Labor: Caste and Class in Late Nineteenth-Century Georgia (Baton Rouge: Louisiana State University Press, 1983), 166.

6. Joseph F. Wall, *Henry Watterson: Reconstructed Rebel* (New York: Oxford University Press, 1956), 6-14.

7. Leonard N. Plummer, "Henry Watterson's Editorial Style: An Interpretive Analysis," *Journalism Quarterly* 23 (March 1946): 58.

8. Wall, *Henry Watterson*, 23-24.

9. Ibid., 39.

10. Ibid., 49; Henry F. Pringle, "Kentucky Bourbon: Marse Henry Watterson," in Edwin H. Ford and Edwin Emery, eds., *Highlights in the History of the American Press* (Minneapolis: University of Minnesota Press, 1954), 218.

11. Wall, *Henry Watterson*, 40.

12. Ibid., 71, 74-76; Writers' Program of the Works Projects Administration in the State of Kentucky, *Louisville, a Guide to the Falls City*, American Guide Series (New York: M. Barrows, 1940), 32; *American Newspaper Annual* (Philadelphia: N.W. Ayer and Son, 1880), 452; George H. Yater, *Two Hundred Years at the Falls of the Ohio: A History of Louisville and Jefferson County* (Louisville: The Heritage Corporation, 1979), 95, 96, 101-2, 122-23; Lawrence H. Larsen, *The Rise of the Urban South* (Lexington: University Press of Kentucky, 1985), 151.

13. Allan Nevins, *American Press Opinion* (Boston: D.C. Heath and Co., 1928), 303.

14. *Courier-Journal*, 8 November 1908, sec. 2: 4.

15. Ibid.; Wall, *Henry Watterson*, 80-81, 84; Henry Watterson, *"Marse Henry"* (New York: George H. Doran Co., 1919), 1: 170-71, 174-75, 178-79; Thomas D. Clark, *A History of Kentucky* (New York: Prentice-Hall, 1937), 345; *Courier-Journal*, "Marse Henry" edition, 2 March 1919, 13; Lena C. Logan, "Henry Watterson, Border Nationalist, 1840-1877" (Ph.D. diss., Indiana University, 1942), 121; Charles F. Wingate, *Views and Interviews on Journalism* (1875; reprint ed., New York: Arno and New York Times, 1970), 22-23. Upon the death of Walter Haldeman, his son assumed his father's duties; thus for his entire career Watterson enjoyed the competent business management of the Haldemans.

16. Wall, *Henry Watterson*, 85; *Courier-Journal*, 8 November 1908, sec. 2: 4.

17. Watterson, *"Marse Henry,"* 1: 171; Logan, "Henry Watterson," 121. The *Courier-Journal*, expressing majority Democratic opinion, stood between the *Louisville Commercial*, a Republican organ, and the *Louisville Ledger*, a Bourbon journal.

18. Watterson, *"Marse Henry,"* 1: 171, 174-75; *Courier-Journal*, 8 November 1908, sec. 2: 4; Editorial Writings, Galley Proofs, n. d. [circa 1913], in Microfilm Edition of a Collection of Henry Watterson Papers, University of Louisville Archives, Lousiville, Kentucky.

19. *Courier-Journal*, 14 November 1870; ibid., 9 November 1868, in Arthur Krock, ed., *The Editorials of Henry Watterson* (New York: George H. Doran Co., 1923), 18; Watterson, *"Marse Henry,"* 1: 239; Isaac F. Marcosson, *Adventures in Interviewing* (London: John Lane Co., 1919), 35.

20. Logan, "Henry Watterson," 363.

21. Ibid., 184, 205-8; *Courier-Journal*, 14 November 1870; C.M. Clay to Henry Watterson, 19 August 1871, Watterson Mss., Library of Congress, Washington, D.C.

22. Wall, *Henry Watterson*, 95; Ballard Smith, "Henry Watterson," *Harper's Weekly*, 20 August 1887, 600.

23. Watterson, *"Marse Henry,"* 1: 240; Oswald Garrison Villard, *Some Newspapers and Newspapermen* (New York: Knopf, 1923), 264; Wingate, *Views and Interviews*, 21; *Courier-Journal*, 8 November 1908, sec. 2: 4.

24. *Louisville Journal*, 13 July 1868; Logan, "Henry Watterson," 212-13.

25. *Courier-Journal*, 8 November 1908, sec. 2: 4; ibid., 3 July 1872, in Krock, *Editorials of Henry Watterson*, 39; Logan, "Henry Watterson," 350.

26. *Courier-Journal*, 12 May 1883.

27. *Mobile Daily Register*, 8 July 1870; 24 August 1870; 6 January 1871.

28. *Louisville Journal*, 13 July 1868; Logan, "Henry Watterson," 199; Wall, *Henry Watterson*, 91.

29. Robert K. Thorp, "'Marse Henry' and the Negro: a New Perspective," *Journalism Quarterly* (Autumn 1969): 467-74; Lawrence J. Friedman, *The White Savage: Racial Fantasies in the Postbellum South* (Englewood Cliffs, N.J.: Prentice-Hall, 1970), chap. 3.

30. Logan, "Henry Watterson," 356.

31. *Atlanta Constitution*, 26 January 1884.

32. Joel Chandler Harris, ed., *Joel Chandler Harris' Life of Henry W. Grady* (New York: Cassell Publishing Co., 1890), 6.

33. *New York Times*, 23 December 1921, 13.

34. Stanley Matthews to Henry Watterson, 2 August 1871, Watterson Mss.; D.G. Croly to Watterson, 17 September 1871, Watterson Mss., Library of Congress, Washington, D.C.

35. Logan, "Henry Watterson," 266, 321.

36. See Watterson Mss.

37. Wall, *Henry Watterson*, 114.

38. Nevins, *American Press Opinion*, 303. See, for example, the *Journalist*'s comment on Henry Watterson: "His locks are as long and thick as usual, and his skill at draw poker as great as ever" (24 October 1885, 6).

39. Krock, *Editorials of Henry Watterson*, 42. The huge number of press clippings in praise of Watterson's editorials in the Microfilm Edition of a Collection of Henry Watterson Papers in the University of Louisville Archives supports Krock's view.

40. Francis Warrington Dawson to his mother, 13 November 1865, Dawson Mss., Perkins Library, Duke University, Durham, North Carolina.

41. *Dictionary of American Biography*, 3: 151; E. Culpepper Clark, *Francis Warrington Dawson and the Politics of Restoration: South Carolina, 1874-1889* (University: University of Alabama Press, 1980), 10-20.

42. Dawson to his mother, 28 July 1866, Dawson Mss.

43. Francis Warrington Dawson, *Reminiscences of Confederate Service, 1861-1865* (Charleston, 1882), 155-62; Dawson to his mother, 28 July 1866, Dawson Mss.; Joseph Walker Barnwell, "Reminiscences of the *Courier* and Its Editors," *News and Courier*, 125th Anniversary edition, 1 May 1928. For Dawson's life during this period, consult his letters to his mother in 1865 and 1866, Dawson Mss.

44. Dawson to his mother, 2 October 1866, Dawson Mss.

45. *DAB*, 3: 151; Dawson to his mother, 15 November 1866, Dawson Mss.

46. *American Newspaper Annual*, (1880), 452.

47. Ibid.; Clark, *Dawson*, 147-49; Robert G. Rhett, *Charleston, An Epic of Car-*

olina (Richmond: Garrett and Massie, 1940), 310-11, 314-23; Don H. Doyle, *New Men, New Cities, New South: Atlanta, Nashville, Charleston, Mobile, 1860-1910* (Chapel Hill: University of North Carolina Press, 1990), 117; idem, "Urbanization and Southern Culture: Economic Elites in Four New South Cities (Atlanta, Nashville, Charleston, Mobile), c. 1865-1910" in Orville Burton and Robert C. McMath, Jr., eds., *Toward a New South? Studies in Post-Civil War Southern Communities* (Westport, Conn.: Greenwood, 1982); idem, "Leadership and Decline in Postwar Charleston, 1865-1910" in Walter J. Fraser, Jr. and Winfred B. Moore, Jr., *From the Old South to the New: Essays in the Transitional South* (Westport, Conn.: Greenwood, 1981).

48. Dawson to his mother, 2 September 1867, Dawson Mss.; Dawson to his father, 30 July 1868, Dawson Mss.

49. Dawson to "My dear Hemphill," 28 June 1876, Hemphill Family Papers, Perkins Library, Duke University, Durham, North Carolina.

50. Clark, *Dawson*, 22.

51. N.G. Gonzales to his sister, 1 December 1882, Elliott-Gonzales Papers, Southern Historical Collection, University of North Carolina; *The Union*, 5 February 188[7], Scrapbook II, 1878-1888, Dawson Mss.

52. Clark, *Dawson*, 1, 9, 23.

53. James Morris Morgan, *Recollections of a Rebel Reefer* (Boston: Houghton Mifflin Co., 1917), 353; Barnwell, "Reminiscences of the *Courier*," *News and Courier*, 1 May 1928, 10-B.

54. Daniel H. Chamberlain to Dawson, 31 July 1874, Dawson Mss.

55. Robert H. Woody, *Republican Newspapers in South Carolina*, Southern Sketches No. 10, 1st ser. (Charlottesville, Va.: Historical Publishing Co., 1936), 51-52.

56. *News and Courier*, 18 February 1876; 8, 9 May 1876; 5, 10, 11, 13 July 1876; Clark, *Dawson*, chap. 3; Jonathan Daniels, *They Will Be Heard* (New York: McGraw-Hill, 1965), 193; Alfred B. Williams, *Hampton and His Red Shirts* (1935; reprint ed., Freeport, N.Y.: Books for Libraries Press, 1970), 33, 41; Joel Williamson, *After Slavery: The Negro in South Carolina During Reconstruction, 1861-1877* (Chapel Hill: University of North Carolina Press, 1965), 267-71; Michael Perman, *The Road to Redemption: Southern Politics, 1869-1879* (Chapel Hill: University of North Carolina Press, 1984), 165; Charles F. Ritter, "The Press in Florida, Louisiana, and South Carolina and the End of Reconstruction, 1865-1877: Southern Men with Northern Interests" (Ph.D. diss., Catholic University, 1976), 203-36.

57. Clark, *Dawson*, 64-65; *News and Courier* (clipping), 25 July 1878, Scrapbook I, 36, Dawson Mss.; Williams, *Hampton and His Red Shirts*, 32-33; Alfred B. Williams, "The Press of South Carolina in the Revolution of 1876," *News and Courier*, 16 June 1907; Daniels, *They Will Be Heard*, 190-93; Lewis P. Jones, "Two Roads Tried—And One Detour," *South Carolina Historical Magazine* 79 (July 1978): 206-18.

58. Daniels, *They Will Be Heard*, 193.

59. Barnwell, "Reminiscences of the *Courier*," *News and Courier*, 1 May 1928, 10-B; Williamson, *After Slavery*, 271, 272; *News and Courier*, 21 December 1876, Scrapbook I, 20, Dawson Mss.; S. Frank Logan, "Francis W. Dawson," 165.

60. Clark, *Dawson*, 75-76, 85-86; Dawson to General John Bratton, 1 June 1888, Letterpress Book, 139, Hemphill Family Papers; *Marlboro Planter* (clipping), Scrap-

book I, 5, Dawson Mss.; *Baltimore American* (clipping) and *Springfield Republican* (clipping), Scrapbook I, 4, Dawson Mss.; William J. Cooper, Jr., *The Conservative Regime: South Carolina, 1877-1890* (Baltimore: Johns Hopkins Press, 1968), 83.

61. Dawson to General John Bratton, 1 June 1888, Letterpress Book, 139, Hemphill Family Papers.

62. *News and Courier*, 16 December 1878; *News and Courier* (clipping), 25 July 1878, Scrapbook I, 36, Dawson Mss.; Clark, *Dawson*, 75-76, 83, 85-87.

63. *News and Courier* (clipping), 25 July 1878, Scrapbook I, 36, Dawson Mss.

64. Lewis Pinckney Jones, *Stormy Petrel: N.G. Gonzales and His State* (Columbia: University of South Carolina Press, 1973), 67.

65. *American Newspaper Annual: 1880.*

66. The press enthusiastically reported the Grady speech. For press clippings on the New South speech, see the Grady scrapbooks in the Grady Mss., Robert W. Woodruff Library, Emory University, Atlanta, Georgia.

67. Raymond B. Nixon, *Henry W. Grady: Spokesman of the New South* (New York: Knopf, 1943), 38-40.

68. Alice E. Reagan, "Promoting the New South: Hannibal I. Kimball and Henry W. Grady," *Atlanta Historical Society Journal* (Fall, 1983): 5-19.

69. Harris, *Life of Henry W. Grady*, 26, 32, 40; Nixon, *Henry W. Grady*, 52-85; Russell Franklin Terrell, *A Study of the Early Journalistic Writings of Henry W. Grady* (1926; reprint ed., New York: Beekman Publishers, 1974), 33; John Donald Wade, "Henry W. Grady," *Southern Review* 3 (Winter 1938): 481.

70. Harris, *Life of Henry W. Grady*, 21.

71. Ibid., 45; Nixon, *Henry W. Grady*, 63.

72. Harris, *Life of Henry W. Grady*, 54.

73. Ibid., 33; Terrell, *Study of the Early Journalistic Writings*, 80; Wade, "Henry W. Grady," 491-92.

74. *Atlanta Constitution*, 21 October 1891.

75. Harris, *Life of Henry W. Grady*, 23.

76. For Grady's early journalistic career in Rome, Georgia, see Scrapbook 1: 6-11, Grady Mss. See also Harris, *Life of Henry W. Grady*, 20, 24-25, 27; Wade, "Henry W. Grady," 484; Nixon, *Henry W. Grady*, 78-79.

77. Nixon, *Henry W. Grady*, 70; Terrell, *Study of the Early Journalistic Writings*, 38-39; Wade, "Henry W. Grady," 483.

78. Clipping, Scrapbook 1: 38, Grady Mss.

79. *Rome Commercial* (clipping), Scrapbook 8: 49, Grady Mss.; Grady to his mother and sister, 21 October 1872, Grady Mss.; Grady to "My dear Mother," December 1872, Grady Mss.

80. Doyle, "Urbanization and Southern Culture," in Burton and McMath, *Toward a New South?*, 12-13; idem, *New Men, New Cities, New South*, 34-38; James Michael Russell, *Atlanta 1847-1890: City Building in the Old South and the New* (Baton Rouge: Louisiana State University Press, 1988), 161-68, 263.

81. Franklin M. Garrett, *Atlanta and Environs* (1954: reprint ed., Athens: University of Georgia Press, 1969), 2: 202, 208; Writers' Program of the Works Projects Administration, *Atlanta: A City of the Modern South*, American Guide Series (New York: Smith and Durrell, 1942), 27-32; Doyle, *New Men, New Cities, New South*, 147.

82. David R. Goldfield, *Cotton Fields and Skyscrapers: Southern City and Region, 1607-1980* (Baton Rouge: Louisiana State University Press, 1982), 103.

83. Harris, *Life of Henry W. Grady*, 25; Nixon, *Henry W. Grady*, 91; Louis Turner Griffith and John Erwin Talmadge, *Georgia Journalism, 1763-1950* (Athens: University of Georgia Press, 1951), 98. Robert Alston was killed in a duel on 12 March 1879 (*Atlanta Constitution*, 12-14 March 1879).

84. *Atlanta Constitution*, 21 October 1891; Scrapbook 2: 1 Grady Mss.; Russell, *Atlanta, 1847-1890*, 183.

85. Harris, *Life of Henry W. Grady*, 25-26; Frank Luther Mott, *American Journalism, A History: 1690-1960*, 3rd ed. (New York: Macmillan, 1962), 454-56.

86. *Atlanta Constitution*, 21 October 1891; Thomas H. Martin, *Atlanta and Its Builders* (New York: Century Memorial Publishing Co., 1902), 2: 372.

87. Griffith and Talmadge, *Georgia Journalism*, 98; Harris, ed., *Life of Henry W. Grady*, 32; Nixon, *Henry W. Grady*, 106-9; Raymond B. Nixon, "Henry Woodfin Grady: Journalistic Leader in Public Affairs" (Ph.D. diss., University of Minnesota, 1942), 150, 161.

88. Nixon, *Henry W. Grady*, chap. 7, 8; Wade, "Henry W. Grady," 485; *Atlanta Constitution*, 15 August 1880.

89. Scrapbook 8: 6, Grady Mss.

90. See Grady Scrapbooks (especially Scrapbook 6), Grady Mss; Harris, *Life of Henry W. Grady*, 26, 61.

91. Nixon, *Henry W. Grady*, 167-70; Harris, *Life of Henry W. Grady*, 30; Wade, "Henry W. Grady," 487.

8. Three Giants of the New South

1. *Courier-Journal*, 2 March 1909; Henry Watterson, *"Marse Henry"* (New York: George H. Doran Co., 1919), 2: 233; Charles F. Wingate, *Views and Interviews on Journalism* (1875; reprint ed., New York: Arno and New York Times, 1970), 15-17.

2. Francis Warrington Dawson, *The Public Press, an Address Delivered before the State Press Association, at Spartanburg, S. C., May 10th, 1876* (Charleston: The News and Courier Job Presses, 1876), 15; Charles F. Ritter, "The Press in Florida, Louisiana, and South Carolina and the End of Reconstruction, 1865-1877: Southern Men with Northern Interests" (Ph.D. diss., Catholic University, 1976), 26, 35. (A copy of the Dawson pamphlet, *The Public Press*, is in the Dawson Mss., Perkins Library, Duke University, Durham, N.C.)

3. Dawson to Sarah Morgan Dawson, 19 September 1886, Dawson Mss.

4. Bernard A. Weisberger, *The American Newspaperman* (Chicago: University of Chicago Press, 1961), 126.

5. Henry Watterson, *The Compromises of Life* (New York: Fox, Duffield and Co., 1903), 246.

6. Ibid., 244.

7. Ibid., 237; Watterson, *"Marse Henry,"* 2: 234; Frank M. O'Brien, *The Story of the Sun* (New York: George H. Doran Co., 1918), 295.

8. *News and Courier*, 25 January 1887.

9. Lewis Pinckney Jones, *Stormy Petrel: N.G. Gonzales and His State* (Columbia: University of South Carolina Press, 1973), 225; Dawson to N.G. Gonzales, 23 July 1883, Dawson Mss.; Dawson to Earle Morris, 25 July 188[5], Letterpress Book, 1884-1887, 133, Dawson Mss.

10. Dawson to Sarah Morgan Dawson, 20 March 1873, 24; 22 April 1877, 29 (typed copies), Dawson Mss.

11. *Louisville Journal*, 13 July 1868; Wingate, *Views and Interviews*, 21; *Courier-Journal*, "Marse Henry" edition, 2 March 1919, 4.

12. Quoted in the *Journalist*, 20 December 1884, 3.

13. *Courier-Journal*, 8 November 1868; 10 February 1887; Dawson, *Public Press*, 10-13; Watterson, *Compromises of Life*, 257; Lena C. Logan, "Henry Watterson, Border Nationalist, 1840-1877" (Ph.D. diss., Indiana University, 1942), 437; Wingate, *Views and Interviews*, 24; *News and Courier* (clipping), Scrapbook 7, Grady Mss., Robert W. Woodruff Library, Emory University, Atlanta, Ga.

14. *Courier-Journal*, 8 November 1908, sec. 2: 4; Watterson, *"Marse Henry,"* 1: 268.

15. R.H. Henry, *Editors I Have Known Since the Civil War* (Jackson, Miss.: Jackson Clarion-Ledger, 1922), 70; Wingate, *Views and Interviews*, 339.

16. Dawson, *Public Press*, 8, 19.

17. Ibid., 16.

18. Ibid., 9.

19. *Courier-Journal*, 7 May 1883.

20. *New York World*, 23 December 1921; Watterson, *Compromises of Life*, 24.

21. Walter C. Johnson and Arthur T. Robb, *The South and Its Newspapers, 1903-1953* (Chattanooga: Southern Newspaper Publishers Association, 1954), 30.

22. *Courier-Journal*, 2 March 1909; Watterson, *Compromises of Life*, 24. "The daily newspaper," wrote Dawson, "should give all the news of the day on all subjects, and cover the whole field of human thought and activity, but more as a chronicler than anything else and with only such comments as illustrate the news and will point its moral." (See Scrapbook II, 1878-1888, Dawson Mss.)

23. Frank Luther Mott, *American Journalism, A History: 1690-1960*, 3rd ed. (New York: Macmillan, 1962), chaps. 23, 24; Edwin Emery, *The Press and America, an Interpretive History of Journalism*, 2nd ed. (Englewood Cliffs, N.J.: Prentice-Hall, 1962), chap. 16.

24. *Courier-Journal*, 2 March 1909. Watterson wrote that even in an age of machine politics the editorial page influenced party managers. See "The leading editorial" in Editorial Writings, Galley Proofs, Reel 2, in Microfilm Edition of a Collection of Henry Watterson Papers, University of Louisville Archives, Louisville, Kentucky.

25. Raymond B. Nixon, *Henry W. Grady: Spokesman of the New South* (New York: Knopf, 1943), 13.

26. "Southern Journalists," *The Union*, 5 February 1887, in Scrapbook II, 1878-1888, Dawson Mss.; Joel Chandler Harris, ed., *Joel Chandler Harris' Life of Henry W. Grady* (New York: Cassell Publishing Co., 1890), 62-63.

27. Nixon, *Henry W. Grady*, 15-16.

28. *Atlanta Constitution*, 18 April 1880.

29. Scrapbook 7: 13-17, Grady Mss.

30. Nixon, *Henry W. Grady*, 158.

31. Harris, *Life of Henry W. Grady*, 11; Louis Turner Griffith and John Erwin Talmadge, *Georgia Journalism, 1763-1950* (Athens: University of Georgia Press, 1951), 97; Nixon, *Henry W. Grady*, 158.

32. Ballard Smith, "Henry Watterson," *Harper's Weekly*, 20 August 1887, 600. See also *Courier-Journal*, "Marse Henry" edition, 2 March 1919, 11.

33. Joseph F. Wall, *Henry Watterson: Reconstructed Rebel* (New York: Oxford University Press, 1956), 308; Joseph M. Rogers, "Henry Watterson," *Booklovers Magazine*, March 1905, 310.

34. Wall, *Henry Watterson*, 178; Henry F. Pringle, "Kentucky Bourbon: Marse Henry Watterson," in Edwin H. Ford and Edwin Emery, eds., *Highlights in the History of the American Press* (Minneapolis: University of Minnesota Press, 1954), 219.

35. Russell Franklin Terrell, *A Study of the Early Journalistic Writings of Henry W. Grady* (1926; reprint ed., New York: Beekman, 1974), 73; *Courier-Journal*, "Marse Henry" edition, 2 March 1919, 6.

36. *Courier-Journal*, "Marse Henry" edition, 2 March 1919, 6.

37. Isaac F. Marcosson, *Adventures in Interviewing* (London: John Lane Co., 1919), 35.

38. Watterson, *"Marse Henry,"* 1: 186; 2: 121-22; *Courier-Journal*, 10 February 1887; Logan, "Henry Watterson," 329.

39. Arthur Krock, ed., *The Editorials of Henry Watterson* (New York: George H. Doran Co., 1923), 62. Later, other phrases, such as "We shall walk through a slaughterhouse into an open grave" (his warning on the party's fate should Cleveland be nominated in 1892) and "No compromise with dishonor" (his rejection of Bryan and free silver in 1896) were less prophetic. See Wall, *Henry Watterson*, 204; *Courier-Journal*, "Marse Henry" edition, 2 March 1919, 8.

40. Paul M. Gaston, *The New South Creed* (New York: Knopf, 1970), 53; Watterson, *"Marse Henry,"* 1: 184; *Courier-Journal*, "Marse Henry" edition, 2 March 1919, 11.

41. Gaston, *New South Creed*, 143.

42. Ibid., 95; C. Vann Woodward, *Origins of the New South 1877-1913* (Baton Rouge: Louisiana State University Press, 1951), 6; Wall, *Henry Watterson*, 97, 99; Logan, "Henry Watterson," 249d, 249e, 300.

43. Logan, "Henry Watterson," 497. See also Wall, *Henry Watterson*, 290. One wonders just how popular Watterson was in Louisville. The *New York Times* noted that "he is not particularly popular in his own ward, where the masses figure to a considerable extent in politics, and oppose him from prejudice, the *Courier-Journal* having always promptly put its foot upon the schemes political of the laboring classes" (12 May 1880).

44. Rogers, "Henry Watterson," 313; Leonard N. Plummer, "Henry Watterson's Editorial Style: An Interpretive Analysis," *Journalism Quarterly* 23 (March 1946): 60; Wingate, *Views and Interviews*, 266; Elisha J. Edwards, "Henry Watterson," *Munsey's Magazine*, January 1906, 438.

45. "Financial Bugaboos," *Courier-Journal*, 24 May 1876, in Krock, *Editorials of Henry Watterson*, 50-51; *Courier-Journal*, January-February 1887.

46. *Courier-Journal*, 3 March 1876, in Krock, *Editorials of Henry Watterson*, 43.

47. *Courier-Journal*, 26 January 1887.

48. Rogers, "Henry Watterson," 320-21.

49. *Courier-Journal*, "Marse Henry" edition, 2 March 1919, 8.

50. *Courier-Journal*, 8 November 1908, sec. 2: 4.

51. Ibid., 14 February 1887.

52. Mark Sullivan, *The Education of an American* (New York: Doubleday, Doran and Co., 1938), 221-23.

53. Plummer, "Henry Watterson's Editorial Style," 60.

54. *Courier-Journal*, "Marse Henry" edition, 2 March 1919, 3; Wingate, *Views and Interviews*, 107; Rogers, "Henry Watterson," 309.

55. Almost all character sketches of Watterson treat this subject. Joseph Rogers concludes that "in spite of his immense popularity and influence, his personality is little known to the world, and most of the ideas afloat concerning him are utterly erroneous" ("Henry Watterson," 306).

56. *New York Times*, 11 August 1887.

57. Marcosson, *Adventures in Interviewing*, 33.

58. *Courier-Journal*, "Marse Henry" edition, 2 March 1919, 20.

59. Rogers, "Henry Watterson," 306, 307, 321.

60. Clearly Watterson lost sight of one of young Grady's dicta which, in dispassionate and reflective moments, he too had endorsed: "Freedom of the press does not imply unbridled license." *Atlanta Daily Herald*, 14 April 1875, quoted in Raymond B. Nixon, "Henry Woodfin Grady: Journalistic Leader in Public Affairs" (Ph.D. diss., University of Minnesota, 1942), 160.

61. *Courier-Journal*, 4 March 1883; 14 April 1883.

62. *News and Courier*, 5 January 1887; 4 February 1887.

63. *Atlanta Constitution*, 26 February 1887; *Atlanta Herald*, 14 September 1875, in Terrell, *Study of the Early Journalistic Writings*, 129.

64. *The Journalist*, 13 December 1884, 5.

65. Logan, "Henry Watterson," 334, 436, 441; Krock, *Editorials of Henry Watterson*, 53-54.

66. Pringle, "Kentucky Bourbon," 222.

67. Ibid.

68. Rogers, "Henry Watterson," 311.

69. *Courier-Journal*, 8 November 1918, in Microfilm Edition of a Collection of Henry Watterson Papers.

70. Allan Nevins, *Grover Cleveland: A Study in Courage* (New York: Dodd, Mead and Co., 1932), 242; Logan, "Henry Watterson," 468-71; *Atlanta Constitution*, 5, 6 February 1887.

71. Dawson to R. T. Logan, 25 July 188[?], Letterpress Book, 1884-1887, Dawson Mss.; clipping, Scrapbook II, 1878-1888, Dawson Mss.; John McElree to Dawson, 25 June 1887, Dawson Mss.; *News and Courier*, 2 January 1882.

72. S. Frank Logan, "Francis W. Dawson, 1840-1889: South Carolina Editor" (M.A. thesis, Duke University, 1947), 77; *The Golden Argosy*, 23 July 1887, in Scrapbook II, 1878-1888, Dawson Mss.; Dawson to J. C. Hemphill, 25 July 1885, Dawson Mss; Ernest Culpepper Clark, "Francis Warrington Dawson in the Era of South Carolina's Conservative Democratic Restoration, 1874-1889" (Ph.D. diss., University of North Carolina, 1974), 313.

73. Clipping, Scrapbook II, 1878-1888, Dawson Mss.

74. Ibid.; Dawson to J.L. Weber, Letterpress Book, 1884-1887, 132, Dawson Mss.

75. Charles Petty to Dawson, 26 November 1887, Dawson Mss.; Gonzales to his aunt, 22 August 1882, Elliott-Gonzales Papers, Southern Historical Collection, University of North Carolina; Jones, *Stormy Petrel*, 94.

76. Jones, *Stormy Petrel*, 94; *News and Courier*, 8, 9, 10, 11 January 1887.

77. *News and Courier*, 29 September 1884. These improvements inspired the condescension of the *Atlanta Constitution*: how gratifying it is "to see our old and valued contemporary wheel into line with the most progressive journals of the day." *Atlanta Constitution*, 3 October 1884; E. Culpepper Clark, *Francis Warrington Dawson and the Politics of Restoration: South Carolina, 1874-1889* (University: University of Alabama Press, 1980), 211.

78. Gonzales to his aunt, 22 August 1882, Elliott-Gonzales Papers; Gonzales to R.E. Elliott, 17 August 1882, Elliott-Gonzales Papers; William Watts Ball, *The State That Forgot* (Indianapolis: Bobbs-Merrill, 1932), 171.

79. Dawson to Earle Morris, 25 July 188[5], Letterpress Book, 1884-1887, 133, Dawson Mss.

80. Clark, *Dawson*, 118; Scrapbook I, 51, 97, 131-37, Dawson Mss; William J. Cooper, Jr., *The Conservative Regime: South Carolina, 1877-1890* (Baltimore: Johns Hopkins Press, 1968), 81-82.

81. James Welch Patton, "The Republican Party in South Carolina, 1876-1895," quoted in Fletcher Melvin Green, ed., *Essays in Southern History* (Chapel Hill: University of North Carolina Press, 1949), 99 n.33.

82. Gonzales to his aunt, 9 April 1882, Elliott-Gonzales Papers; *New York Times*, 30 March 1880.

83. B.W. Edwards to Dawson, 12 July 1888, Dawson Mss.

84. Dawson to Gonzales, 14 December 1887, Letterpress Book, 44, Hemphill Family Papers, Perkins Library, Duke University.

85. Dawson to J.D. Hemphill, 11 September 1888, Hemphill Family Papers. For example, there is the headline from the 1884 presidential campaign: "Blaine and The Letters—How the Plumed Knave Tried to Cover His Foul Tracks" (*News and Courier*, 5 October 1884).

86. Jones, *Stormy Petrel*, 193; Clark, *Dawson*, 172; Woodward, *Origins of the New South*, 134; R.W. Moore to Dawson, 9 November 1880, Scrapbook I, Dawson Mss.; William P. Clyde to Dawson, 14 January 1884; 8 September 1884, Letters, 1874-1885, Dawson Mss.; David L. Carlton, *Mill and Town in South Carolina, 1880-1920* (Baton Rouge: Louisiana State University Press, 1982), 77, 78, 110, 116, 117, 125.

87. Clark, *Dawson*, 33.

88. Paul H. Buck, *The Road to Reunion, 1865-1900* (New York: Knopf, Vintage Books, and Random House, 1937), 193.

89. Nixon, *Henry W. Grady*, 6, 250; *News and Courier*, 31 March 1883; 17, 20 April 1883; 3 May 1883.

90. *News and Courier*, 30 December 1886; Philip E. Chazel to Dawson, 26 February 1887, 81-82, Dawson Mss.

91. *News and Courier*, 8 January 1884. Their contrasting obituaries on Wendell Phillips provide a good example of their different attitudes toward the past. (See *News and Courier*, 4 February 1884; *Atlanta Constitution*, 5 February 1884.)

92. *Atlanta Contitution*, 14, 19, January 1887; *News and Courier*, 4 February 1887; Grady to Dawson, 1 November 1887, Dawson Mss.

93. Dawson to Sarah Morgan Dawson, 8 February 1887, Dawson Mss.; E. Culpepper Clark, "Henry Grady's New South: A Rebuttal from Charleston," *The Southern Speech Communication Journal* 41 (Summer 1976): 353.

94. Dawson to Sarah Morgan Dawson, 11 February 1887, Dawson Mss.; *News and Courier*, 23 February 1887.

95. Clark, *Dawson*, 144-46.

96. Buck, *Road to Reunion*, 154-55; Broadus Mitchell, *The Rise of the Cotton Mills in the South* (Baltimore: Johns Hopkins Press, 1921), 114.

97. Don H. Doyle, *New Men, New Cities, New South: Atlanta, Nashville, Charleston, Mobile, 1860-1910* (Chapel Hill: University of North Carolina Press, 1990), 111, 170-71.

98. Clark, *Dawson*, 147-52, 155; *News and Courier*, 29 October 1891.

99. Griffith and Talmadge, *Georgia Journalism*, 115.

100. Clark, *Dawson*, 90-100, 190-202; *News and Courier*, 13, 24 March 1883; 8 May 1883. For a discussion of liberal reform see John G. Sproat, *"The Best Men": Liberal Reformers in the Gilded Age* (London: Oxford University Press, 1968). Michael Perman has also noted the similarity between Southern good government spokesmen and fusionists and Northern liberal reformers. See *The Road to Redemption: Southern Politics, 1869-1879* (Chapel Hill: University of North Carolina Press, 1984), 166-67.

101. *News and Courier*, 8 May 1880; 1 February 1884.

102. *Philadelphia Press* clipping, Scrapbook II, 1878-1888, 10, Dawson Mss.; *News and Courier*, 14, 17 March 1883; 23 January 1884.

103. *News and Courier*, 1, 7 January 1884.

104. *News and Courier*, 6, 7, 10 March 1883; 28 April 1883; Cooper, *Conservative Regime*, 112, 114; Doyle, *New Men, New Cities, New South*, 272, 291-92, 301, 306-8, 311.

105. *New York Herald* clipping, Scrapbook II, 1878-1888, 104, Dawson Mss. See also *News and Courier* clipping, Scrapbook I, 59, Dawson Mss.

106. Clippings from the *New York Herald, Norfolk Virginian*, and *Boston Herald*, in Scrapbook I, 65, Dawson Mss.; Scrapbook II, 1878-1888, 20, Dawson Mss.

107. "Francis W. Dawson, Knight of the Order of St. Gregory the Great. The Comments of the Press," in Francis Warrington Dawson, *Reminiscences of Confederate Service, 1861-1865* (Charleston, 1882).

108. J.C. Hemphill to the Directors of the News and Courier Co., 8 February 1910, Hemphill Family Papers; "Newspapers in Charleston, S.C.," *The Journalist*, 2 June 1888, 3.

109. See Dawson's letters to William Henry Smith, W.P. Phillips, and James B. Townsend, 1887 and 1888, Dawson Mss.; J.S. Baynard to L.S. Mellichampe, 20 September 1888, Dawson Mss.; "Memorandum—New York Syndicate Bureau," 1 March 1888, Dawson Mss.; Dawson to Gonzales, Dawson to T.R. Gibson, Dawson to T.E. Horton, 8 September 1888, Letterpress Book, 152-54, Hemphill Family Papers; Dawson to W.E. Gonzales, 2 September 1888, Letterpress Book, 117, Hemphill Family Papers; Dawson to R.J. Furlong, 2 May 1888, Letterpress Book, 118, Hemphill Family Papers; Dawson to National Puzzle Bureau, 16 February 1888, Letterpress Book, 74, Hemphill Family Papers.

110. J.C. Hemphill to the Directors of the News and Courier Co., 8 February 1910, Hemphill Family Papers; Dawson to Sarah Morgan Dawson, 29 January 1889, Dawson Mss.

111. Terrell, *Study of the Early Journalistic Writings*, 52; *Atlanta Constitution*, 21 October 1891, in Grady Mss.; Nixon, *Henry W. Grady*, 263; Isaac W. Avery, *History of the State of Georgia from 1850 to 1881* (1881; reprint ed., New York: AMS Press, 1972), 569.

112. Griffith and Talmadge, *Georgia Journalism*, 108; *Remington Brothers' News-*

paper Manual (Pittsburgh: Remington Brothers' Advertising Bureau, 1890), 27; *American Newspaper Annual* (Philadelphia: N.W. Ayer and Son, 1880), 109. In 1885 Grady closed a $12,000 advertising deal with a Philadelphia soap manufacturer.

113. Nixon, *Henry W. Grady*, 187.

114. *Atlanta Constitution*, 25 March 1883; Raymond B. Nixon, "The Qualities of Greatness in Henry W. Grady," *Emory University Quarterly* 21 (Fall 1965): 151.

115. Scrapbook 3: 1, Grady Mss.

116. Scrapbook 11: 69, Grady Mss.; Franklin M. Garrett, *Atlanta and Environs* (1954; reprint ed., Athens: University of Georgia Press, 1969), 1: 790-91; T.W. Reed, "An Early Member of the Constitution Staff Remembers," *Atlanta Constitution Sunday Magazine*, 26 March 1939, 2.

117. *The Journalist*, 18 September 1886, 7.

118. *Atlanta Constitution*, 21 October 1891. See also Harris, *Life of Henry W. Grady*, 30; T.W. Reed, "Henry W. Grady," *Bulletin* (University of Georgia, Athens) 35 (February 1935): 7-8.

119. Emery, *Press and America*, 357-58. See, for example, *Atlanta Constitution*, January 1884 and 1887.

120. Scrapbook 4: 64-65, Grady Mss.

121. H.C. Nixon, *Possum Trot* (Norman: University of Oklahoma Press, 1941), 36.

122. But most of the articles, even the best, were rewritten or in other ways improved. *Athens Banner-Watchman* clipping, Scrapbook 10: 83-84, Grady Mss.

123. *Atlanta Constitution*, 20 February 1887; 27 March 1887; Mott, *American Journalism*, 457; Griffith and Talmadge, *Georgia Journalism*, 106.

124. *Atlanta Constitution*, 20 February 1887.

125. Scrapbook 11: 69, Grady Mss.; *Atlanta Constitution*, 27 March 1887.

126. *Atlanta Constitution*, 21 October 1891; Nixon, *Henry W. Grady*, 257.

127. *Atlanta Constitution*, 30 January 1887.

128. F.A. Richardson, "A Fruitful Life: The Career, Character and Services of Henry Woodfin Grady," 1890, Grady Mss.; Wingate, *Views and Interviews*, 27.

129. Clipping, Scrapbook 11: 69, Grady Mss.; *The Journalist*, 24 May 1884, 2; *Atlanta Constitution*, 3 February 1884.

130. Nixon, *Henry W. Grady*, 235-36, 263.

131. Ibid., 213; Terrell, *Study of the Early Journalistic Writings*, 48. Grady's subject preference is abundantly clear in his scrapbooks.

132. Terrell, *Study of the Early Journalistic Writings*, 12-15. See also the Grady scrapbooks.

133. Terrell, *Study of the Early Journalistic Writings*, 41-43, 58.

134. Clipping, 1877, Scrapbook 3: 11, Grady Mss.

135. *Atlanta Constitution*, 8 January 1882.

136. Terrell, *Study of the Early Journalistic Writings*, 41-43, 58.

137. Wingate, *Views and Interviews*, 110.

138. Harold E. Davis, "Henry W. Grady, Master of the Atlanta Ring, 1880-1886," *Georgia Historical Quarterly* 69 (Spring 1985): 2-5; idem, *Henry Grady's New South: Atlanta, A Brave and Beautiful City* (Tuscaloosa: University of Alabama Press, 1990), 18, 194-97.

139. Nixon, *Henry W. Grady*, 212, 222, 282; Garrett, *Atlanta and Environs*, 2: 167; *Atlanta Constitution*, 18 January 1884; 1 February 1884.

140. Harris, *Life of Henry W. Grady*, 55; Doyle, *New Men, New Cities, New South*, 194, 209-10; James Michael Russell, *Atlanta 1847-1890: City Building in the Old South and New* (Baton Rouge: Louisiana State University Press, 1988), 196, 217, 222.

141. *Atlanta Constitution*, 6, 8 January 1884.

142. Ibid., 8 January 1884.

143. Russell, *Atlanta*, 196-228.

144. *Atlanta Constitution*, 20 January 1887; Goldfield, *Cotton Fields and Skyscrapers: Southern City and Region, 1607-1980* (Baton Rouge: Louisiana State University Press, 1982), 120.

145. Harris, *Life of Henry W. Grady*, 11.

146. Ibid., 60; *Augusta Evening News*, in Scrapbook 9: 2, Grady Mss.; *Eatonton Messenger* [1882], in Scrapbook 6: 97, Grady Mss.

147. Doyle, *New Men, New Cities, New South*, xvi.

148. Griffith and Talmadge, *Georgia Journalism*, 97; Harold E. Davis, "Henry Grady, the Atlanta *Constitution*, and the Politics of Farming in the 1880s," *Georgia Historical Quarterly* 71 (Winter 1987): 584; Harris, *Life of Henry W. Grady*, 61.

149. *News and Courier*, 1 January 1887.

150. Clipping, Scrapbook 3: 29-33, 38-39, Grady Mss.; Nixon, *Henry W. Grady*, 153.

151. William Rutherford to Grady, 9 May 1877, Scrapbook 4: 97, Grady Mss.; Griffith and Talmadge, *Georgia Journalism*, 105.

152. Griffith and Talmadge, *Georgia Journalism*, 115.

153. David R. Goldfield, *Promised Land: The South since 1945* (Arlington Heights, Ill.: Harlan Davidson, 1987), 21; Charles L. Flynn, Jr., *White Land, Black Labor: Caste and Class in Late Nineteenth-Century Georgia* (Baton Rouge: Louisiana State University Press, 1983), 161.

154. *Atlanta Constitution*, 18 May 1883; 9, 13 January 1884; John Donald Wade, "Henry W. Grady," *Southern Review* 3 (Winter 1938): 498. See Grady's famous speeches, "The South and Her Problems," "At the Augusta Exposition," and "At the Boston Banquet," in Harris, *Life of Henry Grady*.

155. Davis, *Henry Grady's New South*, 132-36, 142.

156. Clipping, "Convict Labor," Scrapbook 4: 37, Grady Mss.; *Atlanta Constitution*, 19 January 1882.

157. *Atlanta Constitution*, 22 January 1887.

158. Scrapbook 3: 64-65, Grady Mss.

159. *Atlanta Constitution*, 9, 13 March 1883; 3, 13 April 1883.

160. Davis, "Henry W. Grady, Master of the Atlanta Ring," 1-2, 7; Lewis Nicholas Wynne, *The Continuity of Cotton: Planter Politics in Georgia, 1865-1892* (Macon, Ga.: Mercer University Press, 1986), 143; Ralph L. Eckert, "The Breath of Scandal: John B. Gordon, Henry W. Grady, and the Resignation-Appointment Controversy of May 1880," *Georgia Historical Quarterly* 69 (Fall 1985).

161. Nixon, "Henry W. Grady, Reporter," in Ford and Emery, *Highlights in the History of the American Press*, 229.

162. Scrapbook 7: 9, Grady Mss. *The Springfield Republican* also praised him. (See Scrapbook 7: 29, Grady Mss.)

163. Quoted in *The Journalist*, 15 May 1886, 15.

164. "Will the 'Editorial' Disappear," *The Journalist*, 18 August 1900, 141; Marcosson, *Adventures in Interviewing*, 55; Weisberger, *American Newspaperman*,

115, 121-26, 147; Alfred McClung Lee, *The Daily Newspaper in America: The Evolution of a Social Instrument* (New York: Macmillan, 1937), 630, 632; Michael Schudson, *Discovering the News: A Social History of American Newspapers* (New York: Basic Books, 1978), 98-105; Willard Grosvenor Bleyer, *The Profession of Journalism* (Boston: Atlantic Monthly Press, 1918), 3.

165. Schudson, *Discovering the News*, 106.

166. Patrick J. Hearden, *Independence and Empire: The New South's Cotton Mill Campaign 1865-1901* (DeKalb: Northern Illinois University Press, 1982), 44, and 37-45 *passim*; *News and Courier*, 12, 23, 25, 30 March 1883; 11 April 1883; *Courier-Journal*, 30 March 1883; 12 June 1883; *Atlanta Constitution* 14, 20, 21 March 1883; 4, 10, 13, 21 April 1883; 1 May 1883; 16, 30 June 1884; 30 January 1887; 27 March 1887.

167. *News and Courier*, 10, 14 April 1883; *Courier-Journal*, 27 March 1883; 10, 30 April 1883; *Atlanta Constitution*, 16 May 1883; 2 June 1883.

168. Thomas C. Leonard, *The Power of the Press: The Birth of American Political Reporting* (New York: Oxford University Press, 1986), 109.

169. Jack Claiborne, *The Charlotte Observer* (Chapel Hill: University of North Carolina Press, 1986), 4.

170. John Milton Cooper, Jr., *Walter Hines Page: The Southerner as American, 1855-1918* (Chapel Hill: University of North Carolina Press, 1977), 73-80; Claiborne, *Charlotte Observer*, 62-63; Fred Hobson, *Tell About the South: The Southern Rage to Explain* (Baton Rouge: Louisiana State University Press, 1983), 164-66; Virginius Dabney, *Liberalism in the South* (1932; reprint ed., New York: AMS Press, 1970), 235; Burton J. Hendrick, *The Life and Letters of Walter H. Page* (Garden City: Doubleday, Page and Co., 1922), 1: 42-48. John M. Cooper, Jr., misses the mark in arguing that Page would have been accepted back home because William Allen White had written a similarly sarcastic blast against provincialism and backwardness ("What's the Matter with Kansas") and remained another fifty years at the helm of the *Emporia* (Kansas) *Gazette*. Kansas was not North Carolina; White wrote as a Republican in a community tolerant of two parties; and White's offensive letters emanated from among his own people, not the hated New York City. Page had overstepped outraged local opinion and was viewed, both figuratively and literally, as an outsider.

171. James C. Cobb, "Beyond Planters and Industrialists: A New Perspective on the New South," *Journal of Southern History* 54 (February 1988): 56; idem, *Industrialization and Southern Society 1877-1984* (Lexington: University Press of Kentucky, 1984), 22-24; Perman, *Road to Redemption*, 224, 234-35; Hearden, *Independence and Empire*, 70-75; Flynn, *White Land, Black Labor*, 166; Laurence Shore, *Southern Capitalists: The Ideological Leadership of an Elite, 1832-1885* (Chapel Hill: University of North Carolina Press, 1986), 180-83; Thomas D. Clark, *The Southern Country Editor* (1948; reprint ed., Gloucester, Mass.: Peter Smith, 1964), 26-31.

172. For a brief introduction to the literature on this subject see Cobb, "Beyond Planters and Industrialists," and John J. Beck, "Building the New South: A Revolution from Above in a Piedmont County," *Journal of Southern History* 53 (August 1987): 441-45.

173. Carlton, *Mill and Town in South Carolina*; Lacy K. Ford, "Rednecks and Merchants: Economic Development and Social Tensions in the South Carolina Upcountry, 1865-1900," *Journal of American History* 71 (September 1984): 405-24.

174. Beck, "Building the New South," 445.

175. Cobb, "Beyond Planters and Industrialists," 55.

176. Wynne, *Continuity of Cotton*, 126-29, 142, 159, 171-72, 183-84; Davis, *Henry Grady's New South*, 161-62.

177. Davis, "Henry Grady, the Atlanta *Constitution*, and the Politics of Farming in the 1880s," 573-79; idem, *Henry Grady's New South*, chap. 4.

178. Ibid., 600.

179. Doyle, *New Men, New Cities, New South*, 315-17.

180. Peter Wallenstein has made this point in *From Slave South to New South: Public Policy in Nineteenth-Century Georgia* (Chapel Hill: University of North Carolina, 1987), 213 and "Epilogue."

181. Emery agrees with this judgment (*Press and America*, 316). See also *Courier-Journal*, "Marse Henry" edition, 2 March 1919, 4; Logan, "Henry Watterson," 131.

182. Wall, *Henry Watterson*, 115, 125, 171-73, 181-82; Rogers, "Henry Watterson," 312; George S. Merriam, *The Life and Times of Samuel Bowles* (New York: Century Co., 1885), 2: 134; Tom Wallace, "Old Courier-Journal . . . ," *Louisville Times*, 22 September 1948. The *Courier-Journal* was the first paper outside New York City to adopt Ottmar Mergenthaler's linotype machine, the greatest press innovation of the nineteenth century (*The Journalist*, 14 March 1891, 7).

183. Wall, *Henry Watterson*, 125.

184. *Courier-Journal*, "Marse Henry" edition, 2 March 1919, 3. Among "Watterson's boys" were Ballard Smith and Arthur Krock. See also *The Journalist*, 10 May 1884, 5. See Frederic J. Haskin, "Distinctive Features of American Newspapers," 26 May 1907 in Newspaper Clippings, Reel 5, Microfilm Edition of a Collection of Henry Watterson Papers.

185. Herbert Ravenel Sass, *Outspoken: 150 Years of the Charleston News and Courier* (Columbia: University of South Carolina Press, 1953), 73; *News and Courier*, 12 March 1890; 1 May 1928, 6A.

186. *News and Courier*, 13, 23 April 1883; 8 May 1883.

187. Remarks of Congressman Samuel Dibble, in "In Memoriam: F.W. Dawson," (Charleston: Walker, Evans and Cogswell Co., 1889), 15.

188. Emery, *Press and America*, 354; Nixon, *Henry W. Grady*, 334.

189. Griffith and Talmadge, *Georgia Journalism*, 106.

190. Thomas D. Clark, "The Country Newspaper: A Factor in Southern Opinion, 1865-1930," in George Brown Tindall, ed., *The Pursuit of Southern History: Presidential Addresses of the Southern Historical Association, 1935-1963* (Baton Rouge: Louisiana State University Press, 1964), 218.

191. *New York Times*, 13 March 1889.

192. *Nation*, 21 March 1889, 237.

193. See Harris, *Life of Henry W. Grady*, 443-597.

194. *Atlanta Constitution*, 21 October 1891.

195. *The Journalist*, 28 December 1889, 2.

196. *Courier-Journal*, "Marse Henry" edition, 2 March 1919, 2.

9. Conclusion

1. S.N.D. North, *History and Present Condition of the Newspaper and Periodical Press of the United States* (Washington: Government Printing Office, 1884), 105.

2. Gunther Barth, *City People: The Rise of Modern City Culture in Nineteenth-Century America* (New York: Oxford University Press, 1980); David Paul Nord, "The Public Community: The Urbanization of Journalism in Chicago," *Journal of Urban History* 11 (August 1985): 439 n.32.

3. See, e.g., *Charleston Daily Courier*, 12 April 1858; 9 April 1860; *Charleston Mercury*, 23 September 1859; *Mobile Daily Register*, 27 October 1868; 10 December 1871; 5 April 1874.

4. "Provincial Journalism," *The Journalist*, 31 May 1884, 5.

5. *The Journalist*, 9 January 1886, 4.

6. See, e.g., Julius Wilcox, "Journalism as a Profession," *The Galaxy*, 4 (November 1867): 805.

7. "On a Tennessee Newspaper," *Macmillan's Magazine* 58 (October 1888): 462-63.

8. This colorful quoted phrase is found in John T. Kneebone, *Southern Liberal Journalists and the Issue of Race, 1920-1944* (Chapel Hill: University of North Carolina Press, 1985), 32.

9. The summary that follows is based upon my earlier work on Thompson. See "From the Old South to the New South: The Editorial Career of William Tappan Thompson of the *Savannah Morning News*," *The Southern Quarterly* 14 (April 1976): 237-60.

10. Ibid., 237-38.

11. The Southern response to spiritualism is discussed in Robert W. Delp, "The Southern Press and the Rise of American Spiritualism, 1847-1860," *Journal of American Culture* 7 (Fall 1984): 88-95.

12. George C. Rable, "Bourbonism, Reconstruction, and the Persistence of Southern Distinctiveness," *Civil War History* 29 (June 1983): 146.

13. Fred Hobson, *Tell About the South: The Southern Rage to Explain* (Baton Rouge: Louisiana State University Press, 1983), 204, 205.

14. David R. Goldfield, *Urban Growth in the Age of Sectionalism: Virginia, 1847-1861* (Baton Rouge: Louisiana State University Press, 1977), 277; idem, "Pursuing the American Dream: Cities in the Old South," in Blaine A. Brownell and David R. Goldfield, eds., *The City in Southern History: The Growth of Urban Civilization in the South* (Port Washington, N.Y.: National University Publications, Kennikat Press, 1977), 59-60.

15. Laurence Shore, *Southern Capitalists: The Ideological Leadership of an Elite, 1832-1885* (Chapel Hill: University of North Carolina Press, 1986), 161-68, 179; James Michael Russell, *Atlanta 1847-1890: City Building in the Old South and the New* (Baton Rouge: Louisiana State University Press, 1988), 168.

16. A fine example of this merger appears in the celebration of the opening of the Charleston and Savannah Railroad. What began as a celebration of urban progress and railroad development was transformed into a secession rally emphasizing Southern unity and prosperity. (See *Charleston Daily Courier*, 5 November 1860.)

17. *Charleston Mercury*, 2 February 1858; 10 August 1858; 27 December 1858; 3 October 1859; 24 March 1860; 27, 30 July 1860; 13, 17 August 1860; *Charleston Daily Courier*, 10, 23 April 1858; 9 June 1858; 30 August 1858; 8 October 1858; 13 November 1858; 11 December 1858; 13, 16 September 1859; 8 February 1860; 9, 14 August 1860.

18. Allan Nevins, *The Evening Post: A Century of Journalism* (New York: Boni

and Liveright, 1922), 389; Nord, "The Public Community," 417; James L. Crouth-amel, Bennett's "New York Herald" and the Rise of the Popular Press (Syracuse: Syracuse University Press, 1989), 98-99.

19. William Warren Rogers, "Alabama's Reform Press: Militant Spokesman for Agrarian Revolt," Agricultural History 34 (April 1960): 62-70; Lawrence Good-wyn, Democratic Promise: The Populist Moment in America (New York: Oxford University Press, 1976), 357; Lauren Kessler, The Dissident Press: Alternative Journalism in American History, vol. 13, The Sage Commtext Series (Beverly Hills, Calif.: Sage Publications, 1984), 117.

20. Rogers, "Reform Press," 66; passim; Robert W. Smith, "The People's Party Paper and Georgia's Tom Watson," Journalism Quarterly, 42 (Winter 1965): 110-11.

21. Rogers, "Reform Press," 69; Goodwyn, Democratic Promise, 255, 366-67; Charles Grayson Summersell, "Kolb and the Populist Revolt as Viewed by Newspapers," Alabama Historical Quarterly 19 (Fall and Winter, 1957): 386-88; Edward L. Ayers, The Promise of the New South: Life After Reconstruction (New York: Oxford University Press, 1992), 245.

22. August Meier, Negro Thought in America, 1880-1915 (Ann Arbor: University of Michigan Press, 1963; Ann Arbor Paperbacks, 1966), 79; Henry Lewis Suggs, ed., The Black Press in the South, 1865-1979 (Westport, Conn.: Greenwood, 1983), ix, 8-10, 29, 51, 427; Emma Lou Thornbrough, "American Negro News-papers, 1880-1914," Business History Review 40 (1966): 472; Thornbrough, T. Thomas Fortune, Militant Journalist (Chicago: University of Chicago Press, 1972), 108. For a good introduction to the black press in this period see Betty Lou K. Rathbun, "The Rise of the Modern American Negro Press," (Ph.D. diss., State University of New York at Buffalo, 1978).

23. Meier, Negro Thought, 224-33, 246; Suggs, Black Press, 27-28, 323, 410-11; John M. Matthews, "Black Newspapermen and the Black Community in Georgia, 1890-1930," Georgia Historical Quarterly 68 (1984): 356-63, 380-81.

24. Thornbrough, "American Negro Newspapers," 476-77, 486; Suggs, Black Press, 322.

25. Thornbrough, "American Negro Newspapers," 472, 476-77, 490; Thornbrough, T. Thomas Fortune, passim; Willard B. Gatewood, Jr., "Edward E. Cooper, Black Journalist," Journalism Quarterly 55 (1978): 269-75; Frederick G. Detweiler, The Negro Press in the United States (Chicago: The University of Chicago Press, 1922; reprint, College Park, Md.: McGrath, 1968), 6.

26. Don H. Doyle, New Men, New Cities, New South: Atlanta, Nashville, Charleston, Mobile, 1860-1910 (Chapel Hill: University of North Carolina Press, 1990), 87.

27. "In Memoriam: F.W. Dawson," (Charleston: Walker, Evans and Cogswell Co., 1889), 12.

28. Hobson, Tell About the South, 205.

29. Tennant S. McWilliams, The New South Faces the World: Foreign Affairs and the Southern Sense of Self, 1877-1950 (Baton Rouge: Louisiana State University Press, 1988), 10-11, 48; Doyle, New Men, New Cities, New South, 314-15.

30. Raymond B . Nixon, Henry W. Grady: Spokesman of the New South (New York: Knopf, 1943), 187; John Donald Wade, "Henry W. Grady," Southern Review, 3 (Winter 1938): 489; Melville E. Stone, Fifty Years a Journalist (Garden City, N.Y.: Doubleday, Page, 1921), 44; Francis Warrington Dawson to Sarah Morgan

Dawson, 15 September 1878, Letters, 1874-1885, Dawson Mss., Perkins Library, Duke University.

31. Charles F. Wingate, *Views and Interviews on Journalism* (1875; reprint ed., N.Y.: Arno and New York Times, 1970), 23, 42.

32. Ibid., 86-87; Louis Turner Griffith and John Erwin Talmadge, *Georgia Journalism, 1763-1950* (Athens: University of Georgia Press, 1951), 102-4, 107; Lena C. Logan, "Henry Watterson, Border Nationalist, 1840-1877" (Ph.D. diss., Indiana University, 1942), 117, 118; Nixon, *Henry W. Grady*, 207, 295; *News and Courier*, 3 February 1888; *Atlanta Constitution* clipping in Scrapbook I, 1875-1884, 34, Dawson Mss.

33. North, *History and Present Condition of the Newspaper and Periodical Press*, 65.

34. Griffith and Talmadge, *Georgia Journalism*, 30.

35. A study of the number of English-language daily papers in seven Southern states and three Northern states for the years 1869, 1880, and 1886 reveals a significant increase in the number of Northern dailies but a very mixed condition in the South. Only three of the seven Southern states had an increase in the number of dailies for each of the years examined. Only one Southern state, Kentucky, had a percentage increase comparable to that in the three Northern states. Georgia, the Southern state with the next greatest increase, had 13 dailies in 1869, 15 in 1880, and 18 in 1886. Virginia gained one daily in each of the three years. Alabama's dailies declined from 7 to 4 between 1869 and 1880; Louisiana had eight in both 1880 and 1886, while South Carolina had four in each of these years. Tennessee had 11 in 1869 and 13 in 1880, but only 12 in 1886. For these same years, Connecticut's dailies increased from 13 to 16 to 24, Illinois's from 24 to 58 to 97, and Ohio's from 20 to 34 to 78. *American Newspaper Directory* (New York: Geo. P. Rowell and Co., 1869); *American Newspaper Annual* (Philadelphia: N.W. Ayer and Son, 1880, 1886).

36. *Charleston News and Courier*, 2 January 1882; 3 February 1888. In Chattanooga 15 evening newspapers went to their graves between 1880 and 1888. (See *The Journalist*, 9 June 1888, 13.)

37. Quoted in *Savannah Morning News*, 5 May 1877.

38. Nixon, *Grady*, 295n.

39. J. Cutler Andrews, *The South Reports the Civil War* (Princeton: Princeton University Press, 1970), 36, 39.

40. Griffith and Talmadge, *Georgia Journalism*, 111; Peter R. Knights, "'Competition' in the U. S. Daily Newspaper Industry, 1865-68," *Journalism Quarterly* 45 (Autumn 1968): 473-80; Donald W. Curl, *Murat Halstead and the "Cincinnati Commercial"* (Boca Raton: University Presses of Florida, 1980), 94; Thomas C. Leonard, *The Power of the Press: The Birth of American Political Reporting* (New York: Oxford University Press, 1986), 174-75.

41. "Southern Literary Men," *Independent* [1882], in Scrapbook 7: 16, Grady Mss., Robert W. Woodruff Library, Emory University, Atlanta, Georgia.

42. *The Journalist*, 21 June 1890, 14.

43. Quoted in Scrapbook 10: 41, Grady Mss.

A Note on Sources

It seems redundant to list all of the sources in journalism history and Southern history cited in my footnotes. Nevertheless, a word about those most important for my work is appropriate.

To write newspaper history it is necessary to read newspapers, and I have read lengthy runs of newspapers for all of the editors covered in this study. Manuscript sources are crucial for the interior history of a paper, especially if the emphasis is biographical, as is mine. With one exception noted below, I have read the major collection of manuscripts for each significant editor and other pertinent collections. I make no claim to an exhaustive search for all manuscripts for all editors since, to cite one example, Ritchie, who corresponded with so many of the politicos of his era, has letters in dozens of collections.

In addition to the Ritchie papers in the Library of Congress, there are important letters relating to Thomas Ritchie's political influence and editorial career in the manuscripts holdings of the Alderman Library, University of Virginia, Charlottesville, Virginia. Material on his Washington career can be found in the James K. Polk Papers and Edmund Burke Papers in the Library of Congress. Milo Milton Quaife, ed., *The Diary of James K. Polk*, with an introduction by Andrew Cunningham McLaughlin (Chicago: A.C. McClurg and Co., 1910) also contains information on Ritchie's Washington journalism. The *John P. Branch Historical Papers of Randolph-Macon College* have published manuscripts relating to Ritchie's career; see especially: "Ritchie Letters," 4 (June 1916): 372-418; "Letters of Thomas Ritchie—Glimpses of the Year 1830," 2 (June 1902): 147-154; "Unpublished Letters of Thomas Ritchie," 3 (June 1911): 199-252. The only biography of Ritchie is Charles Ambler's fine study, *Thomas Ritchie: A Study in Virginia Politics* (Richmond: Bell Book and Stationary Co., 1913). Ritchie's early career is the subject of Bert Marsh Mutersbaugh's "Jeffersonian Journalist: Thomas Ritchie and the Richmond 'Enquirer,' 1804-1820," (Ph.D. diss., University of Missouri-Columbia, 1973). For a brief but informative overview of Ritchie's career see Charles T. Thrift, "Thomas Ritchie," *John P. Branch Historical Papers of Randolph-Macon College* 1 (June 1902): 170-187. Lester J. Cappon, *Virginia News-*

papers, 1821-1935, A Bibliography with Historical Introduction and Notes (New York: D. Appleton-Century Co., 1936) provides useful background on Virginia journalism. Among the many studies of pre-Civil War Virginia politics and the Richmond Junto, the most useful were: Harry Ammon, "The Richmond Junto, 1800-1824," *Virginia Magazine of History and Biography* 41 (1953): 395-418; Alison Goodyear Freehling, *Drift Toward Dissolution: The Virginia Slavery Debate of 1831-1832* (Baton Rouge: Louisiana State University Press, 1982); Joseph H. Harrison, Jr., "Oligarchs and Democrats: The Richmond Junto," *Virginia Magazine of History and Biography* 78 (1970): 184-98; and Daniel P. Jordan, *Political Leadership in Jefferson's Virginia* (Charlottesville: University Press of Virginia, 1983). Ritchie's opponents on the *Richmond Whig* and *Southern Press* are covered, respectively, in Robert Hume Tomlinson, "The Origins and Editorial Policies of the Richmond Whig and Public Advertiser, 1824-1865" (Ph.D. diss., Michigan State University, 1971), and Howard C. Perkins, "A Neglected Phase of the Movement for Southern Unity, 1847-1852," *Journal of Southern History* 12 (May 1946): 153-203.

For the careers of George Wilkins Kendall and Francis Asbury Lumsden I had to rely heavily on the files of the *New Orleans Daily Picayune*. A small number of photocopied items relating to Kendall and the *Picayune* were made available to me by the staff of the Louisiana Collection, Tulane University Library, New Orleans, Louisiana. One of the disappointments of my work was that I was unable to locate the George W. Kendall papers that Fayette Copeland used in his biography of the New Orleans editor. Copeland's biography, *Kendall of the Picayune* (Norman: University of Oklahoma Press, 1943), was thus indispensable, as also was Thomas Ewing Dabney, *One Hundred Great Years; The Story of the Times-Picayune from Its Founding to 1940* (Baton Rouge: Louisiana State University Press, 1944). In addition to the Eightieth Anniversary Issue of the *Times-Picayune* (25 January 1917), three other sources were important: John S. Kendall, "George Wilkins Kendall and the Founding of the New Orleans 'Picayune,'" *Louisiana Historical Quarterly* 11 (April 1928): 261-85; Thomas William Reilly, "American Reporters and the Mexican War, 1846-1848," 2 vols. (Ph.D. diss., University of Minnesota, 1975); and Terence P. Smith, "The First of 125 Great Years," *Dixie* (21 January 1962): 6-9.

The chapter on Robert Barnwell Rhett and Richard Yeadon and the contrasting styles of the *Charleston Mercury* and *Charleston Daily Courier* was based on newspaper files and the Rhett papers in the South Caroliniana Library, University of South Carolina, Columbia, South Carolina; the Perkins Library, Duke University, Durham, North Carolina; and the Southern Historical Collection, University of North Carolina, Chapel Hill, North Carolina. The James J. Hammond Papers (microfilm copy) in the Library of Congress provided crucial information critical of the Rhetts' leadership. The Richard Yeadon Scrapbook in the South Caroliniana Library and the "Centennial Edition," *News and Courier*, 1903, were also important. Two studies informed my understanding of the Charleston newspaper scene: William L. King, *The Newspaper Press of Charleston, S.C.* (Charleston: Lucas and Richardson, 1882) and Herbert Ravenel Sass, *Outspoken: 150 Years of The News and Courier* (Columbia: University of South Carolina Press, 1953). The standard biography of Robert Barnwell Rhett is still Laura A. White's *Robert Barnwell Rhett: Father of Secession* (1931; reprint ed., Gloucester, Mass.: Peter Smith, 1965). Four unpublished works were very useful: John Stanford Coussons, "Thirty Years with Calhoun, Rhett, and the Charleston Mercury: A

Chapter in South Carolina Politics" (Ph.D. diss., Louisiana State University and Agricultural and Mechanical College, 1971); William L. T. Crocker, "Richard Yeadon" (M.A. thesis, University of South Carolina, 1927); John Calhoun Ellen, Jr., "Public Life of Richard Yeadon" (M.A. thesis, University of South Carolina, 1953); and Henry Hardy Perritt, "Robert Barnwell Rhett: South Carolina Secession Spokesman" (Ph.D. diss., University of Florida, 1954). John Calhoun Ellen, Jr.'s doctoral dissertation broadened my view of South Carolina political journalism in the 1850s: "Political Newspapers of the Piedmont Carolinas in the 1850s" (Ph.D. diss., University of South Carolina, 1958).

It is somewhat surprising that there is no full-length biography of John M. Daniel. There are small collections of Daniel materials at the Virginia Historical Society, Richmond, Virginia, and the Alderman Library, University of Virginia, Charlottesville, Virginia. Files of the *Richmond Examiner* and the following contemporary accounts were the basis for my study: George W. Bagby, *John M. Daniel's Latch-Key, a Memoir of the Late Editor of the Richmond Examiner* (1868); reprint entitled *The Old Virginia Gentleman and Other Sketches* (New York: Charles Scribner's Sons, 1910); Moncure Daniel Conway, *Autobiography; Memories and Experiences*, 2 vols. (Boston: Houghton, Mifflin and Co., 1905); idem, "Fredericksburg First and Last," *Magazine of American History* 17 (June 1887): 449-69; John Esten Cooke, *Mohun: Or the Last Days of Lee and His Paladins* (1869; reprint ed., Ridgewood, N.J.: Gregg, 1968); John M. Daniel, *The Richmond Examiner during the War; or, The Writings of John M. Daniel, with a Memoir of His Life, by His Brother, Frederick S. Daniel* (1868; reprint ed., Arno, 1970); and Robert W. Hughes, *Editors of the Past* (Richmond: William Ellis Jones, 1897). There are several brief biographical studies: Oscar Penn Fitzgerald, "John M. Daniel and Some of His Contemporaries," *South Atlantic Quarterly* 4 (1905): 13-17; John Moncure, "John M. Daniel: The Editor of the Examiner," *Sewanee Review* 15 (July 1907): 257-70; George F. Mellen, "Famous Southern Editors: John Moncure Daniel," *Methodist Review* (July-August 1897); Andrew Newton Wilkinson, "John Moncure Daniel," *Richmond College Historical Papers* 1, no. 1 (1915): 73-95. Two unpublished master's theses were useful: Michael Houston, "Edward Alfred Pollard and the Richmond Examiner: A Study of Journalistic Opposition in Wartime" (M.A. thesis, American University, 1963), and Emiline L. Stearns, "John M. Daniel and the Confederacy," (M.A. thesis, University of Chicago, 1928). Two works by J. Cutler Andrews summarize much of the history of Civil War journalism North and South: *The North Reports the Civil War* (Pittsburgh: University of Pittsburgh Press, 1955) and *The South Reports the Civil War* (Princeton: Princeton University Press, 1970). I learned much about Richmond newspapers from 1860 to 1865 in the previously cited Lester Cappon, *Virginia Newspapers, 1821-1935*; Marvin Davis Evans, "The Richmond Press on the Eve of the Civil War," *The John P. Branch Historical Papers of Randolph-Macon College*, New Series, 1 (January 1951); and Harrison A. Trexler, "The Davis Administration and the Richmond Press, 1861-1865," *Journal of Southern History* 16 (May, 1950): 177-95. For information on Confederate morale and press freedom I relied on J. Cutler Andrews, "The Confederate Press and Public Morale," *Journal of Southern History* 32 (November 1966): 445-65; Robert Neil Mathis, "Freedom of the Press in the Confederacy: A Reality," *Historian* 37 (August 1975): 633-48; and Quintus Charles Wilson, "Voluntary Press Censorship during the Civil War," *Journalism Quarterly* 19 (September 1942): 251-61.

There are small collections of John Forsyth manuscripts in the Alabama Department of Archives and History, Montogomery, Alabama, and in the Braxton Bragg Papers in the Western Reserve Historical Society in Cleveland, Ohio. The major sources for his career are his newspapers. The only significant studies of Forsyth are the following: David R. Chesnutt, "John Forsyth: A Southern Partisan (1865-1867)," (M.A. thesis, Auburn University, 1967); John Kent Folmar, "Reaction to Reconstruction: John Forsyth and the *Mobile Advertiser and Register*, 1865-1867," *Alabama Historical Quarterly*, 37, no. 4 (Winter 1975): 245-64; Luther N. Steward, Jr., "John Forsyth," *Alabama Review* 14 (April 1961): 98-123. Charles F. Ritter, "The Press in Florida, Louisiana, and South Carolina and the End of Reconstruction, 1865-1877: Southern Men with Northern Interests," (Ph.D. diss., Catholic University, 1976) is a fine study providing background on Reconstruction journalism.

Sources for study of the New South editors are richer than for the others covered in this work. Primary sources for Henry Watterson's career are abundant: the Watterson papers at the Library of Congress, a Microfilm Edition of a Collection of Henry Watterson Papers, University of Louisville Archives, Louisville, Kentucky, and the editorial page of the *Courier-Journal*. Special issues of the *Courier-Journal* (8 November 1908, section 2, and the "Marse Henry" edition, 2 March 1919) were of great value. Watterson was not reluctant to write about himself; see Henry Watterson, *"Marse Henry"*, 2 vols. (New York: George H. Doran Co., 1919). Two fine collections of Watterson's writings are: Henry Watterson, *The Compromises of Life* (New York: Fox, Duffield and Co., 1903); and Arthur Krock, ed., *The Editorials of Henry Watterson* (New York: George H. Doran Co., 1923). I profited from two accounts by his contemporaries: Joseph M. Rogers, "Henry Watterson," *Booklovers Magazine* (March 1905): 305-21; and Ballard Smith, "Henry Watterson," *Harper's Weekly* (20 August 1887): 600. Isaac F. Marcosson authored two important studies, *Adventures in Interviewing* (London: John Lane Co., 1919) and *"Marse Henry": A Biography of Henry Watterson* (Westport, Conn.: Greenwood, 1951). My understanding of Watterson benefited immensely from Joseph Frazier Wall's excellent biography, *Henry Watterson: Reconstructed Rebel* (New York: Oxford University Press, 1956). Henry F. Pringle contributed a delightful essay: "Kentucky Bourbon: Marse Henry Watterson" in Edwin H. Ford and Edwin Emery, eds., *Highlights in the History of the American Press* (Minneapolis: University of Minnesota Press, 1954). Two works by Leonard N. Plummer address different aspects of the Kentucky editor's career: "The Political Leadership of Henry Watterson" (Ph.D. diss., University of Wisconsin, 1940), and "Henry Watterson's Editorial Style: An Interpretive Analysis," *Journalism Quarterly* 23 (March 1946): 58-65. Watterson's early career is the subject of Lena C. Logan, "Henry Watterson, Border Nationalist, 1840-1877," (Ph.D. diss., Indiana University, 1942). Robert K. Thorp addresses a critical subject in "'Marse Henry' and the Negro: a New Perspective," *Journalism Quarterly* 46 (Autumn 1969): 467-74.

The Francis Warrington Dawson manuscripts are rich and voluminous. The major repository is the Perkins Library, Duke University, Durham, North Carolina. Also held there are the important Hemphill Family Papers. The Southern Historical Collection at the University of North Carolina, Chapel Hill, North Carolina, has the Elliot-Gonzales Papers, which contain letters from Dawson's star reporter. Dawson wrote about his Civil War experiences in *Reminiscences of*

Confederate Service, 1861-1865 (Charleston, S.C., 1882). Many details on early history of the *Courier* and the *News and Courier* are contained in Joseph Walker Barnwell, "Reminiscences of the Courier and Its Editors," *News and Courier*, 125th Anniversary edition, 1 May 1928. Two biographies were of great value: E. Culpepper Clark, *Francis Warrington Dawson and the Politics of Restoration: South Carolina, 1874-1889* (University, Alabama: University of Alabama Press, 1980); and Lewis Pinckney Jones, *Stormy Petrel: N.G. Gonzales and His State* (Columbia: University of South Carolina Press, 1973). S. Frank Logan's thesis was also useful: "Francis W. Dawson, 1840-1889: South Carolina Editor" (M.A. thesis, Duke University, 1947).

The literature on Henry Grady is large and growing. His manuscripts at the Robert W. Woodruff Library, Emory University, Atlanta, Georgia, are indispensable. The files of the *Atlanta Constitution* bear witness to his "new journalism." There are a number of collections of Grady essays and speeches; see, e.g., Henry W. Grady, *The New South*, with a character sketch of Henry W. Grady by Oliver Dyer (New York: Robert Bonner's Sons, 1890). Grady's relationship with Joel Chandler Harris was important for his career and also for an early, uncritical assessment of his character and New South campaign. See Joel Chandler Harris, ed., *Joel Chandler Harris' Life of Henry W. Grady* (New York: Cassell Publishing Co., 1890); and Julia Collier Harris, *The Life and Letters of Joel Chandler Harris* (Boston: Houghton Mifflin Co., 1918). The standard Grady biography is Raymond B. Nixon's *Henry W. Grady: Spokesman of the New South* (New York: Knopf, 1943), but Nixon's study should be balanced by Harold E. Davis's recent work, *Henry Grady's New South: Atlanta, A Brave and Beautiful City* (Tuscaloosa, Alabama: University of Alabama Press, 1990), which emphasizes that Grady spoke more for Atlanta than Georgia or the New South. Russell Franklin Terrell's *A Study of the Early Journalistic Writings of Henry W. Grady* (1926, reprint ed., New York: Beekman, 1974) is still useful. A spate of scholarly articles, appearing mostly in the last ten years, enhanced my understanding of Grady and Georgia history: Harold E. Davis, "Henry Grady, the *Atlanta Constitution*, and the Politics of Farming in the 1880s," *Georgia Historical Quarterly* 71, no. 4 (Winter 1987): 571-600; idem, "Henry W. Grady, Master of the Atlanta Ring, 1880-1886," *Georgia Historical Quarterly* 69 (Spring 1985): 1-38; Ralph L. Eckert, "The Breath of Scandal: John B. Gordon, Henry W. Grady, and the Resignation-Appointment Controversy of May 1880," *Georgia Historical Quarterly* 64, no. 3 (Fall 1985): 315-37; Benjamin W. Griffith, "The Piedmont Chatauqua: Henry Grady's Grandiose Scheme," *Georgia Historical Quarterly* 55 (Summer 1971): 254-58; Doris Lanier, "Henry W. Grady and the Piedmont Chautauqua," *Southern Studies* 23, no. 3 (Fall 1984): 216-42; Dennis Joseph Pfennig, "The First Twenty-One Years of the *Atlanta Constitution*, "*Atlanta History* 33 (1989-90): 29-36; Alice E. Reagan, "Promoting the New South: Hannibal I. Kimball and Henry W. Grady," *Atlanta Historical Journal* 27 (Fall 1983): 5-19; Lewis N. Wynne, "New South Rivalry in the 1880s: Gordon versus Bacon," *Atlanta Historical Journal* 27 (Winter 1983-84): 41-55.

Four basic works on journalism history introduced me to this field some years ago: Edwin Emery and Michael Emery, *The Press and America*, 4th ed. (Englewood Cliffs, N.J.: Prentice-Hall, 1978); Alfred McClung Lee, *The Daily Newspaper in America* (New York: Macmillan, 1937); Frank Luther Mott, *American Journalism; A History: 1690-1960*, 3rd ed., (New York: Macmillan, 1962); Bernard A. Weisberger, *The American Newspaperman* (Chicago: University of Chicago Press, 1961). My footnotes refer to a vast literature on the history of journalism (biographies, histories of newspapers, and more specialized studies). Many recent works in newspaper history, especially articles in *Journalism History*, emphasize connections between political journalism and social and economic developments. I especially benefited from the following: William E. Ames and Dwight L. Teeter, "Politics, Economics, and the Mass Media" in Ronald T. Farrar and John D. Stevens, eds., *Mass Media and the National Experience* (New York: Harper and Row, 1971); James L. Crouthamel, *Bennett's New York Herald and the Rise of the Popular Press* (Syracuse: Syracuse University Press, 1989); Donald W. Curl, *Murat Halstead and the "Cincinnati Commercial,"* (Boca Raton: University Presses of Florida, 1980); Lauren Kessler, *The Dissident Press: Alternative Journalism in American History*, vol. 13, The Sage CommText Series (Beverley Hills, Calif.: Sage Publications, 1984); Thomas C. Leonard, *The Power of the Press: The Birth of American Political Reporting* (New York: Oxford University Press, 1986); Dan Schiller, *Objectivity and the News: The Public and the Rise of Commercial Journalism* (Philadelphia: University of Pennsylvania Press, 1981); Michael Schudson, *Discovering the News: A Social History of American Newspapers* (New York: Basic Books, 1978); and Donald Lewis Shaw, "At the Crossroads: Change and Continuity in American Press News 1820-1860," *Journalism History* 8, no. 2 (Summer 1981): 38-53, 76. Frederick B. Marbut, "Decline of the Official Press in Washington," *Journalism Quarterly* 33 (1956): 335-41; James E. Pollard, *The Presidents and the Press* (New York: Macmillan, 1947); and Culver H. Smith, *The Press, Politics, and Patronage* (Athens: University of Georgia Press, 1977) contributed to my understanding of the presidency, newspaper patronage, and offical administration organs.

There are many fine published contemporary accounts which offer insight into newspaper development. Frederic Hudson, managing editor on James Gordon Bennett's *New York Herald*, authored an adulatory text, *Journalism in the United States from 1690 to 1872* (New York: Harper and Brothers, 1873), while Lambert A. Wilmer wrote an indictment, *Our Press Gang* (Philadelphia: J.T. Lloyd, 1859). An important contemporary history is S.N.D. North's report on newspapers and periodicals prepared for the 10th Census (vol. 8., 1880) and also published separately as *History and Present Condition of the Newspapers and Periodical Press of the United States* (Washington: Government Printing Office, 1884). Charles F. Wingate, *Views and Interviews on Journalism* (1875; reprint ed., New York: Arno and the New York Times, 1970) and Julius Wilcox, "Journalism as a Profession," *Galaxy* 4 (November 1867): 796-805 provide critical assessments of the standards of journalism. Among the important memoirs are: Beman Brockway, *Fifty Years in Journalism* (Watertown, N.Y.: n.p., 1891); Charles T. Congdon, *Reminiscences of a Journalist* (Boston: James R. Osgood and Co., 1880); John W. Forney, *Anecdotes of Public Men*, 2 vols. (New York: Harper and Brothers, 1873, 1881); R.H. Henry, *Editors I Have Known Since the Civil War* (Jackson, Miss.: Jackson Clarion-Ledger, 1922); and Melville E. Stone, *Fifty Years a Journalist* (Garden City, N.Y.: Doubleday, Page and Co., 1921). *The Journalist* of the 1880s contains insightful views and professional gossip by practicing newspapermen.

Several newspaper directories provide circulation figures and other pertinent facts. Among these are *American Newspaper Annual* (Philadelphia: N.W. Ayer and Son, 1880, 1886); *Centennial Newspaper Exhibition* (New York: George P. Rowell and Co., 1876); George P. Rowell and Co., *American Newspaper Directory*

(New York: Geo. P. Rowell and Co., 1869); Winifred Gregory, ed., *American Newspapers, 1921-1936: A Union List of Files Available in the United States and Canada* (1937; reprint ed., New York: Kraus Reprint Corp., 1967); J.C.G. Kennedy, *Catalogue of the Newspapers and Periodicals Published in the United States* (New York: J. Livingston, 1852); *Pettengill's Newspaper Directory and Advertiser's Handbook* (New York: S.M. Pettengill and Co., 1878); *Remington Brothers' Newspaper Manual* (Pittsburgh: Remingtron Bros. Advertising Bureau, 1890).

The history of Southern journalism has yet to be written. Donald E. Reynolds, *Editors Make War* (Nashville: Vanderbilt University Press, 1966) is a seminal work. Thomas Harrison Baker, *The Memphis Commercial Appeal* (Baton Rouge: Louisiana State University Press, 1971) is a model newspaper biography. Other studies which influenced me include the following: Earl L. Bell and Kenneth C. Crabbe, *The Augusta Chronicle: Indomitable Voice of Dixie, 1785-1960* (Athens: University of Gerogia Press, 1960); Hodding Carter, *Their Words Were Bullets* (Athens: University of Georgia Press, 1969); Jack Claiborne, *The Charlotte Observer* (Chapel Hill: University of North Carolina Press, 1986); Thomas D. Clark, *The Southern Country Editor* (Indianapolis: Bobbs-Merrill Co., 1948); and Louis Turner Griffith and John Erwin Talmadge, *Georgia Journalism, 1763-1950* (Athens: University of Georgia Press, 1951). Background on Southern newspapers during the War and Reconstruction can be found in Henry T. Malone, "Atlanta Journalism During the Confederacy," *Georgia Historical Quarterly*, 37 (September 1953): 210-19; idem, "The Charleston Daily Courier: Standard-Bearer of the Confederacy," *Journalism Quarterly* 29 (Summer 1952): 307-15; and Fayette Copeland, "The New Orleans Press and the Reconstruction," *Louisiana Historical Quarterly*, 30 (January 1947): 149-337.

The major work on black journalism in the South is Henry Lewis Suggs, ed., *The Black Press in the South, 1865-1979* (Westport, Conn.: Greenwood, 1983). Editorials from the black press can be found in Martin D. Dann, ed., *The Black Press, 1827-1890: The Quest for National Identity*, with an introduction by Martin E. Dann (New York: G.P. Putnam's Sons, 1971). Jean-Charles Houzeau writes of his experiences in Reconstruction New Orleans in *My Passage at the "New Orleans Tribune": A Memoir of the Civil War*, edited, with an introduction by David C. Rankin (Baton Rouge: Louisiana State University Press, 1984). The economics of the black press are the focus of Emma Lou Thornbrough, "American Negro Newspapers, 1880-1914," *Business History Review* 40 (1966): 467-90. An important dissertation on the black press, even though it fails to emphasize distinctions between Northern and Southern journals, is Betty Lou K. Rathbun, "The Rise of the Modern American Negro Press" (Ph.D. diss., State University of New York at Buffalo, 1978).

Many books and articles in Southern history influenced this study; these are cited in the footnotes. A small number in Southern urban history, the history of Reconstruction and the New South, and Southern intellectual history were especially significant in shaping my understanding of the editor's field of journalism: James C. Cobb, "Beyond Planters and Industrialists: A New Perspective on the New South," *Journal of Southern History*, 44 (February 1988): 45-68; Don H. Doyle, *New Men, New Cities, New South: Atlanta, Nashville, Charleston, Mobile, 1860-1910* (Chapel Hill: University of North Carolina Press, 1990); Paul M. Gaston, *The New South Creed* (New York: Knopf, 1970); David R. Goldfield, *Cotton Fields and Skyscrapers: Southern City and Region, 1607-1980* (Baton Rouge: Louisiana State University Press, 1982); idem, *Urban Growth in the Age of Sectionalism: Virginia, 1847-1861* (Baton Rouge: Louisiana State University Press, 1977); Fred Hobson, *Tell About the South: The Southern Rage to Explain* (Baton Rouge: Louisiana State University Press, 1983); Michael Perman, *Reunion Without Compromise* (London: Cambridge University Press, 1973); idem, *The Road to Redemption: Southern Politics, 1869-1879* (Chapel Hill: University of North Carolina Press, 1984); and George C. Rable, "Bourbonism, Reconstruction, and the Persistence of Southern Distinctiveness," *Civil War History* 29 (June 1983): 135-53. Important essays in Southern urban and intellectual history are found in Blaine A. Brownell and David R. Goldfield, eds., *The City in Southern History: The Growth of Urban Civilization in the South* (Port Washington, N.Y.: National University Publications, Kennikat, 1977); Orville Vernon Burton and Robert C. McMath, Jr., eds., *Toward a New South? Studies in Post-Civil War Southern Communities* (Westport, Conn.: Greenwood, 1982); and Walter J. Fraser, Jr. and Winfred B. Moore, Jr., *From the Old South to the New: Essays on the Transitional South* (Westport, Conn.: Greenwood, 1981). Lawrence Goodwyn, *Democratic Promise: The Populist Moment in America* (New York: Oxford University Press, 1976) offers insight into the culture of reform editors.

Index